WILEY

GAAP
Policies and Procedures

SECOND EDITION

Subscriber Update Service

BECOME A SUBSCRIBER!
Did you purchase this product from a bookstore?

If you did, it's important for you to become a subscriber. John Wiley & Sons, Inc. may publish, on a periodic basis, supplements and new editions to reflect the latest changes in the subject matter that you *need to know* in order to stay competitive in this ever-changing industry. By contacting the Wiley office nearest you, you'll receive any current update at no additional charge. In addition, you'll receive future updates and revised or related volumes on a 30-day examination review.

If you purchased this product directly from John Wiley & Sons, Inc., we have already recorded your subscription for this update service.

To become a subscriber, please call **1-877-762-2974** or send your name, company name (if applicable), address, and the title of the product to:

mailing address: **Supplement Department**
                                     John Wiley & Sons, Inc.
                                     One Wiley Drive
                                     Somerset, NJ 08875

e-mail: **subscriber@wiley.com**
fax: **1-732-302-2300**
online: **www.wiley.com**

For customers outside the United States, please contact the Wiley office nearest you:

Professional & Reference Division
John Wiley & Sons Canada, Ltd.
22 Worcester Road
Etobicoke, Ontario M9W 1L1
CANADA
Phone: 416-236-4433
Phone: 1-800-567-4797
Fax: 416-236-4447
Email: canada@jwiley.com

John Wiley & Sons Australia, Ltd.
33 Park Road
P.O. Box 1226
Milton, Queensland 4064
AUSTRALIA
Phone: 61-7-3859-9755
Fax: 61-7-3859-9715
Email: brisbane@johnwiley.com.au

John Wiley & Sons, Ltd.
The Atrium
Southern Gate, Chichester
West Sussex, PO19 8SQ
ENGLAND
Phone: 44-1243-779777
Fax: 44-1243-775878
Email: customer@wiley.co.uk

John Wiley & Sons (Asia) Pte. Ltd.
2 Clementi Loop #02-01
SINGAPORE 129809
Phone: 65-64632400
Fax: 65-64634604/5/6
Customer Service: 65-64604280
Email: enquiry@wiley.com.sg

WILEY

GAAP
Policies and
Procedures

SECOND EDITION

Steven M. Bragg

JOHN WILEY & SONS, INC.

Library of Congress Cataloging-in-Publication Data:

Bragg, Steven M.
   GAAP policies and procedures / Steven M. Bragg – 2nd ed.
       p. cm.
   Title of 1st ed.: GAAP implementation guide
   "Published simultaneously in Canada."
   ISBN 978-0-470-08183-9 (pbk. : alk. paper)
   1. Accounting—Standards—United States. 2. Corporations—Accounting. I. Bragg, Steven M. GAAP implementation guide. II. Title. III. Title: Generally Accepted Accounting Principles implementation guide.
   HF5616. U5B7 2007
   657.02'1873—dc22   2007006578
Printed in the United States of America

10 9 8 7 6 5 4 3 2 1

To Mom, who fulfilled the role wonderfully—a hug when I needed it, warm cookies at dinner, a lunchbox for school every day, and a sympathetic listener.

CONTENTS

PREFACE

There is a considerable amount of literature dealing with the rules of generally accepted accounting principles (GAAP). In all cases, they specify the rules to be applied to various accounting situations and present cogent examples to assist the reader. However, they do not give any advice regarding how to **implement** GAAP. This means that accountants have no way of knowing what controls, policies, procedures, forms, reports, or archiving requirements they should install that properly mesh with the latest GAAP. This book fills that void.

Though there is a brief summarization of GAAP comprising about one-third of each chapter, the primary intent of this book is to add new categories of information designed to assist the accountant in properly applying GAAP. Some of the following sections can be found in each chapter:

Definitions of Terms. Contains the terms most commonly used in the following Concepts and Examples section.

Concepts and Examples. A summary form of the more detailed GAAP found in the *Wiley GAAP 2007* guide.

Decision Trees. Shows the decision factors required to interpret multiple options in the GAAP rules.

Policies. Identifies specific accounting policies a company can adopt in order to comply with GAAP, especially in terms of creating controls that mesh with GAAP.

Procedures. Lists specific procedures for the most common accounting transactions, modified to work within GAAP restrictions. These procedures can be easily modified for inclusion in a company's accounting procedures manual.

Controls. Itemizes specific controls allowing a company to retain the maximum level of control over its accounting systems while remaining in compliance with GAAP.

Forms and Reports. Gives templates for forms and reports that can be used in a GAAP-compliant accounting system.

Footnotes. Gives numerous examples of footnotes that can be used to describe GAAP-mandated financial disclosures.

Journal Entries. Shows hundreds of GAAP-compliant journal entries for most accounting transactions.

Recordkeeping. Notes the types of reports and other information to be retained as part of a comprehensive accounting system.

Chapters are sequenced in the same manner used for the *GAAP 2007* guide published by John Wiley & Sons, covering such topics as receivables, investments, inventory, revenue recognition, liabilities, debt, leases, stockholders' equity, and foreign currency. The more rarely addressed GAAP topics are not included in this volume in the interest of conserving space, but the reader will find that the bulk of the GAAP issues that arise in daily accounting situations are covered.

GAAP Policies and Procedures, 2nd edition is an ideal companion volume for the Wiley GAAP guide. It provides the practical application information needed to ensure that a company's accounting systems are fully capable of incorporating the most recent GAAP.

Steven M. Bragg
Centennial, Colorado
December 2006

ABOUT THE AUTHOR

Steven Bragg, CPA, CMA, CIA, CPIM, has been the chief financial officer or controller of four companies, as well as a consulting manager at Ernst & Young and auditor at Deloitte & Touche. He received a master's degree in finance from Bentley College, an MBA from Babson College, and a Bachelor's degree in Economics from the University of Maine. He has been the two-time President of the Colorado Mountain Club, and is an avid alpine skier, mountain biker, and rescue diver. Mr. Bragg resides in Centennial, Colorado. He has written the following books through John Wiley & Sons:

Accounting and Finance for Your Small Business
Accounting Best Practices
Accounting Control Best Practices
Billing and Collections Best Practices
Business Ratios and Formulas
Controllership
Controller's Guide to Costing
Controller's Guide to Planning and Controlling Operations
Cost Accounting
Design and Maintenance of Accounting Manuals
Essentials of Payroll
Fast Close
Financial Analysis
Inventory Accounting
Inventory Best Practices
Just-in-Time Accounting
Managing Explosive Corporate Growth
Outsourcing
Payroll Accounting
Planning and Controlling Operations
Revenue Recognition
Sales and Operations for Your Small Business
The Controller's Function
The New CFO Financial Leadership Manual
The Ultimate Accountants' Reference
Throughput Accounting

Also:

Advanced Accounting Systems (Institute of Internal Auditors)

ACKNOWLEDGMENTS

A special note of thanks to the acquisitions editor of this project, John DeRemigis, who has been so enthusiastic about it from the start.

FREE ONLINE RESOURCES BY STEVE BRAGG

Steve Bragg issues a free bimonthly accounting best practices newsletter and an accounting best practices podcast. You can sign up for both at www.stevebragg.com, or access the podcast through iTunes.

WILEY

GAAP
Policies and
Procedures

SECOND EDITION

1 RESEARCHING GAAP IMPLEMENTATION PROBLEMS

OVERVIEW

This chapter is designed to give pointers to additional information in areas besides GAAP concepts. Though there are Concepts and Examples sections in each of the following chapters that give summarized versions of the relevant GAAP issues, the primary focus of this book is to provide information about ancillary topics that allow one to implement GAAP, such as accounting policies and procedures, controls, and reporting footnotes. Unfortunately, there are no authoritative sources for these GAAP implementation topics. Instead, the sections of this chapter devoted to each implementation topic list some organizations that can provide additional information, as well as key books that summarize or discuss related topics, including the name of each book's author, publisher, and date of publication. But first, we will address the GAAP hierarchy of accounting standards and rules, followed by the general approach for researching GAAP-related issues.

The GAAP Hierarchy

Generally accepted accounting principles (GAAP) are standards and rules for reporting financial information, as established and approved by the Financial Accounting Standards Board.

There are three primary players in the promulgation of GAAP. First is the Financial Accounting Standards Board (FASB), which plays the lead role in establishing GAAP. Its Web site is located at www.fasb.org. Its mission is to "establish and improve standards of financial accounting for the guidance and education of the public, including issuers, auditors, and users of financial information." A subset of the FASB is the Emerging Issues Task Force (EITF), which (as its name implies) handles emerging accounting issues as soon as they become apparent, so that a standard approach can be created before any competing approaches come into use. This group typically deals with only very narrowly defined accounting issues, and its opinions are considered to be GAAP only if it can first reach a consensus opinion among its members. Finally, the American Institute of Certified Public Accountants (AICPA) is the principal representative body for certified public accountants within the United States. Its Web site is located at www.aicpa.org. It periodically issues research bulletins, audit and accounting guides, statements of position, and practice bulletins that, if approved by the FASB, are considered to be GAAP. Some GAAP is still ascribed to the Accounting Principles Board (APB), though this entity was phased out in 1973.

There are many documents issued by these three accounting entities that are considered part of GAAP. Each one is described in the following bullet points:[1]

- *FASB Statements of Financial Accounting Standards.* The highest form of GAAP, the SFAS series is the primary publication of the FASB, and is the most carefully formulated (and debated) of all GAAP documents.
- *FASB Interpretations.* Used to clarify Statements of Financial Accounting Standards or the pronouncements made by prior accounting entities that are still considered to be GAAP.
- *APB Opinions.* The primary publication of the old Accounting Principles Board, this was the equivalent of an SFAS prior to the formation of the FASB.
- *FASB Technical Bulletins.* Provide guidance on issues not covered by existing standards, and where the guidance is not expected to be costly or create a major change.
- *AICPA Statements of Position.* Provide guidance on financial accounting and reporting issues.
- *AICPA Industry Audit and Accounting Guides.* Provide guidance to auditors in examining and reporting on financial statements of entities in specific industries and provide standards on accounting problems unique to a particular industry.
- *EITF Consensus Positions.* Provide positions on the correct treatment of emerging accounting issues.
- *AICPA Practice Bulletins.* Provide guidance on narrowly defined accounting topics.
- *FASB Implementation Guides.* Provide notes on how to implement specific Statements of Financial Accounting Standards, written by the FASB staff. The guides are organized in a question, background, and answer format.

GAAP is organized in a descending pyramid of authoritative sources, as shown in Exhibit 1-1. It contains the following four categories:[2]

1. Category A is the most authoritative GAAP, containing the Statements of Financial Accounting Standards and related Interpretations (as promulgated by the FASB), as well as AICPA Accounting Research Bulletins and Opinions of the Accounting Principles Board.
2. Category B contains all FASB Technical Bulletins, as well as all AICPA Statements of Position and AICPA Industry Audit and Accounting Guides that have been approved by the FASB.

---

[1] *Adapted with permission from pp. 5–6 of Delaney et al.,* **Wiley GAAP 2003** *(John Wiley & Sons, Inc., Hoboken, NJ, 2002).*

[2] *Adapted with permission from p. 3 of Delaney et al.,* **Wiley GAAP 2003** *(John Wiley & Sons, Inc., Hoboken, NJ, 2002).*

3. Category C includes consensus positions of the FASB's EITF, as well as those Practice Bulletins created by the AICPA's Accounting Standards Executive Committee that have been approved by the FASB. The positions of the EITF tend to cover such specialized topics that there is no more authoritative form of GAAP in Categories A or B, so these positions tend to be the most senior form of GAAP in their topical areas.
4. Category D includes implementation guides published by the FASB staff, as well as AICPA accounting interpretations and prevalent accounting practices.

Exhibit 1-1: The GAAP Source Pyramid

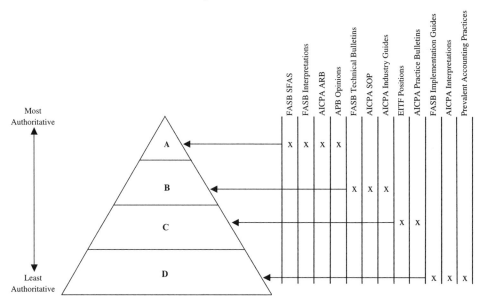

ARB = Accounting Research Bulletin
SFAS = Statement of Financial Accounting Standards
SOP = Statement of Position

Researching GAAP

The simplest approach to researching GAAP is to review the Concepts and Examples sections in this book. If this does not yield a detailed answer, a more comprehensive source of summarized GAAP information is the *Wiley GAAP 2007* guide. The *Wiley GAAP 2007* guide contains a more comprehensive Concepts section than this book, and also contains a list of authoritative pronouncements at its beginning, as well as the applicable page reference leading to a more complete discussion of the issues within the text. If this approach still does not yield a clear answer to a GAAP problem, one should review selected GAAP source documents, of which the most comprehensive is the FASB's Original Pronouncements and Accounting Standards three-volume series (noted in the following book list). It lists all FASB Statements of Standards, as well as AICPA Pronouncements, FASB Interpretations, FASB Concepts Statements, and FASB Technical Bulletins. Of particular use is the topical index located at the end of the third volume, which cross-references each topic to a GAAP source. Other more narrowly defined topics are covered by the other GAAP sources noted in the following book list. If these sources still do not yield a clear answer, one can ask other entities in the same industry how they are handling the issue (if only to obtain alternative solutions). If all else fails, use basic accounting theory to resolve the issue, or consult with a technical expert at a CPA firm. The most useful GAAP source documents are noted in the following book list:

Audit and Accounting Guides

Author: AICPA
Publisher: AICPA
Publication Date: Various

Emerging Issues Task Force Abstracts

Author: FASB
Publisher: FASB
Publication Date: Annually

FASB Staff Implementation Guides

Author: FASB
Publisher: FASB
Publication Date: Annually

Original Pronouncements and Accounting Standards

Author: FASB
Publisher: FASB
Publication Date: Annually

Statements of Position

Author: AICPA
Publisher: AICPA
Publication Date: Various

Researching Accounting Terminology

The best source of information about accounting terminology is the Statements of Financial Accounting Standards (SFAS), as published by the FASB. These Statements generally begin with a definitions section that provides both clear and comprehensive definitions. However, definitions are provided only for the limited topics covered in each SFAS, so it can take some time to locate a specific definition from the various SFAS documents. Definitions are also provided in a variety of lower-level GAAP documents. Another source of definitions is an online glossary of definitions maintained by the AICPA, which can be accessed at www.aicpa.org/members/glossary. Given the minimal time most accountants will allocate to researching accounting definitions, a simpler form of access is the following accounting dictionary:

Dictionary of Accounting Terms

Author: Joel Siegel and Jae Shim
Publisher: Barron's Education Series, Inc.
Publication Date: 2005

Researching Accounting Policies and Procedures

There is no standard set of policies and procedures related to GAAP. This information can be found within the Policies and related Procedures sections of each chapter in this book. Another source is books listing sample policies and procedures for generic company operations, as described in the first two books in the following list. An alternative is to use documentation manuals as guides for the construction of company-specific policies and procedures; the last two books in the following list can assist with this effort:

Bizmanualz Accounting Policies, Procedures, and Forms

Author: Bizmanualz.com Inc.
Publisher: Bizmanualz.com Inc.
Publication Date: 2002

Design and Maintenance of Accounting Manuals

Author: Steven Bragg
Publisher: John Wiley & Sons, Inc.
Publication Date: 2003

Documentation Improvement Methods

Author: Athar Murtuza
Publisher: John Wiley & Sons, Inc.
Publication Date: 2002

Researching Accounting Controls

There is no standard source document itemizing the key control areas related to all types of GAAP. Instead, controls are either described in general terms through the reports issued by various accounting review committees (see the *COSO Implementation Guide* below) or else one must infer the correct types of controls to use based on various types of fraud that may occur (several examples are noted below). A good source for controls-related publications is the Institute of Internal Auditors, whose Web site is www.theiia.org. It is located in Altamonte Springs, Florida, and its phone number is 407-937-1100. Several reference books related to this topic are as follows:

COSO Implementation Guide

Author: James P. Roth
Publisher: Institute of Internal Auditors
Publication Date: 1995

Financial Crime Investigation and Control

Author: K. H. Spencer Pickett, Jennifer M. Pickett
Publisher: John Wiley & Sons, Inc.
Publication Date: 2002

Financial Reporting Fraud

Author: Charles Lundelius Jr.
Publisher: AICPA
Publication Date: 2003

Financial Statement Fraud

Author: Zabihollah Rezaee
Publisher: John Wiley & Sons, Inc.
Publication Date: 2002

Fraud 101

Author: Howard Davia
Publisher: John Wiley & Sons, Inc.
Publication Date: 2000

Internal Control Integrated Frameworks

Author: Coopers & Lybrand
Publisher: AICPA
Publication Date: 1994

Process Development Life Cycle

Author: Albert Marcella Jr.
Publisher: Institute of Internal Auditors
Publication Date: 2001

Researching Accounting Forms and Reports

There is no single book or periodical containing a comprehensive set of forms or reports linked to GAAP. The best source is the Forms and Reports sections within this book. Another alternative is to review publications describing how to construct these documents. Such information can then be used to design forms and reports based on the specific accounting structures unique to a company. The following source book provides information about constructing forms and reports:

Design and Maintenance of Accounting Manuals

Author: Steven Bragg
Publisher: John Wiley & Sons, Inc.
Publication Date: 2003

Some examples of forms and reports can be found scattered through some of the larger accounting "how to" books, an example of which follows:

Controllership

Author: James Willson et al.
Publisher: John Wiley & Sons, Inc.
Publication Date: 2004

Researching Accounting Footnotes

Source documents for GAAP will describe the general contents of footnotes to financial statements, but rarely give more than a few limited examples. A better source of information is a selection of examples culled from financial reports. One of the best sources is the *GAAP Financial Statement Disclosures Manual* listed in the following references. Another option is to access the Web site of the Securities and Exchange Commission at www.sec.gov and review the individual filings of various public companies, which can be accessed through the "Search for Company Filings" option on that Web page. The following source books can be used for additional information about footnote disclosures:

Financial Statement Presentation and Disclosure Practices for Employee Benefit Plans

Author: AICPA
Publisher: AICPA
Publication Date: 2000

Financial Statement Presentation and Disclosure Practices for Not-for-Profit Organizations

Author: Richard F. Larkin
Publisher: AICPA
Publication Date: 1999

GAAP Financial Statement Disclosures Manual

Author: George Georgiades
Publisher: CCH
Publication Date: 2005

The Coopers & Lybrand SEC Manual

Author: Robert Herz et al.
Publisher: John Wiley & Sons, Inc.
Publication Date: 1997

Researching Accounting Journal Entries

Examples of journal entry formats are listed in the Journal Entry sections of each chapter in this book. In addition, one can consult the *Wiley GAAP* guide for the most recent year, which may include different examples of journal entries for a specific topic. Another good source is the most recent edition of the standard textbooks for intermediate accounting, advanced accounting, and cost accounting. The following books can be consulted for this information:

Intermediate Accounting

Author: Donald Kieso et al.
Publisher: John Wiley & Sons, Inc.
Publication Date: 2006

Advanced Accounting

Author: Debra Jeter et al.
Publisher: John Wiley & Sons, Inc.
Publication Date: 2003

Ultimate Accountants' Reference

Author: Steven Bragg
Publisher: John Wiley & Sons, Inc.
Publication Date: 2006

Cost Accounting

Author: Steven Bragg
Publisher: John Wiley & Sons, Inc.
Publication Date: 2001

Researching Accounting Recordkeeping

Information about the proper time period over which to retain accounting documents is difficult to find, as are procedures and documentation for organizing and destroying documents. The principal organization concerning itself with these issues is the Association for Information Management Professionals, whose Web site is located at www.arma.org. It is located in Lenexa, Kansas, and its Web site lists a number of books related to records retention.

2 CASH, RECEIVABLES, AND PREPAID EXPENSES

DEFINITIONS OF TERMS

Accounts receivable. A current asset on the balance sheet, representing short-term amounts due from customers who have purchased on account.

Assignment. Creating a loan document using accounts receivable as the collateral. If the debtor is unable to pay back the loan, the creditor can collect the accounts receivable and retain the proceeds.

Cash. All petty cash, currency, held checks, certificates of deposit, traveler's checks, money orders, letters of credit, bank drafts, cashier's checks, and demand deposits that are held by a company without restriction, and which are readily available on demand.

Collateral. Assets that have been pledged to secure debtor repayment of a loan. If it cannot repay the loan, the creditor can sell the assets and retain the proceeds.

Factoring. The sale of accounts receivable to a third party, with the third party bearing the risk of loss if the accounts receivable cannot be collected.

Factor's holdback. That portion of the payment for an accounts receivable sale retained by the factor in expectation of product returns by customers.

Net realizable value. The expected revenue to be gained from the sale of an item or service, less the costs of the sale transaction.

Pledging. Assigning accounts receivable as collateral on company debt.

Recourse. The right of a creditor under a factoring arrangement to be paid by the debtor for any uncollectible accounts receivable sold to the creditor.

CONCEPTS AND EXAMPLES[1]

Cash

If there is a short-term restriction on cash, such as a requirement that it be held in a sinking fund in anticipation of the payment of a corresponding debt within a year, then it should still be itemized as a current asset, but as a separate line item. If there is a long-term restriction on cash, such as a compensating balance agreement that is linked to debt that will not be paid off within the current year, then the cash must be itemized as a long-term asset. Alternatively, if a compensating balance agreement is tied to a loan that matures within the current period, then it may be recorded separately as a current asset.

If a company issues checks for which there are not sufficient funds on hand, it will find itself in a negative cash situation as reported on its balance sheet. Rather than show a negative cash balance there, it is better to shift the amount of the excess checks back into the accounts payable liability account, thereby leaving the reported cash balance at or near zero.

Cash held in foreign currencies should be included in the cash account on the balance sheet, subject to two restrictions. First, it must be converted to US dollars at the prevailing exchange rate as of the balance sheet date. Second, the funds must be readily convertible into US dollars; if not (perhaps due to currency restrictions by the foreign government), the cash cannot properly be classified as a current asset, and instead must be classified as a long-term asset. This latter item is a key issue for

---

[1] *Some portions of this section are adapted with permission from Chapters 14 and 16 of Bragg,* **Ultimate Accountants' Reference**, *John Wiley & Sons, Inc., Hoboken, NJ, 2006.*

those organizations that want to report the highest possible current ratio by shifting foreign currency holdings into the cash account.

Prepaid Expenses

Prepaid expenses are itemized as current assets on the balance sheet, and should include early payments on any expenditures that would have been made during the next 12 months. For example, prepayments on key man life insurance, rent, or association fees would be charged to this account. There should be a supporting schedule for this account, detailing each line item charged to it and the amortization schedule over which each item will be ratably charged to expense (see the sample report in the Recordkeeping section).

The prepaid expense account does **not** include deposits, since they are typically not converted back to cash until the end of the agreements requiring their original payment, which may be some years in the future. For example, the usual one-month rent deposit required with a building lease agreement cannot be paid back until the lease term has expired. Instead, deposits are usually recorded in the Other Assets or Deposits accounts, which are listed as noncurrent assets on the balance sheet.

Receivables—Presentation

The accounts receivable account tends to accumulate a number of transactions that are not strictly accounts receivable, so it is useful to define what should be stored in this account. An account receivable is a claim that is payable in cash, and which is in exchange for the services or goods provided by the company. This definition excludes a note payable, which is essentially a return of loaned funds, and for which a signed note is usually available as documentary evidence. A note payable should be itemized in the financial statements under a separate account. It also excludes any short-term funds loaned to employees (such as employee advances), or employee loans of any type that may be payable over a longer term. These items may be more appropriately stored in an Other Accounts Receivable or Accounts Receivable from Employees account. Also, one should not create an accrued account receivable to offset an accrued sale transaction (as may occur under the percentage-of-completion method of recognizing revenue from long-term construction projects); on the contrary, the Accounts Receivable account should contain only transactions for which there is a clear, short-term expectation of cash receipt from a customer.

Receivables—Collateral, Assignments, and Factoring

If a company uses its accounts receivable as **collateral** for a loan, then no accounting entry is required. An **assignment** of accounts receivable, where specific receivables are pledged as collateral on a loan and where customer payments are generally forwarded straight to the lender, also requires no accounting entry. However, if a company directly sells receivables with no continuing involvement in their collection, and with no requirement to pay back the creditor in case a customer defaults on payment of a receivable, then this is called **factoring,** and a sale transaction must be recorded (see the Decision Tree section for more information). Typically, this involves a credit to the Accounts Receivable account, a debit to the Cash account for the amount of the buyer's payment, and a Loss on Factoring entry to reflect extra charges made by the factor on the transaction. The amount of cash received from the factor will also be reduced by an interest charge that is based on the amount of cash issued to the company for the period when the factor has not yet received cash from the factored accounts receivable; this results in a debit to the Interest Expense account and a credit to the Accounts Receivable account.

A variation on this transaction is if the company draws down cash from the factor only when needed, rather than at the time when the accounts receivable are sold to the factor. This arrangement results in a smaller interest charge by the factor for the period when it is awaiting payment on the accounts receivable. In this instance, a new receivable is created that can be labeled "Due from Factoring Arrangement."

Another variation is when the factor holds back payment on some portion of the accounts receivable, on the grounds that there may be inventory returns from customers that can be charged back to the company. In this case, the proper entry is to offset the account receivable being transferred to the factor with a holdback receivable account. Once all receipt transactions have been cleared by the factor, any amounts left in the holdback account are eliminated with a debit to Cash (being paid by the factor) and a credit to the Holdback account.

A sample journal entry that includes all of the preceding factoring issues is shown in Exhibit 2-1. In this case, a company has sold $100,000 of accounts receivable to a factor, which requires a 10% holdback provision. The factor also expects to lose $4,800 in bad debts that it must absorb as a result of the transaction, and so pays the company $4,800 less than the face value of the accounts receivable, which forces the company to recognize a loss of $4,800 on the transaction. Also, the company does not elect to take delivery of all funds allowed by the factor in order to save interest costs; accordingly, it only takes delivery of $15,000 to meet immediate cash needs. Finally, the factor charges 18% interest for the thirty-day period that it is expected to take to collect the factored accounts receivable, which results in an interest charge of $200 on the $15,000 of delivered funds.

Exhibit 2-1: Sample Factoring Journal Entry

Cash	15,000	
Accounts receivable—factoring holdback	10,000	
Loss on factoring	4,800	
Interest expense	200	
Due from factoring arrangement	70,000	
Accounts receivable		100,000

If the company factors its accounts receivable, but the factor has recourse against the company for uncollectible amounts (which reduces the factoring fee) or if the company agrees to service the receivables subsequent to the factoring arrangement, then the company still can be construed as having retained control over the receivables. In this case, the factoring arrangement is considered to be a loan, rather than a sale of receivables, resulting in the retention of the accounts receivable on the company's balance sheet, as well as the addition of a loan liability. When receivables are sold with recourse, one should shift the expected amount of bad debts to be incurred from the Allowance for Bad Debts account to a Recourse Obligation account, from which bad debts will be subtracted as incurred.

Receivables—Sales Returns

When a customer returns goods to a company, the accountant should set up an offsetting sales contra account, rather than backing out the original sale transaction. The resulting transaction would be a credit to the Accounts Receivable account and a debit to the Contra account. There are two reasons for using this approach. First, a direct reduction of the original sale would impact the financial reporting in a prior period, if the sale originated in a prior period. Second, a large number of sales returns charged directly against the sales account would be essentially invisible on the financial statements, with management seeing only a reduced sales volume. Only by using (and reporting) an offsetting contra account can management gain some knowledge of the extent of any sales returns. If a company ships products on approval (i.e., customers have the right of return) and there is a history of significant returns, then it should create a reserve for sales returns based on historical rates of return. The offsetting sale returns expense account should be categorized as part of the cost of goods sold.

Example of reserve for sales made on approval

The Dusty Tome Book Company issues new versions of its books to a subscriber list that has purchased previous editions. Historically, it has experienced a 22% rate of return from these sales. In the current month, it shipped $440,000 of books to its subscriber list. Given the historical rate of return, Dusty Tome's controller expects to see $96,800 worth of books returned to the company. Accordingly, she records the following entry:

Sale return expense	96,800	
Reserve for sales returns		96,800

Receivables—Early Payment Discounts

Unless a company offers an exceedingly large early payment discount, it is unlikely that the total amount of this discount taken will have a material impact on the financial statements. Consequently, some variation in the allowable treatment of this transaction can be used. The most theoretically accurate approach is to initially record the account receivable at its discounted value, which assumes that all customers will take the early payment discount. Any cash discounts that are not taken will then be recorded as additional revenue. This results in a properly conservative view of the amount of funds that one can expect to receive from the accounts receivable. An alternative that results in a slightly higher initial revenue figure is to record the full, undiscounted amount of each sale in the accounts receivable, and then record any discounts taken in a sales contra account. One objection to this second approach is that the discount taken will be recognized only in an accounting period that is later than the one in which the sale was initially recorded (given the time delay usually associated with accounts receivable payments), which is an inappropriate revenue recognition technique. An alternative approach that avoids this problem is to set up a reserve for cash discounts taken in the period in which the sales occur, and offset actual discounts against it as they occur.

Receivables—Long-Term

If an account receivable is not due to be collected for more than one year, then it should be discounted at an interest rate that fairly reflects the rate that would have been charged to the debtor under a normal lending situation. An alternative is to use any interest rate that may be noted in the sale agreement. Under no circumstances should the interest rate be one that is less than the prevailing market rate at the time when the receivable was originated. The result of this calculation will be a smaller receivable than is indicated by its face amount. The difference should be gradually accrued as interest income over the life of the receivable.

Example of a long-term accounts receivable transaction

The Carolina Furniture Company (CFC) sells a large block of office furniture in exchange for a receivable of $82,000 payable by the customer in two years. There is no stated interest rate on the receivable, so the CFC controller uses the current market rate of 6% to derive a present value discount rate of 0.8900. She multiplies the $82,000 receivable by the discount rate of 0.8900 to arrive at a present value of $72,980, and makes the following entry:

Notes receivable	82,000	
Furniture revenue		72,980
Discount on notes receivable		9,020

In succeeding months, the CFC controller gradually debits the discount on the notes receivable account and credits interest income, so that the discount is entirely eliminated by the time the note receivable is collected. Also, note that the initial debit is to a notes receivable account, **not** accounts receivable, since this is not considered a current asset.

Receivables—Bad Debts

The accountant must recognize a bad debt as soon as it is reasonably certain that a loss is likely to occur, and the amount in question can be estimated with some degree of accuracy. For financial reporting purposes, the only allowable method for recognizing bad debts is to set up a bad debt reserve as a contra account to the accounts receivable account. Under this approach, one should estimate a long-term average amount of bad debt, debit the bad debt expense (which is most commonly kept in the operating expenses section of the income statement) for this percentage of the period-end accounts receivable balance, and credit the bad debt reserve contra account. When an actual bad debt is recognized, the accountant credits the accounts receivable account and debits the reserve. No offset is made to the sales account. If there is an unusually large bad debt to be recognized that will more than offset the existing bad debt reserve, then the reserve should be sufficiently increased to ensure that the remaining balance in the reserve is not negative.

There are several ways to determine the long-term estimated amount of bad debt for the preceding calculation. One is to determine the historical average bad debt as a proportion of the total credit sales for the past twelve months. Another option that results in a more accurate estimate is to calculate a different historical bad debt percentage based on the relative age of the accounts receivable at the end of the reporting period. For example, accounts aged greater than ninety days may have a historical bad debt experience of 50%, whereas those over thirty days have a percentage of 20%, and those below thirty days are at only 4%. This type of experience percentage is more difficult to calculate, but can result in a considerable degree of precision in the size of the bad debt allowance. It is also possible to estimate the bad debt level based on the type of customer. For example, one could make the case that government entities never go out of business, and so have a much lower bad debt rate than other types of customers. Whatever approach is used must be backed up quantitatively, so that an auditor can trace through the calculations to ensure that a sufficient bad debt reserve has been provided for.

Example of a bad debt reserve calculation

The Granny Clock Company has $120,000 of outstanding accounts receivable. Of that amount, $20,000 is more than ninety days old, while $41,000 is in the sixty- to ninety-day category. The company has historically experienced a loss rate of 25% on receivables more than ninety days old, a loss rate of 10% on receivables in the sixty- to ninety-day category, and 2% on all other receivables. Based on this information, the controller calculates a reserve of $1,180 on the current receivables ($59,000 × 2%), $4,100 for receivables in the sixty- to ninety-day category ($41,000 × 10%), and $5,000 for receivables older than ninety days ($20,000 × 25%), which totals $10,280. The company already has a reserve of $2,000 left over from the previous month, so the new entry is a debit to bad debt expense and a credit to the reserve for bad debts of $8,280 ($10,280 total reserve less the existing balance).

If an account receivable has been already written off as a bad debt and is then collected, the receipt should be charged against the bad debt reserve or to earnings. Incorrect treatment would be to create a new sale and charge the receipt against that, since this would artificially show a higher level of sales than really occurred.

DECISION TREES

Receivables—Ownership Decision

The main issue involving the use of accounts receivable as collateral or for assignment or factoring is how to treat these activities in the financial statements. The illustration in Exhibit 2-2 may be of some assistance. As shown in the exhibit, if receivables are pledged as collateral on a loan, or if they are assigned with recourse, or if the company has some means of forcing their return, then the company essentially has control over the receivables, and should continue to record them as such on its balance sheet. However, if the receivables purchaser has assumed the risk of loss, **and** can pledge or exchange the receivables to a third party, **and** the company or its creditors can no longer access the receivables for any reason, then the purchaser has control over the assets, and the selling company must record the sale of the receivables and remove them from its balance sheet. Thus, if there is any evidence that the selling company retains any aspect of control over the receivables, they must continue to be recorded on the selling company's balance sheet, with additional footnote disclosure of their status as collateral on a loan.

Exhibit 2-2: Reporting Status of Accounts Receivable

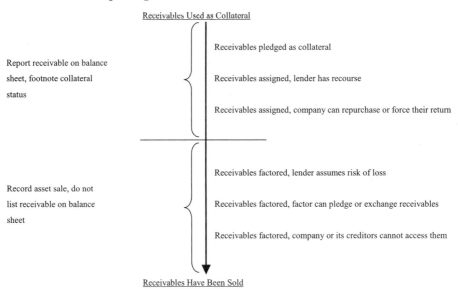

Receivables Used as Collateral

Report receivable on balance sheet, footnote collateral status

Receivables pledged as collateral

Receivables assigned, lender has recourse

Receivables assigned, company can repurchase or force their return

Record asset sale, do not list receivable on balance sheet

Receivables factored, lender assumes risk of loss

Receivables factored, factor can pledge or exchange receivables

Receivables factored, company or its creditors cannot access them

Receivables Have Been Sold

POLICIES

Cash

- **No accounts payable personnel shall be authorized to sign checks or approve money transfers.** This policy is designed to separate the preparation of accounts payable documents from their approval, thereby keeping a single person from falsely creating a payable and authorizing its payment to himself.
- **All check or money transfers exceeding $_____ shall be countersigned by the _____ position.** This policy provides for a second review of very large payments to ensure that they are appropriate, and to reduce the incidence of fraudulent transfers. Unfortunately, many banks do not review the existence of a second signature on a check, making this a less effective policy.
- **All check signers shall be adequately bonded.** This policy requires a company to retain an adequate level of bonding on its check signers to ensure that it will suffer no loss if a signer commits fraud. Bonding companies usually conduct a background review on check signers before agreeing to provide bond, which may give a company warning of previously unknown fraudulent employee activities, thereby allowing it to remove check signing authority from someone before they have the opportunity to commit fraud again.

Prepaid Expenses

- **All advances to employees must be repaid within three months.** This policy keeps a company from becoming a bank for employees. In addition, it rapidly draws down the balances due from employees, so there is a minimal risk of loss to the company if an employee quits work without having paid off the entire balance of an advance.

- **Employee advances shall be limited to __% of their annual pay.** This policy is designed to reduce the amount of money a company can have due from its employees, which mitigates its risk of nonpayment in the event of an employee departure.

Receivables

- **Allow the accounting staff to write off accounts receivable balances under $___ without management approval.** Though one could require management approval of all receivable write-offs in order to reduce the risk of false write-offs, this is not an efficient control point for very small balances. Instead, it is common to allow the write-off of small balances by the accounting staff, thereby avoiding time otherwise wasted by the management staff investigating these write-offs.
- **Require credit manager approval for all prospective sales exceeding customer credit limits.** A common problem for the credit department is to be rushed into granting credit when a salesperson lands a large sale, which tends to result in excessively large credit limits being granted. A better approach is to require an advance review of prospective sales by the credit manager, who can then tell the sales staff the maximum amount of credit the company is willing to grant before any sale is finalized.
- **Require formal annual reviews of all customer credit limits exceeding $_____.** Customer financial situations change over time, making the initial credit limits granted to them incorrect. This is a particular problem when a customer is spiraling down toward bankruptcy, while the company blithely continues to grant it large amounts of credit. Annual reviews of large credit limits can mitigate this problem, though feedback from the collections staff will warn of possible customer problems well before any formal annual review would do so.
- **No factoring arrangements are allowed when receivables are used as collateral for other debts.** This policy prevents a company from violating the terms of a loan agreement under which it must retain its receivables as collateral, rather than reduce them through sale to a factor. Otherwise, the company could be seen as selling assets to the detriment of a secured lender, who would then have the right to call its loan to the company.

PROCEDURES

Cash—Apply Cash to Accounts Receivable

Use this procedure to apply cash received from customers to open accounts receivable balances:

1. Add up all daily cash receipts and match the paper tape of the summarization to the individual payments to ensure that the total is correct.
2. Go to the accounting software and access the cash application screen. At the top of the screen, enter today's date and the total amount to be applied.

3. For each customer payment, enter the customer number, individual check amount, the check number and date, and then tab to the detail section of the screen. The list of all open invoices for the customer will appear. Click on each invoice being paid and enter any discounts taken. After identifying all invoices paid by each customer, complete the transaction and move to the next customer from whom a check was received. Continue in this fashion until all receipts have been entered.
4. Print a daily cash receipts report and verify that the total on the report matches the total amount of cash received on the initial paper tape. Compare the remittance advices attached to individual checks to the daily cash receipts report to find the error, and correct it.
5. Press the "post cash" button to transfer all the receipts information to the general ledger.
6. Photocopy all checks received. Then staple the cash receipts report to the photocopies, and file the set of documents in the applied cash filing cabinet.

Cash—Receive and Deposit Cash

Use this procedure to receive cash from a variety of sources and deposit it into the company bank account.

1. Summarize all cash on an adding machine tape.
2. Enter all checks and cash received on a deposit slip. Verify that the deposit slip total and the adding machine tape total are the same. If not, recount the cash and checks.
3. Give the deposit slip and attached cash and checks to a second cash clerk, who compares the check total to the summary sheet forwarded from the mailroom. Reconcile any differences.
4. Photocopy all checks, including attached remittance advices, as well as the deposit slip. Verify that this packet of information matches the total to be sent to the bank in the deposit. Then send the photocopies to the accounts receivable staff, which will apply these payments to outstanding accounts receivable.
5. Send the completed deposit to the bank by courier.

Cash—Process Credit Card Payments

This procedure is useful for processing credit card payments through an Internet-based processing site.

1. Verify that the customer has supplied all information required for the credit card processing: name on the card, credit card number, expiration date, and billing address. Also retain the customer's phone number in case the payment is not accepted, so corrected information can be obtained.
2. Access the Internet credit card processing site and log in.
3. Enter all customer-supplied information on the Web screen, as well as the invoice number, amount to be billed, and a brief description of the billing.

4. If the transaction is not accepted, call the customer and review all supplied information to determine its accuracy. As an alternative, obtain information for a different credit card from the customer.

5. If the transaction is accepted, go to the accounting computer system and log in the cash receipt associated with the transaction. Date the transaction one day forward, since this more closely corresponds to the settlement date and corresponding receipt of cash.

6. Copy the invoice, stamp it with a "Paid in Full" stamp, and initial the stamp. Mail it to the person whose name was on the credit card (**not** the person listed on the invoice, if any), since this person will need it as a receipt.

Cash—Reconcile Petty Cash

Use this procedure to conduct a manual reconciliation of the petty cash balance in any petty cash box.

1. Access the general ledger account for the petty cash box and determine the amount of cash it should contain as of the last reconciliation.

2. Go to the petty cash box and add up all cash contained in the box. Subtract this amount from the box balance as of the last reconciliation and add any amounts deposited into the box during the interval since the last reconciliation. This calculation reveals the amount of missing cash that should be accounted for by expense vouchers.

3. Add up all vouchers in the box and compare this amount to the predetermined amount of missing cash. If they do not match, review petty cash procedures with the person responsible for it.

4. Create a journal entry summarizing the expenses represented by all vouchers in the box, as well as the amount of any shortfalls or overages. Staple the vouchers to this journal entry and give the packet to the general ledger accountant for entry into the general ledger.

5. Calculate the amount of cash that should be added to the petty cash box, based on usage levels, and recommend to the assistant controller in charge of accounts payable that this amount of cash be forwarded to the person responsible for the petty cash box.

Cash—Reconcile Bank Account

Use this procedure to reconcile any differences between the bank and company records of cash transactions. This procedure assumes that a computerized reconciliation module is available through the accounting software.

1. Verify that the beginning bank balance matches the beginning book record, net of reconciling items. If not, go back and fix the bank reconciliations for earlier periods.

2. Enter the ending bank balance on the computer screen.

3. Check off all company records of deposits in the computer system if they match the bank record of receipts. As you progress through this list, check off the deposit records on the bank statement that have also been checked

off in the computer system. If there are any deposits that cannot be immediately reconciled, pull out the detailed deposit records for the days in question and determine which deposits are in error. Fix any deposit record differences and verify that the total book record of deposits matches the total bank record of deposits.

4. Scan the bank statement for any special charges levied by the bank that have not already been recorded in the company books. Enter these adjustments as a journal entry, and check off all recorded expenses of this type on the bank statement.

5. Check off all company checks in the computer system if they match the amount of checks recorded as having cleared on the bank statement. **It is not good enough to just match check numbers!** You must also verify the amount of each cleared check on the bank statement, since this can be a source of discrepancy.

6. If there are checks still listed on the bank statement that do not appear in the company records, then these are most likely manual checks that were not initially recorded in the company records. Also review these unrecorded checks to see if any were fraudulently created. Enter these items in the computer system as manual checks.

7. If the bank statement reveals transfers between bank accounts, verify that these entries have been recorded in the computer system. If not, make journal entries to match the bank transaction record.

8. Verify that the bank ending balance now matches the company's records, net of any deposits or checks in transit. If not, repeat the foregoing steps. Then print two copies of the reconciliation report, filing one copy in the journal entry binder for the applicable month and one copy in the bank statement binder, next to the applicable bank statement.

Receivables—Print and Issue Invoices

Use this procedure to verify shipment of goods and then create invoices based on the shipments. This procedure assumes that the shipping department is logging out shipped goods from the computer system and tracking back orders, rather than the accounting staff.

1. Locate the shipping paperwork in the "shippers" box in the mailroom. The paperwork should include a copy of the shipping log and a copy of the bill of lading.

2. Verify that there is a bill of lading for every order listed on the shipping log, and also that all bills of lading are listed on the log. Then put the bills of lading in order, first by customer number and then by order number (if there is more than one order per customer). Next, check the "carrier" column on the shipping log—some will indicate shipment pickups by customers. For all other deliveries, the shipping department should have turned in a freight worksheet containing the cost of additional freight for each shipment. Locate these sheets, which will be used to determine the freight charge on each invoice.

3. Locate on each freight sheet the method of delivery, as well as the weight of the order. Cross-reference this information against the standard freight charge table, and write on the freight sheet the price of the freight to be billed to the customer.

4. Locate the signed customer order, which contains the pricing for the items shipped, as well as the bill-to customer name and address and the name of the salesperson to whom a commission will be paid.

5. Go to the computer system and access the customer information screen. Call up the customer name and verify that the invoice-to address and contact name are correct. If not, either change the existing information or add a new invoice-to address for the customer.

6. Go to the invoicing screen in the computer system and enter the customer name verified in the last step. Verify that the default salesperson listed on the screen is correct, or change it to match the salesperson name listed on the signed customer order. Enter the part numbers and quantities shipped that are listed on the shipping log, as well as the prices noted on the customer order. Enter the freight charge listed on the freight sheet.

7. Print two copies of the invoice and mail one to the customer. If the order is complete, also file the bill of lading, invoice, customer order, and freight sheet in the customer file. If the order is not complete, store the customer order form in a pending orders file for cross-referencing purposes when back-ordered items are shipped at a later date.

Receivables—Calculate the Bad Debt Reserve

Use this procedure to alter the bad debt reserve to reflect new billing and bad debt activity in a reporting period.

1. Print the accounts receivable aging report and review all invoices on the report that are at least sixty days old with the collections staff.

2. If the collections staff deems a reviewed invoice to be uncollectible, complete a bad debt authorization form for it and charge it off to the bad debt reserve account (see following procedure).

3. Once all receivables designated as bad debts have been cleared from the aging report, summarize the total amount written off during the reporting period, which can be obtained from the list of written-off invoices listed in the bad debt reserve account in the general ledger.

4. Enter the period's bad debt total as a running balance in an electronic spreadsheet alongside the remaining accounts receivable balance for the reporting period. Calculate the rolling three-month bad debt percentage of accounts receivable on this spreadsheet.

5. Multiply the rolling three-month bad debt percentage calculated from the spreadsheet by the remaining accounts receivable balance to determine the estimated amount of bad debt reserve required.

6. If the amount of estimated bad debt reserve is greater than the actual amount listed in the general ledger, make an entry crediting the bad debt reserve ac-

count for the difference, with the offsetting debit going to the bad debt expense account.

Receivables—Authorize Bad Debt Write-Offs

Use this procedure to formalize the process of writing off bad debts from the accounts receivable aging report.

1. At least once a month, review all outstanding accounts receivable on the accounts receivable aging report with the collections staff to see which invoices or portions of invoices must be written off, taking into account customer bankruptcy, history of collection problems, and the size of the amounts owed.
2. Complete the Bad Debt Write-Off Approval Form (see the Forms section). In particular, note on the form the reason for the write-off. If there is a systemic problem that is causing the write-off to occur, forward a copy of the completed form to the appropriate department for review.
3. Forward the form to the general ledger accountant, who will create a credit based on the information in the form and offset the credit against the outstanding customer invoice.
4. Summarize all completed bad debt forms at the end of each month and send the results to the general manager, showing the total write-off amounts attributable to each type of systemic problem.
5. Store the completed bad debt write-off forms in a separate binder and store them in the archives after year-end.

CONTROLS

Cash

The following controls can be used to reduce the risk of asset theft through the illegal transfer of cash:

- **Control check stock.** This is a key control. All check stock must be locked up when not in use. Otherwise, it is a simple matter for someone to take a check from the bottom of a check stack (where its loss will not be noticed for some time), forge a signature on it, and cash it. Be sure to keep the key or combination to the lock in a safe place, or else this control will be worthless.
- **Control signature plates.** This is a key control. Many companies use either signature plates or stamps to imprint an authorized signature on a check, thereby saving the time otherwise required of a manager to sign checks. If someone obtains access to a signature plate and some check stock, that person can easily pay himself the contents of the entire corporate bank account. The best control is to lock up signature plates in a different storage location than the check stock, so a perpetrator would be required to break into two separate locations in order to carry out a really thorough check fraud.
- **Separate responsibility for the cash receipt and cash disbursement functions.** If a person has access to both the cash receipt and disbursement functions, it is much easier to commit fraud by altering the amount of incoming re-

ceipts, and then pocket the difference. To avoid this, each function should be handled by different people within the organization.

- **Perform bank reconciliations.** Though widely practiced and certainly necessary, this is not a preventive control, and so should be implemented **after** the control of check stock and signature plates. Bank reconciliations are most effective when completed each day; this can be done by accessing the daily log of cash transactions through the company bank's Internet site. By staying up-to-date on reconciliations, evidence of fraudulent check activity can be discovered more quickly, allowing for faster remedial action.

- **Reconcile petty cash.** There tends to be a high incidence of fraud related to petty cash boxes, since money can be more easily removed from them. To reduce the incidence of these occurrences, unscheduled petty cash box reconciliations can be initiated, which may catch perpetrators before they have covered their actions with a false paper trail. This control can be strengthened by targeting those petty cash boxes that have experienced unusually high levels of cash replenishment requests.

- **Require that bank reconciliations be completed by people independent of the cash receipts and disbursement functions.** The bank reconciliation is intended to be a check on the activities of those accounting personnel handling incoming and outgoing cash, so it makes little sense to have the same people review their own activities by completing the reconciliation. Instead, it should be done by someone in an entirely different part of the department, and preferably by a senior person with a proven record of reliability.

- **Require that petty cash vouchers be filled out in ink.** Anyone maintaining a petty cash box can easily alter a voucher previously submitted as part of a legitimate transaction, and remove cash from the petty cash box to match the altered voucher. To avoid this, one should require that all vouchers be completed in ink. To be extra careful, one can even require users to write the amount of any cash transactions on vouchers in words instead of numbers (e.g., "fifty-two dollars" instead of $52.00"), since numbers can be more easily modified.

- **Compare the check register to the actual check number sequence.** If checks are prenumbered, one can compare the check numbers listed in the computer's check register to those on the checks. If a check were to be removed from the check stock, then this action would become apparent when the check number on the check stock no longer matches the check number in the computer system.

    If the check stock is on a continuous sheet, as is used for sheet-fed dot matrix printers, then the more likely way for a perpetrator to steal checks would be to detach them from the top or bottom of the stack of check stock. In this case, one can detect the problem by keeping separate track of the last check number used, as well as of the last check number on the bottom of the stack. Unfortunately, many accounting clerks like to keep this list of check numbers used with the check stock, so a perpetrator could easily alter the last number listed on the sheet while stealing checks at the same time. Consequently, the list of check numbers used should be kept in a separate location.

- **Review uncashed checks.** Review all checks that have not been cashed within ninety days of their check dates. In a few cases, it may be possible to cancel the checks, thereby increasing the available cash balance. This review can also highlight checks that have gone astray. By placing stop payment orders on these checks, one can keep them from being incorrectly cashed by other parties, while new checks can be issued to the proper recipients.
- **Route incoming cash payments through a lockbox.** When customers are told to send payments directly to a bank lockbox, this eliminates a number of control points within a company, since it no longer has to physically handle any forms of cash. Some payments will inevitably still be mailed directly to the company, but the proportion of these payments will drop if customers are promptly asked to send future payments to the lockbox address.
- **Verify amount of cash discounts taken.** A cash receipts person can falsely report that customers are taking the maximum amount of early payment discounts when they have not actually done so, and pocket the amount of the false discount. This can be detected by requiring that photocopies of all incoming checks be made, and then tracing payments on which discounts have been taken back to the copies of the checks. This is a less common problem area, since it requires a perpetrator to have access to both the receipts and payments aspects of the accounting operation, and so is a less necessary control point.

Prepaid Expenses

The largest problem with prepaid expenses is that they tend to turn into a holding area for payments that should have been converted into expenses at some point in the past. There is also a potential for advances to be parked in this area that should have been collected. The following controls address these problems:

- **Reconcile all prepaid expense accounts as part of the month-end closing process.** By conducting a careful review of all prepaid accounts once a month, it becomes readily apparent which prepaid items should now be converted to an expense. The result of this review should be a spreadsheet that itemizes the nature of each prepaid item in each account. Since this can be a time-consuming process involving some investigative work, it is best to review prepaid expense accounts shortly before the end of the month, so that a thorough review can be conducted without being cut short by the time pressures imposed by the usual closing process.
- **Review all employee advances with the payroll and payables staffs at least once a month.** A common occurrence is for an employee to claim hardship prior to a company-required trip, and request a travel advance. Alternatively, an advance may be paid when an employee claims that he or she cannot make it to the next payroll check. For whatever the reason, these advances will be recorded in an employee advances account, where they can sometimes be for-

gotten. The best way to ensure repayment is a continual periodic review, either with the accounts payable staff that process employee expense reports (against which travel advances should be netted) or the payroll staff (which deducts pay advances from future paychecks).

- **Require approval of all advance payments to employees.** The simplest way to reduce the burden of tracking employee advances is not to make them in the first place. The best approach is to require management approval of any advances, no matter how small they may be.

Receivables

- **Confirm payment terms with customers.** Receivable collections can be particularly difficult when the sales staff has established side agreements with customers that alter payment terms—especially when the sales staff does not communicate these new terms to the collections department. One can discover the existence of these deals by confirming payment terms at the time of invoice creation with selected customers, and then working with the sales manager to reprimand those sales staff who have authorized special terms without notifying anyone else in the company.

- **Require approval of bad debt write-offs.** A common form of fraud is for a collections person to write off an invoice as a bad debt and then pocket the customer payment when it arrives. This can be avoided by requiring management approval of all bad debt write-offs (though staffs are usually allowed to write off small balances as an efficiency measure). Management should be particularly wary when a large proportion of bad debt requests come from the same collections person, indicating a possible fraud pattern.

- **Require approval of credits.** Credits against invoices can be required for other reasons than bad debts—incorrect pricing or quantities delivered, incorrect payment terms, and so on. In these cases, management approval should be required not only to detect the presence of false credit claims, but also to spot patterns indicating some underlying problem requiring correction, such as inaccurate order picking in the warehouse.

- **Match invoiced quantities to the shipping log.** It is useful to spot-check the quantities invoiced to the quantities listed on the shipping log. By doing so, one can detect fraud in the billing department caused by invoicing for too many units, with the accounting staff pocketing the difference when it arrives. This is a rare form of fraud, since it generally requires collaboration between the billing and cash receipts staff, and so the control is needed only where the fraud risk clearly exists.

- **Verify invoice pricing.** The billing department can commit fraud by issuing fake invoices to customers at improperly high prices, and then pocketing the difference between the regular and inflated prices when the customer check arrives. Having someone compare the pricing on invoices to a standard price list before invoices are mailed can spot this issue. As was the case for the last control, this form of fraud is possible only when there is a risk of collaboration between the billing and cash receipts staff, so the control is needed only when the fraud risk is present.

FORMS AND REPORTS

Cash—Mailroom Remittance Receipt

In larger companies, all incoming checks are recorded in the mailroom, which summarizes all receipts on a worksheet such as the one shown in Exhibit 2-3. This sheet can then be matched against cash receipts recorded by the accounting department, thereby indicating if any checks were fraudulently removed from the mail delivered by the mailroom staff. The "City and State" column on the report is used to identify which branch of customer has sent in a check, since payments may be received from multiple customer locations. For companies with a smaller number of customers, this column can be omitted.

Exhibit 2-3: Mailroom Remittance Sheet

			Company Name		
			Mailroom Remittance Sheet		
			Receipts of [Month/Day/Year]		
Check Number	Source If Not Check		Sender	City and State	Amount
1602			The Rush Airplane Company	Scranton, PA	$ 126.12
	Cash		Rental Air Service	Stamford, CT	$ 19.50
2402			Automatic Service Company	Los Angeles, CA	$ 316.00
1613			Voe Parts Dealer	Toledo, OH	$ 2.90
9865			Brush Electric Company	Chicago, IL	$ 25.50
2915			Ajax Manufacturing Company	Cleveland, OH	$1,002.60
8512			Apex Machine Tool Co.	New York, NY	$ 18.60
				Total Receipts	$1,511.22
				Prepared by:	_____
				Date:	_____

*SOURCE: Adapted with permission from p. 617 of Willson et al., **Controllership, 6E** (John Wiley & Sons, Inc., Hoboken, NJ, 1999).*

Cash—Bank Reconciliation

The bank reconciliation identifies the differences between a company's record of cash on hand and that of its bank. Preparing the report frequently results in the identification of errors in recorded cash transactions, and can be used as a control to spot fraudulent activities. It should be completed at least once a month, but can be done each day if online bank records are available through the Internet. Many accounting computer systems include a partially automated reconciliation module, along with a bank reconciliation report. If not, the format in Exhibit 2-4 can be used as a model.

Exhibit 2-4: Bank Reconciliation Report

	Company Name			
	Bank Reconciliation			
Bank: _____		Account No: _____		
As of _____				

	Balance 11/30/XX	Receipts	Disbursements	Balance 12/31/XX
Per bank...................	$126,312.50	$92,420.00	$85,119.00	$133,613.50
Add:				
Deposits in transit				
11/30 per book	$ 5,600.00	$ (5,600.00)		
12/31 per book		$12,500.00		$ 12,500.00
Deduct				
Outstanding checks				
November (see list)	$ 4,320.00		$ (4,115.00)	$ 205.00
December (see list)			$ 6,110.00	$ 6,110.00
Other Items:				
Bank charges not recorded			-5.01	5.01
Per books.................	$127,592.50	$99,320.00	$87,108.99	$139,803.51
			Prepared by _____	
			Date _____	

SOURCE: Adapted with permission from p. 623 of Willson et al., **Controllership, 6E** *(John Wiley & Sons, Inc., Hoboken, NJ, 1999).*

Cash—Cash Forecasting Model

The cash forecasting model is the most important report in the controller's arsenal of cash reports, because it gives a detailed forward-looking view of when excess cash can be invested or when new cash inflows are required. A good working model is shown in Exhibit 2-5. The report shows weekly cash flows for each week of the next two months, which are usually fairly predictable in most businesses. The model then switches to monthly forecasts for the following three months, which tend to be increasingly inaccurate for the later months. The first block of information is receipts from sales projections, which is drawn for the corporate sales funnel report. The next block is uncollected invoices, listing larger invoices by customer name and smaller ones at a summary level in a Cash, Minor Invoices category. The collections staff can itemize the weeks in which individual collections are most likely to arise, based on their experience with individual customers. The third block contains the most common categories of expenses, such as payroll, rent, and capital purchases, with all other expenses summarized under the Other Expenses category. By combining cash inflows from the first two blocks with the cash outflows listed in the third block, one can obtain a reasonably accurate picture of cash flows in the near term. These projections can be compared to budgeted cash levels, which are noted at the bottom of the report, in order to gain some idea of the accuracy of the budgeting process.

Exhibit 2-5: Cash Forecasting Model

Cash Forecast												
Date Last Updated	3/9/2007											
	For the Week Beginning on								(partial)			
	3/9/2007	3/16/2007	3/23/2007	3/30/2007	4/6/2007	4/13/2007	4/20/2007	4/27/2007	5/4/2007	May-07	Jun-07	Jul-07
Beginning Cash Balance	**$1,037,191**	$1,034,369	$968,336	$367,918	$918,082	$932,850	$918,747	$829,959	$834,924	$754,124	$808,592	$798,554
Receipts from Sales Projections:												
Coal Bed Drilling Corp.										$ 16,937		$174,525
Oil Patch Kids Corp.								$ 12,965		$ 45,521		$ 28,775
Overfault & Sons Inc.									$ 2,500		$129,000	
Platte River Drillers									$ 3,000	$ 53,000		
Powder River Supplies Inc.									$ 8,700		$ 18,500	$ 14,500
Submersible Drillers Ltd.										$ 2,500	$ 16,250	$ 16,250
Commercial, Various											$ 25,000	$ 25,000
Uncollected Invoices:												
Canadian Drillers Ltd			$ 9,975									
Coastal Mudlogging Co.			$ 6,686									
Dept. of the Interior	$ 1,823			$ 11,629		$ 2,897				$ 18,510		
Drill Tip Repair Co.				$ 5,575								
Overfault & Sons Inc.			$ 9,229									
Submersible Drillers Ltd.				$ 4,245								
U.S. Forest Service		$ 2,967	$ 812	$ 8,715								
Cash, Minor Invoices	$ 2,355	$ --	$ 3,668	$ --	$ 21,768							
Total Cash In	$ 4,178	$ 2,967	$ 30,370	$ 30,164	$ 21,768	$ 2,897	$ --	$ 12,965	$ 14,200	$139,468	$188,750	$259,050
Cash Out:												
Payroll + Payroll Taxes		$ 62,000		$ 65,000			$ 68,000		$ 71,000	$ 71,000	$138,000	$138,000
Commissions				$ 7,000					$ 7,000		$ 8,000	$ 9,000
Rent			$ 10,788				$ 10,788				$ 10,788	$ 10,788
Capital Purchases			$ 10,000			$ 10,000			$ 10,000		$ 10,000	$ 10,000
Other Expenses	$ 7,000	$ 7,000	$ 10,000	$ 8,000	$ 7,000	$ 7,000	$ 10,000	$ 8,000	$ 7,000	$ 14,000	$ 32,000	$ 32,000
Total Cash Out	$ 7,000	$ 69,000	$ 30,788	$ 80,000	$ 7,000	$ 17,000	$ 88,788	$ 8,000	$ 95,000	$ 85,000	$198,788	$199,788
Net Change in Cash	$ (2,822)	$ (66,033)	$ (418)	$ (49,836)	$ 14,768	$(14,103)	$(88,788)	$ 4,965	$ (80,800)	$ 54,468	$ (10,038)	$ 59,262
Ending Cash	$1,034,369	$ 968,336	$967,918	$918,082	$932,850	$918,747	$829,959	$834,924	$754,124	$808,592	$798,554	S857,816
Budgeted Cash Balance:				**897636**				**833,352**		**800,439**	**815,040**	**857,113**

SOURCE: Adapted with permission from p. 600 of Bragg, ***Ultimate Accountants' Reference*** *(John Wiley & Sons, Inc., Hoboken, NJ, 2006)*

Receivables—Bad Debt Authorization Form

The bad debt authorization form is used to itemize the specific invoice to be written off and the reason for doing so, and to obtain management permission for the write-off. Of considerable importance from an operational perspective is the list of reasons used on the form for writing off an invoice, since this information can be summarized and used to improve company systems to ensure that write-offs are reduced in the future. For example, if there are many incidents of "customer unable to pay," then there is a probable need for more intensive credit reviews prior to the acceptance of customer orders. Consequently, the form format shown in Exhibit 2-6 can and should be modified to match the types of bad debt problems being encountered by a business.

Exhibit 2-6: Bad Debt Authorization Form

```
+--------------------------------------------------------------------+
|                          Company Name                              |
|                 Bad Debt Write-Off Approval Form                   |
|                                                                    |
|  Customer Name: _____      Invoice Number: _____     |
|                                                                    |
|  Customer Code: _____      Invoice Amount: _____     |
+--------------------------------------------------------------------+
|                         Reason for Write-Off                       |
|                                                                    |
|         [ ]  Customer unable to pay                                |
|                                                                    |
|         [ ]  Damaged goods                                         |
|                                                                    |
|         [ ]  Incorrect pricing                                     |
|                                                                    |
|         [ ]  Incorrect shipment quantity                           |
|                                                                    |
|         [ ]  Product quality not acceptable                        |
|                                                                    |
|         Other nonstandard reasons for a write-off: _____     |
|                                                                    |
|         _____          |
|                                                                    |
|         _____          |
|                                                                    |
+--------------------------------------------------------------------+
|  Requested Write-off Amount: _____                       |
|                                                                    |
|  Name of Requesting Clerk: _____                         |
|                                                                    |
|  Signature of Requesting Clerk: _____   Date: _____   |
|                                                                    |
|  Name of Approving Manager: _____                        |
|                                                                    |
|  Signature of Approving Manager: _____  Date: _____   |
+--------------------------------------------------------------------+
```

Receivables—Collection Actions Taken

Any reasonably organized collections staff should make notes about the status of their collection activities with each customer account, including the dates of contact, representations made by customers, and when the next collection contact is scheduled to be made. This information may be just handwritten notes, in which case it is quite difficult to summarize into a report. A better approach is to have the entire collections staff use a centralized collections database, from which a variety of re-ports can be printed. With such a system, the report shown in Exhibit 2-7 can be easily printed whenever necessary. It can be sorted by the dollar amount of overdue balances to bring attention to the largest items, or by invoice date in order to focus attention on the oldest collection problems, or by collection staff so that problems with collection techniques can be highlighted.

Exhibit 2-7: Collection Actions Report

Collections Contact	Customer	Invoice Number	Amount	Next Contact Date	Comments
Jones	Alpha Labs	5418	$500.25	5/04	Waiting on controller approval
Jones	Blue Moon	5009	250.00	5/09	Sent bill of lading
Jones	White Ice	5200	375.15	5/03	Sent replacement part
Jones	Zora Inc.	5302	1,005.00	5/12	Meeting in person to discuss
Smith	Chai Tea	5400	2,709.15	5/01	Issued credit for price change
Smith	Deal Time	5417	5,010.00	5/13	Sent claim to bankruptcy court
Smith	Energy Ltd.	5304	128.45	5/08	Faxed new invoice copy
Smith	Foo & Sons	5215	495.31	5/07	Waiting for call back
Smith	Green Way	5450	95.97	5/05	Offered 25% discount to pay

Receivables—Aging Report

The single most used receivables report is the aging report, which divides out-standing invoices into thirty-day time buckets. It is heavily used by the collections staff as their key source of information about old unpaid invoices. The report is standard with all accounting packages, and so would be constructed only if a manual accounting system were used. An example is shown in Exhibit 2-8. The main modification worth considering is shifting the date range on the time buckets to match the terms of company invoices, plus a few days to allow for mail float. For example, altering the current time bucket to contain all invoices issued within the past thirty-five days instead of the usual thirty days would cover all invoices issued under "net thirty" terms, as well as any invoices already paid by customers but in transit to the company. This approach does not bring invoices to the attention of the collections staff until collection activities are truly required.

Exhibit 2-8: Accounts Receivable Aging Report

Customer	Invoice no.	Current	+30 Days	+60 Days	+90 Days
Alpha Labs	5418			$500.25	
	5603		$1,042.75		
	5916	$639.50			
Chai Tea Inc.	5400				$2,709.15
	5511			$25.19	
	5618		$842.68		
	5900	$100.00			
Totals		$739.50	$1,885.43	$525.44	$2,709.15

Receivables—Loan Collateralization Report

Receivables are the most common asset used as loan collateral, since they can be more easily liquidated than other assets. Typically, a lender requires that a loan collateralization report such as the one shown in Exhibit 2-9 be completed at the end of each month. The agreement usually requires that old receivables be stripped from the reported balance to arrive at a core set of receivables most likely to be collected by the lender in the event of default. In addition, each category of assets used as collateral is multiplied by a reduction percentage (shown in bold in the exhibit), reflecting the amount of cash the lender believes it can collect if it were to sell each type of asset. The reduced amount of all asset types is then summarized and compared to the outstanding loan balance; if the collateral amount has dropped below the loan balance, then the company must pay back the difference. The report is typically signed by a company officer.

Exhibit 2-9: Loan Collateralization Report

Company Name		
Loan Collateralization Report		
For the month ended: _____		
Accounts receivable balance	$1,800,000	
Less receivables > 90 days old	-$42,500	
Net accounts receivable	$1,757,500	
80% of net accounts receivable balance		$1,406,000
Raw materials inventory balance	$2,020,000	
40% of raw materials inventory balance		$1,010,000
Finished goods inventory balance	$515,000	
70% of finished goods inventory balance		$360,500
Total collateral		$2,776,500
Total loan balance		$2,000,000
Total collateral available for use		$776,500

I assert that the above calculation is correct, and that all bad debts, work in process, and obsolete inventory have been removed from the above balances.

CFO Signature: _____   Date: _____

FOOTNOTES

Cash—Restrictions on Use

Any restriction on a company's use of its cash should be disclosed in a footnote. An example follows:

Contributors to the organization have specified that their contributions be restricted to one of three funds: conservation, trail maintenance, and mountain properties. As of year-end, approximately $875,000 was restricted in the conservation fund, $520,000 in the trail maintenance fund, and $1,209,000 in the mountain properties fund. This left approximately $2,041,000 in unrestricted cash.

Cash—Restrictions Caused by Compensating Balance Agreements

If there are restrictions on a company's cash balances caused by compensating balance agreements, a footnote should detail the terms of the agreement as well as the amount of cash restricted by the agreement. An example follows:

As part of the company's loan arrangement with the Second National Bank of Boise, it must maintain a compensating balance at the bank of no less than $200,000 at all times. The bank segregates this amount and does not allow drawdowns from it unless the balance of the associated line of credit is less than $500,000. Also, the bank requires an additional compensating balance of 10% of the loan balance; there is no restriction on use of this additional compensating balance, but the company must pay an additional 2% interest on the loan balance whenever its average cash balance drops below the required compensating balance. During the past year, this resulted in an average 0.4% increase in the average interest rate paid on the line of credit.

Cash—Excessive Concentration in Uninsured Accounts

If there is a significant amount of credit risk resulting from the excessive concentration of cash in bank accounts that exceeds federally insured limits, then the excess amounts should be revealed in a footnote. An example follows:

The company concentrates the bulk of its cash at the Second National Bank of Boise for cash management purposes. This typically results in cash investments exceeding Federal Deposit Insurance Corporation (FDIC) insurance limits. As of the balance sheet date, $2,045,000 held as cash reserves at this bank exceeded the FDIC insurance limits.

Receivables—Bad Debt Recognition

The method by which a company derives its bad debt reserves should be noted in a footnote, including the amount of the reserve contained within the balance sheet, and its method for recognizing bad debts. Also note any factors influencing the judgment of management in calculating the reserves. An example follows:

The company calculates a bad debt reserve based on a rolling average of actual bad debt losses over the past three months, divided by the average amount of accounts receivable outstanding during that period. It calculates separate loss percentages for its government and commercial receivables, since government receivables have a significantly lower loss rate. Given the current recession, management has elected to increase this calculated reserve by an additional 1.5%. As of the balance sheet date, the loss reserve percentage for government receivables was 1.1%, while the reserve for commercial receivables was 2.9%. This resulted in a total loss reserve of $329,000 on outstanding accounts receivable of $18,275,000. The company recognizes all receivables as bad debts that have been unpaid for more than ninety days past their due dates, or earlier upon the joint agreement of management and the collections staff, or immediately if a customer declares bankruptcy.

Receivables—Separation of Types

Though different types of receivables may be clustered into a single line item on the balance sheet, one should describe the different types of receivables in a footnote, describing each general category of receivable and the approximate amount of each type. An example follows:

> The ABC Truck Company had approximately $12,525,000 in accounts receivable as of the balance sheet date. Of this amount, $485,000 was a short-term note due from a distributor, while $48,000 was for a cash advance to a company officer and $9,000 was for cash advances to non-key employees. The company expects all cash advances to be paid within ninety days, except for the advance to the company officer, which will be paid back as a single balloon payment in six months.

Receivables—Used as Collateral

When accounts receivable are pledged to a lender as collateral on a loan, the terms of the agreement should be listed in the footnotes, as well as the carrying amount of the receivables. An example follows:

> The XYZ Scuba Supplies Company has entered into a loan agreement with the International Credit Consortium. Under the terms of the agreement, XYZ has pledged the full amount of its trade receivables as collateral on a revolving line of credit carrying a floating interest rate 2% above the prime rate. The amount loaned cannot exceed 80% of all outstanding accounts receivable billed within the past ninety days. As of the balance sheet date, the total amount of accounts receivable subject to this agreement was $2,500,000.

JOURNAL ENTRIES

Cash

Bank reconciliation. To adjust the accounting records to reflect differences between the book and bank records. The cash entry is listed as a credit, on the assumption that bank-related expenses outweigh the interest income.

Bank charges	xxx	
Credit card charges	xxx	
Interest income		xxx
Cash		xxx

Receivables

Accounts receivable, initial entry. To record the creation of a receivable at the point when a sale is made. The entry includes the creation of a liability account for a sales tax. The second entry records the elimination of the account receivable when cash is received from the customer, while the third entry records the payment of sales taxes payable to the relevant government authority.

Accounts receivable	xxx	
Sales		xxx
Sales taxes payable		xxx

Cash	xxx	
Accounts receivable		xxx
Sales taxes payable	xxx	
Cash		xxx

Accounts receivable, recording of long-term payment terms. To record any accounts receivable not due for payment for at least one year. The receivable is discounted at no less than the market rate of interest. The first journal entry shows the initial record of sale, while the second entry shows the gradual recognition of interest income associated with the receivable.

Notes receivable	xxx	
Revenue		xxx
Discount on notes receivable		xxx
Discount on notes receivable	xxx	
Interest income		xxx

Accounts receivable, sale of. To record the outright sale of an account receivable, including the recognition of interest expense and any loss on the transaction due to the expected incurrence of bad debt losses by the factor on the purchased receivables.

Cash	xxx	
Factoring expense	xxx	
Loss on sale of receivables	xxx	
Interest expense	xxx	
Accounts receivable		xxx

Accounts receivable, payment due from factor. To record the outright sale of accounts receivable to a factor, but without taking payment until the due date of the underlying receivables, thereby avoiding interest expenses. The second entry records the eventual payment by the factor for the transferred receivables.

Receivable due from factor	xxx	
Factoring expense	xxx	
Loss on sale of receivables	xxx	
Accounts receivable		xxx
Cash	xxx	
Receivable due from factor		xxx

Accounts receivable, establishment of recourse obligation. To record an obligation to pay back a factor for any bad debts experienced as part of a receivable sale to the factor, for which the company is liable under a factoring with recourse arrangement. The second entry shows the recourse obligation being reduced as bad debts are incurred and the company pays back the factor for the receivables written off as bad debts.

Allowance for bad debts	xxx	
Recourse obligation		xxx
Recourse obligation	xxx	
Cash		xxx

Accounts receivable, write off. To cancel an account receivable by offsetting it against the reserve for bad debts located in the bad debt accrual account.

```
Bad debt accrual                         xxx
    Accounts receivable                              xxx
```

Accrue bad debt expense. To accrue for projected bad debts, based on historical experience.

```
Bad debt expense                         xxx
    Bad debt accrual                                 xxx
```

Account for receipt of written-off receivable. To record the receipt of cash on a sale that had previously been written off as uncollectible.

```
Cash                                     xxx
    Bad debt accrual                                 xxx
```

Accrue for sales returns. To accrue for expected sales returns from sales made on approval, based on historical experience.

```
Sales returns expense                    xxx
    Reserve for sales returns                        xxx
```

Early payment discounts, record receipt of. To record the amount of early payment discounts taken by customers as part of their payments for accounts receivable.

```
Cash                                     xxx
Sales:  Discounts taken                  xxx
    Accounts receivable                              xxx
```

RECORDKEEPING

Detailed and well-organized cash records are needed by all external auditors. Accordingly, all bank statements should be stored in a binder by account number, and by date within each account number. In addition, a copy of the bank reconciliation for each month should be stored alongside each bank statement. If canceled checks are returned by the bank, they can be stored separately and labeled by month of receipt. If canceled checks are stored, one should pay the bank a small additional amount to sort the checks by check number prior to returning them to the company, which makes it much easier to locate checks in the archives.

Prepaid expenses should be reconciled as part of the month-end closing process, so there is no risk of an item continuing to be carried on the books as an asset when it should really have been written off as an expense. This is a common problem that can have serious ramifications at the end of the reporting year if large amounts of prepaid items have been ignored, resulting in large write-offs that drive profits below predicted levels. The best approach is to list not only the detail in the prepaid expense account, but also the date by which it is to be written off (if any) and the calculation method used to write it off over time. The spreadsheet should be retained in the journal entry file for each month in which a balance is maintained in the prepaid expense account. An example of such a reporting format is shown in Exhibit 2-10.

Exhibit 2-10: Itemization of Prepaid Expenses

Origination date	Payee	Description	Termination date	Remaining amount
1/07	MESE LLC	Employers' council annual dues (expense at 1/12 per month)	12/07	3,200.00
7/07	LifeConcepts	Key man life insurance (expense at 1/6 per month)	12/07	5,800.00
8/07	CSE Software	Software maintenance fee (expense at 1/12 per month)	7/08	29,500.00
10/07	Halley & Burns	Annual audit fee (expense at 1/12 per month)	9/08	24,000.00
			Total	$62,500.00

Auditors reviewing a company's accounts receivable balances are primarily interested in an accounts receivable aging report that they can trace back to individual invoices and supporting documents, showing evidence of product shipment or services rendered, such as shipping logs, bills of lading, and employee time sheets showing evidence of time billed to customer projects. Thus, recordkeeping for accounts receivable should include a complete aging as of the fiscal year-end date, while invoices should be stored in order either by customer name or invoice number, so they can be easily traced back from the receivables aging document. The packet of information used to create each invoice, such as freight billing information, time sheets, bills of lading, customers, or shipping logs, should be stapled to each invoice, so that proof of delivery is easily accessible.

Accounts receivable information must also be stored for sales tax auditors. They will want to determine which invoices were billed within their state, so it is useful to have access to a report that sorts invoices by state, though a detailed sales journal is usually acceptable. In addition, one can regularly archive a report listing customer addresses, which government auditors can then use to trace back to the sales journal for those customers whose addresses are in the state for which sales tax remittances are being investigated. These auditors will trace back from the sales journal to individual invoices in order to test sales tax calculations, so the same packets of invoice information described in the previous paragraph must be retained for this purpose, too. Sales tax remittance forms must also be retained, since auditors will want to compare them to the records in the sales tax payable account in the general ledger to ensure that all liabilities are being properly paid to the applicable state sales tax revenue department.

Completed bad debt write-off forms should be sorted by date and stored in a separate binder in the archives. This information is particularly useful in situations where fraud by a collections person is suspected, and evidence is needed detailing the amounts of write-offs requested, the reasons given, and who approved the forms. Given the sensitive nature of this information, the binder should be stored in a secure location.

3 SHORT-TERM INVESTMENTS AND FINANCIAL INSTRUMENTS

DEFINITIONS OF TERMS

Cash flow hedge. The use of an offsetting cash flow from a hedging instrument to reduce the uncertainty of future cash flows.

Derivative. A financial instrument whose fair value is based on changes in a benchmark. It is frequently used as a hedging instrument to offset changes in the fair value of hedged items. Examples of derivatives are interest rate caps and floors, option contracts, letters of credit, swaps, and futures.

Fair value hedge. A hedge designed to protect the fair value of an asset.

Financial instrument. A contract to exchange cash or other financial instruments between entities, or an ownership interest in another entity, or cash.

Forecasted transaction. An expected transaction that has not yet occurred, and for which there is no final commitment.

Foreign currency hedge. A hedge designed to protect against future fluctuations in the value of an investment denominated in a foreign currency.

Hedge. The act of protecting oneself against potentially unfavorable pricing changes, usually by financing an asset with an offsetting liability having a similar maturity, or vice versa.

CONCEPTS AND EXAMPLES

Fair Value Hedges

A hedging transaction qualifies as a fair value hedge only if both the hedging instrument and the hedged item qualify under all of the following criteria:

- **Documentation.** At hedge inception, there is documentation of the relationship between the hedging instrument and the hedged item, the risk management objectives of the hedging transaction, how the hedge is to be undertaken, the method to be used for gain or loss recognition, identification of the instrument used for the hedge, and how the effectiveness calculation is measured.

- **Effectiveness.** There is a high level of expected effectiveness for the transaction to regularly create offsetting fair value changes.
- **Options.** If using a written option, there must be as much potential for a gain as a loss from fair value changes.

A financial asset or liability is considered a hedged item to which a hedging instrument can be matched only if it qualifies under all of the following criteria:

- It is not a held-to-maturity debt security, unless the hedged risk does not include changes in the interest rate or foreign exchange rate.
- It is exposed to fair value changes that can impact earnings.
- The documented hedge risk is comprised of fair value changes in the market interest rates, the total hedged item, foreign currency rates, or the obligor's creditworthiness.
- It is not an equity method investment, minority interest, or firm commitment to acquire or dispose of a business.
- It must be specifically associated with a fair value risk, which must be either changes in the fair value of a total hedged item (or a percentage thereof), specific contractual cash flows, the residual value of a lessor's net investment in a direct financing or sales-type lease, or a call, put, floor, or cap not qualifying as an embedded derivative.

Gains and losses on both the hedging instrument and hedged item are recognized in earnings, while the book value of the hedged item is adjusted by the amount of any gains or losses. The impact of any ineffective amounts or factors excluded from a hedging relationship in its initial documentation is recognized in earnings. This accounting can continue until such time as the criteria for the hedge are no longer met, the hedging designation is canceled, or the derivative instruments used in the hedge are terminated. If any of these circumstances arise, a new hedging relationship can be documented with a different derivative instrument.

The periodic determination of hedging effectiveness first requires the establishment of the method to be used to assess hedge effectiveness, as well as the designation of what type of fair value change in the derivative instrument will be used to assess the hedge effectiveness. Hedge effectiveness must be evaluated at least quarterly, and must include an assessment of both the retrospective and prospective ability of the hedging instrument. Both assessment types can be accomplished through statistical analysis.

There are no quantitative GAAP guidelines for the determination of fair value hedging effectiveness, so a company should create a policy defining the hedging range for different types of hedges (see the Policies and Controls sections).

Cash Flow Hedges

A cash flow hedge is designed to offset uncertain future cash flows. To establish a valid cash flow hedge, one must document the relationship between the hedging instrument and an asset, liability, or forecasted transaction (including expected date of occurrence and amount). The documentation must also describe the hedging strategy, risk management objectives, and how the effectiveness of the transaction shall be measured.

In addition, the hedging relationship must be expected to be highly effective, and evaluated at least quarterly to ensure that this is the case.

If one intends to match a forecasted transaction with a hedging instrument, this is allowable only if the forecasted transaction is probable, is not a held-to-maturity debt security, is specifically identified, could affect earnings, is with an external party, and does not involve a business combination or any equity investment.

One must discontinue a cash flow hedge when the hedge criteria are no longer met, the hedging designation is canceled, or the derivative instruments used in the hedge are terminated. If any of these circumstances arise, a new hedging relationship can be documented with a different derivative instrument.

When reporting derivative gains and losses for a cash flow hedge, the effective portion of the gain or loss is reported in other comprehensive income, while any gains or losses attributable to the ineffective portion of the hedge are reported in earnings. Any remaining gain or loss on the hedging relationship is reported in earnings. Whenever one expects a net loss from the hedging transaction, the amount not expected to be recovered must be shifted in the current period from other comprehensive income to earnings. Also, if a hedging relationship is established for a forecasted cash flow transaction and the transaction is deemed unlikely to occur, any gain or loss thus far recorded in other comprehensive income must be shifted to earnings in the current period.

There are no quantitative GAAP guidelines for the determination of fair value hedging effectiveness, so a company should create a policy defining the hedging range for different types of hedges (see the Policies and Controls sections).

Foreign Currency Hedges

In brief, the accounting for various types of foreign currency hedges is as follows:

- **Available-for-sale security hedge.** One can designate a derivative instrument as a fair value hedge for an available-for-sale **equity** security only if all fair value hedge criteria are met and payments to equity holders are denominated in the same currency to be received upon sale of the security, and the security is not publicly traded in the investor's functional currency. These restrictions do not apply if the available-for-sale security is a debt security.
- **Debt-for-equity swaps.** If a company's foreign debt is legally required to be re-invested in that country, one must first determine the difference between the US dollar values of the debt and the equity in which it is invested. The difference must first be used to reduce the basis of acquired long-term assets and then to reduce the basis of existing long-term assets, with any remaining variance being reported as negative goodwill.
- **Forecasted transaction in foreign currency denomination.** One can designate a derivative instrument as a cash flow hedge of a forecasted transaction denominated in a foreign currency. Cash flow hedge accounting can be used

only if the transaction is not denominated in the functional currency, all cash flow hedge criteria are met, foreign currency inflows and outflows are not included in the same groups of transactions, and one party to the transaction is an operating unit with foreign currency exposure.

- **Net investment hedge.** One can designate a derivative or financial instrument as a foreign currency hedge for an investment in a foreign operation. Any effective gain or loss is reported as a translation adjustment.
- **Unrecognized firm commitment hedge.** One can designate a derivative or financial instrument as a fair value hedge of an unrecognized firm commitment in a foreign currency.

POLICIES

Hedges—General

- **The determination of hedge effectiveness shall always use the same method for similar types of hedges.** GAAP allows one to use different assessment techniques in determining whether a hedge is highly effective. However, changing methods, even when justified, allows the accounting staff room to alter effectiveness designations, which can yield variations in the level of reported earnings. Consequently, creating and consistently using a standard assessment method for each type of hedge eliminates the risk of assessment manipulation.
- **A hedge shall be considered highly effective if the fair values of the hedging instrument and hedged item are at least ___% offset.** GAAP does not quantitatively specify what constitutes a highly effective hedge, so a company should create a policy defining the number. A different hedging range can be used for different types of hedges.

CONTROLS

Hedges—General

- **Include in the hedging procedure a requirement for full documentation of each hedge.** Hedging transactions are allowed under GAAP only if they are fully documented at the inception of the hedge. One can ensure compliance by including the documentation requirement in an accounting procedure for creating hedges.

Fair Value Hedges

- **Include in the closing procedure a requirement to review the effectiveness of any fair value hedges.** GAAP requires that hedging transactions be accounted for as fair value hedges only if a hedging relationship regularly produces offsets to fair value changes. Since this review must be conducted on at least a quarterly basis and every time financial statements are issued, including the requirement in the closing procedure is an effective way to ensure compliance with GAAP.

- **Compare hedging effectiveness assessments to the corporate policy setting forth effectiveness ranges.** GAAP does not specify the exact amount by which hedging instruments and hedged items must offset each other in order to be deemed highly effective, so a corporate policy should be established (see the Policies section) to create such a standard. This control is intended to ensure that the policy is followed when making effectiveness assessments. Comparison to the corporate policy should be included in the assessment procedure.

Cash Flow Hedges

- **Include in the monthly financial statement procedure a review of the recoverability of cash flow hedge losses.** GAAP requires that a nonrecoverable cash flow hedge loss be shifted in the current period from other comprehensive income to earnings. Since this can result only in a reduced level of earnings, accounting personnel tend not to conduct the review. Including the step in the monthly procedure is a good way to ensure prompt loss recognition.

- **Include in the monthly financial statement procedure a review of the likely occurrence of forecasted cash flow transactions.** GAAP requires that any accumulated gain or loss recorded in other comprehensive income be shifted into earnings as soon as it becomes probable that the forecasted cash flow transaction will not take place. Including a standard periodic review of forecasted transactions in the monthly procedure is a good way to ensure prompt inclusion of accumulated gains or losses in earnings.

- **Compare hedging effectiveness assessments to the corporate policy setting forth effectiveness ranges.** GAAP does not specify the exact amount by which hedging instruments and hedged items must offset each other in order to be deemed highly effective, so a corporate policy should be established (see the Policies section) to create such a standard. This control is intended to ensure that the policy is followed when making effectiveness assessments. Comparison to the corporate policy should be included in the assessment procedure.

FOOTNOTES

Short-Term Investments

A company should disclose the types of investments it makes on a short-term basis, as well as their usual term and how they are recorded in the financial records. An example follows:

> The company invests all excess cash over $1 million in marketable stocks and bonds. All stocks held are required by company policy to be of companies listed on the New York Stock Exchange, while all bonds must be of investment grade. Given the company's high tax bracket, it keeps at least 50% of all excess cash invested in investment-grade tax-free municipal bonds. These investments are carried at cost, which approximates market pricing.

Restricted Short-Term Investments

If there is a restriction on the ability of a company to access its invested funds, this information should be disclosed, along with the reason for the restriction, the amount restricted, and the duration of the restriction period. An example follows:

> The company is required by the terms of its building term loan with the Second National Bank of Milwaukee to restrict all investments related to its loan for the construction of a new corporate headquarters. Accordingly, the Second National Bank has custody over these funds, which are invested in short-term US Treasury funds yielding approximately 3.25%. The restricted amount is $4,525,000 as of the balance sheet date, and is expected to be eliminated as of year-end, when the headquarters building will be completed and all contractors paid.

Disclosure of Objectives for Derivative Use

If a company is party to a derivative financial instrument, it should state its objective and related strategies for using such an instrument and what specific risks are being hedged with its use. The following additional disclosures are required for fair value and cash flow hedges:

- **Fair value hedge.** One must disclose the net gain or loss recognized in earnings during the period stemming from the ineffective portion of a fair value hedge, as well as any derivative instrument's gain or loss excluded from the assessment of hedge effectiveness. If a hedged firm commitment no longer qualifies as a fair value hedge, then disclosure must also include the resulting gain or loss shown in earnings.
- **Cash flow hedge.** One must disclose the net gain or loss recognized in earnings during the period stemming from the ineffective portion of a cash flow hedge, as well as any derivative instrument's gain or loss excluded from the assessment of hedge effectiveness. Also note the future events that will result in the reclassification of gains or losses from other comprehensive income into earnings, as well as the net amount expected to be reclassified in the next year.

    Further, itemize the maximum time period over which the company hedges its exposure to cash flows from forecasted transactions (if any). Finally, if forecasted transactions are considered unlikely to occur, note the amount of gains or losses shifted from other comprehensive income into earnings as a result of canceling the hedge.

The first footnote sample is for a fair value hedge, while the second addresses a cash flow hedge:

1. The Company designates certain futures contracts as fair value hedges of firm commitments to purchase coal for electricity generation. Changes in the fair value of a derivative that is highly effective and that is designated and qualifies as a fair value hedge, along with the loss or gain on the hedged asset or liability that is attributable to the hedged risk are recorded in current period earnings. Ineffectiveness results when the change in the fair value of the hedge instruments differs from the change in fair value of the hedged item. Ineffectiveness recorded related to the Company's fair value hedges was not significant during fiscal 2007.

2. If a derivative instrument used by the Company in a cash flow hedge is sold, terminated, or exercised, the net gain or loss remains in accumulated other comprehensive income and is reclassified into earnings in the same period when the hedged transaction affects earnings. Accordingly, accumulated other comprehensive income at September 30, 2007, includes $6.5 million of the loss realized upon termination of derivative instruments that will be reclassified into earnings over the original term of the derivative instruments, which extend through December 2011. As of September 30, 2007, the Company had entered into contracts for derivative instruments, designated as cash flow hedges, covering 200,000 tons of coal with a floor price of $58 per ton and a ceiling price of $69 per ton, resulting in other current assets of $0.7 million and $0.7 million of accumulated other comprehensive income representing the effective portion of unrealized hedge gains associated with these derivative instruments.

Valuation of Financial Instruments

If a company has outstanding financial instruments, it must describe the method and assumptions used to estimate their fair value. If it is impossible to determine fair value, then it must disclose the carrying amount, effective interest rate, and maturity of the instruments, as well as why it is not possible to determine their fair value.

The Company's significant financial instruments include cash and cash equivalents, investments and debt. In evaluating the fair value of significant financial instruments, the Company generally uses quoted market prices of the same or similar instruments or calculates an estimated fair value on a discounted cash flow basis using the rates available for instruments with the same remaining maturities. As of December 31, 2007, the fair value of financial instruments held by the Company approximated the recorded value except for long-term debt. Fair value of long-term debt was $2.9 billion on December 31, 2007.

Hedging of Foreign Operation Investment

When a company hedges its investment in a foreign operation, it must disclose the net gain or loss incorporated within the cumulative translation adjustment. This applies to any derivative or hedging instruments that may cause foreign currency gains or losses. An example follows:

The company has invested $40 million in a manufacturing facility in Dubai. It has entered into certain foreign currency derivative instruments that are designed to hedge its investment in this facility. The cumulative translation adjustment includes a net loss of $1,240,000 from these derivative instruments.

RECORDKEEPING

At the inception of a fair value hedge, GAAP requires documentation of the relationship between the hedging instrument and the hedged item, the risk management objectives of the hedging transaction, how the hedge is to be undertaken, the method to be used for gain or loss recognition, identification of the instrument used for the hedge, and how the effectiveness calculation is measured. Since hedge accounting cannot be used unless this documentation exists, it is important to store a complete set of documentation for each hedge for the duration not only of the hedge, but also through the audit following the hedge termination. It can then be included in the archives with accounting documentation for the year in which the transaction terminated.

4 INVENTORY

DEFINITIONS OF TERMS

Book inventory. The amount of money invested in inventory, as per a company's accounting records. It consists of the beginning inventory balance, plus the cost of any receipts, less the cost of sold or scrapped inventory. It may be significantly different from the actual on-hand inventory if the two are not periodically reconciled.

Consignment inventory. Inventory that has been shifted to the location of a third party by the owning entity in order to sell it. The inventory continues to be recorded on the books of the owning entity until it has been sold.

Cycle counting. The ongoing incremental counting of perpetual inventory records, with the intent of correcting record inaccuracies and determining the underlying causes of those errors.

Finished goods. Completed manufactured goods that have not yet been sold.

First-in, first-out. A process costing methodology that assigns the earliest cost of production and materials to units being sold, while the latest costs of production and materials are assigned to units still retained in inventory.

Inventory. Tangible items held for sale, or that are being produced for this purpose, or that will be used during the manufacturing process to create these items.

Last-in, first-out. An inventory costing methodology that bases the recognized cost of sales on the most recent costs incurred, while the cost of ending inventory is based on the earliest costs incurred. The underlying reasoning for this costing system is the assumption that goods are sold in the reverse order of their manufacture.

Lower of cost or market. An accounting valuation rule used to reduce the reported cost of inventory to its current resale value if that cost is lower than its original cost of acquisition or manufacture.

Periodic inventory. An inventory tracking system that determines inventory levels only at fixed points in time through the use of physical inventory counts.

Perpetual inventory. An inventory tracking system that determines inventory levels on an ongoing basis by making incremental adjustments to inventory records based on individual production transactions.

Raw materials. Materials kept on hand prior to their use in the manufacturing process.

Scrap. The excess unusable material left over after a product has been manufactured.

Spoilage, abnormal. Spoilage arising from the production process that exceeds the normal or expected rate of spoilage. Since it is not a recurring or expected cost of ongoing production, it is expensed to the current period.

Spoilage, normal. The amount of spoilage that naturally arises as part of a production process, no matter how efficient the process may be.

Work in process. Inventory that is partway through the conversion process that will transform it into finished goods.

CONCEPTS AND EXAMPLES

Goods in Transit

Inventory that is in transit to the buyer continues to be owned by the seller as long as that entity is responsible for the transportation costs. If the seller is paying for transportation only to a certain point, such as to a third-party shipper, then its ownership stops at that point and is transferred to the buyer.

In reality, companies do not usually track goods in transit, preferring instead to not count them if they either have already left the facility (in the case of the seller) or have not yet arrived at the facility (in the case of the buyer). The reason for avoiding this task is the difficulty in determining the amount of goods in transit that belong to the company, especially when the accounting staff is trying to close the books very quickly and does not want to keep the books open long enough to make a proper determination. This avoidance has minimal impact on the receiving company's recordkeeping, since a missing inventory item would have required both a debit to an inventory account and a credit to a liability account, which cancel each other out. This is more of an issue for the shipping firm, since it is probably recognizing revenue at the point of shipment, rather than at some later point in transit, which can potentially overstate revenue if this occurs near the end of the reporting period.

Examples of different types of transit scenarios

- If goods are shipped under a cost, insurance and freight (C&F) contract, the buyer is paying for all delivery costs, and so acquires title to the goods as soon as they leave the seller's location.
- If goods are shipped Free Alongside (FAS), the seller is paying for delivery of the goods to the side of the ship that will transport the goods to the buyer. If so, it retains ownership of the goods until they are alongside the ship, at which point the buyer acquires title to the goods.
- If goods are shipped Free on Board (FOB) destination, then transport costs are paid by the seller, and ownership will not pass to the buyer until the carrier delivers the goods to the buyer.
- As indicated by the name, an Ex-Ship delivery means that the seller pays for a delivery until it has departed the ship, so it retains title to the goods until that point.
- If goods are shipped FOB shipping point, then transport costs are paid by the buyer, and ownership passes to the buyer as soon as the carrier takes possession of the delivery from the seller.
- If goods are shipped FOB a specific point, such as Nashville, then the seller retains title until the goods reach Nashville, at which point ownership transfers to the buyer.

Accounting for Inventories

The type and quantity of items stored in inventory can be accounted for on a periodic basis by using the **periodic inventory system,** which requires one to conduct a complete count of the physical inventory in order to obtain a calculation of the inventory cost. A more advanced method that does not require a complete inventory count is the perpetual inventory system; under this approach, one incrementally adds or subtracts inventory transactions to or from a beginning database of inventory records in order to maintain an ongoing balance of inventory quantities. The accuracy of the inventory records under this latter approach will likely degrade over time, so an ongoing cycle counting program is needed to maintain its accuracy level.

The perpetual inventory system is highly recommended, because it avoids expensive periodic inventory counts, which also tend not to yield accurate results. Also, it allows the purchasing staff to have greater confidence in what inventory is on hand for purchasing planning purposes. Further, accountants can complete period-end financial statements more quickly, without having to guess at ending inventory levels.

Perpetual inventory example

A company wishes to install a perpetual inventory system, but it has not established tight control over the warehouse area with fencing or gate control. Accordingly, production employees are able to enter the warehouse and remove items from the shelf for use in the manufacturing process. Because of this issue, inventory balances in the perpetual inventory system are chronically higher than is the really the case, since removed items are not being logged out of the system.

The scenario changes to one where the company has not assigned responsibility for inventory accuracy to anyone in the company, but still creates a perpetual inventory system. As a result, the employees charged with entering inventory transactions into the computer system have no reason to do so, and no one enforces high accuracy levels. In this case, inventory accuracy levels rapidly worsen, especially for those items being used on a regular basis, since they are most subject to transactional inaccuracies. Only the inventory of slow-moving items remains relatively accurate.

The scenario changes to one where transactional procedures have not been clearly established, and employees entering inventory transactions have not been properly trained. This results in the worst accuracy levels of the three scenarios, since employees are not even certain if they should be adding or subtracting quantities, what units of measure to enter, or what special transactions call for what types of computer entries.

Consigned inventory is any inventory shipped by a company to a reseller, while retaining ownership until the product is sold by the reseller. Until sold, the inventory remains on the books of the originating company and is not on the books of the reseller. A common cause of inventory valuation problems is the improper recording of consignment inventory on the books of a reseller. Inventory that has been sold with a **right of return** receives treatment similar to consignment inventory if the amount of future inventory returns cannot be reasonably estimated. Until the probability of returns is unlikely, the inventory must remain on the books of the selling company, even though legal title to the goods has passed to the buyer.

Right of return example

A company has sold a large shipment of refrigerators to a new customer. Included in the sales agreement is a provision allowing the customer to return one-third of the refrigerators within the next ninety days. Since the company has no experience with this customer, it cannot record the full amount of the sale. Instead, it records that portion of the sale associated with the refrigerators for which there is no right of return, and waits ninety days until the right of return has expired before recording the remainder of the sale.

Valuation of Inventories

Overhead costs allocable to inventory. All costs can be assigned to inventory that are incurred to put goods in a salable condition. For raw materials, this is the purchase price, inbound transportation costs, insurance, and handling costs. If inventory is in the work-in-process or finished goods stages, then an allocation of the overhead costs shown in Exhibit 4-1 must be added:

Exhibit 4-1: Costs to Allocate to Overhead

Depreciation of factory equipment	Quality control and inspection
Factory administration expenses	Rent, facility and equipment
Indirect labor and production supervisory wages	Repair expenses
Indirect materials and supplies	Rework labor, scrap and spoilage
Maintenance, factory and production equipment	Taxes related to production assets
Officer salaries related to production	Uncapitalized tools and equipment
Production employees' benefits	Utilities

Allocation of overhead costs can be made by any reasonable measure, but must be consistently applied across reporting periods. Common bases for overhead allocation are direct labor hours or machine hours used during the production of a product.

Overhead allocation example

A company manufactures and sells Product A and Product B. Both require considerable machining to complete, so it is appropriate to allocate overhead costs to them based on total hours of standard machine time used. In March, Product A manufacturing required a total of 4,375 hours of machine time. During the same month, all units of Product B manufactured required 2,615 hours of machine time. Thus, 63% of the overhead cost pool was allocated to Product A and 37% to Product B. This example results in a reasonably accurate allocation of overhead to products, especially if the bulk of expenses in the overhead pool relate to the machining equipment used to complete the products. However, if a significant proportion of expenses in the overhead cost pool could be reasonably assigned to some other allocation measure, then these costs could be stored in a separate cost pool and allocated in a different manner. For example, if Product A was quite bulky and required 90% of the storage space in the warehouse, as opposed to 10% for Product B, then 90% of the warehouse-related overhead costs could be reasonably allocated to Product A.

Lower of cost or market rule. A company is required to recognize an additional expense in its cost of goods sold in the current period for any of its inventory whose replacement cost (subject to certain restrictions) has declined below its carrying cost. If the market value of the inventory subsequently rises back to or above its original carrying cost, its recorded value cannot be increased back to the original carrying amount.

More specifically, the lower of cost or market (LCM) calculation means that the cost of inventory cannot be recorded higher than its replacement cost on the open market; the replacement cost is bounded at the high end by its eventual selling price, less costs of disposal, nor can it be recorded lower than that price, less a normal profit percentage. The concept is best demonstrated with the four scenarios listed in the following example:

Item	Selling price	–	Completion/ selling cost	=	Upper price boundary	–	Normal profit	=	Lower price boundary	Existing inventory cost	Replacement cost [1]	Market value [2]	LCM
A	$15.00		$ 4.00		$ 11.00		$ 2.20		$ 8.80	$ 8.00	$12.50	$11.00	$ 8.00
B	40.15		6.00		34.15		5.75		28.40	35.00	34.50	34.15	34.15
C	20.00		6.50		13.50		3.00		10.50	17.00	12.00	12.00	12.00
D	10.50		2.35		8.15		2.25		5.90	8.00	5.25	5.90	5.90

[1] *The cost at which an inventory item could be purchased on the open market*
[2] *Replacement cost, bracketed by the upper and lower price boundaries*

In the example, the numbers in the first six columns are used to derive the upper and lower boundaries of the market values that will be used for the lower of cost or market calculation. By subtracting the completion and selling costs from each product's selling price, we establish the upper price boundary (in bold) of the market cost calculation. By then subtracting the normal profit from the upper cost boundary of each product, we establish the lower price boundary. Using this information, the LCM calculation for each of the listed products is as follows:

- **Product A, replacement cost higher than existing inventory cost.** The market price cannot be higher than the upper boundary of $11.00, which is still higher than the existing inventory cost of $8.00. Thus, the LCM is the same as the existing inventory cost.
- **Product B, replacement cost lower than existing inventory cost, but higher than upper price boundary.** The replacement cost of $34.50 exceeds the upper price boundary of $34.15, so the market value is designated at $34.15. This is lower than the existing inventory cost, so the LCM becomes $34.15.
- **Product C, replacement cost lower than existing inventory cost, and within price boundaries.** The replacement cost of $12.00 is within the upper and lower price boundaries, and so is used as the market value. This is lower than the existing inventory cost of $17.00, so the LCM becomes $12.00.
- **Product D, replacement cost lower than existing inventory cost, but lower than lower price boundary.** The replacement cost of $5.25 is below the lower price boundary of $5.90, so the market value is designated as $5.90. This is lower than the existing inventory cost of $8.00, so the LCM becomes $5.90.

Specific identification inventory valuation method. When each individual item of inventory can be clearly identified, it is possible to create inventory costing records for each one, rather than summarizing costs by general inventory type. This approach is rarely used, since the amount of paperwork and effort associated with developing unit costs is far greater than under all other valuation techniques. It is most applicable in businesses such as home construction, where there are very few units of inventory to track, and where each item is truly unique.

First-in, first-out (FIFO) inventory valuation method. A computer manufacturer knows that the component parts it purchases are subject to extremely rapid rates of obsolescence, sometimes rendering a part worthless in a month or two. Accordingly, it will be sure to use up the oldest items in stock first, rather than running the risk of scrapping them a short way into the future. For this type of environment, the first-in, first-out (FIFO) method is the ideal way to deal with the flow of costs. This method assumes that the oldest parts in stock are always used first, which means that their associated old costs are used first, as well.

The concept is best illustrated with an example, which we show in Exhibit 4-2. In the first row, we create a single layer of inventory that results in 50 units of inventory, at a per-unit cost of $10.00. So far, the extended cost of the inventory is the same as we saw under the LIFO, but that will change as we proceed to the second row of data. In this row, we have monthly inventory usage of 350 units, which FIFO assumes will use the entire stock of 50 inventory units that were left over at the end of the preceding month, as well as 300 units that were purchased in the current month. This wipes out the first layer of inventory, leaving us with a single new layer that is composed of 700 units at a cost of $9.58 per unit. In the third row, there is 400 units of usage, which again comes from the first inventory layer, shrinking it down to just 300 units. However, since extra stock was purchased in the same period, we now have an extra inventory layer that is comprised of 250 units, at a cost of $10.65 per unit. The rest of the exhibit proceeds using the same FIFO layering assumptions.

Exhibit 4-2: FIFO Valuation Example

LIFO Costing
Part Number BK0043

Col. 1	Col. 2	Col. 3	Col. 4	Col. 5	Col. 6	Col. 7	Col. 8	Col. 9
Date purchased	*Quantity purchased*	*Cost per unit*	*Monthly usage*	*Net inventory remaining*	*Cost of 1st inventory layer*	*Cost of 2nd inventory layer*	*Cost of 3rd inventory layer*	*Extended inventory cost*
05/03/07	500	$ 10.00	450	50	(50 × $10.00)	--	--	$ 500
06/04/07	1,000	9.58	350	700	(700 × $9.58)	--	--	6,706
07/11/07	250	10.65	400	550	(300 × $9.58)	(250 × $10.65)	--	5,537
08/01/07	475	10.25	350	675	(200 × $10.65)	(475 × $10.25)	--	6,999
08/30/07	375	10.40	400	650	(275 × $10.40)	(375 × $10.40)	--	6,760
09/09/07	850	9.50	700	800	(800 × $9.50)	--	--	7,600
12/12/07	700	9.75	900	600	(600 × $9.75)	--	--	5,850
02/08/08	650	9.85	800	450	(450 × $9.85)	--	--	4,433
05/07/08	200	10.80	0	650	(450 × $9.85)	(200 × $10.80)	--	6,593
09/23/08	600	9.85	750	500	(500 × $9.85)	--	--	4,925

There are several factors to consider before implementing a FIFO costing system.

- **Fewer inventory layers.** The FIFO system generally results in fewer layers of inventory costs in the inventory database. For example, the LIFO model shown in Exhibit 4-3 contains four layers of costing data, whereas the FIFO model shown in Exhibit 4-2, which used exactly the same data, resulted in no more than two inventory layers. This conclusion generally holds true, because a LIFO system will leave some layers of costs completely untouched for long time periods, if inventory levels do not drop; whereas a FIFO system will continually clear out old layers of costs, so that multiple costing layers do not have a chance to accumulate.

- **Reduces taxes payable in periods of declining costs.** Though it is very unusual to see declining inventory costs, it sometimes occurs in industries where there is either ferocious price competition among suppliers, or else extremely high rates of innovation that in turn lead to cost reductions. In such cases, using the earliest costs first will result in the immediate recognition of the highest possible expense, which reduces the reported profit level, and therefore reduces taxes payable.

- **Shows higher profits in periods of rising costs.** Since it charges off the earliest costs first, any very recent increase in costs will be stored in inventory, rather than being immediately recognized. This will result in higher levels of reported profits, though the attendant income tax liability will also be higher.

- **Less risk of outdated costs in inventory.** Because old costs are used first in a FIFO system, there is no way for old and outdated costs to accumulate in inventory. This prevents the management group from having to worry about the adverse impact of inventory reductions on reported levels of profit, either with excessively high or low charges to the cost of goods sold. This avoids the dilemma noted earlier for LIFO, where just-in-time systems may not be implemented if the result will be a dramatically different cost of goods sold.

In short, the FIFO cost layering system tends to result in the storage of the most recently incurred costs in inventory and higher levels of reported profits. It is most useful for those companies whose main concern is reporting high profits rather reducing income taxes.

Last-in, first-out (LIFO) inventory valuation method. In a supermarket, the shelves are stocked several rows deep with products. A shopper will walk by and pick products from the front row. If the stocking person is lazy, he will then add products to the front row locations from which products were just taken, rather than shifting the oldest products to the front row and putting new ones in the back. This concept of always taking the newest products first is called last-in, first-out.

The following factors must be considered before implementing a LIFO system:

- **Many layers.** The LIFO cost flow approach can result in a large number of inventory layers, as shown in the exhibit. Though this is not important when a computerized accounting system is used that will automatically track a large number of such layers, it can be burdensome if the cost layers are manually tracked.

- **Alters the inventory valuation.** If there are significant changes in product costs over time, the earliest inventory layers may contain costs that are wildly different from market conditions in the current period, which could result in the recognition of unusually high or low costs if these cost layers are ever accessed. Also, LIFO costs can never be reduced to the lower of cost or market (see the Lower of Cost or Market Rule), thereby perpetuating any unusually high inventory values in the various inventory layers.

- **Reduces taxes payable in periods of rising costs.** In an inflationary environment, costs that are charged off to the cost of goods sold as soon as they are incurred will result in a higher cost of goods sold and a lower level of profitability, which in turn results in a lower tax liability. This is the principle reason why LIFO is used by most companies.

- **Requires consistent usage for all reporting.** Under IRS rules, if a company uses LIFO to value its inventory for tax reporting purposes, then it must do the same for its external financial reports. The result of this rule is that a company cannot report lower earnings for tax purposes and higher earnings for all other purposes by using an alternative inventory valuation method. However, it is still possible to mention what profits would have been if some other method had been used, but only in the form of a footnote appended to the financial statements. If financial reports are only generated for internal management consumption, then any valuation method may be used.

- **Interferes with the implementation of just-in-time systems.** As noted in the last bullet point, clearing out the final cost layers of a LIFO system can result in unusual cost of goods sold figures. If these results will cause a significant skewing of reported profitability, company management may be put in the unusual position of opposing the implementation of advanced manufacturing concepts, such as just-in-time, that reduce or eliminate inventory levels (with an attendant, and highly favorable, improvement in the amount of working capital requirements).

In short, LIFO is used primarily for reducing a company's income tax liability. This single focus can cause problems, such as too many cost layers, an excessively low inventory valuation, and a fear of inventory reductions due to the recognition of inventory cost layers that may contain very low per-unit costs, which will result in high levels of recognized profit and therefore a higher tax liability. Given these issues, one should carefully consider the utility of tax avoidance before implementing a LIFO cost layering system.

LIFO inventory valuation example

The Magic Pen Company has made 10 purchases, which are itemized in Exhibit 4-3. In the exhibit, the company has purchased 500 units of a product with part number BK0043 on May 3, 2007 (as noted in the first row of data), and uses 450 units during that month, leaving the company with 50 units. These 50 units were all purchased at a cost of $10.00 each, so they are itemized in column 6 as the first layer of inventory costs for this product. In the next row of data, an additional 1,000 units were bought on June 4, 2007, of which only 350 units were used. This leaves an additional 650 units at a purchase price of $9.58, which are placed in the second inventory layer, as noted in column 7. In the third row, there is a net decrease in the amount of inventory, so this reduction comes out of the second (or last) inventory layer in column 7; the earliest layer, as described in column 6, remains untouched, since it was the first layer of costs added, and will not be used until all other inventory has been eliminated. The exhibit continues through seven more transactions, at one point increasing to four layers of inventory costs.

Exhibit 4-3: FIFO Valuation Example

LIFO Costing
Part Number BK0043

Col. 1	Col.2	Col.3	Col.4	Col.5	Col.6	Col.7	Col.8	Col.9
Date purchased	Quantity purchased	Cost per unit	Monthly usage	Net inventory remaining	Cost of 1st inventory layer	Cost of 2nd inventory layer	Cost of 3rd inventory layer	Extended inventory cost
05/03/07	500	$ 10.00	450	50	(50 × $10.00)	--	--	$ 500
06/04/07	1,000	9.58	350	700	(50 × $10.00)	(650 × $9.58)	--	6,727
07/11/07	250	10.65	400	550	(50 × $10.00)	(500 × $9.58)	--	5,290
08/01/07	475	10.25	350	675	(50 × $10.00)	(500 × $9.58)	(125 × $10.25)	6,571
08/30/07	375	10.40	400	650	(50 × $10.00)	(500 × $9.58)	(100 × $10.25)	6,315
09/09/07	850	9.50	700	800	(50 × $10.00)	(500 × $9.58)	(100 × $10.25)	7,740
12/12/07	700	9.75	900	600	(50 × $10.00)	(500 × $9.58)	(50 × $9.58)	5,769
02/08/08	650	9.85	800	450	(50 × $10.00)	(400 × $9.58)	--	4,332
05/07/08	200	10.80	0	650	(50 × $10.00)	(400 × $9.58)	(200 × $10.00)	6,492
09/23/08	600	9.85	750	500	(50 × $10.00)	(400 × $9.58)	(50 × $9.85)	4,825

Dollar-value LIFO inventory valuation method. This method computes a conversion price index for the year-end inventory in comparison to the base year cost. This index is computed separately for each company business unit. The conversion price index can be computed with the **double-extension method.** Under this approach, the total extended cost of the inventory at both base year prices and the most recent prices are calculated. Then the total inventory cost at the most recent prices is divided by the total inventory cost at base year prices, resulting in a conversion price percentage, or index. The index represents the change in overall prices between the current year and the base year. This index must be computed and retained for each year in which the LIFO method is used.

There are two problems with the double-extension method. First, it requires a massive volume of calculations if there are many items in inventory. Second, tax regulations require that any new item added to inventory, no matter how many years after the establishment of the base year, have a base year cost included in the LIFO database for purposes of calculating the index. This base year cost is supposed to be the one in existence at the time of the base year, which may require considerable research to determine or estimate. Only if it is impossible to determine a base year cost can the current cost of a new inventory item be used as the base year cost. For these reasons, the double-extension inventory valuation method is not recommended in most cases.

Double-extension inventory valuation example

A company carries a single item of inventory in stock. It has retained the following year-end information about the item for the past four years:

Year	Ending unit quantity	Ending current price	Extended at current year-end price
1	3,500	$32.00	$112,000
2	7,000	34.50	241,500
3	5,500	36.00	198,000
4	7,250	37.50	271,875

The first year is the base year upon which the double-extension index will be based in later years. In the second year, we extend the total year-end inventory by both the base year price and the current year price, as follows:

Year-end quantity	Base-year cost	Extended at base-year cost	Ending current price	Extended at ending current price
7,000	$32.00	$224,000	$34.50	$241,500

To arrive at the index between year 2 and the base year, we divide the extended ending current price of $241,500 by the extended base year cost of $224,000, yielding an index of 107.8%.

The next step is to calculate the incremental amount of inventory added in year 2, determine its cost using base year prices, and then multiply this extended amount by our index of 107.8% to arrive at the cost of the incremental year 2 LIFO layer. The incremental amount of inventory added is the year-end quantity of 7,000 units, less the beginning balance of 3,500 units, which is 3,500 units. When multiplied by the base year cost of $32.00, we arrive at an incremental increase in inventory of $112,000. Finally, we multiply the $112,000 by the price index of 107.8% to determine that the cost of the year 2 LIFO layer is $120,736.

Thus, at the end of year 2, the total double-extension LIFO inventory valuation is the base year valuation of $112,000 plus the year 2 layer's valuation of $120,736, totaling $232,736.

In year 3, the amount of ending inventory has declined from the previous year, so no new layering calculation is required. Instead, we assume that the entire reduction of 1,500 units during that year were taken from the year 2 inventory layer. To calculate the amount of this reduction, we multiply the remaining amount of the year 2 layer (5,500 units less the base year amount of 3,500 units, or 2,000 units) times the ending base year price of $32.00 and the year 2 index of 107.8%. This calculation results in a new year 2 layer of $68,992.

Thus, at the end of year 3, the total double-extension LIFO inventory valuation is the base layer of $112,000 plus the reduced year 2 layer of $68,992, totaling $180,992.

In year 4, there is an increase in inventory, so we can calculate the presence of a new layer using the following table:

Year-end quantity	Base-year cost	Extended at base-year cost	Ending current price	Extended at ending current price
7,250	$32.00	$232,000	$37.50	$271,875

Again, we divide the extended ending current price of $271,875 by the extended base year cost of $232,000, yielding an index of 117.2%. To complete the calculation, we then multiply the incremental increase in inventory over year 3 of 1,750 units, multiply it by the base year cost of $32.00/unit, and then multiply the result by our new index of 117.2% to arrive at a year-4 LIFO layer of $65,632.

Thus, after four years of inventory layering calculations, the double-extension LIFO valuation consists of the following three layers:

Layer type	Layer valuation	Layer index
Base layer	$112,000	0.0%
Year 2 layer	68,992	107.8%
Year 4 layer	65,632	117.2%
Total	$246,624	--

Another way to calculate the dollar-value LIFO inventory is to use the **link-chain method.** This approach is designed to avoid the problem encountered during double-extension calculations, where one must determine the base year cost of each new item added to inventory. However, tax regulations require that the link-chain method be used for tax reporting purposes only if it can be clearly demonstrated that all other dollar-value LIFO calculation methods are not applicable due to high rates of churn in the types of items included in inventory.

The link-chain method creates inventory layers by comparing year-end prices to prices at the beginning of each year, thereby avoiding the problems associated with comparisons to a base year that may be many years in the past. This results in a rolling cumulative index that is linked (hence the name) to the index derived in the preceding year. Tax regulations allow one to create the index using a representative sample of the total inventory valuation that must comprise at least one-half of the total inventory valuation. In brief, a link-chain calculation is derived by extending the cost of inventory at both beginning-of-year and end-of-year prices to arrive at a pricing index within the current year; this index is then multiplied by the ongoing cumulative index from the previous year to arrive at a new cumulative index that is used to price out the new inventory layer for the most recent year.

Link-chain inventory valuation example

This example assumes the same inventory information just used for the double-extension example. However, we have also noted the beginning inventory cost for each year and included the extended beginning inventory cost for each year, which facilitates calculations under the link-chain method.

Year	Ending unit quantity	Beginning-of-year cost/each	End-of-year cost/each	Extended at beginning-of-year price	Extended at end-of-year price
1	3,500	$ ---	$32.00	$ ---	$112,000
2	7,000	32.00	34.50	224,000	241,500
3	5,500	34.50	36.00	189,750	198,000
4	7,250	36.00	37.50	261,000	271,875

As was the case for the double-extension method, there is no index for year 1, which is the base year. In year 2, the index will be the extended year-end price of $241,500 divided by the extended beginning-of-year price of $224,000, or 107.8%. This is the same percentage calculated for year 2 under the double-extension method, because the beginning-of-year price is the same as the base price used under the double-extension method.

We then determine the value of the year 2 inventory layer by first dividing the extended year-end price of $241,500 by the cumulative index of 107.8% to arrive at an inventory valuation restated to the base year cost of $224,026. We then subtract the year-1 base layer of $112,000 from the $224,026 to arrive at a new layer at the base year cost of $112,026, which we then multiply by the cumulative index of 107.8% to bring it back to current year prices. This results in a year 2 inventory layer of $120,764. At this point, the inventory layers are as follows:

Layer type	Base-year valuation	LIFO layer valuation	Cumulative index
Base layer	$112,000	$112,000	0.0%
Year 2 layer	112,026	120,764	107.8%
Total	$224,026	$232,764	--

In year 3, the index will be the extended year-end price of $198,000 divided by the extended beginning-of-year price of $189,750, or 104.3%. Since this is the first year in which the base year was not used to compile beginning-of-year costs, we must first derive the cumulative index, which is calculated by multiplying the preceding year's cumulative index of 107.8% by the new year 3 index of 104.3%, resulting in a new cumulative index of 112.4%. By dividing year 3 extended year-end inventory of $198,000 by this cumulative index, we arrive at inventory priced at base year costs of $176,157.

This is less than the amount recorded in year 2, so there will be no inventory layer. Instead, we must reduce the inventory layer recorded for year 2. To do so, we subtract the base year layer of $112,000 from the $176,157 to arrive at a reduced year 2 layer of $64,157 at base year costs. We then multiply the $64,157 by the cumulative index in year 2 of 107.8% to arrive at an inventory valuation for the year 2 layer of $69,161. At this point, the inventory layers and associated cumulative indexes are as follows:

Layer type	Base-year valuation	LIFO layer valuation	Cumulative index
Base layer	$112,000	$112,000	0.0%
Year 2 layer	64,157	69,161	107.8%
Year 3 layer	--	--	112.4%
Total	$176,157	$181,161	--

In year 4, the index will be the extended year-end price of $271,875 divided by the extended beginning-of-year price of $261,000, or 104.2%. We then derive the new cumulative index by multiplying the preceding year's cumulative index of 112.4% by the year 4 index of 104.2%, resulting in a new cumulative index of 117.1%. By dividing year 4 extended year-end inventory of $271,875 by this cumulative index, we arrive at inventory priced at base year costs of $232,173. We then subtract the preexisting base year inventory valuation for all previous layers of $176,157 from this amount to arrive at the base year valuation of the year 4 inventory layer, which is $56,016. Finally, we multiply the $56,016 by the cumulative index in year 4 of 117.1% to arrive at an inventory valuation for the year 4 layer of $62,575. At this point, the inventory layers and associated cumulative indexes are as follows:

Layer type	Base-year valuation	LIFO layer valuation	Cumulative index
Base layer	$112,000	$112,000	0.0%
Year 2 layer	64,157	69,161	107.8%
Year 3 layer	--	--	112.4%
Year 4 layer	56,016	62,575	117.1%
Total	$232,173	$243,736	--

Compare the results of this calculation to those from the double-extension method. The indexes are nearly identical, as are the final LIFO layer valuations. The primary differences between the two methods is the avoidance of a base year cost determination for any new items subsequently added to inventory, for which a current cost is used instead.

Weighted-average inventory valuation method. The weighted-average costing method is calculated in accordance with its name—it is a weighted-average of the costs in inventory. It has the singular advantage of not requiring a database that itemizes the many potential layers of inventory at the different costs at which they were acquired. Instead, the weighted-average of all units in stock is determined, at which point **all** of the units in stock are accorded that weighted-average value. When parts are used from stock, they are all issued at the same weighted-average cost. If new units are added to stock, then the cost of the additions are added to the weighted-average of all existing items in stock, which will result in a new, slightly modified weighted average for **all** of the parts in inventory (both the old and new ones).

This system has no particular advantage in relation to income taxes, since it does not skew the recognition of income based on trends in either increasing or declining costs. This makes it a good choice for those organizations that do not want to deal with tax planning. It is also useful for very small inventory valuations, where there would not be any significant change in the reported level of income even if the LIFO or FIFO methods were to be used.

Weighted-average inventory valuation example

Exhibit 4-4 illustrates the weighted-average calculation for inventory valuations, using a series of 10 purchases of inventory. There is a maximum of one purchase per month, with usage (reductions from stock) also occurring in most months. Each of the columns in the exhibit shows how the average cost is calculated after each purchase and usage transaction.

Exhibit 4-4: Weighted-Average Costing Valuation Example

Part Number BK0043

Col. 1	Col. 2	Col. 3	Col. 4	Col. 5	Col. 6	Col. 7	Col. 8	Col. 9
Date purchased	*Quantity purchased*	*Cost per unit*	*Monthly usage*	*Net inventory remaining*	*Net change in inventory during period*	*Extended cost of new inventory layer*	*Extended inventory cost*	*Average inventory cost/unit*
05/03/07	500	$10.00	450	50	50	$ 500	$ 500	$ 10.00
06/04/07	1,000	9.58	350	700	650	6,227	6,727	9.61
07/11/07	250	10.65	400	550	(150)	0	5,286	9.61
08/01/07	475	10.25	350	675	125	1,281	6,567	9.73
08/30/07	375	10.40	400	650	(25)	0	6,324	9.73
09/09/07	850	9.50	700	800	150	1,425	7,749	9.69
12/12/07	700	9.75	900	600	(200)	0	5,811	9.69
02/08/08	650	9.85	800	450	(150)	0	4,359	9.69
05/07/08	200	10.80	0	650	200	2,160	6,519	10.03
09/23/08	600	9.85	750	500	(150)	0	5,014	10.03

We begin the illustration with the first row of calculations, which shows that we have purchased 500 units of item BK0043 on May 3, 2007. These units cost $10.00 per unit. During the month in which the units were purchased, 450 units were sent to production, leaving 50 units in stock. Since there has been only one purchase thus far, we can easily calculate, as shown in column 7, that the total inventory valuation is $500, by multiplying the unit cost of $10.00 (in column 3) by the number of units left in stock (in column 5). So far, we have a per-unit valuation of $10.00.

Next we proceed to the second row of the exhibit, where we have purchased another 1,000 units of BK0043 on June 4, 2007. This purchase was less expensive, since the purchasing volume was larger, so the per-unit cost for this purchase is only $9.58. Only 350 units are sent to production during the month, so we now have 700 units in stock, of which 650 are added from the most recent purchase. To determine the new weighted-average cost of the total inventory, we first determine the extended cost of this newest addition to the inventory. As noted in column 7, we arrive at $6,227 by multiplying the value in column 3 by the value in column 6. We then add this amount to the existing total inventory valuation ($6,227 plus $500) to arrive at the new extended inventory cost of $6,727, as noted in column 8. Finally, we divide this new extended cost in column 8 by the total number of units now in stock, as shown in column 5, to arrive at our new per-unit cost of $9.61.

The third row reveals an additional inventory purchase of 250 units on July 11, 2007, but more units are sent to production during that month than were bought, so the total number of units in inventory drops to 550 (column 5). This inventory reduction requires no review of inventory layers, as was the case for the LIFO and FIFO calculations. Instead, we simply charge off the 150-unit reduction at the average per-unit cost of $9.61. As a result, the ending inventory valuation drops to $5,286, with the same per-unit cost of $9.61. Thus, reductions in inventory quantities under the average costing method require little calculation—just charge off the requisite number of units at the current average cost.

The remaining rows of the exhibit repeat the concepts just noted, alternatively adding units to and deleting them from stock. Though there are a number of columns noted in this exhibit that one must examine, it is really a simple concept to understand and work with. The typical computerized accounting system will perform all of these calculations automatically.

DECISION TREES

The decision tree in Exhibit 4-5 shows how to determine who owns inventory that is in transit. The "ex-ship" transportation noted in the tree refers to the practice of the seller paying for delivery up to the point when the product is removed from a ship on its way to the buyer.

Exhibit 4-5: Decision Tree for Ownership of Inventory in Transit

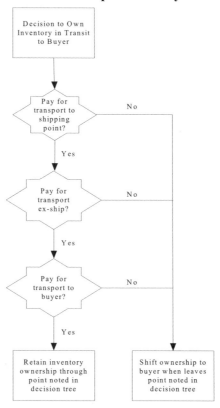

The decision tree in Exhibit 4-6 assists in determining which inventory tracking system to install, based on the presence of several items that are required to achieve an accurate perpetual inventory system.

Exhibit 4-6: Decision Tree for Type of Inventory Tracking System to Use

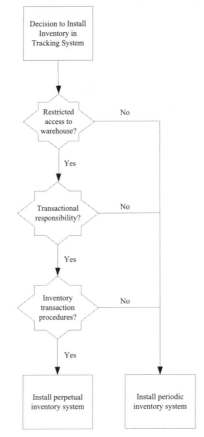

The decision tree in Exhibit 4-7 assists in determining which inventory valuation system to use, based on the type of inventory, the type of business, and the preferences of management in reporting financial information.

Exhibit 4-7: Decision Tree for Type of Inventory Valuation System to Use

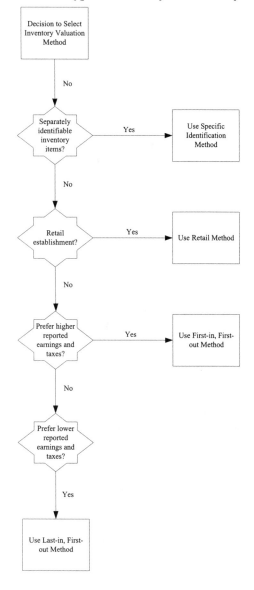

POLICIES

This section lists the policies that should be used in relation to the handling, accounting for, and valuation of inventory. Though some are mutually exclusive, most can be copied directly into a company's policy manual.

Goods in Transit

- **Revenue shall be recognized on goods in transit based on the point when the company no longer has title to the goods.** This policy ensures that there is a consistent cutoff at the point at which a company records revenue on shipments of finished goods to customers.

- **Incoming inventory shall be recorded after it has been received and inspected.** This policy ensures that the quantity and quality of incoming inventory has been verified prior to recording it in the inventory database, thereby avoiding later problems with having incorrect usable quantities on hand.
- **Goods received on consignment shall be identified and stored separately from company-owned inventory.** This policy keeps a company from artificially inflating its inventory by the amount of incoming consignment inventory, which would otherwise increase reported profits.
- **Consignment inventory shipped to reseller locations shall be clearly identified as such both in the shipping log and the inventory tracking system.** This policy keeps a company from inflating its sales through the recognition of shipments sent to resellers that are actually still owned by the company.

Accounting for Inventories

- **A complete physical inventory count shall be conducted at the end of each reporting period.** This policy ensures that an accurate record of the inventory is used as the basis for a cost of goods sold calculation.
- **The materials manager is responsible for inventory accuracy.** This policy centralizes control over inventory accuracy, thereby increasing the odds of it being kept at a high level.
- **Cycle counters shall continually review inventory accuracy and identify related problems.** This policy is intended for perpetual inventory systems, and results in a much higher level of inventory accuracy and attention to the underlying problems that cause inventory errors.
- **No access to the inventory is allowed by unauthorized personnel.** This policy generally leads to the lockdown of the warehouse, yielding much greater control over the accurate recording of inventory issuance transactions.
- **No inventory transaction shall occur without being immediately recorded in the perpetual inventory database.** This policy keeps the inventory database accurate at all times, preventing errors from arising when employees adjust the database on the incorrect assumption that the current record is correct.
- **Only designated personnel shall have access to the inventory database and item master file.** This policy not only ensures that only trained employees adjust inventory records, but also that the responsibility for their accuracy can be traced to designated people.

Valuation of Inventories

- **Only designated personnel shall have access to the labor routing and bill of materials databases.** This policy ensures that untrained employees are kept away from the critical computer files needed to value inventory quantities.

- **Standard cost records shall be updated at least annually.** This policy ensures that standard costs used in inventory valuations do not stray too far from actual costs.
- **Lower of cost or market calculations shall be conducted at least annually.** This policy ensures that excessively high inventory costs are stripped out of the inventory before they can become an excessively large proportion of it. This policy may be modified to require more frequent reviews, based on the variability of market rates for various inventory items.
- **Formal inventory obsolescence reviews shall be conducted at least annually.** This policy requires an inventory review team to periodically scan the inventory for obsolete items, which not only removes the cost of such items from stock, but also gives management a chance to profitably dispose of older inventory items before they become worthless.
- **Management shall actively seek out, identify, and dispose of scrap as soon as possible.** This policy requires the production team to remove scrap from the manufacturing process immediately, thereby keeping it from being recorded in the inventory records and artificially inflating profits.
- **Changes in production processes shall be immediately reflected in labor routings.** This policy ensures that the costs assigned to products through labor routings accurately reflect the actual production process, equipment usage, and production staffing.
- **Changes in product components shall be immediately reflected in the associated bills of material.** This policy ensures that the costs assigned to a product through a bill of materials accurately reflect the current product configuration as designed by the engineering staff.

PROCEDURES

Goods in Transit—Receiving Procedure

Take the following steps to ensure that received goods are properly inspected and recorded in the accounting system:

1. When the shipper arrives, compare the shipment to the description on the bill of lading and the authorizing purchase order. If there are significant discrepancies, reject the shipment.
2. Sign a copy of the bill of lading to accept the delivery.
3. Access the authorizing purchase order on the corporate computer system and record both the received quantity and the warehouse location in which they will be stored. If portable bar code scanners are used, then record this transaction at the time the warehouse move is made.
4. Store a copy of the bill of lading in an indexed file.
5. Forward a copy of the bill of lading to the accounting department or digitize the image in a scanner and enter the document into the corporate accounting system.

NOTE: If items are received during a physical inventory count, clearly mark them as not being available for counting and segregate them. Either wait to enter the transaction in the corporate accounting system until after the count has been completed, or make the entry but list the received goods as being unavailable for counting in the database.

Accounting for Inventories—Physical Count Procedure for Periodic Inventory

Take the following steps one week before the physical count:

1. Contact the printing company and order a sufficient number of sequentially numbered count tags. The first tag number should always be "1000." The tags should include fields for the product number, description, quantity count, location, and the counter's signature.
2. Review the inventory and mark all items lacking a part number with a brightly colored piece of paper. Inform the warehouse manager that these items must be marked with a proper part number immediately.
3. Clearly mark the quantity on all sealed packages.
4. Count all partial packages, seal them, and mark the quantity on the tape.
5. Prepare "Do Not Inventory" tags and use them to mark all items that should not be included in the physical inventory count.
6. Issue a list of count team members, with a notice regarding where and when they should appear for the inventory count.

Take the following steps one day before the physical count:

1. Remind all participants that they are expected to be counting the next day.
2. Notify the warehouse manager that all items received during the two days of physical counts must be segregated and marked with "Do Not Inventory" tags.
3. Notify the manager that no shipments are allowed for the duration of the physical count.
4. Notify the warehouse manager that all shipments for which the paperwork has not been sent to accounting by that evening will be included in the inventory count on the following day.
5. Notify the warehouse manager that all shipping and receiving documentation from the day before the count must be forwarded to the accounting department that day, for immediate data entry. Likewise, any pick information must be forwarded at the same time.
6. Notify all outside storage locations to fax in their inventory counts.

Take the following steps on the morning of the physical count:

1. Enter all transactions from the previous day.
2. Assemble the count teams. Issue counting instructions to them, as well as blocks of tags, for which they must sign. Give each team a map of the warehouse with a section highlighted on it that they are responsible for counting. Those teams with forklift experience will be assigned to count the top racks; those without this experience will be assigned the lower racks.
3. Call all outside storage warehouses and ask them to fax in their counts of company-owned inventory.
4. The count supervisor assigns additional count areas to those teams that finish counting their areas first.

5. The tag coordinator assigns blocks of tags to those count teams that run out of tags, tracks the receipt of tags, and follows up on missing tags. All tags should be accounted for by the end of the day.
6. The data entry person enters the information on the tags into a spreadsheet, and then summarizes the quantities for each item and pencils the totals into the cycle count report that was run earlier in the day.
7. The count supervisor reviews any unusual variances with the count teams to ensure that the correct amounts were entered.
8. Review the test count with an auditor, if necessary. Give the auditor a complete printout of all tags, as well as the cycle counting spreadsheet, showing all variances.

The following job descriptions apply to the inventory counting procedure:

- The **count supervisor** is responsible for supervising the count, which includes assigning count teams to specific areas and ensuring that all areas have been counted and tagged. This person also waits until all count tags have been compared to the quantities listed in the computer, and then checks the counts on any items that appear to be incorrect.
- The **tag coordinator** is responsible for tracking the blocks of count tags that have been issued, as well as for accounting for all tags that have been returned. When distributing tags, mark down the beginning and ending numbers of each block of tags on a tracking sheet, and obtain the signature of the person who receives the tags. When the tags are returned, put them in numerical order and verify that all tags are accounted for. Once the verification is complete, check off the tags on the tracking sheet as having been received. Once returned tags have been properly accounted for, forward them to the extension calculation clerk.
- The **extension calculation clerk** is responsible for summarizing the amounts on the tags (if there are multiple quantities listed) to arrive at a total quantity count on each tag. This person also compares the part numbers and descriptions on each tag to see if there are any potential identification problems. This person forwards all completed tags to the data entry person.
- The **data entry person** is responsible for entering the information on all count tags into the computer spreadsheet. When doing so, enter all the information on each tag into a spreadsheet. Once a group of tags has been entered, stamp them as having been entered, clip them together, and store them separately. Once all tags are entered in the spreadsheet, sort the data by part number. Print out the spreadsheet and summarize the quantities by part number. Transfer the total quantities by part number to the cycle count report. If there are any significant variances between the counted and cycle count quantities, bring them to the attention of the count supervisor for review.

Accounting for Inventories—Cycle Counting Procedure for Perpetual Inventory

Take the following steps to ensure that a perpetual inventory database is properly cycle counted:

1. Print a portion of the inventory report, sorted by location. Block out a portion of the physical inventory locations shown on the report for cycle counting purposes.
2. Go to the first physical inventory location to be cycle counted and compare the quantity, location, and part number of each inventory item to what is described for that location in the inventory report. Mark on the report any discrepancies between the on-hand quantity, location, and description for each item.
3. Also use the reverse process to ensure that the same information listed for all items on the report matches the items physically appearing in the warehouse location. Note any discrepancies on the report.
4. Verify that the noted discrepancies are not caused by recent inventory transactions that have not yet been logged into the computer system.
5. Correct the inventory database for all remaining errors noted.
6. Calculate the inventory error rate and post it in the warehouse.
7. Call up a history of inventory transactions for each of the items for which errors were noted, and try to determine the cause of the underlying problem. Investigate each issue and recommend corrective action to the warehouse manager, so the problems do not arise again.

Accounting for Inventories—Part Logging Procedure for Perpetual Inventory

Use this procedure to ensure that all transactions associated with the use of inventory are properly logged into the inventory database, thereby ensuring the ongoing existence of accurate perpetual inventory records.

1. The materials management department will issue a parts request form to the warehouse for each new job to be produced. Upon receipt, the warehouse staff should set up a pallet on which to store the requested items.
2. The warehouse staff collects the requested items from the warehouse, checking off each completed part number on the list and noting the quantity removed and the location from which they were removed.
3. The warehouse staff accesses the inventory database record for each removed item and logs out the quantities taken from the appropriate warehouse locations.
4. The warehouse staff delivers the filled pallet to the production floor.
5. If any parts remain after the production job is complete, the warehouse staff accepts them at the warehouse gate, logs them back into the computer system, and notifies the materials management department of the overage, so they can adjust the bill of material for the products being produced.
6. If any parts are returned in a damaged condition, the warehouse staff logs them in with a damaged code and stores them in the review area where the

Materials Review Board can easily access them. The warehouse staff periodically prints out a report listing all items stored in this area, and forwards it to the Materials Review Board, so they will be aware that items require their attention.

Accounting for Inventories—Inbound Consignment Inventory

Use this procedure to properly track consignment inventory owned by other parties but stored in the company's warehouse.

1. Upon receipt of consigned inventory, prominently label the inventory with a colored tag, clearly denoting its status.
2. Record the inventory in the computer system using a unique part number to which no valuation is assigned. If a consignment flag is available in the database, flag the part number as being a consignment item.
3. Store the item in a part of the warehouse set aside for consigned inventory.
4. Include the consigned inventory in a review by the materials review board (see next procedure), which should regularly determine the status of this inventory and arrange for its return if there are no prospects for its use in the near future.

Accounting for Inventories—Obsolete Inventory Review

Use this procedure to periodically review the inventory for obsolete items and account for items considered to be obsolete.

1. Schedule a meeting of the materials review board, to meet in the warehouse.
2. Prior to the meeting, print enough copies of the Inventory Obsolescence Review Report (see the Forms and Reports section) for all members of the committee.
3. Personally review all items on the report for which there appear to be excessive quantities on hand.
4. Determine the proper disposal of each item judged to be obsolete, including possible returns to suppliers, donations, inclusion in existing products, or scrap.
5. Have the warehouse staff mark each item as obsolete in the inventory database.
6. Have the accounting staff write down the value of each obsolete item to its disposal value.
7. Issue a memo to the materials review board, summarizing the results of its actions.

Valuation of Inventories—Period-End Inventory Valuation

Use this procedure to ensure that the inventory valuation created by a computerized accounting system is accurate, as well as to update it with the latest overhead costs.

1. Following the end of the accounting period, print out and review the computer change log for all bills of material and labor routings. Review them

with the materials manager and production engineer to ensure their accuracy. Revise any changes made in error.

2. Go to the warehouse and manually compare the period-end counts recorded on the inventory report for the most expensive items in the warehouse to what is in the warehouse racks. If there are any variances, adjust them for any transactions that occurred between the end of the period and the date of the review. If there are still variances, adjust for them in the inventory database.

3. Print a report that sorts the inventory in declining extended dollar order and review it for reasonableness. Be sure to review not only the most expensive items on the list but also the least expensive, since this is where costing errors are most likely to be found. Adjust for any issues found.

4. Review all entries in the general ledger during the reporting period for costs added to the cost pool, verifying that only approved costs have been included. Also investigate any unusually large overhead entries.

5. Verify that the overhead allocation calculation conforms to the standard allocation used in previous reporting periods, or that it matches any changes approved by management.

6. Verify that the journal entry for overhead allocation matches the standard journal entry listed in the accounting procedures manual.

7. Print out the inventory valuation report and compare its results by major category to those of the previous reporting period, both in terms of dollars and proportions. Investigate any major differences.

Valuation of Inventories—Lower of Cost or Market Calculation

Use this procedure to periodically adjust the inventory valuation for those items whose market value has dropped below their recorded cost.

1. Export the extended inventory valuation report to an electronic spreadsheet. Sort it by declining extended dollar cost, and delete the 80% of inventory items that do not comprise the top 20% of inventory valuation. Sort the remaining 20% of inventory items by either part number or item description. Print the report.

2. Send a copy of the report to the materials manager, with instructions to compare unit costs for each item on the list to market prices, and be sure to mutually agree on a due date for completion of the review.

3. When the materials management staff has completed its review, meet with the materials manager to go over its results and discuss any major adjustments. Have the materials management staff write down the valuation of selected items in the inventory database whose cost exceeds their market value.

4. Have the accounting staff expense the value of the write-down in the accounting records.

5. Write a memo detailing the results of the lower of cost or market calculation. Attach one copy to the journal entry used to write down the valuation, and issue another copy to the materials manager.

CONTROLS

Goods in Transit

The following controls should be installed to ensure that goods in transit are properly accounted for:

- **Audit shipment terms.** Certain types of shipment terms will require that a company shipping goods must retain inventory on its books for some period of time after the goods have physically left the company, or that a receiving company record inventory on its books prior to its arrival at the receiving dock. Though in practice most companies will record inventory only when it is physically present, this is technically incorrect under certain shipment terms. Consequently, a company should perform a periodic audit of shipment terms used to see if there are any deliveries requiring different inventory treatment. The simplest approach is to mandate no delivery terms under which a company is financially responsible for transportation costs.
- **Audit the receiving dock.** A significant problem from a recordkeeping perspective is that the receiving staff may not have time to enter a newly received delivery into the corporate computer system, so the accounting and purchasing staffs have no idea that the items have been received. Accordingly, one should regularly compare items sitting in the receiving area to the inventory database to see if they have been recorded. One can also compare supplier billings to the inventory database to see if items billed by suppliers are not listed as having been received.
- **Reject all purchases that are not preapproved.** A major flaw in the purchasing systems of many companies is that all supplier deliveries are accepted at the receiving dock, irrespective of the presence of authorizing paperwork. Many of these deliveries are verbally authorized orders from employees throughout the company, many of whom are not authorized to make such purchases, or who are not aware that they are buying items at high prices. This problem can be eliminated by enforcing a rule that all items received must have a corresponding purchase order on file that has been authorized by the purchasing department. By doing so, the purchasing staff can verify that there is a need for each item requisitioned, and that it is bought at a reasonable price from a certified supplier.

Accounting for Inventories

The following controls should be installed to ensure that inventories are properly accounted for:

- **Conduct inventory audits.** If no one ever checks the accuracy of the inventory, it will gradually vary from the book inventory, as an accumulation of errors builds up over time. To counteract this problem, one can schedule either a complete recount of the inventory from time to time, or else an ongoing cycle count of small portions of the inventory each day. Whichever method is used, it is important to conduct research in regard to why errors are occurring, and attempt to fix the underlying problems.

- **Control access to bill of material and inventory records.** The security levels assigned to the files containing bill of material and inventory records should allow access to only a very small number of well-trained employees. By doing so, the risk of inadvertent or deliberate changes to these valuable records will be minimized. The security system should also store the keystrokes and user access codes for anyone who has accessed these records, in case evidence is needed to prove that fraudulent activities have occurred.
- **Keep bill of material accuracy levels at a minimum of 98%.** The bills of material are critical for determining the value of inventory as it moves through the work-in-process stages of production and eventually arrives in the finished goods area, since they itemize every possible component that comprises each product. These records should be regularly compared to actual product components to verify that they are correct, and their accuracy should be tracked.
- **Pick from stock based on bills of material.** An excellent control over material costs is to require the use of bills of material for each item manufactured, and then requiring that parts be picked from the raw materials stock for the production of these items based on the quantities listed in the bills of material. By doing so, a reviewer can hone in on those warehouse issuances that were **not** authorized through a bill of material, since there is no objective reason why these issuances should have taken place.
- **Require approval to sign out inventory beyond amounts on pick list.** If there is a standard pick list used to take raw materials from the warehouse for production purposes, then this should be the standard authorization for inventory removal. If the production staff requires any additional inventory, they should go to the warehouse gate and request it, and the resulting distribution should be logged out of the warehouse. Furthermore, any inventory that is left over after production is completed should be sent back to the warehouse and logged in. By using this approach, the cost accountant can tell if there are errors in the bills of material that are used to create pick lists, since any extra inventory requisitions or warehouse returns probably represent errors in the bills.
- **Require transaction forms for scrap and rework transactions.** A startling amount of materials and associated direct labor can be lost through the scrapping of production or its occasional rework. This tends to be a difficult item to control, since scrap and rework can occur at many points in the production process. Nonetheless, the manufacturing staff should be well trained in the use of transaction forms that record these actions, so that the inventory records will remain accurate.
- **Restrict warehouse access to designated personnel.** Without access restrictions, the company warehouse is like a large store with no prices—just take all you want. This does not necessarily mean that employees are taking items from stock for personal use, but they may be removing excessive inventory quantities for production purposes, which leads to a cluttered production floor.

Also, this leaves the purchasing staff with the almost impossible chore of trying to determine what is in stock and what needs to be bought for immediate manufacturing needs. Consequently, a mandatory control over inventory is to fence it in and closely restrict access to it.

- **Segregate customer-owned inventory.** If customers supply a company with some parts that are used when constructing products for them, it becomes very easy for this inventory to be mingled with the company's own inventory, resulting in a false increase in its inventory valuation. Though it is certainly possible to assign customer-specific inventory codes to these inventory items in order to clearly identify them, a more easily discernible control is to physically segregate these goods in a different part of the warehouse.

Valuation of Inventories

The following controls should be installed to ensure that the correct costs are assigned to inventory items:

- **Audit inventory material costs.** Inventory costs are usually assigned either through a standard costing procedure or as part of some inventory layering concept such as LIFO or FIFO. In the case of standard costs, one should regularly compare assigned costs to the actual cost of materials purchased to see if any standard costs should be updated to bring them more in line with actual costs incurred. If it is company policy to update standard costs only at lengthy intervals, then one should verify that the variance between actual and standard costs is being written off to the cost of goods sold.

    If inventory layering is used to store inventory costs, then one should periodically audit the costs in the most recently used layers, tracing inventory costs back to specific supplier invoices.

- **Audit production setup cost calculations.** If production setup costs are included in inventory unit costs, there is a possibility of substantial costing errors if the assumed number of units produced in a production run is incorrect. For example, if the cost of a production setup is $1,000 and the production run is 1,000 units, then the setup cost should be $1 per unit. However, if someone wanted to artificially increase the cost of inventory in order to create a jump in profits, the assumed production run size could be reduced. In the example, if the production run assumption were dropped to 100 units, the cost per unit would increase tenfold to $10. A reasonable control over this problem is to regularly review setup cost calculations. An early warning indicator of this problem is to run a report comparing setup costs over time for each product to see if there are any sudden changes in costs. Also, access to the computer file storing this information should be strictly limited.

- **Compare unextended product costs to those for prior periods.** Product costs of all types can change for a variety of reasons. An easy way to spot these changes is to create and regularly review a report that compares the unextended cost of each product to its cost in a prior period. Any significant changes can then be traced back to the underlying costing information to see exactly what caused each change. The main problem with this control is that many less expensive accounting systems do not retain historical inventory records. If so, the information should be exported to an electronic spreadsheet or separate database once a month, where historical records can then be kept.

- **Review sorted list of extended product costs in declining dollar order.** This report is more commonly available than the historical tracking report noted in the previous bullet point, but contains less information. The report lists the extended cost of all inventory on hand for each inventory item, sorted in declining order of cost. By scanning the report, one can readily spot items that have unusually large or small valuations. However, finding these items requires some knowledge of what costs were in previous periods. Also, a lengthy inventory list makes it difficult to efficiently locate costing problems. Thus, this report is inferior to the unextended historical cost comparison report from a control perspective.

- **Control updates to bill of material and labor routing costs.** The key sources of costing information are the bill of material and labor routing records for each product. One can easily make a few modifications to these records in order to substantially alter inventory costs. To prevent such changes from occurring, one should impose strict security access to these records. If the accounting software has a change-tracking feature that stores data about who made changes and what changes were made, then be sure to use this feature. If used, periodically print a report (if available) detailing all changes made to the records, and scan it for evidence of unauthorized access.

- **Review inventory for obsolete items.** The single largest cause of inventory valuation errors is the presence of large amounts of obsolete inventory. To avoid this problem, periodically print a report that lists which inventory items have **not** been used recently, including the extended cost of these items. A more accurate variation is to print a report itemizing all inventory items for which there are no current production requirements (possible only if a material requirements planning system is in place). Alternatively, one can use a report that compares the amount of inventory on hand to annual historical usage of each item. With this information in hand, one should then schedule regular meetings with the materials manager to determine what inventory items should be scrapped, sold off, or returned to suppliers.

- **Review inventory layering calculations.** Most inventory layering systems are automatically maintained through a computer system and cannot be altered. In these cases, there is no need to verify the layering calculations. However, if the layering information is manually maintained, one should schedule periodic reviews of the underlying calculations to ensure proper cost layering. This usually involves tracing costs back to specific supplier invoices. However, one should also trace supplier invoices forward to the layering calculations, since it is quite possible that invoices have been excluded from the calculations. Also verify consistency in the allocation of freight costs to inventory items in the layering calculations.

• **Verify the calculation and allocation of overhead cost pools.** Overhead costs are usually assigned to inventory as the result of a manually derived summarization and allocation of overhead costs. This can be a lengthy calculation, subject to error. The best control over this process is a standard procedure that clearly defines which costs to include in the pools and precisely how these costs are to be allocated. In addition, one should regularly review the types of costs included in the calculations, verify that the correct proportions of these costs are included, and ensure that the costs are being correctly allocated to inventory. A further control is to track the total amount of overhead accumulated in each reporting period—any sudden change in the amount may indicate an error in the overhead cost summarization.

FORMS AND REPORTS

Goods in Transit

If a company has a fully integrated computer system into which the receiving staff can directly enter all receipts, there will be no forms required for goods in transit. If not, a receiving log will be used, such as the one shown in Exhibit 4-8. The report may contain additional room for notations by the receiving staff, such as the condition of the items received.

Exhibit 4-8: Receiving Log

Date	*Supplier*	*Item*	*Quantity shipped*	*Quantity received*
9/10/07	Acme Acorn Co.	Pistachio Nuts	3 barrels	3 barrels
9/10/07	Acme Acorn Co.	Pine Nuts	2 barrels	2 barrels
9/10/07	Durango Nut Co.	Pine Cones	100 pounds	98 pounds

The same information is commonly used in receiving reports, which are sorted by either date, supplier, part number, or part description.

Accounting for Inventories

A physical inventory count is usually taken by using a tag to be affixed to each lot. The tags are numbered serially in advance, and since a portion of the tag is left on the stock, it serves as a means of assuring that all lots are counted. A sample inventory tag is shown in Exhibit 4-9. This is a two-part tag, with the lower section being collected for summarization. Space is provided on the reverse side for noting movements so that slow-moving items can be counted in advance of the regular count.

Exhibit 4-9: Inventory Tag

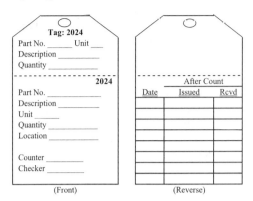

A cycle counting report is used by cycle counters to compare inventory records from the accounting database to physical counts in the warehouse. The sample report in Exhibit 4-10 is usually sorted by warehouse location code, so that counters can verify all items within a small area, which is the most efficient accounting method. The report has space on it to record physical inventory counts, though one can also write in any adjustments to part descriptions or units of measure, as well.

Exhibit 4-10: Cycle Counting Report

Location	Item no.	Description	U/M	Quantity
A-10-C	Q1458	Switch, 120V, 20A	EA	
A-10-C	U1010	Bolt, Zinc, 3 x 1/4	EA	
A-10-C	M1458	Screw, Stainless Steel, 2 x 3/8	EA	

Once cycle counting information has been collected, accuracy levels for each part of the inventory should be recorded on a trend line, preferably on a wall-mounted display board. By doing so, management makes a statement that this information is extremely important, and that it wishes to see improvement in the accuracy statistics. An example of an inventory accuracy report is shown in Exhibit 4-11.

Exhibit 4-11: Inventory Accuracy Report

Aisles	Responsible person	2 Months ago	Last month	Week 1	Week 2	Week 3	Week 4
A-B	Fred P.	82%	86%	85%	84%	82%	87%
C-D	Alain Q.	70%	72%	74%	76%	78%	80%
E-F	Davis L.	61%	64%	67%	70%	73%	76%
G-H	Jeff R.	54%	58%	62%	66%	70%	74%
I-J	Alice R.	12%	17%	22%	27%	32%	37%
K-L	George W.	81%	80%	79%	78%	77%	76%
M-N	Robert T.	50%	60%	65%	70%	80%	90%

Most inventory to be used on the production floor is kitted by the warehouse staff based on bills of material and issued on pallets to the production floor. However, if the amount listed on the bill of materials is too low, more inventory will be requested from the warehouse. Alternatively, if the bill of materials is too high, some inventory will be returned. More inventory may also be requested if parts are damaged on the production floor. When any of these issues arise, the warehouse staff should record all related transactions on an inventory sign-out and return a form such as the one shown in Exhibit 4-12. It is useful not only as a written record of transactions that must be entered into the inventory database, but also as a record of prospective adjustments to erroneous bills of material.

Exhibit 4-12: Inventory Sign-Out and Return Form

Description	Part no.	Quantity issued	Quantity returned	Job no.	Date

Production operations frequently result in either scrapped inventory or inventory that must be reworked in some manner before it can be completed. The accounting department needs to know as soon as scrap is created, so it can charge off the related cost to the cost of goods sold. Many companies give the same treatment to items requiring rework, only reassigning a cost to them once they are fixed and sent back into production. The two-part form shown in Exhibit 4-13 can be filled out by the production or materials management staffs whenever scrap or rework occurs, with one copy being attached to the inventory and the other being forwarded to accounting. The form is prenumbered, in case the accounting staff wants to verify that all forms are submitted. If the "Scrapped" block is filled out, accounting charges off the inventory cost to the cost of goods sold. If the "Sent to Rework" block is filled out, accounting must also shift the related inventory to a rework inventory category in the inventory database, where it will stay until rework activities are completed. The form can be sent later to the production or engineering managers, in case they wish to review the reasons why scrap or rework occurred.

Exhibit 4-13: Scrap/Rework Transaction Form

	7403
Date: _____ Item Number: _____ Description: _____	

Scrapped	Sent to Rework
Quantity Scrapped: _____ Reason: _____ _____ _____ Signature: _____	Quantity to Rework: _____ Reason: _____ _____ _____ Signature: _____

Valuation of Inventories

When standard costs are used to create an inventory valuation, there will inevitably be some differences between standard and actual costs that will create variances that appear in the cost of goods sold. The report shown in Exhibit 4-14 itemizes these variances.

Exhibit 4-14: Standard to Actual Cost Comparison Report

Part description	Standard cost ($)	Actual cost ($)	Variance ($)	Unit volume	Extended variance ($)
Antenna	1.20	2.00	–0.80	500	–400.00
Speaker	0.50	0.70	–0.20	375	–75.00
Battery	2.80	3.10	–0.30	201	–60.30
Plastic case, top	0.41	0.50	–0.09	14,000	–1,260.00
Plastic case, bottom	0.23	0.41	–0.18	11,000	–1,980.00
Base unit	4.00	4.25	–0.25	820	–205.00
Cord	0.90	0.91	–0.01	571	–5.71
Circuit board	5.78	4.00	+1.78	1,804	+3,211.12
Total	--	--	--	--	–774.89

Standard costs will be altered from time to time in order to bring them more in line with actual costs. When this happens, it is useful to show the changes on a report, along with the reasons why costs were changed. If management is particularly sensitive about altering standard costs, one could also add a manager sign-off section to the report in order to record formal approval of the changes. An example of this report is shown in Exhibit 4-15.

Exhibit 4-15: Standard Cost Changes Report

Part description	Beginning standard cost	Cost changes	Ending standard costs	Remarks
Power unit	820.00	+30.00	850.00	Price increase
Fabric	142.60		142.60	
Paint	127.54	–22.54	105.00	Modified paint type
Instruments	93.14	–1.14	92.00	New altimeter
Exhaust stock	34.17		34.17	
Rubber grommet	19.06	–.06	19.00	New material
Aluminum forging	32.14	–2.00	30.14	Substitute forging
Cushion	14.70		14.70	
Total	1,283.35	4.26	1,287.61	

More parts than are normally needed may be taken from stock to complete various items in production, which will unexpectedly reduce inventory levels and increase the cost of goods sold. Given its potentially large impact on inventory valuation, this issue may require a separate report such as the one shown in Exhibit 4-16. If excess parts usage continues over time, the report can also be used as proof of a need for changes to an item's underlying bill of materials.

Exhibit 4-16: Excess Material Usage Report

Material used	Standard usage (units)	Actual usage (units)	Excess usage (units)	Unit cost	Total excess cost	Comments
A	3,960	4,110	150	$4.75	$712.50	(a)
B	15,840	15,960	120	2.00	240.00	(b)
C	3,960	4,000	40	21.50	860.00	(c)
D	3,960	3,970	10	65.40	654.00	(d)
E	15,840	15,920	80	3.25	260.00	(e)
Total	--	--	--	--	$2,726.50	

(a) Parts defective
(b) Careless workmanship
(c) Power down
(d) Wrong speed drilling
(e) Maintenance technician dropped case

One of the easiest ways to detect obsolete inventory is to create a list of inventory items for which there has been no usage activity. The version shown in Exhibit 4-17 compares total inventory withdrawals to the amount on hand, which by itself may be sufficient information to conduct an obsolescence review. It also lists planned usage, which calls for information from a material requirements planning system, and which informs one of any upcoming requirements that might keep one from otherwise disposing of an inventory item. An extended cost for each item is also listed, in order to give report users some idea of the write-off that might occur if an item is declared obsolete. In the exhibit, the subwoofer, speaker bracket, and wall bracket appear to be obsolete based on prior usage, but the planned use of more wall brackets would keep that item from being disposed of.

Exhibit 4-17: Inventory Obsolescence Review Report

Description	Item no.	Location	Quantity on hand	Last year usage	Planned usage	Extended cost
Subwoofer case	0421	A-04-C	872	520	180	$9,053
Speaker case	1098	A-06-D	148	240	120	1,020
Subwoofer	3421	D-12-A	293	14	0	24,724
Circuit board	3600	B-01-A	500	5,090	1,580	2,500
Speaker, bass	4280	C-10-C	621	2,480	578	49,200
Speaker bracket	5391	C-10-C	14	0	0	92
Wall bracket	5080	B-03-B	400	0	120	2,800
Gold connection	6233	C-04-A	3,025	8,042	5,900	9,725
Tweeter	7552	C-05-B	725	6,740	2,040	5,630

FOOTNOTES

Disclosure of Inventory

If a company uses the LIFO valuation method, it should note the financial impact of any liquidation in LIFO inventory layers. Also, if a company uses other methods of valuation in addition to LIFO, then the extent to which each method is used should be described. Also, irrespective of the type of valuation method used, a company must reveal whether it is using the lower of cost or market adjustment (and the extent of any losses), whether any inventories are recorded at costs above their acquisition costs, whether any inventory is pledged as part of a debt arrangement, and the method of valuation being used. An example follows:

> The company uses the LIFO valuation method for approximately 65% of the total dollar value of its inventories, with the FIFO method being used for all remaining inventories. The company experienced a loss of $1.50 per share during the period that was caused by the elimination of LIFO inventory layers. The company also lost $.74 per share during the period as a result of a write-down of inventory costs to market. The company records no inventories above their acquisition costs. As of the balance sheet date, the company had pledged $540,000 of its inventory.

JOURNAL ENTRIES

This section describes the most common inventory-related journal entries. The first block of entries are for goods in transit, beginning with the receipt of raw material, and progressing through the various types of inventory to their eventual sale to customers. The next block of entries lists common adjustments to inventory, including obsolescence, physical count adjustments, and abnormal scrap. The final block of entries shows how to shift indirect costs of various kinds into the overhead cost pool, and then to allocate these costs back out to either the cost of goods sold or inventory. For each journal entry there is a sample description, as well as the most likely debit and credit for each account used within the entry.

Goods in Transit

Record received goods. To increase inventory levels as a result of a supplier delivery.

Raw materials inventory	xxx	
Accounts payable		xxx

Move inventory to work-in-process. To shift the cost of inventory to the work-in-process category once production work begins on converting it from raw materials to finished goods.

Work-in-process inventory	xxx	
Raw materials inventory		xxx

Move inventory to finished goods. To shift the cost of completed inventory from work-in-process inventory to finished goods inventory.

Finished goods inventory	xxx	
Work-in-process inventory		xxx

Sell inventory. To record the elimination of the inventory asset as a result of a product sale, shifting the asset to an expense and also recording the creation of an accounts receivable asset to reflect an unpaid balance from the customer on sale of the product.

Cost of goods sold	xxx	
Finished goods inventory		xxx
Accounts receivable	xxx	
Revenues		xxx
Overhead cost pool		xxx

Accounting for Inventories

Adjust inventory for obsolete items. To charge an ongoing expense to the cost of goods sold that increases the balance in a reserve against which obsolete inventory can be charged (**first entry**). The **second entry** charges off specific inventory items against the reserve.

Cost of goods sold	xxx	
Obsolescence reserve		xxx
Obsolescence reserve	xxx	
Raw materials inventory		xxx
Work-in-process inventory		xxx
Finished goods inventory		xxx

Adjust inventory to lower of cost or market. To reduce the value of inventory to a market price that is lower than the cost at which it is recorded in the company records.

Loss on inventory valuation	xxx	
Raw materials inventory		xxx
Work-in-process inventory		xxx
Finished goods inventory		xxx

Adjust inventory to physical count. To adjust inventory balances, either up or down, as a result of changes in the inventory quantities that are noted during a physical count. The following entries assume that there are increases in inventory balances. If there are declines in the inventory balances, then the debits and credits are reversed.

Raw materials inventory	xxx	
Work-in-process inventory	xxx	
Finished goods inventory	xxx	
Cost of goods sold		xxx

Write off abnormal scrap/spoilage. To shift unexpected, one-time scrap or spoilage costs directly to the cost of goods sold, effectively writing off this amount in the current period.

Cost of goods sold	xxx	
Work-in-process inventory		xxx

Valuation of Inventories

Record indirect expenses incurred. To add to the overhead cost pool the amount of indirect expenses related to the production process.

Overhead cost pool	xxx	
Accounts payable		xxx

Record indirect wages incurred. To add to the overhead cost pool the amount of indirect wages related to the production process.

Overhead cost pool	xxx	
Wages payable		xxx

Record receipt of supplies. To add the cost of incidental manufacturing supplies to the overhead cost pool for eventual allocation to inventory.

Overhead cost pool	xxx	
Accounts payable		xxx

Record normal scrap/spoilage. To shift the normal, expected amount of scrap or spoilage cost to the overhead cost pool, from whence it is allocated as a part of overhead to inventory.

Overhead cost pool	xxx	
Work-in-process inventory		xxx

Allocate overhead costs to inventory. To shift the amount of costs built up in the overhead cost pool to the work-in-process and finished goods inventory categories, as well as to the cost of goods sold for any inventory sold during the period.

Cost of goods sold	xxx	
Work-in-process inventory		xxx
Finished goods inventory		xxx

RECORDKEEPING

Goods in Transit

A company receiving inventory typically records it as soon as it arrives, so that both the inventory and liability accounts increase at the same time, thereby resulting in no net change in the balance sheet and no impact on the income statement. Consequently, there is no particular need for recordkeeping.

The situation is different for companies shipping goods for which they retain title until some point in the shipment process. Shipping documents, such as a shipping log or bill of lading, should be stored that indicate the date of shipment from the facility, and preferably also a notification form from the shipping entity that describes the date on which title passed to the buyer. The shipping log or bill of lading can be used to estimate the date on which title passes by adding a standard number of days to the ship date, based on the distance of the buyer from the shipper's facility, and so is a critical document for affirming the timing of any revenue transactions.

A particular problem for adequate recordkeeping is the tracking of consignment inventory. A company receiving such inventory should make a notation in its computer system at the time of receipt that clearly identifies this inventory. Preferably, there should also be a flag in the software that prevents the consignment inventory from being assigned a value. If the consignment inventory matches company-owned inventory, then it will be particularly difficult to segregate it, so one should create a unique inventory number for the item. For example, a wash basin might normally be inventory number 11478, so an identical item received on consignment could be given the number 11478-C.

If a company has sent inventory on consignment to a third-party location, then the inventory tracking system in its software should contain an **offsite** inventory location code clearly identifying where it has been sent. A reasonable location code would be the name of the company to whom it was sent, truncated to match the size of the inventory location field in the computer system.

Accounting for Inventories

Recordkeeping for perpetual inventory systems is most easily accomplished by having the computer system store a transaction log that shows what transactions were entered, who made the entries and the date on which they were made. This can be subdivided into a variety of reports that reveal only certain types of transactions, or transactions only for particular inventory items. If the perpetual records are stored on paper, then these documents should be kept for at least one year following year-end, so inventory levels can be manually reconstructed at a later date. Also, US tax regulations require at least one physical inventory count per year, so these records should be stored in the event of a tax audit. If continuous cycle counting is used instead of a single physical inventory count, then these records must also be stored.

Recordkeeping for periodic systems is more complex, since they are usually manual systems. First, the counting records for each physical inventory count must be stored. Also, all purchasing records for the year should be retained, which can be as minimal as the general ledger detail for the purchasing account. However, this approach reveals nothing about who ordered goods, what goods were ordered, and from whom they were bought. Accordingly, one should also retain purchase order and receiving documentation, which can be quite voluminous. The reason for this much document retention is that the calculation of the cost of goods sold requires one to add purchases to the beginning inventory and then subtract out the ending inventory, which calls for backup information on all three parts of the calculation.

If inventory is tracked using the specific identification method, then the computer system should contain a unique identifying number for each item tracked, such as a serial number. This identification number should be included in the standard inventory valuation report, which should be printed at the fiscal year-end and stored.

Valuation of Inventories

There are a number of recordkeeping issues related to the valuation of inventory. In all cases, the main issue is creating a paper trail that can be traced back to the source documents at any point in the future, so that anyone (especially an auditor) can easily determine the reason why a specific cost was assigned to an inventory item. The following discussion covers recordkeeping issues for the standard costing of work-in-process and finished goods inventory, as well as inventory layering, spoilage, and the cost reductions for the lower of cost or market rule. In all cases, it is crucial to maintain accurate records of these transactions, which have a major impact on corporate expenses.

When auditors review the raw material costs listed on the balance sheet, their first source of evidentiary material for affirming this cost will be the invoices received from suppliers. These are normally stored in the accounts payable files, and so no additional recordkeeping is necessary. The main point is to ensure that the supplier name and invoice number are recorded in the raw materials valuation report, or can be easily traced from there, so the auditors have a clear documentation path from the inventory valuation report to the backup materials.

Many manufactured goods move through the production process so fast that there is no reason to track their progress from workstation to workstation, since they arrive in finished goods inventory so quickly. In other cases, materials may plod through the production process for weeks or months, traveling from workstation to workstation. In these latter cases, their recorded work-in-process (WIP) cost will gradually increase as value is added to them. If so, there must be a way to record the stage of completion of all WIP inventory at the end of a reporting period, and to consistently assign a value to each stage of completion. This is done through a labor routing, which is usually a computer record assigned to each product in the computer system's item master file, itemizing the work processes that must be performed on the product and the cost of those processes. When a reporting period ends, the accounting staff must itemize in the computer system the last workstation through which work has been completed on each inventory item; the computer then increases the cost of the inventory by the incremental production work completed, based on the standard costs used in the labor routings. Accordingly, one must store copies of the labor routings used for the period-end report, either in the computer system or as printed copies. If they are to be stored on the computer, then there should be an archiving function or a change-tracking feature, so that one can find the correct version of a routing.

Once completed units of production are shifted into finished goods inventory, they are assigned a cost that is usually based on a bill of materials, which is a list of standard parts included in each product. Given its importance in the valuation process, one should keep a record of the bill of materials as proof of how costs were derived at the end of each accounting period. The bills can be printed and kept separately, or stored in the computer under an appropriate archiving or change control methodology, so that one can scroll back in time through various changes to the bills in order to find the version used to calculate the cost of inventory on a specific date.

Both labor routings and bills of materials assign a standard amount of cost to either WIP or finished goods inventories, using a standard list of work centers and parts that are comprised of standard costs. Actual costs may vary somewhat from the standard costs used, due to variations in the market prices of parts, changing labor rates, different parts or work center configurations, and so on. The standard costs used in a labor routing and a bill of materials are always incrementally varying from actual costs, which requires periodic adjustments to the standards in order to bring them more in line with actual costs. Whenever this happens, one should create and store a record of the changes made, or use a computer system that stores this information whenever changes are made.

When the actual amount of material scrap used to create a product varies substantially from the amount included in a bill of materials, this is considered abnormal scrap, and will drop directly into the cost of goods sold in the current period. There is no need from an accounting perspective to track the exact items lost to scrap, since they are no longer stored in inventory. Nonetheless, it may be useful for operational reasons to know where this scrap is occurring, so it may be useful to track such information as which products are most likely to generate scrap or the workstations in which scrap is most likely to occur. By tracking this information on a trend line, one can direct the attention of production engineers to those areas of the production process where their efforts can result in the greatest decrease in scrap costs. There is no further need to retain records in this area, however.

Overhead is a major component of inventory cost, in some cases comprising far more than the cost of labor or materials in a product. The overhead rate is compiled in one or more cost pools within the general ledger and then allocated to either work-in-process, finished goods, or the cost of goods sold using some sort of activity measure, such as the amount of direct labor or machine time used by a product, or perhaps a combination of several activity measures. Given the large amount of money being allocated, this is an extremely important area in which to have accurate recordkeeping. Records should itemize what costs are included in the overhead cost pool and the exact derivation of the allocation methodology. The method by which the allocated costs are assigned to inventory, such as through a journal entry or an alteration in the standard overhead rate used in the bills of material, should also be noted.

As noted earlier in the Concepts and Examples section, there are a variety of inventory layering concepts that can be used to value inventory. In all such cases, the computer system should maintain a database of all cost layers used to derive the inventory valuation. Unless the inventory is very small, it is usually very labor intensive to maintain this information manually, and so it is not recommended. However, computer databases typically store data for only a few years into the past, so adequate recordkeeping in this area will require one to eventually print out the layering records when old computer files are about to be deleted from the system. If there are many inventory items, these printed records will be voluminous.

If a lower of cost or market (LCM) review is made that results in a reduction in the recorded cost of inventory, then the adjustment is typically made as a journal entry that reduces the cost of inventory in a single lump sum. If so, there is no way to tell which costs were reduced or what calculation was used to determine the reduction. Consequently, the journal entry records should include complete documentation of the comparison of standard costs to market costs, unfavorable variances between the two, and the total cost of these variances incorporated into the journal entry.

If the purchasing department has entered into any material long-term purchasing commitments with suppliers, the amount of these commitments must be included in the footnotes to the financial statements. Accordingly, the purchasing staff should be recording all of its purchase orders in the corporate computer system, while all receipts against those purchase orders should be logged into the system by the receiving staff. By netting out the receipts against the purchase orders, one can easily determine the total amount of long-term purchasing commitments. This report should be printed and stored at the fiscal year-end.

The one problem with this recordkeeping approach is when long-term commitments are only contained within legal agreements and have not yet been converted into purchase orders. Though some companies have stored this information in separate computer databases, many more keep legal agreements only in paper format, making them much more difficult to summarize (or even locate). If this is the case, the accounting staff should either maintain the master file of legal contracts or at least be given access to it, and schedule regular reviews of new or modified contracts in order to determine the amount of purchase commitments. Notes from these reviews should be stored as supporting documentation for the footnote disclosure.

5 REVENUE RECOGNITION

DEFINITIONS OF TERMS

Completed contract method. An accounting method under which no income is recognized until all work associated with a project has been completed.

Construction in progress. An inventory account in which costs are accumulated for ongoing work related to separately identifiable construction projects.

Cost recovery method. The most conservative method for accounting for installment sales, where the recognition of all gross profit is deferred until the entire cost of sales has first been recognized.

Cost-to-cost method. The division of cost incurred to date on a project by the total estimated project cost to derive the overall project percentage of completion for incremental billing purposes.

Deferred gross profit. The gross profit associated with a sale whose recognition is deferred due to the uncertainty of final cash collection.

Initiation fee. An up-front fee charged as part of a service or membership agreement, entitling the customer to specific services or if additional periodic payments are made.

Installation fee. An up-front fee required to install equipment.

Installment method. A method for recognizing the profit on an installment sale when cash is received.

Installment transaction. When a customer pays for a purchase through a series of periodic payments.

Percentage-of-completion method. An accounting method under which a percentage of the income associated with a project is recognized in proportion to the estimated percentage of completion of the project.

Revenue. An inflow of cash, accounts receivable, or barter from a customer in exchange for the provision of a service or product to that customer by a company.

Right of return. The right of a customer to return goods to the seller within a specific time period.

Substantial completion. The point at which essentially all work has been completed and major risks incurred in relation to a project.

Unearned revenue. A payment from a customer that cannot yet be recognized as earned revenue, because the offsetting services or products for which the money was paid have not yet been delivered.

CONCEPTS AND EXAMPLES[1]

The accountant should not recognize revenue until it has been earned. There are a number of rules regarding exactly when revenue can be recognized, but the key concept is that revenue occurs at the point when substantially all services and deliveries related to the sale transaction have been completed. Within this broad requirement, here are a number of more precise rules regarding revenue recognition.

- **Recognition at point of delivery.** One should recognize revenue when the product is delivered to the customer. For example, revenue is recognized in a retail store when a customer pays for a product and walks out of the store with it in hand. Alternatively, a manufacturer recognizes revenue when its products are placed onboard a conveyance owned by a common carrier for delivery to a customer; however, this point of delivery can change if the company owns the method of conveyance, since the product is still under company control until it reaches the customer's receiving dock.
- **Recognition at time of payment.** If payment by the customer is not assured, even after delivery of the product or service has been completed, then the most appropriate time to recognize revenue is upon receipt of cash. For example, if a book publisher issues new editions of books to the buyers of the previous edition without any indication that they will accept the new shipments, then waiting for the receipt of cash is the most prudent approach to the recognition of revenue.
- **Other rules.** In addition to the above rules, there are a few others that are applicable in all instances. The first is that the seller should have no obligation to assist the buyer in reselling the product to a third party; if this were the case, it would imply that the initial sale had not yet been completed. The second is that any damage to the product subsequent to the point of sale will have no impact on the buyer's obligation to pay the seller for the full price of the product; if this were the case, one would reasonably assume that at least some portion of the sale price either includes a paid warranty that should be separated from the initial sale price and recognized at some later date, or that the sale cannot be recognized until the implied warranty period has been completed. The third rule is that the buying and selling entities cannot be the same entity, or so closely related that the transaction might be construed as an intercompany sale; if this were the case, the intercompany sale would have to be eliminated from the financial statements of both the buyer and the seller for reporting purposes, since the presumption would be that no sale had occurred.

---

[1] *Some portions of this section are adapted with permission from Chapter 20 of Bragg,* **Accounting Reference Desktop** *(John Wiley & Sons, Inc. Hoboken, NJ, 2002).*

Revenue Recognition Scenarios

The most common revenue recognition system is based on the **accrual method.** Under this approach, if the revenue recognition rules presented in the previous section have been met, then revenue may be recognized in full. In addition, expenses related to that revenue, even if supplier invoices have not yet been received, should be recognized and matched against the revenue.

Example of revenue recognition

If the High Pressure Dive Company sells a set of face masks for $500 and recognizes the revenue at the point of shipment, then it must also recognize at the same time the $325 cost of those masks, even if it has not yet received a billing from the supplier that sold it the masks. In the absence of the billing, the cost can be accrued based on a purchase order value, market value, or supplier price list.

The **installment method** is used when there is a long string of expected payments from a customer that are related to a sale, and for which the level of collectibility of individual payments cannot be reasonably estimated. This approach is particularly applicable in the case of multiyear payments by a customer. Under this approach, revenue is recognized only in the amount of each cash receipt, and for as long as cash is received. Expenses can be proportionally recognized to match the amount of each cash receipt, creating a small profit or loss at the time of each receipt.

An alternative approach, called the **cost recovery method**, uses the same revenue recognition criterion as the installment sales method, but the amount of revenue recognized is exactly offset by the cost of the product or service until all related costs have been recognized; all remaining revenues then have no offsetting cost, which effectively pushes all profit recognition out until near the end of the installment sale contract.

It is generally not allowable to record inventory at market prices at the time when production has been completed. However, this is allowed in the few cases where the item produced is a commodity, has a ready market, and can be easily sold at the market price. Examples of such items are gold, silver, and wheat. In these cases, the producer can mark up the cost of the item to the market rate at the point when production has been completed. However, this amount must then be reduced by the estimated amount of any remaining selling costs, such as would be required to transport the commodity to market. In practice, most companies prefer to recognize revenue at the point of sale. Consequently, this practice tends to be limited to those companies that produce commodities, but that have difficulty in calculating an internal cost at which they can record the cost of their production (and so are forced to use the market price instead).

When property is sold on a conditional basis, where the buyer has the right to cancel the contract and receive a refund up until a prespecified date, the seller cannot recognize any revenue until the date when cancellation is no longer allowed. Until that time, all funds are recorded as a deposit liability. If only portions of the contract can be canceled by the buyer, then revenue can be recognized at once by the seller for just those portions not subject to cancellation.

Bill and Hold Revenue Transactions

When a company is striving to reach difficult revenue goals, it will sometimes resort to bill and hold transactions, under which it completes a product and bills the customer, but then stores the product rather than sending it to the customer (who may not want it yet). Though there are a limited number of situations where this treatment is legitimate (perhaps the customer has no storage space available), there have also been a number of cases where bill and hold transactions have been subsequently proven to be a fraudulent method for recognizing revenue. Consequently, the following rules must now be met before a bill and hold transaction will be considered valid:

- **Completion.** The product being stored under the agreement must be ready for shipment. This means that the seller cannot have production staff in the storage area, making changes to the product subsequent to the billing date.
- **Delivery schedule.** The products cannot be stored indefinitely. Instead, there must be a schedule in place for the eventual delivery of the goods to the customer.
- **Documentation.** The buyer must have signed a document in advance clearly stating that it is buying the products being stored by the seller.
- **Origination.** The **buyer** must have requested that the bill and hold transaction be completed, and have a good reason for doing so.
- **Ownership.** The buyer must have taken on all risks of ownership, so the seller is now simply the provider of storage space.
- **Performance.** The terms of the sales agreement must not state that there are any unfulfilled obligations on the part of the seller at the time when revenue is recognized.
- **Segregation.** The products involved in the transaction must have been split away from all other inventory and stored separately. They must also not be made available for the filling of orders from other customers.

Recording Revenues at Gross or Net

Some companies that act as brokers will overreport their revenue by recognizing not just the commission they earn on brokered sales, but also the revenue earned by their clients. For example, if a brokered transaction for an airline ticket involves a $1,000 ticket and a $20 brokerage fee, the company will claim that it has earned revenue of $1,000, rather than the $20 commission. This results in the appearance of enormous revenue (albeit with very small gross margins), which can be quite misleading. Consequently, one should apply the following rules to see if the full amount of brokered sales can be recognized as revenue:

- **Principal.** The broker must act as the principal who is originating the transaction.
- **Risks.** The broker must take on the risks of ownership, such as bearing the risk of loss on product delivery, returns, and bad debts from customers.

- **Title.** The broker must obtain title to the product being sold at some point during the sale transaction.

There are several key indicators in a transaction that reveal whether it should be recorded at gross or net. It should be recorded at gross if the following indicators are present:

- The company adds value to products sold, perhaps through alteration or added services.
- The company can establish a selling price to the customer.
- The company is responsible to the customer for order fulfillment.
- The company takes title to inventory before shipping it to the customer.

The transaction should be recorded at net if the answer to any of the preceding indicators is "no." In addition, it should be recorded at net if the following indicators are present:

- The company earns a fixed fee (such as a commission payment) from a transaction.
- The company has only one source of supplier for the product it sells.
- The supplier cannot obtain payment from the company if the customer does not pay.

If a specific transaction contains indicators pointing in either direction, the decision to record at gross or net should be based on the preponderance of evidence pointing in a particular direction.

Example of recording revenues at gross or net

The Aboriginal Travel Agency (ATA), which sells trips to Australia, purchases blocks of tickets from the airlines and resells them to customers as part of its package deals. If it cannot find purchasers for the tickets, it must absorb the cost of the tickets. In this case, ATA should record as revenues the entire amount of the airline tickets, since it has taken title to the tickets, bears the risk of loss, and is originating the transaction.

ATA also reserves airline seats on behalf of its clients, charging a $30 fee for this service. Since it is acting only as an agent for these transactions, it can record only the $30 fee as revenue, not the price of the airline tickets.

Reducing Revenue by Cash Paid to Customers

If a company pays cash consideration to its customers, this is presumed to be a reduction in the company's revenue. The only exception is when a clearly identifiable benefit is being passed from the customer to the company, and the fair value of that benefit can be estimated. If the fair value of the benefit is less than the amount of cash paid, the difference must be deducted from revenue. This approach is designed to keep companies from inflating their reported revenue levels through delayed cash-back payments to customers as part of sales deals. Alternatively, if the company pays its customers with goods or services, the transaction should be recorded as an expense.

Example of revenue reduction based on cash payments to customers

An international customer of the ABC Widget Company has operations in a country that has imposed foreign exchange controls. As part of an agreement to sell widgets to this customer, ABC agrees to overbill the customer by 10% and rebate this amount to a customer location in a third country. Whenever this transaction occurs, ABC should credit its cash account and debit its revenue account by the amount of the overbilling.

Example of expense incurrence based on noncash payments to customers

The XYZ Technology Company sells a variety of software packages to its customers, and offers free training classes at its in-house university to purchasers. In a recent sale, the company promised ten days of free training, which equated to twenty days of instructor time at a payroll cost of $7,000. Accordingly, this cost was shifted from the training department's payroll expense and charged to the sale as a cost of goods sold.

Long-Term Construction Contracts

In the construction industry, one option for revenue recognition is to wait until a construction project has been completed in all respects before recognizing any related revenue. This is called the **completed contract method.** It makes the most sense when the costs and revenues associated with a project cannot be reasonably tracked, or when there is some uncertainty regarding either the addition of costs to the project or the receipt of payments from the customer. However, this approach does not reveal the earning of any revenue on the financial statements of a construction company until its projects are substantially complete, which gives the reader of its financial statements very poor information about its ability to generate a continuing stream of revenues (except for projects of such short duration that they will be initiated and completed within the same accounting period). Consequently, the percentage-of-completion method is to be preferred when costs and revenues can be reasonably estimated.

The **percentage-of-completion method** is most commonly used in the construction industry, where very long-term construction projects would otherwise keep a company from revealing any revenues on its financial statements until its projects are completed, which might occur only at long intervals. Under this approach, the accounting staff creates a new asset account for each project, in which it accumulates all related expenses. At the end of each reporting period, the budgeted gross margin associated with each project is added to the total expenses accumulated in each account, and subtracted from the accumulated billings to date. If the amount of expenses and gross profit exceeds the billings figure, then the company recognizes revenue matching the difference between the two figures. If the expenses and gross profit figure are less than the amount of billings, the difference is stored in a liability account.

Example of the percentage-of-completion method

The ABC Construction Company is constructing a log cabin–style office building for a company specializing in rustic furniture. Thus far, it has accumulated $810,000 in expenses on the project and billed the customer $1 million. The estimated gross margin on the project is 28%. The total of expenses and estimated gross profit is therefore $1,125,000, which is calculated as $810,000 divided by $(1 - 0.28)$. Since this figure exceeds the billings to date of $1 million, the company can recognize additional revenue of $125,000. The resulting journal entry would be

Unbilled contract receivables	125,000	
Contract revenues earned		125,000

Since ABC must also recognize a proportional amount of expenses in relation to the revenues recognized, it should credit the construction in progress account and debit the cost of goods sold account for $90,000. This cost of goods sold is derived by multiplying the recognized revenue figure of $125,000 by one minus the gross margin, or 72%.

Under an alternative scenario, ABC Construction has billed the customer $1,200,000, while all other information remains the same. In this case, the amount of revenue earned is $1,125,000, which is $75,000 less than the amount billed. Consequently, the company must record a $75,000 liability for the incremental amount of work it must still complete before it can recognize the remaining revenue that has already been billed. The resulting journal entry would be

Contract revenues earned	75,000	
Billings exceed projects costs and margin		75,000

An alternative approach for measuring the percentage of completion is the **cost-to-cost method.** Under this approach, we measure the percentage of completion by dividing the total amount of expenses incurred to date by the total estimated project cost. This method works well only if the total estimated project cost is regularly revised to reflect the most accurate expense information. Also, it tends to result in proportionately greater amounts of revenue recognition early in a project, since this is when most of the materials-related costs are incurred. A more accurate way to calculate the percentage of completion when there are large up-front materials costs is to include the materials costs only when the aspects of the project in which they are used are completed.

Example of the cost-to-cost method

The ABC Construction Company is building a hotel, and has elected to purchase the materials for the air conditioning system, costing $200,000, at the beginning of the project. The total estimated project cost is $2 million and the amount billable to the customer is $2.5 million. After one month, ABC has incurred a total of $400,000 in costs, including the air conditioning equipment. This is 20% of the total project cost, and would entitle ABC to recognize $500,000 of revenue (20% of $2.5 million). However, because the air conditioning equipment has not yet been installed, a more accurate approach would be to exclude the cost of this equipment from the calculation, resulting in a project completion percentage of 10% and recognizable revenue of $250,000.

The trouble with these methods is that one must have good cost tracking and project planning systems in order to ensure that all related costs are being properly accumulated for each project, and that cost overruns are accounted for when deriving the percentage of completion. For example, if poor management results in a doubling of the costs incurred at the halfway point of a construction project, from $5,000 up to $10,000, this means that the total estimated cost for the entire project (of $10,000) would already have been reached when half of the project had not yet been completed. In such a case, one should review the remaining costs left to be incurred and change this estimate to ensure that the resulting percentage of completion is accurate.

If the percentage-of-completion calculation appears suspect when based on costs incurred, one can also use a percentage of completion that is based on a Gantt chart or some other planning tool that reveals how much of the project has actually been completed. For example, if a Microsoft Project plan reveals that a construction project has reached the 60% milestone, then one can reasonably assume that 60% of the project has been completed, even if the proportion of costs incurred may result in a different calculation.

Costs that may be included in the construction-in-progress account include direct labor, materials, and overhead related to the project. Expenses included in overhead should be consistently applied across multiple projects, as should the method of applying overhead to jobs; this keeps one from arbitrarily shifting overhead expenses between project accounts.

If the estimate of costs left to be incurred plus actual costs already incurred exceeds the total revenue to be expected from a contract, then the full amount of the difference should be recognized in the current period as a loss, and presented on the balance sheet as a current liability. If the percentage-of-completion method has been used on the project, then the amount recognized will be the total estimated loss on the project plus all project profits previously recognized. If, after the loss estimate has been made, the actual loss turns out to be a smaller number, the difference can be recognized in the current period as a gain.

Example of project loss recognition

The ABC Construction Company's cost accountant has determined that its construction of a military barracks building will probably result in a loss of $80,000, based on his most recent cost estimates. The company uses the percentage-of-completion method, under which it had previously recorded gross profits of $35,000 for the project. Thus, the company must record a loss of $115,000 in the current period, both to record the total estimated loss and to back out the formerly recognized profit. The entry is as follows:

Loss on uncompleted project	115,000	
Estimated loss on uncompleted contract		115,000

If costs are incurred prior to the signing of a project contract, these costs must be charged to expense at once, rather than storing them in the construction-in-progress account as an asset. It is not allowable to retroactively shift these costs from an expense account into the construction-in-progress account.

Service Revenues

Service revenues differ from product sales in that revenue recognition is generally based on the performance of specific activities, rather than on the shipment of a product. There are four ways in which service revenues can be recognized. They are presented as follows, in ascending order from the most conservative to the most liberal approaches:

1. **Collection method.** Used when there is significant uncertainty about the collection of payment from customers.
2. **Completed performance method.** Used when the primary service goal is not achieved until the end of a contract, or if there are no intermediate milestones upon which revenue calculations can be based.
3. **Specific performance method.** Used when revenue is tied to the completion of a specific act.
4. **Proportional performance method.** Used when a number of specific and clearly identifiable actions are taken as part of an overall service to a customer. Rather than waiting until all services have been performed to recognize any revenue, this approach allows one to proportionally recognize revenue as each individual action is completed. The amount of revenue recognized is based on the proportional amount of direct costs incurred for each action to the estimated total amount of direct costs required to complete the entire service. However, if the service involves many identical actions (such as delivering the newspaper for a year), then revenue can be based on the proportion of actions completed thus far under the contract. Alternatively, if the service period is fixed but the amount of service provided cannot be determined (such as annual customer support for a software package), then service revenue can be ratably recognized over the service period.

Example of the proportional performance method using direct costs

If a service contract for $100,000 involved the completion of a single step that required $8,000 of direct costs to complete, and the total direct cost estimate for the entire job were $52,000, then the amount of revenue that could be recognized at the completion of that one action would be $15,385 = ($8,000/$52,000) × $100,000.

Example of the proportional performance method using a fixed period

A software company sells annual support agreements along with its software packages. A typical support agreement costs $2,400 per year. The company has no obligation other than to respond to customer calls, whose timing, duration, and frequency cannot be predicted. Accordingly, it ratably recognizes $200 of revenue per month for each agreement, which is 1/12 of the total amount.

Costs related to service contracts generally should be charged to expense when incurred. The exception is for direct costs, which are stored in a prepaid expenses account until revenue is recognized, at which point they are charged to expense. This treatment of direct costs is complicated somewhat under the proportional performance method, where costs are charged to expense only in proportion to the amount of revenue being recognized.

Recognition of Losses on Service Contracts

If the amount of direct costs incurred on a services project plus the estimate of remaining costs to be incurred exceeds the net revenue estimate for a project, the excess cost should be charged to expense, with the offsetting credit first being used to eliminate any deferred costs and any remainder being stored in a liability account.

Example of loss recognition on a services contract

The ABC Software Development Company expects to earn $100,000 in revenues from the sale of a new computer game it is developing. Unfortunately, its incurred direct expenses of $64,000 and estimated remaining costs of $50,000 exceed projected revenues by $14,000. The company had stored an additional $3,500 of incurred costs related to the project in an asset account. The following entry records the initial loss transaction:

Loss on service contract	14,000	
Unrecognized contract costs		3,500
Estimated loss on service contracts		10,500

As actual losses are incurred in later periods, the Estimated Loss on Service Contracts account is debited to reduce the outstanding liability.

Recording Initiation Fees as Service Revenue

A company may charge an initiation fee as part of a service contract, such as the up-front fee that many health clubs charge to new members. This fee should be recognized immediately as revenue only if there is a discernible value associated with it that can be separated from the services provided from ongoing fees that may be charged at a later date. However, if the initiation fee does not yield any specific value to the purchaser, then revenue from it can be recognized only over the term of the agreement to which the fee is attached. For example, if a health club membership agreement were to last for two years, then the revenue associated with the initiation fee should be spread over two years.

Recording Out-of-Pocket Expense Reimbursements

It is a common occurrence for service companies to bill their customers for any out-of-pocket expenses incurred, such as photocopying and delivery charges. It is not acceptable to record customer reimbursement of these expenses as a reduction in expenses. Instead, revenue must be credited for the amount of any reimbursements made.

Example of treatment of out-of-pocket expense reimbursements

The ABC Legal Services LLP entity charges a client for $552.00 in document delivery charges. It incorporates this charge into its standard monthly customer billing, crediting revenues for $552.00 and debiting receivables for $552.00.

Sales When Collection Is Uncertain

There are two methods used to record sales when the collection of those sales is uncertain. The first approach is the **installment method,** under which both revenue and the associated cost of goods sold are recognized at the time of the initial sale, but gross profit recognition is deferred until cash payments are received. This method requires one to track the gross margin percentage for each reporting period, so the correct percentage can be recognized when the associated cash receipts arrive at a later date. The second approach is the **cost recovery method,** under which the recognition of all gross profit is delayed until cash payments have been received that equal the entire cost of goods sold. The cost recovery method is the more conservative method, and should be used only when the collection of sales is highly uncertain.

For both recognition methods, installment accounts receivable are recognized as current assets, since the full term of the installment sale represents the normal operating cycle of the company. However, if installment sales are not a part of normal company operations, then the receivables are classified as long-term assets. In either case, installment accounts receivable should be itemized on the balance sheet by year. For example, all outstanding receivables due for payment in 2007 would be listed next to the title "Installment Receivables Due in 2007" in the balance sheet.

A typical component of installment sales is interest income, which is included in the periodic installment payments. Since installment payments are typically designed to be in equal amounts, the interest income component of these billings will comprise a gradually decreasing amount as more of the installment receivable is paid off. In order to properly account for the interest income component of installment sales, interest income must be stripped out of each payment made and credited to the interest income account, leaving the remaining balance of the payment subject to accounting under either the installment or cost recovery method. For the cost recovery method, interest income related to any long-term installment sales increases the unrecognized gross profit until the aggregate customer payments exceed the asset cost, after which the interest income is recognized.

Example of the installment method

The Gershwin Music Company sells musical instruments in bulk to school districts. Under one recent deal, it sold $10,000 of instruments to a district in Indiana at a gross profit of 30%. The district paid for the instruments in four annual installments that included 8% interest. The following table illustrates the recognition of both interest income and gross profit under the deal. Equal cash payments of $3,019.21 were made at the end of each year (column 1), from which interest income was separated and recognized (column 2), leaving an annual net receivable reduction (column 3). The gross profit on the deal (column 5) was recognized in proportion to the amount of accounts receivable reduction each year, which was 30% of column 3.

	(1)	*(2)*	*(3)*	*(4)*	*(5)*
	Cash	*Interest*	*Receivable*	*Receivable*	*Profit*
Date	*payment*	*@ 8%*	*reduction*	*balance*	*realized*
1/1/2005				$10,000.00	
12/31/2005	$ 3,019.21	$ 800.00	$2,219.21	$7,780.79	$ 665.76
12/31/2006	$ 3,019.21	$ 622.46	$2,396.75	$5,384.04	$ 719.02
12/31/2007	$ 3,019.21	$ 430.72	$2,588.49	$2,795.56	$ 776.55
12/31/2008	$ 3,019.20	$ 223.64	$2,795.56	$0.00	$ 838.67
		$2,076.83			$3,000.00

In short, Gershwin recognized 30% of the deferred gross profit contained within each cash payment, net of interest income. As an example of the journal entry made with each cash receipt, the company made the following entry to record the cash payment received on 12/31/2005:

Cash	3,019.21	
Interest income		800.00
Accounts receivable		2,219.21
Deferred gross profit	665.76	
Recognized gross profit		665.76

Example of the cost recovery method

We use the same assumptions for the Gershwin Music Company under the cost recovery method. Cash payments are the same, as are the interest charges and beginning balance. However, no gross profit or interest income is realized until all $7,000 of product costs have been recovered through cash payments net of interest income. Instead, interest income is shifted to a deferred account. To reflect these changes, column 5 shows a declining balance of unrecovered costs that are eliminated when the third periodic payment arrives. This allows Gershin's controller to recognize a small amount of deferred interest income in the third year, representing the net amount of cash payment left over after all costs have been recovered. In the final year, all remaining deferred interest income can be recognized, leaving the deferred gross margin as the last item to be recognized.

	(1)	(2)	(3)	(4)	(5)	(6)	(7)
	Cash	*Interest*	*Receivable*	*Receivable*	*Unrecovered*	*Profit*	*Interest*
Date	*payment*	*@ 8%*	*reduction*	*balance*	*cost*	*realized*	*realized*
1/1/2005				$10,000.00	$7,000.00		
12/31/2005	$3,019.21	$ 800.00	$2,219.21	$7,780.79	$4,780.79		
12/31/2006	$3,019.21	$ 622.46	$2,396.75	$5,384.04	$2,384.04		
12/31/2007	$3,019.21	$ 430.72	$2,588.49	$2,795.56	$ --		$ 204.43
12/31/2008	$3,019.20	$ 223.64	$2,795.56	$ 0.00	$ --	$3,000.00	$1,872.40
		$2,076.83				$3,000.00	$2,076.83

Repossession of Goods under Installment Sales

It is acceptable to recognize bad debts only under installment sales, since the seller can usually repossess the underlying goods. However, when the goods are repossessed, their value must be adjusted to their fair market value, which in most cases calls for the recognition of a loss.

Example of goods repossession

The Hudson's Bay Trailer Company has repossessed a construction trailer, for which $40,000 of accounts receivable is still outstanding, as well as $10,000 of deferred gross profit. The trailer has a fair market value of $28,000, so the company records the following entry to eliminate the receivable and deferred gross profit, while recognizing a loss of $2,000 on the write-down of the construction trailer:

Deferred gross margin	10,000	
Finished goods inventory	28,000	
Loss on inventory write-down	2,000	
Accounts receivable		40,000

Revenue Recognition When Right of Return Exists

If a sale transaction allows the buyer to return goods to the seller within a stated time period, then the transaction should be recognized only when one can reasonably estimate the amount of returns. If so, a sales return allowance should be established at the time of the sale, and coincident with the recognition of the sale. In practice, many companies do not record a returns allowance because the amount of sales returns is so small.

If the amount of sales returns cannot be reasonably estimated, then revenue recognition must be delayed until the expiration date of the return privilege has passed.

Revenue Recognition for Multiple Deliverables

Arrangements between vendors and their customers often include the sale of multiple products and services (deliverables). A multiple deliverable arrangement (MDA) can be structured using fixed, variable, or contingent pricing or combinations thereof. Product delivery and service performance can occur at different times and in different locations, and customer acceptance can be subject to various return privileges or performance guarantees.

Three steps must be followed when determining revenue recognition for an MDA arrangement:

1. Separate the components of the MDA into separate units of accounting, which can only occur if each component to be tracked separately has standalone value to the customer and there is objective evidence of its fair value.
2. Allocate proceeds from the total sale arrangement to the separate units of accounting based on their relative fair values.
3. Apply revenue recognition criteria separately to each unit of accounting.

When determining the fair value of each of the units of accounting in an MDA, it is best to use vendor-specific objective evidence (VSOE), which is the price at which the vendor has sold these units elsewhere in the marketplace on a stand-alone basis.

Example of multiple deliverable revenue recognition

Peach Company sells an MP3 player, which it calls the Nectarine. Peach prefers to sell the Nectarine with a bundled annual support package, which sells for $320. Without the service package, the Nectarine retails for $250, and Peach sells the servicing package separately for $120 per year.

Peach splits apart the two revenue elements of the bundled annual support package by allocating revenue to the Nectarine, based on the fair values of the Nectarine and its support package, which it calculates as follows:

$$\frac{(\$250 \text{ product price})}{(\$250 \text{ product price} + \$120 \text{ servicing price})} \times \$320 \text{ bundled price} = \$216.22$$

Peach also allocates revenue to the support package in the same manner with the following calculation:

$$\frac{(\$120 \text{ servicing price})}{(\$250 \text{ product price} + \$120 \text{ servicing price})} \times \$320 \text{ bundled price} = \$103.78$$

Based on these calculations, Peach can recognize $216.22 of revenue every time it sells the bundled Nectarine support package. However, because Peach must provide one year of service under the support package, the remaining $103.78 of revenue associated with the servicing contract can be only incrementally recognized on a monthly basis over the twelve-month life of the service contract, which is $8.65 per month.

Franchise Sales

Franchise operations are generally subject to the same accounting principles as other commercial enterprises. Special issues arise out of franchise agreements, however, which require the application of special accounting rules.

Revenue is recognized, with an appropriate provision for bad debts, when the franchisor has substantially performed all material services or conditions. Only when revenue is collected over an extended period of time and collectibility cannot be predicted in advance would the use of the cost recovery or installment methods of revenue recognition be appropriate. Substantial performance means

1. The franchisor has no remaining obligation to either refund cash or forgive any unpaid balance due.
2. Substantially all initial services required by the agreement have been performed.
3. No material obligations or conditions remain.

Even if the contract does not require initial services, the pattern of performance by the franchisor in other franchise sales will impact the time period of revenue recognition. This can delay such recognition until services are either performed or it can reasonably be assured they will not be performed. The franchisee operations will be considered as started when such substantial performance has occurred.

If initial franchise fees are large compared to services rendered and continuing franchise fees are small compared to services to be rendered, then a portion of the initial fee is deferred in an amount sufficient to cover the costs of future services plus a reasonable profit, after considering the impact of the continuing franchise fee.

Example of initial franchise fee revenue recognition

Shanghai Oriental Cuisine sells a Quack's Roast Duck franchise to Toledo Restaurants. The franchise is renewable after two years. The initial franchise fee is $50,000, plus a fixed fee of $500 per month. In exchange, Shanghai provides staff training, vendor relations support, and site selection consulting. Each month thereafter, Shanghai provides $1,000 of free local advertising. Shanghai's typical gross margin on franchise start-up sales is 25%.

Because the monthly fee does not cover the cost of monthly services provided, Shanghai defers a portion of the initial franchise fee and amortizes it over the two-year life of the franchise agreement, using the following calculation:

Cost of monthly services provided $1,000 × 24 months	=	$24,000
÷ Markup to equal standard 25% gross margin	=	.75
= Estimated revenue required to offset monthly services provided	=	$32,000
Less: Monthly billing to franchise $500 × 24 months	–	$12,000
= Amount of initial franchise fee to be deferred	=	$20,000

Shanghai's entry to record the franchise fee deferral follows:

Franchise fee revenue	20,000	
Unearned franchise fees (liability)		20,000

Shanghai recognizes one twenty-fourth of the unearned franchise fee liability during each month of the franchise period on a straight-line basis, which amounts to $833.33 per month.

Motion Picture Revenues

An entity recognizes revenue from a sale or licensing arrangement only when all of the following conditions are met:

1. Persuasive evidence exists of a sale or licensing arrangement with a customer. This requires documented evidence of the license period, films covered by the agreement, the rights transferred, and the payment terms.
2. The film is complete and, in accordance with the terms of the arrangement, has been delivered or is available for immediate and unconditional delivery. This requirement is not fulfilled if the customer requires significant changes to the film.
3. The license period for the arrangement has started and the customer can begin exploitation, exhibition, or sale.
4. The arrangement fee is fixed or determinable. If there are multiple films in the agreement, this may require allocation of the fee to each film based on the relative fair values of the rights to exploit each film. If relative fair values cannot be determined, then the company cannot recognize revenue until those determinations can be made.
5. Collection of the arrangement fee is reasonably assured.

If any of the above conditions has not been met, the company defers revenue recognition until all of the conditions are met. If the company recognizes a receivable on its balance sheet for advances under an arrangement for which all of the above conditions have not been met, a liability for deferred revenue of the same amount is to be recognized until such time as all of the conditions have been met.

DECISION TREES

Recording Revenues at Gross or Net

Given the large company valuations that can be achieved by recording the largest possible amount of revenue, it is no surprise that companies have a tendency to record revenue even when they are only acting as brokers, rather than the initiators of revenue transactions. The decision tree in Exhibit 5-1 is designed to show the criteria that a company must pass before it can record revenue at the gross amount; all three criteria must be satisfied, otherwise only the commission or broker fee associated with the sale can be recorded as revenue.

Exhibit 5-1: Decision Tree for Recording Revenue at Gross or Net

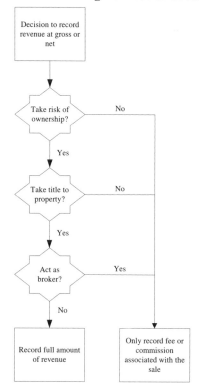

Recording Service Revenues

Service revenues can be recorded using four methods, one of which is most appropriate depending on the underlying factors of a specific service contract. Exhibit 5-2 shows the criteria under which one should use either the collection, completed performance, specific performance, or proportional performance methods. The flowchart is designed to show that, unless various revenue-related problems exist in a service contract, the proportional performance method is the default revenue recording method.

Exhibit 5-2: Decision Tree for Recording Service Revenues

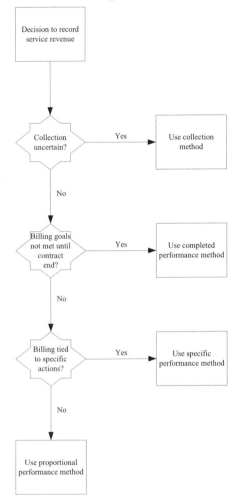

POLICIES

Revenue—General

- **Preliminary revenue summaries shall be issued no later than one day following the close of an accounting period.** This policy is designed to prevent the accounting staff from artificially keeping the books open past the end of the reporting period, since it must commit to a specific revenue figure within a day of closing.
- **Extended rights of return shall not be allowed.** This policy limits the ability of the sales staff to engage in "channel stuffing," since it cannot offer special rights of return to customers in exchange for early sales. The policy keeps a company from gyrating between large swings in sales caused by channel stuffing.

- **Special sale discounts shall not be allowed without senior management approval.** This policy prevents large bursts in sales caused by special price discounts that can stuff a company's distribution channels, causing rapid sales declines in subsequent periods.
- **The company shall not use bill and hold transactions.** Though bill and hold transactions are allowable under clearly defined and closely restricted circumstances, they are subject to abuse, and so should generally be avoided. This policy ensures that bill and hold transactions would require Board approval before being used.
- **Estimated profits on service contracts shall be reviewed monthly.** This policy ensures that estimated losses on service contracts are identified and recognized promptly, rather than being delayed until the contracts are closed.

Barter Revenues

- **The company shall not engage in barter transactions whose sole purpose is the creation of revenue.** This policy informs the accounting staff that it is unacceptable to create barter swap transactions whose sole purpose is to create additional revenue without the presence of any economic reason for the transaction.
- **All expenses associated with barter transactions shall be recognized in the same proportions as related revenues.** This policy is designed to keep expenses associated with barter swap transactions from being significantly delayed while revenues are recognized up front. The policy will keep profits from being incorrectly recorded in advance.

Long-Term Construction Contracts

- **Construction contract revenue shall be calculated using the percentage-of-completion method.** This policy allows a company to calculate all construction revenues using a consistent methodology, so there is no question of using one method over another to gain a short-term advantage in reporting the amount of revenue.
- **Accounts used in overhead pools shall be reviewed annually and altered only with management approval.** This policy keeps the accounting staff from arbitrarily altering the contents of overhead cost pools. Overhead pool alterations are a classic approach for shifting expenses out of the current period and into construction-in-process asset accounts.

Sales When Collection Is Uncertain

- **A single revenue recognition method shall be used for all installment sales.** This policy keeps an accounting department from switching back and forth between the installment method and cost recovery method for recognizing this type of revenue, which would otherwise allow it to manipulate reported levels of profitability.

Revenue Recognition When Right of Return Exists

- **A sales return allowance shall be maintained for all goods sold with a right of return.** This policy ensures that profits are not initially overstated by the amount of any potential returns by requiring an initial reserve to be established.

Franchising Revenues

- **The initial franchise fee shall not be recognized until substantially all startup services to be provided by the franchisor have been completed.** This policy keeps the accounting staff from recognizing revenue too early.
- **The estimated number of total franchise locations shall be regularly reviewed and updated.** Under an area franchise sale agreement, the franchisor typically recognizes initial fee revenue based on the proportion of actual franchise locations completed within the area as a proportion of the total estimated number to be completed. Thus, the number of estimated locations directly impacts revenue recognition, and should be kept as accurate as possible.
- **Deferred franchise costs shall be matched against franchise fees as part of the monthly closing process.** If deferred costs related to a franchise exceed the amount of the franchise fee, then the excess costs must be recognized at once. This policy ensures that any excess costs will be found and charged to expense in a timely manner.

PROCEDURES[2]

Issue a Customer Credit Rating

Use this procedure to both create and subsequently adjust a customer's credit rating.

1. Pull the standard credit references form (see the Customer Credit Application in the Forms and Reports section) from the forms cabinet and fax it to the customer requesting credit.
2. Once the completed form is returned, verify with each customer reference the maximum and average amounts of credit granted and used, as well as any issues with slow payment.
3. Obtain the names of other credit references from these references, if possible, and record the answers to the same questions from them.
4. Contact Dun & Bradstreet's automated credit reporting system, enter the customer's contact information, and specify that you want to receive the Business Information Report.
5. To determine an appropriate credit level, ignore any exceedingly high credit amounts granted by other companies and pick the average level of the remainder. Then reduce this amount by 5% for every additional day of late payments as reported for the customer by Dun & Bradstreet.

---

[2] *Many of the procedures in this section were reprinted with permission from Chapter 5 of Bragg,* **Design and Maintenance of Accounting Manuals** *(John Wiley & Sons, Inc. Hoboken, NJ, 2003).*

6. If there has been some sales experience with a customer, consult with the collections staff to obtain their opinion of the most appropriate credit level. Also review the Dun & Bradstreet bankruptcy early warning notification system to see if there are any recent customer problems. Revise the credit level based on this information.
7. Enter the credit level in the accounting system's customer file.
8. Notify the sales staff of the credit level granted.

Process a Shipment

Use this procedure to ensure that the proper paperwork and computer transactions are completed when product is shipped to a customer.

1. Access the daily schedule of shipments in the computer system and print the report.
2. Verify that all finished goods listed on the daily schedule are on hand and available for shipment.
3. If the required quantities are not available, contact the customer service staff to ascertain customer wishes regarding partial orders, or contact the production scheduling staff to ensure that the production department will complete the missing products as soon as possible.
4. Mark all other items on the daily schedule as being ready for delivery.
5. Using the daily schedule, remove all targeted items from the warehouse bins and relocate them to the shipping area.
6. Contact freight carriers regarding scheduled pickup times.
7. Prepare bills of lading and packing slips for all shipments.
8. Load shipments on trucks for delivery.
9. Complete the shipping log.
10. Send copies of the bills of lading and packing slips to the accounting department by interoffice mail. Include a copy of the day's shipping log, which should match all other documentation sent.
11. Access the computer system and enter the customer, ship date, part number, and quantity shipped for each shipment sent out that day.

Create an Invoice

Use this procedure to create invoices based on shipping and pricing information.

1. Receive the daily packet of shipping information from the warehouse manager. The paperwork should include a handwritten shipping log, as well as two copies of the bills of lading. Print the customer order from the computer system. Separate these documents into different piles.
2. Verify that there is a bill of lading for every order listed on the shipping log, and also that **all** bills of lading are listed on the log. Then put the bills of lading in order, first by customer name and then by order number (if there is more than one order per customer), and match the order forms to them.
3. Check the "carrier" column on the shipping log. There is no shipping charge if "customer pickup" is noted. Otherwise, if a carrier name is listed,

calculate a freight rate based on the standard freight rate schedule. Note the amount of the freight charge on the order form.

4. Go to the invoicing module in the accounting software and access the invoicing screen. Enter the customer name and verify that the Bill To name in the system is correct. If not, change it to match the name listed on the order. Then enter the part number, quantity, and price listed on the order form. Add the freight rate to the bottom of the invoice. Also verify that the sales tax code is correct. Save the invoice record and repeat until all invoices have been entered.

5. Verify that the invoice form is correctly positioned in the printer. Run a test invoice if necessary to ensure that the form is properly aligned. Then print the daily invoice batch.

6. Burst all printed invoices, with the pink copies going to the alphabetical filing bin, the white copies going to customers, and the goldenrod copies going to the numerical filing bin.

7. Stuff the white invoice copies into envelopes and mail them to customers.

8. Attach the pink invoice copies to the bills of lading, packing slip, and customer orders, and file them by customer name. File the goldenrod copies in numerical order.

Compare Billings to the Shipping Log

Use this procedure to verify that shipments are matched by the same number of invoices, thereby ensuring that no invoices are missing or duplicated.

1. Go to the warehouse and make a copy of the shipping log for the previous week. Alternatively (if available), access this information on-line through the receiving system and print out the shipping log.

2. Match the shipments listed on the shipping log to invoices issued during the same period. Note all exceptions in the shipping log for missing billings. Also, note on invoices any incorrect quantities that were billed, as well as "leftover" invoices for which there is no shipping record.

3. Using the list of shipments for which there are no corresponding invoices, go to the shipping department and obtain bills of lading for the unbilled shipments. If these are not available, determine which freight carrier shipped the items and obtain shipping traces on them. Then create invoices, mail a copy to the customer, and attach proof of delivery to the company's copy of the invoice. File the company's copy in the accounting files.

4. Using the list of invoices for which no corresponding shipment is recorded in the shipping log, go back to the company's copy of these invoices and see if there is any bill of lading or other proof of delivery attached to the invoice. If not, call the shipping department to verify that no such documentation exists there. If not, issue a credit to eliminate these invoices.

5. Using the list of invoices for which the quantity of product billed is different from the quantity shipped, go back to the company's copy of the invoice and check the attached bill of lading to determine the actual quantity shipped. If the quantity is different, verify this with the shipping department and then

either issue a credit (if the quantity billed was too high) or an additional invoice (if the quantity billed was too low).

Review Pricing Errors

Use this procedure to locate all invoice pricing errors occurring during a fixed time period, determine underlying problems, and report on the results to management.

1. Go to the accounting software and access the invoice register for the past month.
2. Convert the invoice register to an Excel file. Open the Excel file and sort the invoice list by dollar order. Delete all invoices from the list that do not have a credit balance.
3. Search the description field for each credit for wording regarding corrections of pricing errors. Retain these records and delete all others. Print the spreadsheet.
4. Transfer the following information to a separate spreadsheet report: credit number, credit amount, customer name, correct price, actual price charged, the quantity of product to which the correction applies, the grand total pricing error, and the initials of the customer service person who processed the credit.
5. Go to the customer service person who processed the credit and determine the cause of the pricing error. Include this information on the spreadsheet.
6. Print the spreadsheet and distribute it to the sales manager, controller, and chief operating officer.
7. Enter the total number of pricing errors and the total dollar error in the monthly corporate statistics report.

Process Bill and Hold Transactions

Though, as noted under the Policies section, bill and hold transactions are generally to be discouraged, they can be used under very specific circumstances. When this occurs, a separate procedure is needed, since invoices are not triggered by a shipping transaction. The following steps show the proper approach:

1. Access the warehouse database on a specific recurring date and call up the report listing all bill and hold items currently in stock. Take the report to the warehouse and verify that all items listed on the report match what is in stock, and also trace all items in stock back to the report. Investigate any variances.
2. If the invoice number associated with each bill and hold item is not already listed in the report, retrieve this information from the file containing the last period's bill and hold transactions. Compare this information to the validated warehouse report and note any items that have not yet been billed.
3. For all bill and hold items not yet billed, print the Acknowledgment of Bill and Hold Transaction form (see the Forms and Reports section for a sample

version) and fax it to the authorized customer representative, with a request that it be signed and sent back.

4. Once the signed form has been received, verify that all signature spots have been signed. Then attach a copy of the customer's purchase order to the form, copy both, and send them to the billing staff for invoicing. Put the originals in a pending file.

5. Once the accounting staff creates the invoice, it will return an invoice copy. Attach this copy to the signed form and customer purchase order, staple them together, and file them by customer name.

6. When bill and hold items are eventually shipped to the customer, the warehouse staff removes them from the inventory database and sends the bill of lading to the accounting person handling the bill and hold transactions. This person removes the transaction's previously filed invoice packet from the files, attaches to it the bill of lading, and forwards the complete package to the billings staff, which then files the packet in the completed invoices file.

Process Sales Returns

Use this procedure to issue a sales return authorization number to a customer, log the authorization into the accounting system, and record the receipt upon arrival.

1. **Customer service staff.** When a customer calls to ask for a return authorization number, call up the return authorization screen in the computer system. Verify that the part numbers and quantities to be returned were previously ordered and received by the customer. If not, deny return authorization. If so, enter the part numbers and quantities to be returned into the system and issue a return authorization number.

2. **Receiving staff.** When products are returned from a customer, verify the existence of a return authorization number on the delivery. If not, reject the delivery. If so, enter it into the computer system and verify that the items included in the delivery were authorized. If not, reject the order. If so, enter the amounts actually received into the computer, and close the authorization if all items received match the amounts authorized.

3. **Accounting staff.** The computer system will create a credit based on the amount of product returned. Offset this amount against the relevant outstanding accounts receivable. If the computer system does not automatically create credits for sales returns, then calculate the credit due, net of any return and restocking charges, and enter the amount in the sales journal. All related documentation should be retained in the customer file.

4. **Warehouse staff.** Move all returned merchandise to the returned goods section of the warehouse. Open and test all returned items, replacing them in new packaging. Log them into the inventory database and move them to the finished goods section of the warehouse.

Collect Overdue Accounts

Use this procedure to manage the collections process, as well as to determine the causes of collection problems and correct them.

1. Go to the accounting database and access the accounts receivable module. Print the accounts receivable aging report.
2. Review the printed report and circle all invoices more than forty days old.
3. Return to the accounts receivable module and print the customer master file, showing contact information for each customer.
4. Using the contact information on the customer master file, use the following four-step sequence of escalating contacts to ensure that customers are aware of nonpayment situations:
   a. Send a fax to the customer noting a payment problem, including a copy of the invoice.
   b. Send an e-mail to the customer noting a payment problem, including an Adobe Acrobat PDF version of the invoice.
   c. Call the customer and verify receipt of the prior information. If no one answers, then leave a message.
   d. If there was no direct contact during the last step, send an overnight delivery package containing the same information.
5. Upon making contact with a customer, determine why payment has not been made. If a customer states that a payment is on the way, verify exactly what invoices are being paid and then inquire about any overdue invoices that will continue to be open after the payment.
6. Go to the customer contact log and enter the date of each customer contact, who was contacted, and what information was gained. Use this information as a reference whenever calling the customer again in the future. Also, if there is new customer contact information as a result of the most recent customer contact, update the customer file with this information.
7. If it is necessary to adjust a customer's credit limit to more properly reflect its ability to pay, go to the credit department and review the credit status with the credit manager. If new credit terms are agreed upon, contact the customer with this information.
8. If customer contacts reveal that internal problems are causing collection difficulties, then assign a problem code to each collection issue in the collections database, as well as a brief description of the issue. Periodically run a summary report sorted by problem code and send this information to the controller or CFO for further action.

Long-Term Construction Contracts—Percentage-of-Completion Calculation

Use this procedure to determine the amount of revenue to be recognized on a construction project.

1. Access the approved project bid file and determine the estimated gross profit percentage for the project.

2. Discuss the estimated gross margin with the project manager to verify that the percentage is still valid. If not, use the project manager's revised estimate.

3. Access the general ledger and note the total amount of expenses accumulated to date in the project's construction-in-progress account.

4. Divide the total project expenses by one minus the estimated gross profit percentage to arrive at total expenses plus the estimated gross profit.

5. Access the project billing records and determine the total amount of billings made to the customer thus far.

6. Subtract the total expenses and estimated gross profit from the billings figure. If the amount of expenses and gross profits is larger than the billed amount, debit the Unbilled Contract Receivables account and credit the Contract Revenues Earned account for the difference. If the amount of expenses and gross profits is less than the billed amount, debit the Contract Revenues Earned account and credit the Billings Exceeding Project Costs and Margin account for the difference.

Service Revenues—Advance Recognition of Losses

Use this procedure to periodically review service contracts to determine the existence of any projected contract losses.

1. Summarize all project-to-date direct costs from the relevant general ledger account.

2. Go to the project manager and review the amount of estimated costs yet to be incurred on the project. Compare this amount to the estimated completion cost from the last review to see if there are any unusual changes, and discuss the differences. Also verify the cost estimated against any project planning database, such as a Gantt or Critical Path Method chart.

3. Summarize all project billings to date, and verify the amount of remaining billings, adjusted for any contract modifications.

4. Combine the actual and estimated costs and subtract them from the total expected project revenues. If the costs exceed revenues, notify the controller of the difference with a memo, outlining the reasons for the loss.

5. Debit the Loss on Contracts account for the amount of the estimated loss. Use the offsetting credit to eliminate any unrecognized costs stored in an asset account, and credit the remaining loss to the Estimated Loss on Service Contracts account.

Sales When Collection Is Uncertain—Goods Repossession

Use this procedure to process back into inventory any goods received as part of a repossession from an installment sale on which the customer has failed to make payments.

1. Upon the return of goods, the warehouse staff segregates the inventory and contacts the materials review board for an evaluation.

2. The materials review board periodically examines all returned goods to determine if they can be returned directly to finished goods inventory at full valuation, refurbished, or donated.

    a. If the goods are returned to finished goods stock, they are entered into inventory at full cost, and the accounting department is notified of the transaction so it can record the inventory valuation as an offset to the receivable being canceled as part of the repossession.

    b. If the goods are to be refurbished, they are entered into inventory at their current fair value, and the accounting department is notified of the reduced valuation so it can record the reduced inventory valuation as a smaller offset to the receivable being canceled as part of the repossession.

    c. If the inventory is donated, the warehouse manager fills out the Asset Donation form and sends the original to the accounting department, which retains it for use by the tax department in determining charitable donations. The accounting staff also records a full loss on the returned inventory.

3. Based on the treatment of the returned inventory, the accounting staff credits the accounts receivable account to eliminate the unpaid balance of the account receivable, debits the Finished Goods account for the fair value of the returned inventory, debits the Deferred Gross Profit account to eliminate the unpaid balance of unearned gross profit on the transaction, and debits the Loss on Repossessed Inventory account to charge off any difference between these entries.

Revenue Recognition When Right of Return Exists

Use this procedure to determine the amount of sales returns to record at the end of each reporting period:

1. Summarize all sales occurring during the period for which a right of return exists, using subcategories if there are significant differences in sales returns for different products.
2. Calculate the sales return percentage for each category of products on a one-year rolling basis.
3. Multiply the sales return percentage by sales in each category to arrive at the required sales return allowance.
4. Debit the revenue account for the amount of the allowance to be added, while crediting the associated cost of goods sold and deferred gross profit accounts.

CONTROLS

General

- **Investigate all journal entries increasing the size of revenue.** Any time a journal entry is used to increase a sales account, this should be a red flag indicating the potential presence of revenues that were not created through a normal sales journal transaction. These transactions can be legitimate cases of incremental revenue recognition associated with prepaid services, but can also be barter swap transactions or fake transactions whose sole purpose is to increase revenues.

It is especially important to review all sales transactions where the offsetting debit to the sales credit is **not** accounts receivable or cash. This is a prime indicator of unusual transactions that may not really qualify as sales. For example, a gain on an asset sale or an extraordinary gain may be incorrectly credited to a sales account that would mislead the reader of a company's financial statements that its operating revenues have increased.

- **Compare the shipping log and shipping documents to invoices issued at period-end.** This control is designed to spot billings on transactions not completed until after the reporting period had closed. An invoice dated within a reporting period whose associated shipping documentation shows the transaction as having occurred later is clear evidence of improper revenue reporting. If invoices are based on services instead of goods provided, then invoices can be matched to service reports or timesheets instead.

- **Issue financial statements within one day of the period-end.** By eliminating the gap between the end of the reporting period and the issuance of financial statements, it is impossible for anyone to create additional invoices for goods shipping subsequent to the period-end, thereby automatically eliminating any cutoff problems.

- **Compare customer-requested delivery dates to actual shipment dates.** If customer order information is loaded into the accounting computer system, run a comparison of the dates on which customers have requested delivery to the dates on which orders were actually shipped. If there is an ongoing tendency to make shipments substantially early, there may be a problem with trying to create revenue by making early shipments. Of particular interest is when there is a surge of early shipments in months when revenues would otherwise have been low, indicating a clear intention to increase revenues by avoiding customer-mandated shipment dates. It may be possible to program the computer system to not allow the recording of deliveries if the entered delivery date is prior to the customer-requested delivery date, thereby effectively blocking early revenue recognition.

- **Compare invoice dates to the recurring revenue database.** In cases where a company obtains a recurring revenue stream by billing customers periodically for maintenance or subscription services, there can be a temptation to create early billings in order to record revenue somewhat sooner. For example, a billing on a 12-month subscription could be issued after 11 months, thereby accelerating revenue recognition by one month. This issue can be spotted by comparing the total of recurring billings in a month to the total amount of recurring revenue for that period as compiled from the corporate database of customers with recurring revenue. Alternatively, one can compare the recurring billing dates for a small sample of customers to the dates on which invoices were actually issued.

- **Identify shipments of product samples in the shipping log.** A product that is shipped with no intention of being billed is probably a product sample being sent to a prospective customer, marketing agency, and so on. These should be noted as product samples in the shipping log, and the internal audit staff should verify that each of them was properly authorized, preferably with a signed document.

- **Verify that a signed Acknowledgment of Bill and Hold Transaction has been received for every related transaction.** If a company uses bill and hold transactions, then this control is absolutely mandatory. By ensuring that customers have agreed in advance to be billed for items to be kept in the company's warehouse, one can be assured of being in compliance with the strict GAAP rules applying to these transactions. Also, a continual verification of this paperwork (as shown in the Forms and Reports section) will keep managers from incorrectly inflating revenues by issuing false bill and hold transactions.

- **Confirm signed Acknowledgment of Bill and Hold Transactions with customers.** If a company begins to match bill and hold acknowledgment letters to invoices issued to customers (see previous control), the logical reaction of any person who wants to fraudulently continue issuing bill and hold invoices is to create dummy acknowledgments. Consequently, it is useful to contact the persons who allegedly signed the acknowledgments to verify that they actually did so.

- **Do not accept any product returns without an authorization number.** Customers will sometimes try to return products if there is no justification required, thereby clearing out their inventories at the expense of the company. This can be avoided by requiring a return authorization number, which must be provided by the company in advance and prominently noted on any returned goods. If the number is not shown, the receiving department is required to reject the shipment.

- **Compare related company addresses and names to customer list.** By comparing the list of company subsidiaries to the customer list, one can determine if any intercompany sales have occurred, and if these transactions have all been appropriately backed out of the financial statements. Since employees at one subsidiary may conceal this relationship by using a false company name or address, one can verify the same information at all the other subsidiaries by matching subsidiary names and addresses to their supplier lists, since it is possible that the receiving companies are **not** trying to hide the intercompany sales information.

Barter Revenues

- **Require a written business case for all barter transactions.** Require the creation of a business case detailing why a barter transaction is required, and what type of accounting should be used for it. The case should be approved by a senior-level manager before any associated entry is made in the general ledger. The case should be attached to the associated journal entry and filed. This approach makes it less likely that sham barter swap transactions will be created.

Cash Payments to Customers

- **Verify that cash-back payments to customers are charged to sales.** Compare the customer list to the cash disbursements register to highlight all cash payments made to customers. Investigate each one and verify that the revenue account was debited in those instances where cash-back payments were made. This should not apply to the return of overpayments made by customers to the company.

Recording Revenues at Gross or Net

- **Create a revenue accounting procedure to specify the treatment of gross or net transactions.** When a company deals with both gross and net revenue transactions on a regular basis, there should be a procedure that clearly defines for the accounting staff the situations under which revenues shall be treated on a gross or net basis. This reduces the need for internal audit reviews (see next control) to detect revenue accounting problems after the fact.
- **Review the revenue accounting for potential pass-through transactions.** In situations where there is an extremely high cost of goods sold (indicating a possible pass-through transaction) or where there is no clear evidence of the company acting as principal, taking title to goods, or accepting risk of ownership, the internal audit staff should review the appropriateness of the transaction.
- **Trace commission payments back to underlying sale transactions.** One can keep a list of all business partners who pay the company commissions, and run a periodic search on all payments made by them to the company. The internal audit staff can then trace these payments back to the underlying sales made by the company, and verify that they were recorded at net, rather than at gross.

Long-Term Construction Contracts

- **Compare declared percentage of completion to estimated work required to complete projects.** A very common way to record excessive revenue on a construction project is to falsely state that the percentage of completion is greater than the actual figure, thereby allowing the company to record a greater proportion of revenues in the current period. Though difficult to verify with any precision, a reasonable control is to match the declared percentage of completion to a percentage of the actual hours worked, divided by the total estimated number of hours worked. The two percentages should match.
- **Ensure that project expenses are charged to the correct account.** A common problem with revenue recognition under the percentage-of-completion method is that extra expenses may be erroneously or falsely loaded into a

project's general ledger account, which can then be used as the justification for the recognition of additional revenue related to that project. Auditing expenses in active project accounts can spot these problems.

- **Promptly close project accounts once projects are completed.** It is not a difficult matter to incorrectly store project-related expenses in the wrong accounts, and may be done fraudulently in order to avoid recognizing losses related to excessive amounts of expenses being incurred on specific projects. This problem can be resolved by promptly closing general ledger project accounts once the related projects are complete. Closing project accounts can be included in the month-end closing procedure, thereby ensuring that this problem will be addressed on a regular basis.

- **Control access to general ledger accounts.** Employees are less likely to shift expenses between general ledger construction accounts if they are unable to access the accounts, or if they have no way of reopening closed accounts. This can be achieved by tightly restricting account access, and especially access to the closed or open status flag for each account.

- **Compare the dates on supplier invoices in the construction-in-progress account to the project start date.** Since precontract costs must be charged to expense, there is a temptation to hold these supplier invoices until after the project contract has been signed, so they can be stored in the construction-in-progress account instead as an asset. To detect this problem, examine a selection of invoiced expenses in the account to see if any are dated prior to the project's contract date.

- **Review journal entries shifting expenses into construction-in-progress accounts.** Since precontract costs must be charged to expense, there is a temptation to increase short-term profits by shifting these expenses into the construction-in-progress account with a journal entry. To spot this problem, review all journal entries adding expenses to the construction-in-progress account.

- **Consistently aggregate expenses into overhead accounts and charge them to individual projects.** One could charge different overhead expenses to various projects, or apply the same pool of overhead costs inconsistently to the accounts, thereby effectively shifting expenses to those projects that would result in the greatest revenue increase under the percentage of completion revenue recognition method. To avoid this problem, periodically verify that the same expenses are being consistently charged to overhead cost pools over time, and that the same allocation method is used to shift these expenses from the overhead cost pools to project accounts.

- **Exclude the cost of unused materials from cost-to-cost percentage of completion calculations.** More materials than are initially needed are typically purchased at the beginning of a project. This increases the amount of recognizable revenue early in a project when the cost-to-cost percentage-of-completion method is used. To avoid this problem, remove all unused materials from the calculation.

- **Compare the percentage of revenues recognized to expenses recognized.** When revenues associated with a project are recognized, one must also make a second entry to shift costs from the construction-in-progress account to the cost of goods sold. If this second entry is missed for any reason, profits will be unusually high. To spot this problem, compare the amount of recognized revenue to recognized expenses for each project and verify that it matches the most recent gross profit estimate for the project. If the percentage is higher, some expenses have probably not been recognized.
- **Review prospective project issues with the construction manager.** A common fraud involving project accounting is to shift the timing and amount of recognized losses on projects. These losses can be delayed in order to make the current period's results look better, or made excessively large or small in order to meet reporting targets. Though it is quite difficult to ascertain if the size of a loss is correct, it is possible to guess **when** a loss should be recognized. By having regular discussions with a project's construction manager regarding ongoing and upcoming project-related issues, it is possible to see when significant unbudgeted costs are to be incurred, thereby giving some insight into the need for loss recognition.
- **Watch for expense loading on cost-plus contracts.** When a company is guaranteed by the customer to pay for all expenses incurred, there exists a temptation to load extra expenses into an account. These expense additions can be spotted by looking for charges from suppliers whose costs are not normally charged to a specific type of contract, as well as by looking for expense types that increase significantly over expenses incurred in previous periods, and by investigating any journal entries that increase expense levels.

Service Revenues

- **Review underlying contract terms for all proportional performance revenue calculations.** The proportional performance method is the most aggressive service revenue calculation method, in that revenues can be recognized earlier than with most other revenue recognition methods. For this control, trace each revenue-creation journal entry back to the related service contract and verify that collection is reasonably assured and that billings are not tied to specific actions. If either of these cases holds true, other more conservative revenue recognition methods must be used that may reduce the amount of revenue recognized.
- **Regularly review service contracts for potential losses.** Losses on service contracts must be recognized as expenses immediately, even if the losses are only estimated. Since there is a natural reluctance to recognize losses in advance of the actual event, a good control is to include a standard review of estimated losses on service contracts as part of the monthly closing process.

Sales When Collection Is Uncertain

- **Verify that the correct gross margin percentage is used for the recognition of gross margins upon the receipt of cash.** The gross margins associated with installment sales should be deferred until the related cash payments are received from customers. This margin is typically aggregated for all sales within a specific time period, and used for all receipts related to that time period. If the gross margin percentage for a different period were to be incorrectly used to recognize gross margin dollars, there would be an impact on the reported level of profitability. The best control over this issue is a procedure clearly stating how to calculate, track, and apply gross margins when cash is received. A secondary control is a regular review of all calculations made to recognize gross margins.

Revenue Recognition When Right of Return Exists

- **Include a sales return allowance calculation in the standard closing procedure.** By requiring someone to address the issue of return allowances as part of every period-end close, there is a much greater chance that the allowance amount will be verified against actual returns, resulting in an accurate return allowance.
- **Verify the amount of the return allowance against actual experience.** One can examine the basis for a specific returns allowance amount being recorded, comparing it to actual experience with the same or similar products in the recent past. However, this is an after-the-fact control that must be repeated regularly to ensure that allowance levels are reasonable.
- **Review the condition of returned inventory.** Sales returns tend not to be in pristine condition, so a company must record a write-down to their fair value at the time of the return. However, the warehouse staff tends to place them back in stock without any consideration of condition, resulting in the overstatement of finished goods inventory. A good control is to have all sales returns set to one side for review, after which they are either shifted back to stock at full value, thrown away, donated, or reclassified as used stock and assigned a reduced inventory value.

Multiple Deliverable Arrangements (MDAs)

- **Review clusters of invoices issued to individual customers.** A company can circumvent the MDA rules by issuing separate contracts for each element of a sale that would normally be considered to have multiple deliverables. One way to spot this issue is to conduct a periodic audit that searches for clusters of contracts entered into with a single customer within a short period of time. The audit program should include a review of these contracts to determine if they are in fact associated with a single sale transaction.
- **Review definitions of units of accounting.** If a company has multiple sale arrangements that include multiple deliverables, it is possible that it will not separate the various elements into separate units of accounting in a consistent manner. To guard against this issue, a periodic audit should compare the documentation of the various MDAs to locate any inconsistencies in the definition of units of accounting.

- **Compare billings to unbilled costs.** A control problem arises when a company records a combination of revenue and "costs and estimated earnings in excess of billings" that exceed the total amount a customer has agreed to pay. A billing procedure should require the accounting staff to compare the combination of billings and unbilled costs to the customer's contractual agreement to pay, and record a loss for any costs incurred that exceed this amount.

Franchise Revenues

- **Compare gross margins earned on initial and ongoing franchise fees.** To ensure that revenue recognition is not accelerated through the use of an excessively high initial franchise fee in proportion to services generated, a periodic audit could calculate and compare the gross margins earned on initial and ongoing franchise fees.
- **Compare completion of services to fee recognition.** It is also possible that revenue could be recognized on an initial franchise fee before all related services have been completed, thereby falsely accelerating revenue recognition. To detect this problem, a periodic audit could compare the completion of services to the recognition of initial franchise fee revenue for each franchise agreement.
- **Compare actual to estimated franchise locations.** It is possible to incorrectly accelerate the recognition of initial franchise fees when area franchise sales have been made, simply by underestimating the number of franchise locations to be situated within the area franchise. A periodic audit can investigate the number of actual and estimated franchise locations used in the revenue recognition calculation to determine if improperly low estimates have been used.
- **Review the timing of franchise revenue recognition.** The franchisor may recognize ongoing franchise fees automatically, without regard to whether related services have been provided at the same time. This is most likely to occur when certain activities, such as advertising campaigns, are only conducted at long intervals, and therefore do not coincide with the receipt of franchisee payments. As a result, revenue is incorrectly recognized prior to the completion of all related services by the franchisor. To detect this issue, a periodic audit should review the calculations used to recognize ongoing franchise revenue, and whether some revenue recognition is withheld pending the completion of such services.

FORMS AND REPORTS

Customer Credit Application

A key control point over the granting of customer credit is a formal credit application, which the treasury department's credit staff then evaluates to determine an appropriate credit level. An example of this form is shown in Exhibit 5-3. The form contains three blocks of information. The contact block requires the customer to list its address information, which allows the credit staff to run a credit report on the customer through a third-party credit analysis agency. The credit block reveals the customer's general financial status, while the references block contains information about the customer's trade references, who can be contacted for further information.

Acknowledgment of Bill and Hold Transaction

External auditors frown upon the use of bill and hold transactions, since there is a high probability of improper revenue recording associated with them. To anticipate their heightened level of investigation, it is best to have customers initial and sign the form in Exhibit 5-4, indicating customer acknowledgment of all aspects of each bill and hold transaction. Please note that the form is designed for individual purchase orders—it is not sufficient to have a customer sign a blanket acknowledgment covering all transactions over a long time period.

Sales Return Authorization Form

Requiring customers to fill out a sales return authorization form, or to at least obtain a sales return authorization number prior to returning goods, is an effective approach for reducing the number of returns. It also assists with the categorization of reasons why sales returns are being made. Otherwise, sales returns would appear at the company receiving dock with no explanation for the return, making it difficult to determine what problems are causing the returns. An example of a sales return authorization form is shown in Exhibit 5-5. The standard list of reasons for product returns listed on the sample form should be regularly reviewed and revised to reflect changes in product-related problems.

Exhibit 5-3: Customer Credit Application

Customer Credit Application

Contact

		For Company Use
Company Name:		
Address:		Customer No:
Address:		Credit Limit:
City:	State: ___ Zip: _____	Date Approved:
Date Started: _____ State of Incorporation: _____		Approved By:

Parent Company Name and Address:

Contact Name: _____ Phone: _____

Web Site: _____ Fax: _____

- -

Credit

Credit Requested: $ _____	Annual Sales: $ _____
Annual Profit: $ _____	Total Cash: $ _____
Total Debt: $ _____	Retained Earnings: $ _____

Bank Name: _____ Bank Contact: _____

Bank Address: _____

Checking Account Number: _____ Savings Account Number: _____

- -

References

Reference Name: _____ Phone: _____

Reference Address: _____

Reference Name: _____ Phone: _____

Reference Address: _____

Reference Name: _____ Phone: _____

Reference Address: _____

I hereby authorize the above-referenced bank and trading partners to release credit information to the Company for use in reviewing this credit application.

Officer Signature: _____

Print Officer Name: _____ Officer Title: _____

Return to The Company
Address
City State, Zip Code

Exhibit 5-4: Acknowledgment of Bill and Hold Transaction Form

Acknowledgment of
Bill and Hold Transaction

Customer Name: _____

This document indicates your acknowledgment that a bill and hold transaction exists in regard to purchase order number _____, which you ordered from [company name]. Please indicate your acknowledgment of this transaction by initialing next to each of the following statements and signing at the bottom of the page. If you disagree with any of the statements, please indicate your concerns at the bottom of the page. Thank you!

_____   I agree that I ordered the items noted in the purchase order.
(initial)

_____   I agree that [company name] is storing the items noted in the purchase order on my behalf.
(initial)

_____   I acknowledge that I have taken on all risks of ownership related to this purchase order.
(initial)

_____   I agree that I requested the bill and hold transaction, and my reason for doing so is as
(initial)   follows:

          _____

          _____

_____   I agree that all performance issues related to this purchase order were completed no
(initial)   later than _____.

_____   I agree that the held goods will be delivered to me no later than _____.
(initial)

I disagree with some or all of the statements on this page. My concerns are as follows:

_____

_____

_____

_____   _____
          Signature   Date

_____   _____
      Name (Please Print)   Title

Exhibit 5-5: Sales Return Authorization Form

```
                              Company Name
                       Sales Return Authorization Form

  Customer Name: _____        Date: _____

  Sales Return Authorization Number: _____ (Required)
_____

                        Product Being Returned                Reason for
    Number              Quantity        Description              Return

  _____       _____  _____      _____

  _____       _____  _____      _____

  _____       _____  _____      _____

  _____       _____  _____      _____

  Standard Reason Codes:
    1 = Product damaged in transit
    2 = Product quality below required level
    3 = Incorrect product shipped
    4 = Incorrect quantity shipped
    5 = Shipment made to wrong location
    6 = Other (describe below)
_____

  Other reasons for return: _____

  _____

  _____
```

Sales Return Credit Calculation Form

Companies rarely take back prior sales at full credit. Instead, they charge restocking fees, transaction processing charges, damage credits, or some combination in order to give customers an incentive to keep what they have bought. Since some of these calculations can be difficult to follow, it is best to neatly categorize the information in a credit calculation form. This is an invaluable document when discussing the proper amount of receivables still owed by a customer after a return has been made. The customer needs to see the calculation before paying whatever net amount is left on the related receivable. An example is shown in Exhibit 5-6.

Exhibit 5-6: Sales Return Credit Calculation Form

Company Name
Sales Return Credit Calculation Form

Customer Name: _____   Date: _____

Sales Return Authorization Number: _____

Product Number	Quantity	Description	Unit Price	Extended Price	Damage Credit
_____	_____	_____	_____	_____	_____
_____	_____	_____	_____	_____	_____
_____	_____	_____	_____	_____	_____
_____	_____	_____	_____	_____	_____
_____	_____	_____	_____	_____	_____

Totals _____   _____

Less: _____

20% Restocking Fee   _____

Total Damage Credit   _____

$25 Transaction Fee $ 25

Net Credit Granted _____

_____   _____
Clerk Signature   Clerk Name

FOOTNOTES

Disclosure of Revenue Recognition Policy

The general principles followed by company management in recognizing revenue should be stated in a footnote. This can include the amount of time over which revenue from maintenance agreements is followed, how the company handles different types of products and services bundled into the same pricing packages, and at what point revenues are recognized in the revenue generating process. Here are some sample footnotes.

1. The company sells maintenance agreements along with its home air conditioning units. Maintenance revenue is recognized ratably over the term specified within each agreement, which can range from twelve to sixty months. In cases where maintenance agreements are offered to customers at a discount, the company assumes that the discounts really apply to the complete package of air conditioning products and related maintenance agreements, and so recalculates the discount as a

percentage of the entire package. This results in approximately 65% of the discounts being assigned to product sales and the remaining 35% to maintenance sales. The adjusted maintenance revenues are then recognized ratably over the term specified within each agreement. As of the balance sheet date, $1,389,000 of maintenance revenues had not been recognized.

2. The company sells electrical appliance monitoring devices to large industrial manufacturers. It charges a nominal amount for each unit sold, and takes 5% of the electricity savings generated from the use of each unit for the first three years after each unit is installed, up to a maximum of $5,000 per quarter. Given the uncertainty of the savings to be generated from electricity cost savings, the company does not feel that it can reasonably recognize any revenue until after cost savings have been determined at the end of each quarter. Also, since cost savings tend to be disputed by recipients, making cash receipts problematic, management has elected to further delay revenue recognition until after cash has been received from each customer.

In the case of service-related revenues, disclosures should also include information about unearned revenues, such as the amount billed but not earned, and where it is placed on the balance sheet. Related expenses that have been deferred should also be described, including their amount and where they are itemized on the balance sheet. Two examples follow:

1. The company recognizes revenue under the proportional performance method, whereby revenue is recognized based on the hours charged to a project as a percentage of the total hours required to complete the job. Billings occur at quarterly intervals on most contracts, resulting in recognized but unbilled revenue. At the end of 2007, there was $1,895,000 of recognized but unbilled revenue, as compared to $2,905,000 in 2006. This asset is listed in the Unbilled Revenue current asset account.

2. The company recognizes revenue under the specific performance method, whereby revenue is recognized only after specific project milestones have been approved by customers. When costs are incurred prior to a revenue recognition event, they are stored in the Unrecognized Project Expense current asset account. At the end of 2007, there was $1,505,000 of unrecognized project expense, as compared to $1,759,000 in 2006.

Disclosure of Bill and Hold Transactions

Bill and hold transactions are generally frowned upon, given the risk of abuse by companies that can use this technique to inflate their revenues. Consequently, if any bill and hold transactions are used, it is best to reveal this information in a footnote, clearly stating that the company follows all GAAP requirements for such transactions, and also noting the dollar amount and percentage of revenues involved, and any change in the level of bill and hold revenue from the preceding year. An example is as follows:

During the past year, the company sold $172,000 of stoves to its restaurant customers under "bill and hold" transactions. Under these arrangements, restaurant owners asked the company to retain stoves in its warehouse facilities until new restaurants had been built to accommodate them. All these customers acknowledged in writing that they had ordered the inventory that the company was storing the stoves on their behalf, that they had taken on all risks of ownership, and that the stoves would be delivered in no more than three months. Total bill and hold transactions were $15,000 lower than the $187,000 in similar transactions that occurred in the preceding year. In both years, bill and hold transactions comprised 14% of total company revenues.

Disclosure of Contract Revenue Recognition

If a company recognizes revenue based on the percentage-of-completion method, it should state how it makes this calculation, how it is recorded on the balance sheet, when claims against customers are recognized, and how changes in estimates can impact reported profits or losses on contracts. If there is a change in the method of contract revenue recognition, the reason for doing so should be revealed, as well as the net effect of the change. Several examples follow:

1. The company recognizes all revenue in its construction division using the percentage-of-completion method, under which it ascertains the completion percentage by dividing costs incurred to date by total estimated project costs. It revises estimated project costs regularly, which can alter the reported level of project profitability. If project losses are calculated under this method, they are recognized in the current reporting period. Claims against customers are recorded in the period when payment is received. If billings exceed recognized revenue, the difference is recorded as a current liability, while any recognized revenues exceeding billings are recorded as a current asset.
2. The company recognizes claims against customers when cash receipt is probable, the claim is legally justified, and the amount of the claim can be proven. If any of these factors cannot be reasonably proven, then claims are only recognized upon the receipt of cash. Since claims involve the use of estimates, it is reasonable to record some changes to the initially reported revenue figure upon the eventual receipt of cash, or sooner if there is a firm basis for this information.
3. The company has switched to the percentage-of-completion method from the completed-contract method for recording the results of its construction projects. Management authorized the change due to the increasingly long-term nature of its contracts, which have increased from single-month to multimonth durations. The net impact of this change was an increase in profits of $218,000 in 2007. The change was carried back to 2006, resulting in a profit increase of $12,000 in that period.

Disclosure of Barter Revenue

Barter transactions should be recognized at the fair market value of the assets received in an exchange. The nature of any such transactions should be noted in a footnote, as well as the approximate value of the transactions, and how they are recorded in the financial statements. An example follows:

> The company provides aerial traffic reports to a number of radio stations, for which they give air time to the company. The company then obtains advertising to run on these free minutes, from which it collects the proceeds. The company recognizes revenue from these barter transactions only after advertisements have been obtained and have been run on the participating radio stations. No asset is recorded on the company balance sheet when air time is received from radio stations, since there is still significant uncertainty that the company will be able to convert the air time into paid advertisements. In 2007, the revenue recognized from these transactions was $1,745,000.

Disclosure of Consignment Revenue

Shipments made to a distributor on consignment are not truly sales until sold by the distributor. The exact method of revenue recognition should be clearly stated in a footnote, so readers can be sure that revenue is not recognized too soon in the sales process. Also, inventory may be shipped to a company by its customers on a consignment basis, to be included in custom products that are then sold back to the customers. Only the value added to these custom products should be recognized as revenue. The following footnotes show proper disclosure of these situations:

1. The company ships its eyewear products to a number of distributors, having no direct sales function of its own. All shipments to distributors continue to be recorded as inventory by the company until notification of shipment is received from distributors. In selected cases where there has been a problematic payment history by distributors, the company does not record revenue until cash has been received.
2. The company produces custom rockets for its payload launch customers. Several customers prefer to supply rocket engines to be incorporated into the company's rockets. Accordingly, these engines are recorded as consignment inventory when received and assigned a zero cost. When the completed rockets are shipped to customers, the price of the consigned engines are not included in the amount billed, thereby reducing the total revenue recognized by the company.

Disclosure of Gain or Loss on Asset Sale

When a company recognizes a material gain or loss on the sale of an asset or a group of assets, it should disclose in a footnote the general transaction, its date, the gross amount of the sale, the amount of the gain or loss, and its presentation in the financial statements. An example follows:

The company sold its printing press in August 2007 for $5.3 million as part of a plan to reduce the capacity of its printing facilities in the United States. Net of its original cost, less depreciation and tax effects, this resulted in a net gain of $420,000, which is itemized as a Gain on Sale of Assets in the financial statements.

Disclosure of Life Insurance Proceeds

If a company receives a payout from a life insurance policy, it should disclose in a footnote the amount of the payout, the event that caused the payout to be earned, and how the transaction was presented in the financial statements. An example follows:

The company received a payout of $20 million upon the death of a major shareholder in May 2007. The payout is recognized in the income statement under the Life Insurance Receipts line item. Under the terms of a stock buyback agreement with this shareholder, the company intends to use the proceeds to purchase all company shares held by the shareholder's estate.

Disclosure of Research and Development Revenue

Research and development contracts are typically accounted for in the same manner as any other construction project, though sometimes product profit-sharing terms will require a company to incur an up-front loss against the promise of future earnings. The primary disclosure is the method used to recognize revenue. A sample footnote follows:

> The company's research division enters into research and development contracts with a variety of organizations, typically on a fixed fee basis. The company recognizes revenue from these contracts on a percentage of completion basis. In some instances, customers offer profit-sharing agreements from future product proceeds, rather than up-front payments. In these cases, the company recognizes a loss when contracts begin, based on anticipated costs, and updates this loss information as projects progress. The company records revenue from these profit-sharing arrangements only when profit-sharing payments are received from customers.

Disclosure of Warranty Revenue Recognition

As is the case with any long-term service revenue contract, the period over which warranty revenues are calculated should be described, if this is a significant proportion of revenues. For many companies, this is a small revenue component not requiring separate disclosure. If it is disclosed, note the term over which warranty revenues are recognized and the amount of unrecognized warranty revenues. A sample footnote follows:

> The company sells a one-year warranty agreement with its kitchen appliances; warranty revenues comprise approximately 8% of total revenues. These revenues are recognized ratably over their service periods, with the unrecognized balance listed as a short-term liability in the Unrecognized Warranty Revenues account. The unrecognized balance of these sales was $850,000 as of the balance sheet date.

Disclosure of Membership Fee Recognition

A membership organization should describe the types of membership fees charged and the method used to recognize revenue. The footnote can also reveal the amount of unrecognized revenue currently listed as a liability. Two examples follow:

1. The club charges a onetime nonrefundable membership fee of $10,000, as well as monthly dues of $300. Since members have no right to the return of the initial fee, the club recognizes this amount in its entirety when paid. Monthly dues are recognized when billed. There is no liability associated with unrecognized revenue shown on the balance sheet.
2. The club charges a onetime membership fee of $10,000, which can be repaid to members if they choose to resign from the club, less a $500 termination fee. The club holds all membership fees in escrow and recognizes the termination fee only when members resign from the club. The total amount of membership fees currently held in escrow is $1,620,000, and is listed under the Membership Fees Held in Reserve liability account. The club also charges $300 monthly dues, which are recognized when billed.

Disclosure of Sales Return Allowance

There is no specific GAAP requirement that a company state its policy regarding the use of an allowance for sales returns. However, if a reserve has been created, then a footnote should detail how the amount of the reserve was derived. An example follows:

> The company recorded an allowance for sales returns of $148,000. This amount is based on a historical average rate of return of 12% of the company's subscription book sale business.

Disclosure of Warranty Expense Allowance

If there is a history or expectation of significant warranty expenses, one should accrue an appropriate amount when related revenues are recognized. The footnote should describe the basis for the warranty expense calculation, as well as the current amount of the reserve. An example follows:

> The company recognizes a warranty expense when it recognizes the sale of its amusement park bumper cars. This expense is based on the most recent one year of actual warranty claims, which is currently 1.9% of sales. The current warranty expense reserve, as listed in the Warranty Reserve liability account on the balance sheet, is $302,000.
>
> The company has just released a completely reengineered bumper car, containing 90% new parts. Given the large number of changes in this new product, there exists considerable uncertainty in regard to probable future warranty claims, which could be materially larger than the amount previously reserved, and which could have a material impact on the company's financial results in the near term.

Disclosure of Computer Software Sales

When a company sells computer software, it must split the sale into product and service components and recognize the service portion of the sale ratably over the maintenance period covered by the sales contract. This information should be included in a footnote. An example follows:

> Approximately 80% of the company's sales are from computer software and related maintenance agreements. The company splits these sales into their software and maintenance components and recognizes the software portion of the sales at once. The maintenance portion of the sales are initially recorded in an Unrecognized Maintenance Service Agreements liability account and recognized ratably over the term of the agreements, which are either three or twelve months. In cases where the software and maintenance components of a sale are not clearly differentiated in a sale contract, the company estimates the relative price of each component based on its separate retail price. As of the balance sheet date, there was approximately $725,000 of unrecognized maintenance sales in the Unrecognized Maintenance Service Agreements account.

Disclosure of Customers

If a company has revenues from individual customers that amount to at least 10% of total revenues, then it must report the amount of revenues from each of these customers, as well as the name of the business segment with which these customers are doing business. An example follows:

> The company does a significant amount of its total business with two customers. One customer, comprising 15% of total revenues for the entire company, also comprises 52% of the revenues of the Appliances segment. The second customer, comprising 28%

of total revenues for the entire company, also comprises 63% of the revenues of the Government segment.

Disclosure of Foreign Customers

If sales are concentrated in foreign locations where there are risks of sales re-ductions due to political issues, then the extent of these sales and the types of risks should be disclosed. An example follows:

> The company sells 55% of its customer relationship management software through a distributor in Iran. Given the large proportion of company sales attributable to this supplier, any unrest in the region, such as wars, terrorist activity, or an enforced shut-down in business activities by the Iranian government would have a material impact on the company's financial results.

Disclosure of Installment Sales

If installment sales comprise a significant proportion of corporate sales, a foot-note should disclose the revenue recognition policy used, as well as the amounts of gross profit recognized from the current and prior years, the total amount of deferred gross profit, and its placement on the balance sheet. An example follows:

> The company sells kitchen appliances on various installment payment plans. Given the extreme uncertainty associated with the collection of receivables under this plan, the company uses the cost recovery method to recognize profits, under which it recognizes no gross profit until all costs of goods sold have been paid back through cash receipts. In 2007, the company recognized $397,000 of gross profit earned in the current year, as well as $791,000 deferred from prior years. An additional $2,907,000 of deferred gross profits is classified as a current liability in the Unrecognized Gross Profit on Installment Sales account.

Disclosure of Sales with Significant Rights of Return

If there is considerable uncertainty regarding the amount of potential sales re-turns, such as may be caused by a new product, potential product obsolescence, or heightened competition, then a company may be forced to not recognize any revenue at all until the right of product return has passed. Since this can cause a substantial reduction in recognized revenue, a footnote describing the reason for the recognition delay would be in order. The information in the following footnotes illustrates a sufficient level of disclosure:

1. The company is in the beta testing phase of its new crop planting system, and so has granted an unconditional right of return to the first ten customers who have agreed to purchase the product. The right of return privilege extends for six months from the shipment date. Since there is no return history for this new product, the com-pany has recorded the total amount of all ten sales in an Unearned Sales liability ac-count, and will not recognize the revenue until the right of return period has expired. The total amount in this account is $328,000. Of this amount, $275,000 will be rec-ognizable in March 2007, and the remaining $53,000 in May 2007, assuming that no products are returned in the interim.
2. The company's light saber product is entirely new and is being introduced into a new market, so management feels that it cannot estimate potential levels of product

returns. Consequently, the company has not recognized any revenues related to recent shipments of the product until the three-month right of return period has passed. The company plans to reevaluate this policy after a sufficient amount of time has passed for it to make a better estimate of potential sales returns. The initial amount of light saber revenues that would otherwise have been recognized in the first month of shipments was $1,750,000.

Disclosure of Multiple Deliverables

The financial statements of a vendor are to include the following disclosures, when applicable:

1. The nature of the vendor's MDAs including provisions relative to performance, cancellation, termination, or refund.
2. The vendor's accounting policy with respect to the recognition of revenue from MDAs (e.g., whether deliverables are separable into units of accounting.)

An example of this disclosure requirement follows:

The company enters into multiple-element revenue arrangements, which may include any combination of services, software, hardware, and/or financing. A multiple-element arrangement is separated into more than one unit of accounting if all of the following criteria are met: (1) the delivered item has value to the client on a stand-alone basis; (2) there is no objective and reliable evidence of the fair value of the undelivered item; (3) if the arrangement includes a right of return relative to the delivered item, delivery is considered probable and is under the company's control. If these criteria are met for each element and there is objective and reliable evidence of fair value for all units of accounting in an arrangement, the arrangement consideration is allocated to the separate units of accounting based on each unit's relative fair value. There may be cases, however, in which there is objective and reliable evidence of fair value of the undelivered item but no such evidence for the delivered item. In those cases, the residual method is used to allocate the arrangement consideration. Under the residual method, the amount of consideration allocated to the delivered item equals the total arrangement consideration less the aggregate fair value of the undelivered item. The revenue policies described below are then applied to each unit of accounting, as applicable. If the allocation of consideration in a profitable arrangement results in a loss on an element, that loss is recognized at the earlier of (1) delivery of that element, (2) when the first dollar of revenue is recognized on that element, or (3) when there are no remaining profitable elements in the arrangement to be delivered.

Disclosure of Franchise Revenues

There are several disclosures required for franchise fee transactions. They include:

- The types of significant commitments resulting from franchising arrangements, as well as franchisor services not yet performed
- The franchise sale price
- The amount of deferred revenue and costs
- The periods when fees become payable by the franchisee

- The amounts of revenue initially deferred due to collectibility uncertainties, but then recognized due to resolution of the uncertainties
- The number of franchises sold, purchased, and in operation during the period (which shall segregate the number of franchisor-owned outlets in operation from the number of franchisee-owned operations)
- Segregating the reporting of initial franchise fees from other franchise fee revenue, if they are significant
- Segregating the revenues and costs of franchisor-owned outlets from those of franchisees, when practicable
- If there is no reasonable basis for estimating the ability of the franchisor to collect franchise fees, the type of accounting method used to recognize franchise fee revenue (either the installment or cost recovery method) must be disclosed.
- If initial franchise fee revenue is likely to decline because of market saturation, this issue should be disclosed.

Here are several examples of company disclosures that follow some of the preceding reporting requirements:

1. The Company's revenues consist of sales by Company-operated restaurants and fees from restaurants operated by franchisees and affiliates. Sales by Company-operated restaurants are recognized on a cash basis. Fees from franchised and affiliated restaurants include continuing rent and service fees, initial fees, and royalties received from foreign affiliates and developmental licensees. Continuing fees and royalties are recognized in the period earned. Initial fees are recognized upon opening of a restaurant, which is when the Company has performed substantially all initial services required by the franchise arrangement.

2. The Company enters into franchise agreements committing to provide franchisees with various marketing services and limited rights to utilize the Company's registered trademarks. These agreements typically have an initial term of ten years with provisions permitting franchisees to terminate after five years under certain circumstances. In most instances, initial franchise fees are recognized upon execution of the franchise agreement because the initial franchise fee is nonrefundable and the Company has no continuing obligations related to the franchisee. The initial franchise fee related to executed franchise agreements, which include incentives such as future potential rebates, are deferred and recognized when the incentive criteria are met or the agreement is terminated, whichever occurs first.

3. The following are changes in the Company's franchised locations for each of the fiscal years 2005 through 2007:

	2007	2006	2005
Franchises in operation—beginning of year	7,958	7,637	7,322
Franchises opened	355	425	470
Franchises closed	(121)	(122)	(104)
Net transfers within the system	(1)	18	(51)
Franchises in operation—end of year	8,191	7,958	7,637
Company-owned stores	1,758	1,748	1,672
Total system-wide stores	9,949	9,706	9,309

Disclosure of Motion Picture Revenues

A company should disclose its methods of accounting for revenue. Sample disclosures are as follows:

1. Revenue from the sales of home video units is recognized at the later of when product is made available for retail sale or when video sales to customers are reported by third parties, such as fulfillment service providers or distributors. Management calculates an estimate of future returns of product by analyzing a combination of historical returns, current economic trends, projections of consumer demand for the Company's product, and point-of-sale data available from certain retailers. Based on this information, a percentage of each sale is reserved, provided that the customer has the right of return. Actual returns are charged against the reserve.
2. Long-term noninterest-bearing receivables arising from television licensing agreements are discounted to present value, net of an allowance for doubtful accounts.
3. The Company recognizes revenues from its films net of reserves for returns, rebates, and other incentives after it has retained a distribution fee of ___% and recovered all of its distribution and marketing costs on a title-by-title basis.

JOURNAL ENTRIES

Revenue—General

Record sales return allowance. To create a reserve for expected sales returns. This entry is not normally made unless there is an expectation of an appreciable amount of returns. The second entry records the actual return of products by eliminating the related account receivable and charging this amount to the allowance for sales returns.

Sales returns expense	xxx	
Allowance for sales returns		xxx
Allowance for sales returns	xxx	
Accounts receivable		xxx

Bill and Hold Transactions

A common problem with bill and hold transactions is that the sale is recorded, but the subtraction from inventory of the items sold is not, resulting in a sale with a 100% gross margin. To avoid this, use the second part of the following journal entry to shift the sold inventory items into a special cost of goods sold account that clearly identifies the items sold. When the items are eventually shipped to the customer, the third journal entry is used to shift the expense into the regular cost of goods sold account. By using this approach, one can monitor the "Cost of Goods Sold—Bill and Hold" account to determine which billed inventory items have not yet been shipped.

Accounts receivable	xxx	
Sales		xxx
Cost of goods sold—bill and hold	xxx	
Inventory		xxx
Cost of goods sold	xxx	
Cost of goods sold—bill and hold		xxx

Cash Payments to Customers

When cash-back payments are made to customers, the offset to the cash reduction should be a corresponding reduction in the revenue earned from that customer, as is recorded in the first of the following two entries. If the company receives some benefit back from the customer, then only the difference between the fair value of the benefit and the cash payment shall be charged against the revenue account. This later scenario is covered in the second journal entry.

Revenue	xxx	
Cash		xxx
Revenue	xxx	
Expense account (various)	xxx	
Cash		xxx

Long-Term Construction Contracts

Record additional revenues under percentage-of-completion method. To record the amount of extra revenues thus far not recognized, comprising the difference between project expenses and the estimated gross profit margin, less prior billings. The second entry is the recording of a proportional amount of offsetting cost of goods sold, so that the principle of matching revenues to expenses is observed.

Unbilled contract receivables	xxx	
Contract revenues earned		xxx
Cost of recognized revenues	xxx	
Construction-in-progress		xxx

Record excessive billings under percentage-of-completion method in a liability account. To record the amount of excess billings over the amount of project expenses and the estimated gross profit margin in a liability account.

Contract revenues earned	xxx	
Billings exceeding project costs and margin		xxx

Record amount of costs exceeding the total project billing. To record the estimated amount of expenses incurred on a project that will exceed the total billable amount of the contract. This is a loss recognizable in the current period.

Loss on uncompleted project	xxx	
Estimated loss on uncompleted contract		xxx

Service Revenues

Record unearned service revenue. To record a liability when a sales transaction for unearned services work is recorded. The first entry records the offset to an account receivable in a liability account, while the second entry records incremental revenue recognition from the liability account as services are completed.

Accounts receivable	xxx	
Unearned service contracts		xxx
Unearned service contracts	xxx	
Service revenue		xxx

Record earned revenue under the proportional performance method. Under the proportional performance method, one can recognize revenue in proportion to the amount of direct cost incurred on a service job. The first entry is the simplest, showing a basic sale transaction under which the customer is billed for the same amount of proportional revenue recognized by the company. The second entry assumes there is no customer billing yet to match the revenue recognized, so the sales offset is stored in an asset account. The third entry shows the reduction of the asset account when a customer billing eventually occurs.

Accounts receivable	xxx	
Sales		xxx
Earned revenue asset account	xxx	
Sales		xxx
Accounts receivable	xxx	
Earned revenue asset account		xxx

Recognize a loss on a service contract. This entry is used when it becomes apparent that actual and estimated expenses on a service contract will exceed related revenue. An estimated loss is recognized, while the offsetting credit is first used to eliminate any unrecognized contract costs, with the remainder being credited to an estimated loss account that is later drawn down as actual losses are incurred.

Loss on service contract	xxx	
Unrecognized contract costs		xxx
Estimated loss on service contracts		xxx

Installment Revenues

Revenue (installment basis). To record the initial installment sale, as noted in the **first entry.** As cash is received over time in payment of installment accounts receivable, the **second entry** is used to recognize portions of the gross profit and interest income from the installment sale.

Installment receivables collectible in (year)	xxx	
Inventory		xxx
Deferred gross profit		xxx
Cash	xxx	
Deferred gross profit	xxx	
Installment receivables collectible in (year)		xxx
Interest income		xxx
Recognized gross profit		xxx

Repossession of goods sold under installment plans. When goods are repossessed due to lack of payment under an installment sales plan, the deferred gross profit associated with the initial sale must be reversed, while the repossessed goods should be transferred back into inventory at their fair market value. If there is a difference between the book value and fair value of the goods, then a gain or loss should be recognized on the difference. The following entry illustrates the transaction:

Finished goods inventory	xxx	
Loss on repossessed inventory	xxx	
Deferred gross profit	xxx	
Accounts receivable		xxx

Revenue Recognition When Right of Return Exists

To record predictable amounts of sales returns. When the amount of sales returns can be reasonably estimated, one should record an estimate of returns, which is noted in the first journal entry. The second entry notes the offsetting of an actual return against the sales return reserve, while the third entry notes the elimination of any remaining amount left in the reserve after the right of return has expired.

NOTE: In the case of sales where the amount of sales returns is not predictable, the same entries are used, but they will apply to the entire amount of sales made, rather than just an estimated amount of returns.

Revenue	xxx	
Cost of goods sold		xxx
Deferred gross profit		xxx
Finished goods inventory	xxx	
Deferred gross profit	xxx	
Loss on returned inventory	xxx	
Accounts receivable		xxx
Cost of goods sold	xxx	
Deferred gross profit	xxx	
Revenue		xxx

RECORDKEEPING

When a company engages in barter swap transactions, there is a strong likelihood that auditors will want to review the transactions to see if any related revenue recognition is reasonable. Accordingly, business cases should be written for each such transaction, and then filed for later review. A copy of the business case should be attached to the journal entry used to record each of these transactions. It may also be useful to store a second copy of each business case in the legal department, since the legal staff may need to monitor the progress of each such transaction to ensure that it is properly completed.

If credits are manually calculated for sales returns from customers, this information should be retained in the customer file, since it may be subject to dispute by the customer. The documentation should include the amounts of any return-related charges, such as restocking fees. It is best to use a formal credit calculation worksheet, such as the one shown in the Forms and Reports section, since this results in a more organized calculation that can be more easily understood by customers.

Any journal entries increasing the reported level of sales should be stored in the journal entries binder, with documentation of the reasons why specific entries were made. These are very likely to be examined by auditors when they review the appropriateness of any journal entries that increase sales. This is especially common for service revenues recognized under the proportional performance method, since the amount of revenue recognized may be higher than the amount billed to the customer. In this case, the specific proportional performance calculation should be retained for each service contract on which revenue is recognized.

If a company engages in bill and hold transactions, then it should have its customers sign the Acknowledgment of Bill and Hold Transaction form shown earlier in the Forms and Reports section. These completed forms will be reviewed by the external auditors as part of their auditing of the revenue portion of the income statement, so they should be sorted by date and stored in a binder in the accounting archives.

When long-term installment sales covering multiple years are made, all information regarding the annual calculation of the gross margin percentage associated with each year of installment sales should be retained until all collections related to that year have been made. Similarly, records for cash receipts, repossessions, and the recognition of bad debts should be retained for the duration of all installment sales.

If repossessed goods from installment sales are considered to be not worth reconditioning for resale, they may possibly be donated. If so, all asset donation forms should be given to the taxation department for consideration in the creation of the annual corporate income tax return. If so used, the forms should be archived with all other source documents used to create the tax returns.

6 LONG-LIVED ASSETS

DEFINITIONS OF TERMS

Amortization. The write-off of an asset over the period when the asset is used. This term is most commonly applied to the gradual write-down of intangible items, such as goodwill or organizational costs.

Asset retirement obligation. A legal requirement to retire assets at a certain date, such as leasehold improvements as of the termination date of the lease.

Book value. An asset's original cost, less any depreciation that has been subsequently incurred.

Boot. The monetary portion of an exchange involving similar assets.

Capitalization limit. The minimum threshold of expenditure beyond which a purchased asset will be recorded as a fixed asset. Below this limit, the expenditure will be recorded as an expense.

Depreciation. Both the decline in value of an asset over time, as well as the gradual expensing of an asset over time, roughly in accordance with its level of usage or decline in value through that period.

Development. The enhancement of existing products or processes, or the creation of entirely new ones.

Fixed assets. An item with a longevity greater than one year, and which exceeds a company's minimum capitalization limit. It is not purchased with the intent of immediate resale, but rather for productive use within a company.

Impairment. When the carrying amount of a fixed asset exceeds its net present value. This condition usually requires a write-down in the recorded value of the asset.

Intangible assets. A nonphysical asset with a life greater than one year. Examples are goodwill, patents, trademarks, and copyrights.

Leasehold improvements. Improvements made by a company to its leased properties, exceeding the corporate capitalization limit, that have an expected life of greater than one year.

Research. The planned search for the discovery of new knowledge.

Retirement. The stoppage of regular use of a fixed asset. This event is typically followed by the idling, disposal, or sale of the asset.

CONCEPTS AND EXAMPLES[1]

Fixed Assets—Purchases

When a company purchases a fixed asset, there are a number of expenditures it is allowed to include in the capitalized cost of the asset. These costs include the sales tax and ownership registration fees (if any). Also, the cost of all freight, insurance, and duties required to bring the asset to the company can be included in the capitalized cost. Further, the cost required to install the asset can be included. Installation costs include the cost to test and break in the asset, which can include the cost of test materials.

If a **fixed asset is acquired for nothing but cash,** then its recorded cost is the amount of cash paid. However, if the asset is acquired by taking on a payable, such as a stream of debt payments (or taking over the payments that were initially to be made by the seller of the asset), then the present value of all future payments yet to be made must also be rolled into the recorded asset cost. If the stream of future payments contains no stated interest rate, then one must be imputed based on market

---

[1] *Much of the information in this section is adapted with permission from Chapter 17 of Bragg,* **Ultimate Accountant's Reference** *(John Wiley & Sons, Inc., Hoboken, NJ, 2006).*

rates when making the present value calculation. If the amount of the payable is not clearly evident at the time of purchase, then it is also admissible to record the asset at its fair market value.

If an **asset is purchased with company stock,** one may assign a value to the asset acquired based on either the fair market value of the stock or the asset, whichever is more easily determinable.

Example of an asset acquired with stock

The St. Louis Motor Car Company issues 500 shares of its stock to acquire a sheet metal bender. This is a publicly held company, and on the day of the acquisition its shares were trading for $13.25 each. Since this is an easily determinable value, the cost assigned to the equipment is $6,625 (500 shares times $13.25/share). A year later, the company has taken itself private, and chooses to issue another 750 shares of its stock to acquire a router. In this case, the value of the shares is no longer so easily determined, so the company asks an appraiser to determine the router's fair value, which she sets at $12,000. In the first transaction, the journal entry was a debit of $6,625 to the fixed asset equipment account and a credit of $6,625 to the common stock account, while the second transaction was to the same accounts, but for $12,000 instead.

If a company **obtains an asset through an exchange involving a dissimilar asset,** it should record the incoming asset at the fair market value of the asset for which it was exchanged. However, if this fair value is not readily apparent, the fair value of the incoming asset can be used instead. If no fair market value is readily obtainable for either asset, then the net book value of the relinquished asset can be used.

Example of an exchange for a dissimilar asset

The Dakota Motor Company swaps a file server for an overhead crane. Its file server has a book value of $12,000 (net of accumulated depreciation of $4,000), while the overhead crane has a fair value of $9,500. The company has no information about the fair value of its file server, so Dakota uses its net book value instead to establish a value for the swap. Dakota recognizes a loss of $2,500 on the transaction, as noted in the following entry:

Factory equipment	9,500	
Accumulated depreciation	4,000	
Loss on asset exchange	2,000	
Factory equipment		16,000

A common transaction is for a company to **trade in an existing asset for a new one, along with an additional payment** that covers the incremental additional cost of the new asset over that of the old one being traded away. The additional payment portion of this transaction is called the "boot." When the boot comprises at least 25% of the exchange's fair value, both entities must record the transaction at the fair value of the assets involved. If the amount of boot is less than 25% of the transaction, the party receiving the boot can recognize a gain in proportion to the amount of boot received.

Example of an asset exchange with at least 25% boot

The Dakota Motor Company trades in a copier for a new one from the Fair Copy Company, paying an additional $9,000 as part of the deal. The fair value of the copier traded away is $2,000, while the fair value of the new copier being acquired is $11,000 (with a book value of $12,000, net of $3,500 in accumulated depreciation). The book value of the copier being traded away is $2,500, net of $5,000 in accumulated depreciation. Because Dakota has paid a combination of $9,000 in cash and $2,500 in the net book value of its existing copier ($11,500 in total) to acquire a new copier with a fair value of $11,000, it must recognize a loss of $500 on the transaction, as noted in the following entry:

Office equipment (new asset)	11,000	
Accumulated depreciation	5,000	
Loss on asset exchange	500	
Office equipment (asset traded away)		7,500
Cash		9,000

On the other side of the transaction, Fair Copy is accepting a copier with a fair value of $2,000 and $9,000 in cash for a replacement copier with a fair value of $11,000, so its journal entry is as follows:

Cash	9,000	
Office equipment (asset acquired)	3,500	
Loss on sale of asset	1,000	
Office equipment (asset traded away)		15,500

Example of an asset exchange with less than 25% boot

As was the case in the last example, the Dakota Motor Company trades in a copier for a new one, but now it pays $2,000 cash and trades in its old copier, with a fair value of $9,000 and a net book value of $9,500 after $5,000 of accumulated depreciation. Also, the fair value of the copier being traded away by Fair Copy remains at $11,000, but its net book value drops to $10,000 (still net of accumulated depreciation of $3,500). All other information remains the same. In this case, the proportion of boot paid is 18% ($2,000 cash, divided by total consideration paid of $2,000 cash plus the copier fair value of $9,000). As was the case before, Dakota has paid a total of $11,500 (from a different combination of $9,000 in cash and $2,500 in the net book value of its existing copier) to acquire a new copier with a fair value of $11,000, so it must recognize a loss of $500 on the transaction, as noted in the following entry:

Office equipment (new asset)	11,000	
Accumulated depreciation	5,000	
Loss on asset exchange	500	
Office equipment (asset traded away)		14,500
Cash		2,000

The main difference is on the other side of the transaction, where Fair Copy is now accepting a copier with a fair value of $9,000 and $2,000 in cash in exchange for a copier with a book value of $10,000, so there is a potential gain of $1,000 on the deal. However, because it receives boot that is less than 25% of the transaction fair value, it recognizes a pro rata gain of $180, which is calculated as the 18% of the deal attributable to the cash payment, multiplied by the $1,000 gain. Fair Copy's journal entry to record the transaction is as follows:

Cash	2,000	
Office equipment (asset acquired)	8,180	
Accumulated depreciation	3,500	
Office equipment (asset traded away)		13,500
Gain on asset transfer		180

In this entry, Fair Copy can recognize only a small portion of the gain on the asset transfer, with the remaining portion of the gain being netted against the recorded cost of the acquired asset.

If **a group of assets are acquired** through a single purchase transaction, the cost should be allocated among the assets in the group based on their proportional share of their total fair market values. The fair market value may be difficult to ascertain in many instances, in which case an appraisal value or tax assessment value can be used. It may also be possible to use the present value of estimated cash flows for each asset as the basis for the allocation, though this measure can be subject to considerable variability in the foundation data, and also requires a great deal of analysis to obtain.

Example of a group asset acquisition

The Dakota Motor Company acquires three machines for $80,000 as part of the Chapter 7 liquidation auction of a competitor. There is no ready market for the machines. Dakota hires an appraiser to determine their value. She judges machines A and B to be worth $42,000 and $18,000, respectively, but can find no basis of comparison for machine C, and passes on an appraisal for that item. Dakota's production manager thinks the net present value of cash flows arising from the use of machine C will be about $35,000. Based on this information, the following costs are allocated to the machines:

Machine Description	*Value*	*Proportions*	*Allocated Costs*
Machine A	$42,000	44%	$35,200
Machine B	18,000	23%	18,400
Machine C	35,000	33%	26,400
Totals	$95,000	100%	$80,000

Fixed Assets—Improvements

Once an asset is put into use, the majority of expenditures related to it must be charged to expense. If expenditures are for basic maintenance, not contributing to an asset's value or extending its usable life, then they must be charged to expense. If expenditures are considerable in amount and increase the asset's value, then they are charged to the asset capital account, though they will be depreciated only over the predetermined depreciation period. If expenditures are considerable in amount and increase the asset's usable life, then they are charged directly to the accumulated depreciation account, effectively reducing the amount of depreciation expense incurred.

If an existing equipment installation is moved or rearranged, the cost of doing so is charged to expense if there is no measurable benefit in future periods. If there is a measurable benefit, then the expenditure is capitalized and depreciated over the periods when the increased benefit is expected to occur.

If an asset must be replaced that is part of a larger piece of equipment, one should remove the cost and associated accumulated depreciation for the asset to be replaced from the accounting records and recognize any gain or loss on its disposal. If there is no record of the subsidiary asset's cost, then ignore this step. In addition, the cost of the replacement asset should be capitalized and depreciated over the remaining term of the larger piece of equipment.

An example of current period expenditures is routine machine maintenance, such as the replacement of worn-out parts. This expenditure will not change the ability of an asset to perform in a future period, and so should be charged to expense within the current period. If repairs are effected in order to repair damage to an asset, this is also a current period expense. Also, even if an expenditure can be proven to impact future periods, it may still be charged to expense if it is too small to meet the corporate capitalization limit. If a repair cost can be proven to have an impact covering more than one accounting period, but not many additional periods into the future, a company can spread the cost over a few months or all months of a single year by recording the expense in an allowance account that is gradually charged off over the course of the year. In this last case, there may be an ongoing expense accrual throughout the year that will be charged off, even in the absence of any major expenses in the early part of the year—the intention being that the company knows that expenses will be incurred later in the year and chooses to smooth out its expense recognition by recognizing some of the expense prior to its actually being incurred.

If a company incurs costs to avoid or mitigate environmental contamination (usually in response to government regulations), these costs generally must be charged to expense in the current period. The only case in which capitalization is an alternative is when the costs incurred can be demonstrated to reduce or prevent future environmental contamination, as well as improve the underlying asset. If so, the asset life associated with these costs should be the period over which environmental contamination is expected to be reduced.

Fixed Assets—Capitalization of Interest

When a company is constructing assets for its own use or as separately identifiable projects intended for sale, it should capitalize as part of the project cost all associated interest expenses. Capitalized interest expenses are calculated based on the interest rate of the debt used to construct the asset or (if there was no new debt) at the weighted-average interest rate the company pays on its other debt. Interest is not capitalized when its addition would result in no material change in the cost of the resulting asset, or when the construction period is quite short (since there is little time over which to accrue interest), or when there is no prospect of completing a project.

The interest rate is multiplied by the average capital expenditures incurred to construct the targeted asset. The amount of interest expense capitalized is limited to an amount less than or equal to the total amount of interest expense actually incurred by the company during the period of asset construction.

Example of an interest capitalization transaction

The Carolina Astronautics Corporation (CAC) is constructing a new launch pad for its suborbital rocket launching business. It pays a contractor $5,000,000 up front and $2,500,000 after the project completion six months later. At the beginning of the project, it issued $15,000,000 in bonds at 9% interest to finance the project, as well as other capital needs. The calculation of interest expense to be capitalized is as follows:

Investment amount	Months to be capitalized	Interest rate	Interest to be capitalized
$5,000,000	6	9%/12	$225,000
2,500,000	0	---	0
		Total	$225,000

There is no interest expense to be capitalized on the final payment of $2,500,000, since it was incurred at the very end of the construction period. CAC accrued $675,000 in total interest expenses during the period when the launch pad was built ($15,000,000 × 9%/12 × 6 months). Since the total expense incurred by the company greatly exceeds the amount of interest to be capitalized for the launch pad, there is no need to reduce the amount of capitalized interest to the level of actual interest expense incurred. Accordingly, CAC's controller makes the following journal entry to record the capitalization of interest:

Assets (launch pad)	225,000	
Interest expense		225,000

Fixed Assets—Dispositions

When a company disposes of a fixed asset, it should completely eliminate all record of it from the fixed asset and related accumulated depreciation accounts. In addition, it should recognize a gain or loss on the difference between the net book value of the asset and the price at which it was sold. For example, Company ABC is selling a machine, which was originally purchased for $10,000, and against which $9,000 of depreciation has been recorded. The sale price of the used machine is $1,500. The proper journal entry is to credit the Fixed Asset account for $10,000 (thereby removing the machine from the fixed asset journal), debit the Accumulated Depreciation account for $9,000 (thereby removing all related depreciation from the accumulated depreciation account), debit the Cash account for $1,500 (to reflect the receipt of cash from the asset sale) and credit the Gain on Sale of Assets account for $500.

There may be identifiable costs associated with an asset disposition that are required by a legal agreement, known as an **asset retirement obligation** (ARO). For example, a building lease may require the lessee to remove all equipment by the termination date of the lease; the cost of this obligation should be recognized at the time the lease is signed. As another example, the passage of legislation requiring the cleanup of hazardous waste sites would require the recognition of these costs as soon as the legislation is passed.

The amount of ARO recorded is the range of cash flows associated with asset disposition that would be charged by a third party, summarized by their probability weightings. This amount is then discounted at the company's credit-adjusted risk-free interest rate. The risk-free interest rate can be obtained from the rates at which zero-coupon US Treasury instruments are selling.

If there are upward adjustments to the amount of the ARO in subsequent periods, these adjustments are accounted for in the same manner, with the present value for each one being derived from the credit-adjusted risk-free rate at the time of the transaction. These incremental transactions are then recorded separately in the fixed asset register, though their depreciation periods and methods will all match that of the underlying asset. If a reduction in the ARO occurs in any period, this amount should be recognized as a gain in the current period, with the amount being offset pro rata against all layers of ARO recorded in the fixed asset register.

When an ARO situation arises, the amount of the ARO is added to the fixed asset register for the related asset, with the offset to a liability account that will eventually be depleted when the costs associated with the retirement obligation are actually incurred. The amount of the ARO added to the fixed asset is then depreciated under the same method used for the related asset. In subsequent periods, one must also make an entry to accretion expense to reflect ongoing increases in the present value of the ARO, which naturally occurs as the date of the ARO event comes closer to the present date. These transactions are shown in more detail in the Journal Entries section.

Example of an ARO transaction

The Ever-Firm Tire Company installs a tire molding machine in a leased facility. The lease expires in three years, and the company has a legal obligation to remove the machine at that time. The controller polls local equipment removal companies and obtains estimates of $40,000 and $60,000 of what it would cost to remove the machine. She suspects the lower estimate to be inaccurate, and so assigns probabilities of 25% and 75% to the two transactions, resulting in the following probability-adjusted estimate:

Cash flow estimate	Assigned probability	Probability-adjusted cash flow
$40,000	25%	$10,000
60,000	75%	45,000
	100%	$55,000

She assumes that inflation will average 4% in each of the next three years, and so adjusts the $55,000 amount upward by $6,868 to $61,868 to reflect this estimate. Finally, she estimates the company's credit-adjusted risk-free rate to be 8%, based on the implicit interest rate in its last lease, and uses the 8% figure to arrive at a discount rate of 0.7938. After multiplying this discount rate by the inflation- and probability-adjusted ARO cost of $61,868, she arrives at $49,111 as the figure to add to the machinery asset account as a debit and the asset retirement obligation account as a credit.

In the three following years, she must also make entries to increase the asset retirement obligation account by the amount of increase in the present value of the ARO, which is calculated as follows:

Year	Beginning ARO	Inflation multiplier	Annual accretion	Ending ARO
1	$49,111	8%	$3,929	$53,041
2	53,041	8%	4,243	57,285
3	57,285	8%	4,583	61,868

After three years of accretion entries, the balance in the ARO liability account matches the original inflation- and probability-adjusted estimate of the amount of cash flows required to settle the ARO obligation.

Fixed Assets—Inbound Donations

If an asset is donated to a company (common only in the case of a not-for-profit corporation), the receiving company can record the asset at its fair market value, which can be derived from market rates on similar assets, an appraisal, or the net present value of its estimated cash flows.

Fixed Assets—Outbound Donations

When a company donates an asset to another company, it must recognize the fair value of the asset donated, which is netted against its net book value. The difference between the asset's fair value and its net book value is recognized as either a gain or loss.

Example of an outbound donation

The Nero Fiddle Company has donated to the local orchestra a portable violin repair workbench from its manufacturing department. The workbench was originally purchased for $15,000, and $6,000 of depreciation has since been charged against it. The workbench can be purchased on the eBay auction site for $8,500, which establishes its fair market value. The company uses the following journal entry to record the transaction:

Charitable donations	8,500	
Accumulated depreciation	6,000	
Loss on property donation	1,000	
Machinery asset account		15,000

Fixed Assets—Construction in Progress

If a company constructs its own fixed assets, it should capitalize all direct labor, materials, and overhead costs that are clearly associated with the construction project. In addition, one should charge to the capital account those fixed overhead costs considered to have "discernible future benefits" related to the project. From a practical perspective, this makes it unlikely that a significant amount of fixed overhead costs should be charged to a capital project.

If a company constructs its own assets, it should compile all costs associated with it into an account or journal, commonly known as the construction-in-progress (CIP) account. There should be a separate account or journal for each project that is currently under way, so there is no risk of commingling expenses among multiple projects. The costs that can be included in the CIP account include all costs normally associated with the purchase of a fixed asset, as well as the direct materials and direct labor used to construct the asset. In addition, all overhead costs that are reasonably apportioned to the project may be charged to it, as well as the depreciation expense associated with any other assets that are used during the construction process.

One may also charge to the CIP account the interest cost of any funds that have been loaned to the company for the express purpose of completing the project. If this approach is used, one can use either the interest rate associated with a specific loan that was procured to fund the project, or the weighted-average rate for a number of company loans, all of which are being used for this purpose. The amount of interest charged in any period should be based on the cumulative amount of expenditures thus far incurred for the project. The amount of interest charged to the project should not exceed the amount of interest actually incurred for all associated loans through the same time period.

Once the project has been completed, all costs should be carried over from the CIP account into one of the established fixed asset accounts, where the new asset is recorded on a summary basis. All of the detail-level costs should be stored for future review. The asset should be depreciated beginning on the day when it is officially completed. Under no circumstances should depreciation begin prior to this point.

Fixed Assets—Land

Land cannot be depreciated, and so companies tend to avoid charging expenses to this account on the grounds that they cannot recognize taxable depreciation expenses. Nonetheless, those costs reasonably associated with the procurement of land, such as real estate commissions, title examination fees, escrow fees, and accrued property taxes paid by the purchaser should all be charged to the fixed asset account for land. This should also include the cost of an option to purchase land. In addition, all subsequent costs associated with the improvement of the land, such as draining, clearing, and grading, should be added to the land account. The cost of interest that is associated with the development of land should also be capitalized. Property taxes incurred during the land development process also should be charged to the asset account, but should be charged to current expenses once the development process has been completed.

Fixed Assets—Leasehold Improvements

When a lessee makes improvements to a property that is being leased from another entity, it can still capitalize the cost of the improvements (subject to the amount of the capitalization limit), but the time period over which these costs can be amortized must be limited to the lesser of the useful life of the improvements or the length of the lease.

If the lease has an extension option that would allow the lessee to increase the time period over which it can potentially lease the property, the total period over which the leasehold improvements can be depreciated must still be limited to the initial lease term, on the grounds that there is no certainty that the lessee will accept the lease extension option. This limitation is waived for depreciation purposes only if there is either a bargain renewal option or extensive penalties in the lease contract that would make it highly likely that the lessee would renew the lease.

Fixed Assets—Depreciation Base

The basis used for an asset when conducting a depreciation calculation should be its capitalized cost less any salvage value that the company expects to receive at the time when the asset is expected to be taken out of active use. The salvage value can be difficult to determine, for several reasons. First, there may be a removal cost associated with the asset, which will reduce the net salvage value that will be realized (see the earlier ARO discussion). If the equipment is especially large (such as a printing press) or involves environmental hazards (such as any equipment involving the use of radioactive substances), then the removal cost may exceed the salvage value. In this latter instance, the salvage value may be negative, in which case it should be ignored for depreciation purposes.

A second reason why salvage value is difficult to determine is that asset obsolescence is so rapid in some industries (especially in relation to computer equipment) that a reasonable appraisal of salvage value at the time an asset is put into service may require drastic revision shortly thereafter. A third reason is the lack of a ready market for the sale of used assets in many instances. A fourth reason is the cost of conducting an appraisal in order to determine a net salvage value, which may be excessive in relation to the cost of the equipment being appraised. For all these reasons, a company should certainly attempt to set a net salvage value in order to arrive at a cost base for depreciation purposes, but it will probably be necessary to make regular revisions to its salvage value estimates in a cost-effective manner in order to reflect the ongoing realities of asset resale values.

In the case of low-cost assets, it is rarely worth the effort to derive salvage values for depreciation purposes; as a result, these items are typically fully depreciated on the assumption that they have no salvage value.

Fixed Assets—Depreciation

Depreciation is designed to spread an asset's cost over its entire useful service life. Its service life is the period over which it is worn out for any reason, at the end of which it is no longer usable, or not usable without extensive overhaul. Its useful life also can be considered terminated at the point when it no longer has a sufficient productive capacity for ongoing company production needs, rendering it essentially obsolete.

Anything can be depreciated that has a business purpose, has a productive life of more than one year, gradually wears out over time, and whose cost exceeds the corporate capitalization limit. Since land does not wear out, it cannot be depreciated.

There are a variety of depreciation methods, as outlined in the following sections. Straight-line depreciation provides for a depreciation rate that is the same amount in every year of an asset's life, whereas various accelerated depreciation methods (such as sum-of-the-years' digits and double-declining balance) are oriented toward the more rapid recognition of depreciation expenses, on the grounds that an asset is used most intensively when it is first acquired. Perhaps the most accurate depreciation methods are those that are tied to actual asset usage (such as the units of production method), though they require much more extensive recordkeeping in relation to units of usage. There are also depreciation methods based on compound interest factors, resulting in delayed depreciation recognition; since these methods are rarely used, they are not presented here.

If an asset is present but is temporarily idle, then its depreciation should be continued using the existing assumptions for the usable life of the asset. Only if it is permanently idled should the accountant review the need to recognize impairment of the asset (see the later section discussing impairment).

An asset is rarely purchased or sold precisely on the first or last day of the fiscal year, which brings up the issue of how depreciation is to be calculated in these first and last partial years of use. There are a number of alternatives available, all of which are valid as long as they are consistently applied. One option is to record a full year of depreciation in the year of acquisition and no depreciation in the year of sale. Another option is to record a half-year of depreciation in the first year and a half-year of depreciation in the last year. One can also prorate the depreciation more precisely, making it accurate to within the nearest month (or even the nearest day) of when an acquisition or sale transaction occurs.

Fixed Assets—Straight-Line Depreciation

The straight-line depreciation method is the simplest method available, and is the most popular one when a company has no particular need to recognize depreciation costs at an accelerated rate (as would be the case when it wants to match the book value of its depreciation to the accelerated depreciation used for income tax calculation purposes). It is also used for all amortization calculations.

It is calculated by subtracting an asset's expected salvage value from its capitalized cost, and then dividing this amount by the estimated life of the asset. For example, a candy wrapper machine has a cost of $40,000 and an expected salvage value of $8,000. It is expected to be in service for eight years. Given these assumptions, its annual depreciation expense is as follows:

$$= \text{(Cost – salvage value) / number of years in service}$$
$$= (\$40,000 – \$8,000) / 8 \text{ years}$$
$$= \$32,000 / 8 \text{ years}$$
$$= \$4,000 \text{ depreciation per year}$$

Fixed Assets—Double-Declining Balance Depreciation

The double-declining balance method (DDB) is the most aggressive depreciation method for recognizing the bulk of the expense toward the beginning of an asset's useful life. To calculate it, determine the straight-line depreciation for an asset for its first year (see the previous section for the straight-line calculation). Then double this amount, which yields the depreciation for the first year. Then subtract the first-year depreciation from the asset cost (using no salvage value deduction), and run the same calculation again for the next year. Continue to use this methodology for the useful life of the asset.

For example, a dry cleaning machine costing $20,000 is estimated to have a useful life of six years. Under the straight-line method, it would have depreciation of $3,333 per year. Consequently, the first year of depreciation under the 200% DDB method would be double that amount, or $6,667. The calculation for all six years of depreciation is noted in the following table:

Year	Beginning cost basis	Straight-line depreciation	200% DDB depreciation	Ending cost basis
1	$24,000	$3,333	$6,667	$17,333
2	17,333	2,889	5,778	11,555
3	11,555	1,926	3,852	7,703
4	7,703	1,284	2,568	5,135
5	5,135	856	1,712	3,423
6	3,423	571	1,142	2,281

Note that there is still some cost left at the end of the sixth year that has not been depreciated. This is usually handled by converting over from the DDB method to the straight-line method in the year in which the straight-line method would result in a higher amount of depreciation; the straight-line method is then used until all of the available depreciation has been recognized.

Fixed Assets—Sum-of-the-Years' Digits Depreciation

This depreciation method is designed to recognize the bulk of all depreciation within the first few years of an asset's depreciable period, but does not do so quite as rapidly as the double-declining balance method described in the previous section. Its calculation can be surmised from its name. For the first year of depreciation, one adds up the number of years over which an asset is scheduled to be depreciated, and then divides this into the total number of years remaining. The resulting percentage is used as the depreciation rate. In succeeding years, simply divide the reduced number of years left into the same total number of years remaining.

For example, a punch press costing $24,000 is scheduled to be depreciated over five years. The sum-of-the-years' digits is 15 (Year 1 + Year 2 + Year 3 + Year 4 + Year 5). The depreciation calculation in each of the five years is as follows:

$$
\begin{aligned}
\text{Year } 1 &= (5/15) \times \$24,000 &= \$\ 8,000 \\
\text{Year } 2 &= (4/15) \times \$24,000 &= \$\ 6,400 \\
\text{Year } 3 &= (3/15) \times \$24,000 &= \$\ 4,800 \\
\text{Year } 4 &= (2/15) \times \$24,000 &= \$\ 3,200 \\
\text{Year } 5 &= (1/15) \times \$24,000 &= \$\ \underline{1,600} \\
& & \underline{\$24,000}
\end{aligned}
$$

Fixed Assets—Units of Production Depreciation Method

The units of production depreciation method can result in the most accurate matching of actual asset usage to the related amount of depreciation that is recognized in the accounting records. Its use is limited to those assets to which some estimate of production can be attached. It is a particular favorite of those who use activity-based costing systems, since it closely relates asset cost to actual activity.

To calculate it, one should first estimate the total number of units of production that are likely to result from the use of an asset. Then divide the total capitalized asset cost (less salvage value, if this is known) by the total estimated production to arrive at the depreciation cost per unit of production. Then the depreciation recognized is derived by multiplying the number of units of actual production during the period by the depreciation cost per unit. If there is a significant divergence of actual production activity from the original estimate, the depreciation cost per unit of production can be altered from time to time to reflect the realities of actual production volumes.

As an example of this method's use, an oil derrick is constructed at a cost of $350,000. It is expected to be used in the extraction of 1 million barrels of oil, which results in an anticipated depreciation rate of $0.35 per barrel. During the first month, 23,500 barrels of oil are extracted. Under this method, the resulting depreciation cost is

= (Cost per unit of production) × (Number of units of production)
= ($0.35 per barrel) × (23,500 barrels)
= $8,225

This calculation also can be used with service hours as its basis, rather than units of production. When used in this manner, the method can be applied to a larger number of assets for which production volumes would not be otherwise available.

Fixed Assets—Asset Impairment

A company is allowed to write down its remaining investment in an asset if it can be proven that the asset is impaired. Impairment can be proven if an asset's net book value is greater than the sum of the undiscounted cash flows (including proceeds from its sale) expected to be generated by it in the future. Having an asset's net book value be greater than its fair value is not a valid reason for an asset write-down, since the asset may still have considerable utility within the company, no matter what its market value may be.

There is no requirement for the periodic testing of asset impairment. Instead, it should be done if there is a major drop in asset usage or downgrading of its physical condition, or if government regulations or business conditions will likely result in a major drop in usage. For example, if new government regulations are imposed that are likely to significantly reduce a company's ability to use the asset, such as may be the case for a coal-fired electricity-generating facility that is subject to pollution controls, then an asset impairment test would be necessary. The test also can be conducted if there are major cost overruns during the construction of an asset, or if there is a history or future expectation of operating losses associated with an asset. An expectation of early asset disposition can also trigger the test.

To calculate an impairment loss, determine an asset's fair value, either from market quotes or by determining the expected present value of its future cash flows. Then write off the difference between its net book value and its fair value. This action may also result in a change in the method or duration of depreciation. For example, if an asset impairment write-down is made because an asset's life is expected to be shortened by five years, then the period over which its associated depreciation will be calculated should also be reduced by five years. If asset impairment is being calculated for a group of assets (such as an entire assembly line or production facility), then the amount of the asset impairment is allocated to the assets within the group based on their proportional net book values (though not below the separately identifiable fair value of any asset within the group).

If an asset is no longer in use and there is no prospect for it to be used at any point in the future, then it must be written down to its expected salvage value. Since there will then be no remaining asset value to depreciate, all depreciation stops at the time of the write-down.

Intangible Assets

When an intangible asset is purchased, it should be capitalized on the company books at the amount of cash that was paid for it. If some other asset was used in exchange for the intangible, then the cost should be set at the fair market value of the asset given up. A third alternative for costing is the present value of any liability that is assumed in exchange for the intangible asset. It is also possible to create an intangible asset internally (such as the creation of a customer list), as long as the detail for all costs incurred in the creation of the intangible asset is adequately tracked and summarized.

If an intangible asset has an indefinite life, as demonstrated by clearly traceable cash flows well into the future, then it is not amortized. Instead, it is subject to an annual impairment test, resulting in the recognition of an impairment loss if its net book value exceeds its fair value. If an intangible asset in this category were to no longer have a demonstrably indefinite life, then it would convert to a normal amortization schedule based on its newly defined economic life.

If any intangible asset's usefulness is declining or evidently impaired, then its remaining value should be written down to no lower than the present value of its remaining future cash flows.

When a company acquires another company or its assets, any excess of the purchase price over the fair value of tangible assets should be allocated to intangible assets to the greatest degree possible. Examples of such assets are customer lists, patents, trademarks, and brand names. When some value is assigned to these intangible assets, they will then be amortized over a reasonable time period. If the excess purchase price cannot be fully allocated to intangible assets, the remainder is added to the goodwill account.

Goodwill cannot be amortized. Instead, it is subject to annual impairment testing, or more frequently if circumstances indicate that impairment is likely. The impairment test is based on the lowest level of business entity to which the goodwill can be assigned. For example, if Company A purchases another business and renames it as an operating division of Company A, then the impairment test will be conducted on the results of only that division. Alternatively, if the purchased business is merged into the operations of Company A in such a manner that its operating results no longer can be tracked, then the impairment test will be conducted on the results of all of Company A.

Goodwill impairment testing is conducted by comparing the net book value (including goodwill) of the subject business unit to its fair value. If the fair value figure is greater, then no adjustment is required. However, if the fair value figure is lower than the net book value, take the following steps:

1. Determine the fair value of the subject business unit.
2. Determine the fair value of the individual assets and liabilities, excluding goodwill, within the business unit.
3. Subtract the fair value of the individual assets and liabilities determined in step 2. from the fair value of the subject business unit determined in step 1. to arrive at the carrying value of the goodwill.
4. Subtract the goodwill carrying value from the amount at which it is recorded on the company books. Write off any excess goodwill amount remaining on the company books.

If there is any subsequent increase in the fair value of the subject business unit, the impairment amount already written off cannot be recovered.

Example of intangible amortization

Mr. Mel Smith purchases cab license #512 from the city of St. Paul for $20,000. The license term is for five years, after which he can renew it with no anticipated difficulties. The cash flows from the cab license can be reasonably shown to extend into the indefinite future, so there is no amortization requirement. However, the city council then changes the renewal process to a lottery where the odds of obtaining a renewal are poor. Mr. Smith must now assume that the economic life of his cab license will end in five years, so he initiates amortization to coincide with the license renewal date.

Example of an intangible asset purchase

An acquirer spends $1 million more to purchase a competitor than its book value. The acquirer decides to assign $400,000 of this excess amount to the patent formerly owned by the competitor, which it then amortizes over the remaining life of the patent. If the acquirer assigns the remaining $600,000 to a customer list asset, and the customer loss rate is 20% per year, then it can reasonably amortize the $600,000 over five years to match the gradual reduction in value of the customer list asset.

Research and Development (R&D) Costs

Any R&D costs incurred by a company must be charged to expense in the current period, unless they have alternative future uses (such as fixed assets). R&D costs cannot be included in an overhead cost pool, since these costs might then be deferred into a future period. The total amount of R&D expense must be reported in the financial statements. The following list includes the R&D costs that must be expensed:

- **Contract services.** R&D work performed by an outside entity on behalf of the company, and for which the company pays, must be charged to expense as an R&D cost.
- **Indirect costs.** Any costs that can be reasonably allocated to R&D activities through a consistently applied cost allocation system shall be charged to R&D expense.
- **Materials, equipment, and facilities.** Any that are acquired for R&D work, and which have no alternative future value, must be expensed. If they do have an alternative future value, then they must be capitalized and depreciated over time as a cost of R&D.
- **Personnel.** Any personnel costs, such as salaries, wages, benefits, and payroll taxes, that are associated with personnel engaged in R&D work shall be charged as an R&D expense.

This rule covers all research, plus testing and modification of product alternatives, prototypes and models, the design of new tools and dies, pilot plants not commercially feasible, or any engineering work conducted prior to being ready for manufacture.

There are also a number of costs that are **not** to be included in the R&D expense category. They are nearly always costs that must be expensed as incurred, rather than capitalized, and so are not different from R&D costs in terms of their treatment. However, companies would artificially increase their reported R&D expense (which is a separate line item in the financial statements) if they were to include these items in the R&D category, which may give investors an artificial impression of the size of funding being directed toward R&D activities. The costs not to be included in R&D are as follows:

- **Engineering costs.** Includes efforts to make minor incremental enhancements to existing products, or to make minor customized adjustments to products for existing customers, as well as the design of tools and dies on a routine basis.
- **Facility costs.** Includes the startup cost of new facilities that are not intended for use as R&D facilities.
- **Legal costs.** Includes the cost of patent applications, the cost of litigation to support them, and the costs associated with their licensing to or from other parties.
- **Production costs.** Includes industrial engineering, quality, and troubleshooting work engaged in during the commercial production of a product.

If a company purchases its R&D work from some other entity, then the cost of this work to the company must be expensed in the period incurred. However, if a company acquires intangibles that may be used in R&D activities (such as through a corporate acquisition), and which have alternative future uses, the intangibles must be amortized over time. For example, if a company were to purchase another entity, then under the purchase method of accounting, it could assign intangible costs to identifiable assets that are related to R&D, such as patents, formulas, and new product designs, as well as to more concrete items, such as equipment used in R&D experiments.

This latter case has given rise to inconsistent accounting treatment, for acquiring companies are sometimes making the assumption that some acquired intangibles are directly associated with R&D costs (rather than being capitalized under the assumption that they have alternative future uses), and are using this assumption as the basis for writing them off at once, rather than amortizing their cost over a number of years. Under this scenario, if there is any doubt regarding the proper treatment of intangibles associated with R&D, it is best to amortize the cost.

If a company specializes in the provision of R&D to other businesses, the accounting for these costs will essentially be determined by the contents of each R&D contract signed. For example, if a contract states that R&D work will be billed to a client on a time and materials basis, then the expense can easily be recorded in conjunction with any associated billings. A more common case is that the R&D organization receives a large amount of initial funding; if there is no obligation to return the funds, they may be recorded at once as revenue. However, if there is a requirement that the funds be used for specific R&D work or else be returned, then the funds must be recorded as a liability that will gradually be drawn down as offsetting R&D costs are incurred.

DECISION TREES

There are a variety of decision points involved in the determination of how to treat an expenditure related to a fixed asset. The decision tree shown in Exhibit 6-1 can be used to determine the correct accounting treatment of these expenditures. There may be some uncertainty about whether an expenditure adds to an asset's future value or extends its useful life, which results in different treatments, as indicated at the bottom of the decision tree. When this situation arises, choose the decision point corresponding to the most dominant impact of the expenditure. For example, switching to a concrete roof from a wooden one may extend the life of a structure, but its dominant impact is to increase the building's future value.

Exhibit 6-1: Asset Acquisition Capitalization or Expense Decision

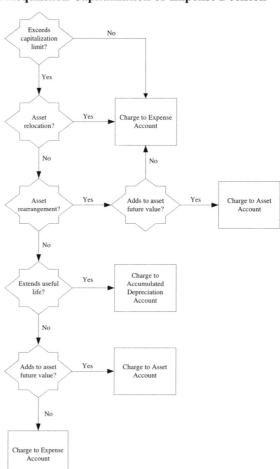

There are a number of ways to handle asset transactions where there is either no exchange of money for the assets or where money is only part of the consideration given. The decision tree in Exhibit 6-2 can be used to determine the correct accounting treatment for the various scenarios.

Exhibit 6-2: Accounting for Nonmonetary Exchanges Involving Assets

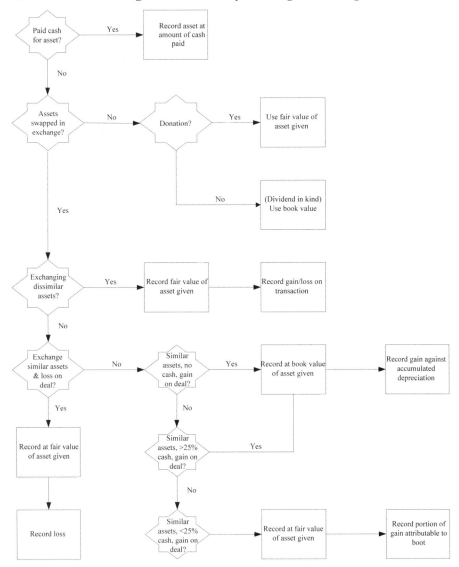

POLICIES

Fixed Assets

- **Management must approve all asset additions through a formal review process.** This policy requires the management team to follow a formal review process, preferably using a capital investment proposal form such as the one shown in the Forms and Reports section that requires both the use of cash flow analysis and a hierarchy of approvals depending on the size of the proposed expenditure.

- **All assets with a purchase price exceeding $1,000 shall be recorded as fixed assets.** This policy reduces the amount of paperwork associated with fixed asset tracking by shifting smaller assets into the expense category.
- **The capitalization limit shall be reviewed annually.** This policy requires the controller to verify that the existing capitalization limit represents a reasonable balance of minimized recordkeeping for fixed assets and not an excessive amount of charges to expense for lower-cost assets.
- **Capital investment results shall be reviewed annually.** This policy requires a company to compare the actual results of a capital investment to what was predicted in its capital investment proposal form (see the Forms and Reports section). The intent is to highlight incorrect assumptions that still may be used for other capital investment proposals, which then can be corrected to ensure better ongoing capital investment decisions.
- **Conduct an annual inventory of all fixed assets.** This policy requires the accounting staff to compare the record of fixed assets to their actual locations, typically resulting not only in adjustments to their recorded locations, but also a determination of the need to dispose of selected assets.
- **A detailed record shall be maintained of each fixed asset acquired.** This policy forces one to centralize the recordkeeping for each asset, making it much easier to identify, locate, cost, and determine the warranty provisions associated with each one.
- **All asset valuations associated with dissimilar asset exchanges shall be reviewed by an outside appraiser.** This policy prevents the accounting staff from intentionally creating gains or losses on asset exchange transactions by assuming incorrect asset fair values.
- **Copies of property records shall be maintained in an off-site location.** This policy reduces the risk of lost records by requiring a periodic shifting of record copies to a secure outside location.
- **All asset transfers and disposals require management approval.** This policy brings any asset movements to the attention of the accounting department, which can then record the revised asset locations in the accounting records. The policy also allows one to review the proposed prices to be obtained from the sale or disposal of assets.
- **Periodically review all fixed assets for impairment.** This policy ensures that the accounting staff will regularly compare the book value of all fixed assets to their fair value, and write down the book value to the fair value if this is the lower amount.

Intangible Assets

- **All transactions involving the recording of intangible assets must be approved by the external auditors in advance.** Intangible assets are subject to a considerable degree of scrutiny by auditors. By gaining advance approval of these transactions, it is much less likely that there will be significant audit adjustments related to them after the end of the fiscal year.

- **Periodically review all intangible assets for impairment.** This policy ensures that the accounting staff will regularly compare the book value of all intangible assets to their fair value, and write down the book value to the fair value if this is the lower amount.

Research and Development Costs

- **All research and development costs must be recorded under unique general ledger account codes.** Because GAAP requires that all R&D costs be charged to expense in the current period, it is imperative that these costs be segregated for easy review. Otherwise, it is likely that the costs will be mixed into other general ledger accounts and possibly capitalized, thereby incorrectly increasing reported profits.

PROCEDURES

Fixed Assets—Calculate Depreciation

Use this procedure to ensure that the correct depreciation type and period is used for each capitalized asset.

1. Compare the type of asset to the company policy statement on asset types in the accounting policy manual.
2. Go to the fixed assets register in the computer database and enter the asset under the correct asset category.
3. When adding the asset to the database, set the number of years of depreciation in accordance with the standard listed in the company policy statement on asset types.
4. Set the first-year depreciation at the half-year convention.
5. Set the depreciation method as the _____ method.
6. Print the transaction and store it in the fixed assets records manual.
7. Print the depreciation register and verify that the system has correctly calculated the depreciation expense for the newly added asset.

Fixed Assets—Conduct Inventory of Fixed Assets

Use this procedure to periodically verify the existence of fixed assets in the locations listed in the computer system.

1. Obtain a list of all assets in a company location that is scheduled to be reviewed.
2. Check off all assets on the list as they are found and their tag numbers matched to the list.
3. Make note of the tag numbers of all physical assets found that are not on the computer list for this location.
4. Inquire of the staff in the target location as to where the missing assets might be located. Enter these notes in the computer database, to be included in subsequent physical counts.
5. Go to the computer database and enter the correct physical location code for those assets found at the review location that were not listed on the report.

6. Go to the computer database and reset the location code to "Pending" for those assets not found in the location that were listed on the report.
7. If inquiries indicate that assets have been disposed of or transferred, refer the matter to the internal audit staff for review of potential control problems.
8. If assets have been disposed of or transferred, record a gain or loss based on the remaining net book value of the assets in question, and retire them from the fixed assets register.

Fixed Assets—Enter Fixed Asset Payments

Use this procedure to process fixed asset transactions by the accounts payable clerk.

1. Determine if an asset purchase exceeds the corporate capitalization limit. If so, code the purchase into the appropriate asset account. If not, contact the assistant controller to verify which expense account is to be charged for the purchase.
2. Open the purchasing module and create a purchase transaction. Include in the asset account all expenses required to bring the asset to the company and install it. In the case of the current invoice in question, this means including the listed sales tax, delivery charges, and shipping insurance in the asset account.
3. Open the fixed assets register and enter the asset's name, account type, and location within the company. Also enter the fixed asset tag number, if available. The system will automatically assign a depreciation calculation method and period to the asset based on the account type to which it was assigned.
4. Verify that the amount listed in the fixed asset register matches the amount entered for the purchase transaction.

Fixed Assets—Evaluate Capital Purchase Proposals

Use this procedure to verify the assumptions, cash flows, and net present value of all capital proposals.

1. Review each submitted capital expenditure form to ensure that all fields have been completed. If not, return the form to the sender with a note regarding the missing information.
2. Review all assumptions, which are noted at the bottom of the form. If these vary significantly from assumptions used for previous approved capital budgets, or if there are reasonable grounds for doubt, review them with the originating person, and modify them if necessary, as well as all underlying numerical data.
3. Review all itemized cash flows with the project manager, purchasing staff, sales staff, and anyone else with a reasonable degree of knowledge regarding the amount or timing of the cash flows.
4. Adjust the amount or timing of cash flows in the capital expenditure analysis based on the preceding cash flow review.

5. Obtain the cost of capital from the controller, and use this to discount the stream of cash flows noted in the capital expenditure proposal.
6. If the project seems unusually risky, also recalculate the net present value using a higher discount rate, to be determined by the controller.
7. If the net present value is positive, then issue a favorable project recommendation to the controller and project sponsor.
8. If the net present value is negative, state the amount by which it is negative, and the internal rate of return, so that the project sponsor can rework the assumptions and possibly arrive at a positive net present value.

Fixed Assets—Record Gain/Loss on Sale of an Asset

Use this procedure to calculate the gain or loss on the sale or disposal of any capital assets.

1. Receive documentation from the purchasing department regarding the sale of assets. This should include a signed Asset Disposition form that authorized someone to sell an asset. If the document is not signed by an authorized person, return it with a note asking for the appropriate signature. The document should be accompanied by a copy of the bill of sale, and a copy of the check or other document that shows proof of the amount paid.
2. Once the sale documentation is complete, go to the fixed asset database and call up the record for the asset being sold. The easiest way is to conduct a search based on the name of the asset, though the documentation may contain the asset number, which can also be used to find the correct record.
3. Write down the original asset cost and total accumulated depreciation, which is located in the record in the fixed asset database.
4. Subtract the sale amount and accumulated depreciation from the original asset cost. If there is a positive amount left over, this is a loss on the sale of the asset. If there is a negative amount left over, this is a gain on the sale of the asset.
5. Obtain a journal entry form and complete it for the gain or loss transaction. The asset's original cost goes in the "Credit Column," while the accumulated depreciation amount goes in the "Debit Column." The sale amount is a debit to cash. If there is a gain, this is recorded as a credit. A loss is recorded as a debit.
6. Access the fixed asset database and record the sale of the asset. Print the fixed asset database after this transaction is recorded and compare the total for the account to the general ledger, to ensure that the information is recorded in the same amounts in both locations.
7. File a copy of the gain or loss calculation in the journal entry book, and also in the permanent file documenting the addition or removal of fixed assets.

Fixed Assets—Test Assets for Impairment

Use this procedure to determine if the fair value of a fixed asset has dropped below its book value, and to adjust the book value down to the fair value if this is the case. Most assets have book values clustered near the corporate capitalization limit, and therefore are so small that impairment testing would not result in significant as-set valuation changes. Accordingly, this procedure is designed to test the values of only the largest assets.

1. Sort the fixed asset register by declining net book value (e.g., original pur-chase price less accumulated depreciation).
2. Select for impairment testing those 20% of the listed assets containing 80% of the total book value of the asset register.
3. Determine the total undiscounted cash flows expected to be generated from each of the selected assets (including net salvage value) and list this amount next to their net book values.
4. Compare the net book value figure to the undiscounted cash flow figure and highlight those assets for which the book value is higher.
5. For the highlighted assets, determine the amount of the variance between the net book value and the undiscounted cash flow figure, and record an adjust-ment in the general ledger for this amount (see the Journal Entries section for the entry format).
6. Reduce the net book values of all adjusted assets in the fixed asset register to match the amount of their undiscounted cash flows.
7. Calculate depreciation based on the new reduced book value figures and ad-just any recurring depreciation journal entries to include these changes.

Intangible Assets—Test Assets for Impairment

Use this procedure to determine if the fair value of an intangible asset is less than its book value, and to adjust its book value downward if this is the case. As opposed to the impairment testing on fixed assets, impairment testing should be conducted on all intangible assets.

1. Print the fixed asset register, selected only for intangible assets.
2. Determine the total undiscounted cash flows expected to be generated from each of the intangible assets. If intangible assets can be grouped by business unit, this information may be obtained by reviewing the budget for that business unit.
3. Compare the book value figure for each intangible asset or related group of assets to its expected undiscounted cash flow figure.
4. Reduce the book values of all adjusted intangible assets in the fixed asset register to match the amount of their undiscounted cash flows.

CONTROLS

Fixed Assets

The following controls should be installed to ensure that fixed assets are properly accounted for:[2]

---

[2] *Selected controls for fixed assets have been copied with permission from pp. 463–465 of Bragg,* **Ultimate Accountants' Reference** *(John Wiley & Sons, Inc., Hoboken, NJ, 2006).*

- **Ensure that fixed asset purchases have appropriate prior authorization.** A company with a capital-intensive infrastructure may find that its most important controls are over the authorization of funds for new or replacement capital projects. Depending on the potential amount of funding involved, these controls may include a complete net present value (NPV) review of the cash flows associated with each prospective investment, as well as multilayered approvals that reach all the way up to the Board of Directors. A truly comprehensive control system will also include a post-completion review that compares the original cash flow estimates to those actually achieved, not only to see if a better estimation process can be used in the future, but also to see if any deliberate misrepresentation of estimates was initially made.
- **Compare capital investment projections to actual results.** Managers have been known to make overly optimistic projections in order to make favorable cases for asset acquisitions. This issue can be mitigated by conducting regular reviews of the results of asset acquisitions in comparison to initial predictions, and then tracing these findings back to the initiating managers. This approach can also be used at various milestones during the asset construction to ensure that costs incurred match original projections.
- **Verify that correct depreciation calculations are being made.** Though there is no potential loss of assets if incorrect depreciation calculations are being made, it can result in an embarrassing adjustment to the previously reported financial results at some point in the future. This control should include a comparison of capitalized items to the official corporate capitalization limit, in order to ensure that items are not being inappropriately capitalized and depreciated. The control should also include a review of the asset categories in which each individual asset has been recorded, in order to ensure that an asset has not been misclassified and therefore incorrectly depreciated.
- **Verify the fair value assumptions on dissimilar asset exchanges.** Accounting rules allow one to record a gain or loss on the exchange of dissimilar assets. Since this calculation is based on the fair value of the assets involved (which is not already clearly stated in the accounting records), the possibility exists for someone to artificially create an asset fair value that will result in a gain or loss. This situation can be avoided by having an outside appraiser review the fair value assumptions used in this type of transaction.
- **Ensure that capital construction projects are not delayed for accounting reasons.** Accounting rules require one to capitalize the interest expense associated with the construction of certain types of assets. By artificially delaying the completion date of an asset, or by delaying the official completion date for accounting purposes, one can improperly extend the time period over which interest expense can be ascribed to a project and capitalized as part of its cost, thereby reducing the overall corporate interest expense and increasing profits. This problem can be avoided by personally reviewing the physical status of construction projects in relation to planning documents, such as Gantt charts, and determining the validity of reasons for delays in completion.

- **Verify that fixed asset disposals are properly authorized.** A company does not want to have a fire sale of its assets taking place without any member of the management team knowing about it. Consequently, the sale of assets should be properly authorized prior to any sale transaction being initiated, if only to ensure that the eventual price paid by the buyer is verified as being a reasonable one.

- **Verify that all changes in asset retirement obligation assumptions are authorized.** A company can artificially increase its short-term profitability by altering the assumed amount of future cash flows associated with its asset retirement obligations. Since downward revisions to these assumptions will be reflected in the current period's income statement as a gain, any changes to these assumptions should be approved prior to implementation.

- **Verify that cash receipts from asset sales are properly handled.** Employees may sell a company's assets, pocket the proceeds, and report to the company that the asset was actually scrapped. This control issue can be reduced by requiring that a bill of sale or receipt from a scrapping company accompany the file for every asset that has been disposed of.

- **Verify that fixed assets are being utilized.** Many fixed assets are parked in a corner and neglected, with no thought to their being profitably sold off. To see if this problem is occurring, the accounting staff should conduct a periodic review of all fixed assets, which should include a visual inspection and discussion with employees to see if assets are no longer in use.

- **Test for asset impairment.** There are a variety of circumstances under which the net book value of an asset should be reduced to its fair value, which can result in significant reductions in the recorded value of an asset. This test requires a significant knowledge of the types of markets in which a company operates, the regulations to which it is subject, and the need for its products within those markets. Consequently, only a knowledgeable person who is at least at the level of a controller should be relied on to detect the presence of assets whose values are likely to have been impaired.

Intangible Assets

- **Verify that excess acquisition purchase costs are fully allocated to intangible assets.** Companies have a major incentive to park the excess amount of acquisition purchase costs greater than the fair values of the tangible assets purchased in the goodwill account. By doing so, they avoid extra depreciation or amortization expenses (subject to periodic impairment tests), but also avoid GAAP rules to shift this excess amount to other types of intangible assets that can be amortized. Thus, perhaps the major control point resulting from an acquisition is ensuring that all intangible assets acquired as part of an acquisition are fully valued, leaving the minimum possible amount to be charged to the goodwill account.

Research and Development Costs

- **Preconfigure account codes for R&D suppliers to expense accounts.** When setting up the account codes for suppliers of R&D services and products to a company, always configure the records to an expense account, thereby reducing the chance that an R&D expense will find its way into an asset account and be capitalized.
- **Compare R&D expenses over multiple periods to spot expense changes.** By creating a multiperiod report that tracks all R&D expenses by cost category, one can see when expenses suddenly drop, which can be indicative of an incorrect charge to an asset account.

FORMS AND REPORTS

Fixed Assets

When a company is considering the purchase or construction of an expensive asset, it typically summarizes all relevant cash flow information pertaining to it on a form such as the one shown in Exhibit 6-3. This form clearly reveals the ability of an asset to generate a return to the company. In addition, if the asset is required for other reasons than the generation of cash flow, this information is noted in the lower left corner. Finally, the form requires an increasing number of management approvals, depending on its size. The approval matrix is noted in the lower right corner of the form.

Exhibit 6–3: Capital Investment Proposal Form

Name of Project Sponsor: *H. Henderson*   **Submission Date:** *Date*

Investment Description:
Additional press for newsprint

Cash Flows:

Year	Equipment	Working Capital	Maintenance	Tax Effect of Annual Depreciation	Salvage Value	Revenue	Taxes	Total
0	–5,000,000	–400,000		800,000				–5,400,000
1			–100,000	320,000		1,650,000	–700,000	1,170,000
2			–100,000	320,000		1,650,000	–700,000	1,170,000
3			–100,000	320,000		1,650,000	–700,000	1,170,000
4			–100,000	320,000		1,650,000	–700,000	1,170,000
5		400,000	–100,000	320,000	1,000,000	1,650,000	–700,000	1,170,000
Totals	–5,000,000		–500,000	2,400,000	1,000,000	8,250,000		1,850,000

Tax Rate: **40%**
Hurdle Rate: **10%**

Payback Period: 4.28%

Net Present Value: (86,809)

Internal Rate of Return: 9.4%

Type of Project (check one):   **Approvals:**

Legal requirement		Amount	Approver	Signature
New product-related		<$5,000	Supervisor	
Old product extension	Yes	$5–19,999	General Manager	
Repair/replacement		$20–49,999	President	
Safety issue		$50,000+	Board	

*SOURCE: Adapted with permission from p. 24 of Bragg, **Financial Analysis: A Controller's Guide** (John Wiley & Sons, Inc., Hoboken, NJ, 2000).*

If a company has a large project under construction that will result in a fixed asset in the accounting records, such as a new headquarters building, it must accumulate all information pertaining to it on a project cost sheet such as the one noted in Exhibit 6-4. Though some of this information could be solely accumulated in a separate general ledger account, that approach results in less storage of detailed information about a project. In general, the larger the project, the more need for a form of this type.

Exhibit 6-4: Project Cost Sheet

						Form 2-520
PROJECT COST SHEET						
Balance Sheet Account No. _____					Project No. _____	
Project Name: _____						
Project Description: _____						
Start Date: _____					Budgeted Total $: _____	

Item	Date	Invoice No.	Supplier or Payroll	Item or Service	Amount	
Materials						
Direct Labor						
Contractors						
Project Completion Date _____				Total Materials		
				Total Direct Labor		
Transferred to Balance Sheet Account No. _____				Total Contractors		
				Total Project		

Whenever a company acquires land, it should record all pertinent information on a land record form such as the one shown in Exhibit 6-5. Any title or surveying information should be attached to this form for easy reference. By consolidating this information, one will have easy access to zoning, assessment, easement, and other information critical for taxation and subsequent construction purposes.

Exhibit 6-5: Land Record Form

```
                                                              Form 2-530
                              LAND RECORD

                                Property number: _____

1.  General description: _____


2.  Cost: _____         Date purchased: _____

3.  Address: _____

4.  City, State, Zip Code: _____

5.  Township: _____         County: _____


6.  Approximate size: _____

7.  Legal description: _____


8.  Zoning classification: _____

9.  Easements: _____


10. Restrictions on use: _____


11. Assessed valuation:   Year: _____   Amount: _____

                          Year: _____   Amount: _____

                          Year: _____   Amount: _____

                          Year: _____   Amount: _____


12. Land improvements: _____


13. Buildings on property: _____
```

When any kind of improvement is made to land, such as septic systems or landscaping, this information should be recorded on a separate land improvement form, such as the one shown in Exhibit 6-6. By clearly stating the size, cost, and type of constructions installed, a company not only has a better chance of defending itself from adverse tax valuations, but also can compile a reasonable land value for resale purposes.

Exhibit 6-6: Land Improvement Form

```
                                                              Form 2-540
                          LAND IMPROVEMENT RECORD


                                        Property number: _____


   1.  General description: _____


   2.  Cost: _____


   3.  Date put in use: _____


   4.  Approximate size: _____


   5.  Construction materials: _____


   6.  Useful life: _____


   7.  Assessed valuation:      Year: _____     Amount: _____
                                Year: _____     Amount: _____
                                Year: _____     Amount: _____
                                Year: _____     Amount: _____
```

The documentation of the expenses associated with the construction of company-owned buildings and later upgrades to them are frequently disorganized, and sometimes nonexistent. This can be a problem when the accounting staff attempts to determine which expenses can be shifted into a fixed asset account, or when to begin depreciation of the asset, or to determine trends in assessed values for property tax purposes. This problem can be avoided with the use of a building record form, such as the one shown in Exhibit 6-7.

Exhibit 6-7: Building Form

```
                                                            Form 2-550
                          BUILDING RECORD

                                    Property number: _____

 1.  Building name/number: _____

 2.  General description: _____

 3.  Type of construction: _____

 4.  General use of building: _____

 5.  Cost: _____     Date put in use: _____  Useful life: _____

 6.  Approximate size:      Length: _____ Width: _____

                            Number of floors: _____

                            Square footage: _____

 7.  Assessed valuation:    Year: _____      Amount: _____

                            Year: _____      Amount: _____

                            Year: _____      Amount: _____

                            Year: _____      Amount: _____
```

Of all company assets, the type suffering from the least documentation is equipment, which can include factory, office, or computer equipment. The usual approach is to keep a copy of the purchase invoice in a separate file for the external auditors to peruse, and keep no other records besides a depreciation calculation. This presents problems when someone attempts to locate the equipment, determine what period is covered by its warranty, when it was first put into use, and so on. This information should be summarized on an equipment record form similar to the one shown in Exhibit 6-8. The form should be the lead document in a separate file on each piece of equipment that also contains all warranty and related maintenance information.

Exhibit 6-8: Equipment Form

```
                                                          Form 2-560
                        EQUIPMENT RECORD

                             Property number: _____

 1.  General description: _____

 2.  Purpose of equipment: _____

 3.  Fixed or portable: _____

 4.  Location, building and room: _____

 5.  Cost: _____      Date put in use: _____ Useful life: _____

 6.  Model: _____ Serial number: _____

 7.  Supplier name: _____
     Supplier address: _____

 7.  Warranty coverage period: _____
     Warranty provisions: _____

 8.  Property tag number: _____
```

Leases frequently appear in the accounting records as nothing more than a series of monthly lease payments. This tells one nothing about any required maintenance by the lessor, nor about term of the lease or any bargain purchase options. This information should be stored on a lease record form such as the one shown in Exhibit 6-9. The form should be the lead document in a separate file on each lease that also contains a copy of the lease. If a company also maintains a contracts database, lease terms should be noted there, so the legal department can plan for lease expirations and renewals.

Exhibit 6-9: Lease Record

```
                                                            Form 2-570
                          LEASE RECORD

                                        Number: _____

  1.  Description of leased property: _____

  2.  Serial number: _____

  3.  Location of property: _____

  4.  Lessor name: _____
      Lessor address: _____

  5.  Lease begin date: _____
      Lease end date: _____

  6.  Monthly rental amount: _____
      Annual rental amount: _____

  7.  Maintenance by lessee: _____
                              (type and frequency)

  8.  Lease renewal/extension terms: _____

  9.  Lease termination terms: _____
```

Nearly all computerized accounting systems contain a standard fixed asset report itemizing the asset type, cost, and periodic and accumulated depreciation for each asset. A typical format is shown in Exhibit 6-10. More detailed formats can also include the date in which an asset was put into service, the type of depreciation method used, the depreciation duration, and assumed salvage value. Most accounting systems will allow this format to be presented in a variety of different data sorts, such as by asset type, general ledger account, or asset book value. This basic report format is quite useful for verifying recurring depreciation calculations, and is required by external auditors as part of their review of one's financial statements.

Exhibit 6-10: Fixed Asset Depreciation Report

Account no.	Asset type	Description	Net cost	Periodic depreciation	Accumulated depreciation	Net book value
13000	Computers	Dell laptop	$ 3,500	$ 97.22	$ 291.66	$ 3,208.34
	Computers	HP laptop	3,000	83.33	749.97	2,250.03
	Computers	Compaq server	10,000	277.78	4,166.70	5,833.30
	Computers	IBM server	42,000	1,166.67	19,833.39	22,166.61
14000	Software	Quark license	3,800	105.56	2,744.56	1,055.44
	Software	Office license	1,000	27.78	833.40	166.60
	Software	Windows license	2,500	69.44	2,360.96	139.04
15000	Equipment	50-ton press	45,000	375.00	14,250.00	30,750
	Equipment	150-ton press	220,000	1,833.33	76,999.86	143,000.14

When the accounting staff is conducting a periodic audit of fixed assets, it is useful to print a report of assets by location that also includes such identifying information as model and serial numbers, with a notation field allowing them to make notes about changes in fixed asset locations. An example of this report is shown in Exhibit 6-11. In the example, the location code begins with a letter to identify the building, followed by the floor and room numbers in which an asset is located.

Exhibit 6-11: Fixed Asset Audit Report

Location	Tag number	Description	Model no.	Serial no.	Notes
A-02-13	05432	Dell laptop	Dim 43	IE75J	
A-02-01	05021	HP laptop	HP 312	06M14	
A-02-14	04996	Compaq server	CQ 007	MK14J	
A-02-07	04985	IBM server	A31	A09J5	
A-02-11	04900	Quark license	Ver 4.0	MM047	
A-02-15	04730	Office license	Ver. 2004	F4KQW	
A-02-08	04619	Windows license	Ver. XP	9M4G7	
C-01-01	01038	50-ton press	G42	Z9G2K	
C-01-01	01004	150-ton press	G90	V12L9	

FOOTNOTES

Disclosure of Asset Impairments

If a company writes down the value of assets due to the impairment of their value, the accountant should describe the assets, note which segment of the business is impacted by the loss, and disclose the amount of the loss, how fair value was determined, where the loss is reported in the income statement, the remaining cost assigned to the assets, and the date by which the company expects to have disposed of them (if it expects to do so). An example follows:

> The company has written down the value of its server farm, on the grounds that this equipment has a vastly reduced resale value as a result of the introduction of a new generation of microprocessor chips. The services of an appraiser were used to obtain a fair market value, net of selling costs, to which their cost was reduced. The resulting loss of $439,500 was charged to the application service provider segment of the company, and is contained within the "Other Gains and Losses" line item on the income statement. The remaining valuation ascribed to these assets as of the balance sheet date is $2,450,000. There are no immediate expectations to dispose of these assets.

Disclosure of Goodwill

If a company elects to immediately write down some or all of the goodwill recorded on its books, there must be disclosure of the reasons for doing so. The footnote should specify why an impairment of goodwill has occurred, the events that have caused the impairment to take place, those portions of the business to which the impaired goodwill is associated, and how the company measured the amount of the loss. Any calculation assumptions used in determining the amount of the write-down should be noted. An example follows:

> The company has taken a write-down of $1.2 million in its goodwill account. This write-down is specifically tied to the increase in competition expected from the approval of a competing patent, given to Westmoreland Steel Company, which will allow it to produce steel much more efficiently than the company's Arbuthnot Foundry, to which the $1.2 million in goodwill is associated. This write-down is based on the assumption that the Arbuthnot Foundry will not be able to compete with Westmoreland Steel for longer than four years—consequently, the present value of all goodwill that will remain on the company's books four years from the date of these financial statements has been written off.

Disclosure of Intangibles

If a company has a material amount of intangible assets on its books, the accountant should describe the types of intangibles, the amortization period and method used to offset their value, and the amount of accumulated amortization. An example follows:

> The company has $1.5 million of intangible assets on its books that are solely comprised of the estimated fair market value of patents acquired through the company's acquisition of the R.C. Goodnough Company under the purchase method of accounting. This intangible asset is being amortized over fifteen years, which is the remaining term of the acquired patents. The accumulated amortization through the reporting period is $300,000.

JOURNAL ENTRIES

Fixed Assets

Depreciation. To record the depreciation incurred during the month. The amortization account is used to write off intangible assets.

Depreciation, computer equipment	xxx	
Depreciation, computer software	xxx	
Depreciation, furniture and fixtures	xxx	
Depreciation, leasehold improvements	xxx	
Depreciation, manufacturing equipment	xxx	
Amortization expense	xxx	
Accumulated depreciation, computer equipment		xxx
Accumulated depreciation, computer software		xxx
Accumulated depreciation, furniture and fixtures		xxx
Accumulated depreciation, leasehold improvements		xxx
Accumulated depreciation, manufacturing equipment		xxx
Intangible assets		xxx

Fixed asset (capitalization of interest). To capitalize interest expense associated with the construction of a qualified asset.

Asset account	xxx	
Interest expense		xxx

Fixed asset (impairment of). To record the reduction in book value when an asset's fair value is less than its book value.

Impairment loss	xxx	
Accumulated depreciation		xxx

Fixed asset (retirement obligation). To record legally mandated asset retirement costs. The **first** entry records the initial ARO liability, while the **second** entry shows ongoing adjustments to the present value of the ARO liability as the termination date of the liability approaches and its present value increases. The **third** entry records a gradual reduction in the asset retirement liability account as actual expenses are incurred to remove an asset. The **fourth** entry records the final settlement of the liability; a loss will be incurred if the actual expense exceeds the amount of the initial liability, while a gain will be recorded if the reverse is true.

Asset account	xxx	
Asset retirement obligation		xxx
Accretion expense	xxx	
Asset retirement obligation		xxx
Asset retirement obligation	xxx	
Accounts payable		xxx
Asset retirement obligation	xxx	
Loss on settlement of ARO liability	xxx	
Gain on settlement of ARO liability		xxx

Fixed asset (sale of). To record the cash received from the sale of an asset, as well as any gain or loss in its sale. This entry also eliminates all associated accumulated depreciation that has built up over the term of the company's ownership of the asset.

Cash	xxx	
Accumulated depreciation	xxx	
Loss on sale of assets	xxx	
(Various fixed asset accounts)		xxx
Gain on sale of assets		xxx

Fixed asset (outbound donation). To record the donation of a company asset to a charitable organization. This entry clears the original asset and depreciation entries from the company's records, and also records a gain or loss on the transaction in relation to the asset's fair market value after being netted against the asset's net book value.

Charitable donations	xxx	
Accumulated depreciation	xxx	
Loss on property donation	xxx	
Gain on property donation		xxx
Asset account		xxx

Fixed asset (purchase with stock). To record the acquisition of an asset with company stock. The amount of the stock paid out must be split between the par value and paid-in capital accounts, depending on the predetermined par value of each share issued.

Asset account	xxx	
Stock, par value		xxx
Stock, additional paid-in capital		xxx

Fixed asset (exchange for a dissimilar asset). To record the trade of a company asset for a different type of asset, including a cash payment. Any loss on this transaction is caused by the remaining net book value of the asset being relinquished being higher than its fair value, with the reverse being true for a gain. The debit to accumulated depreciation is used to clear from the accounting records the accumulated depreciation associated with the asset being traded away.

Asset account for new asset	xxx	
Accumulated depreciation	xxx	
Loss on asset exchange	xxx	
Gain on asset exchange		xxx
Asset account for asset traded away		xxx
Cash		xxx

Fixed asset (write-off). To record the unreimbursed disposal of an asset. This entry also eliminates all associated accumulated depreciation that has built up over the term of the company's ownership of the asset.

Accumulated depreciation	xxx	
Loss on disposal of assets	xxx	
(Various fixed asset accounts)		xxx

Intangible Assets

Goodwill, write-down. To record a reduction in the amount of recorded goodwill caused by impairment of the asset value.

Loss due to goodwill impairment	xxx	
Goodwill (asset account)		xxx

RECORDKEEPING[3]

The amount of recordkeeping recommended here may appear voluminous, but it is necessary to maintain sufficient information about the warranties, maintenance, vendor contact information, and other items about each asset. However, one can reduce the amount of recordkeeping by using a relatively high capitalization limit, below which assets are immediately charged to expense, rather than being recorded as an asset.

Depreciation records used to be manually calculated for each of the records noted in this chapter, and stored with them. However, the advent of inexpensive computerized depreciation software has rendered this approach inefficient. Instead,

---

[3] *Much of the information in this section and the Forms and Reports section is adapted with permission from Chapter 8 of Bragg,* **Design and Maintenance of Accounting Manuals, 4th ed.** *(John Wiley & Sons, Inc., Hoboken, NJ, 2003).*

one should record all depreciable asset information in a central database, from which depreciation calculations can be easily made.

Fixed asset records, such as purchasing documents, title records, related warranties, and the detailed records noted in the following paragraphs should be retained for as long as the company retains the asset. The records may be archived once the assets have been disposed of, and may then be destroyed on the same schedule used for other accounting records. The calculation of capitalized interest associated with the construction of qualified assets should be fully documented and included with these records.

If any capital assets are acquired or constructed that need additional work, one should use a project cost sheet to accumulate the changes. To complete the form for each asset, enter the descriptive heading information such as the name of the project or asset, assigned project number with a prefix letter to indicate the asset category (**L**and, **B**uilding, **F**actory Equipment, etc.), the balance sheet account where the item will be recorded, and a brief description of the project. Additional information recorded on the form should include the following:

- Date project is initiated
- Budget approval amount
- Asset serial number
- Materials used, including description, supplier, and cost
- Labor used, including date incurred and cost
- Contractors, including date incurred and cost
- Date of project completion
- Account number to which accumulated costs were transferred
- Summary totals for all cost categories

Maintain a record of the purchase price of land, including tax stamps, recording fees, surveys, title insurance, and any state fees. However, this should not include property taxes or the cost of land improvements. Information about each land purchase should be maintained on a separate property accounting record, which should contain the following information:

- General description of the land site
- Purchase cost
- Postal address of the location
- Township (if in a western state) and county location
- Approximate size
- Legal description
- Zoning classification, such as residential single or multiple unit, commercial retail, or light or heavy industry
- Easements for electricity, water, sewers, or gas lines
- Use restrictions
- Year of valuation and assessed value

Land improvements are depreciable. Examples of land improvements are fences and gates, parking lots, roads, sewage ponds, and signs. Information about each land improvement should be maintained on a separate property accounting record, which should contain the following information:

- General description
- Purchase cost
- Date put into use
- Approximate size
- Construction materials used
- Useful life
- Assessed valuation

In the category of "construction materials used," the description for fences and gates should note whether they are constructed of wood, brick, or chain link. If for roads or parking lots, the description should note the use of gravel, asphalt, or concrete.

A record of each company-owned building should be maintained. Use a sufficiently high capitalization limit to ensure that small additions, such as a small wall or shed attachment, do not become part of the building asset. Each building should have a name or number for reference purposes. Information about each building should be maintained on a separate property accounting record, which should contain the following information:

- Building name or number
- General description
- Type of construction
- Intended use
- Cost, date put into use, and useful life
- Approximate size
- Assessed valuation

In a manufacturing environment, the factory equipment will be the largest-dollar asset category, and therefore requires special attention, especially in regard to asset warranty information that may very well be used. Information about each piece of factory equipment should be maintained on a separate property accounting record, which should contain the following information:

- General description
- Purpose of the equipment
- Fixed or portable equipment designation
- Location by building and room number
- Cost, date put into use, and useful life
- Model and serial number
- Vendor name and address
- Warranty provisions and the period covered
- Property tag number

The increasing uses of technology in the modern office mean that the volume of office equipment can make this the largest asset category, especially in service industries where the entire staff is equipped with computers. Examples of office equipment are personal computers, video presentation equipment, fax machines, and copiers. Information about each piece of office equipment should be maintained on a separate property accounting record, which should contain the following information:

- General description
- Purpose of the equipment
- Fixed or portable equipment designation
- Location by building and room number
- Cost, date put into use, and useful life
- Model and serial number
- Vendor name and address
- Warranty provisions and the period covered
- Property tag number

Anything that is portable and can be ridden upon by a person is a vehicle. A car, truck, trailer, motorcycle, boat, airplane, lift truck, snowmobile, riding lawnmower, construction equipment and so forth are all vehicles. Information about each vehicle should be maintained on a separate property accounting record, which should contain the following information:

- General description
- Serial or vehicle identification number
- Purpose of equipment
- Location where stored
- Cost
- Vendor name and address
- Warranty provisions and period covered
- Property tag number
- Person assigned to

Leasehold improvements are additions to leased land and buildings. Examples are storage cabinets, shelves, counters, refrigeration units, drapes, air conditioning, parking lots, roads, signs, fences and gates, or anything else that will be abandoned when the lease contract expires. The amortization of these improvements is recorded over the time period of the lease agreement, unless the lease term exceeds the useful life—in this case, calculate depreciation only through the useful life of the asset. Information about each leasehold improvement should be maintained on a separate property accounting record, which should contain the following information:

- General description
- Serial number (if available)
- Purpose of improvement
- Location where stored
- Cost, date put into use, and useful life
- Vendor name and address
- Warranty provisions and period covered

- Property tag number
- Lease record number

Maintain a separate record for each lease entered into by the organization. All leasehold improvements recorded elsewhere are tied to these lease records by the item number of the lease. If the company is required to have annual financial statements prepared by a certified public accountant, the lease information is needed for a footnote disclosure in the financial statements, itemizing the future lease payments for each of the following five years. Information about each lease should be maintained on a separate property accounting record, which should contain the following information:

- Description of the leased property
- Serial number (if available)
- Location of property
- Name and address of lessor
- Beginning and ending dates of the lease
- Lease amount
- Required maintenance by the lessee
- Lease renewal provisions
- Termination provisions

7 INVESTMENTS

DEFINITIONS OF TERMS

Available for sale. The classification of debt securities not intended to be "trading" or "held-to-maturity" investments, or of equity investments not intended to be "trading" investments.

Cost method. The recognition of income by an investor in that entity's investment in another entity, solely based on dividends received from the investee.

Equity method. The recognition of an investor's share of the profits and losses reported by an investee, based on the ownership percentage of the investor.

Goodwill. The total amount paid for an investment in an investee, less that portion of the investment clearly assigned to specific assets, minus liabilities assumed. Essentially the premium paid for the investee.

Held to maturity. Debt securities purchased with the express intention and ability to hold until the maturity date.

Marketable security. An easily traded investment, such as Treasury bills, that is easily convertible into cash. It is recorded as a current asset.

Significant influence. An investor's ability to alter the operating or financial policies of an investee.

Trading securities. Either debt or equity securities bought with the express intention of being sold in the short term for a profit.

CONCEPTS AND EXAMPLES[1]

Accounting for Marketable Equity Securities

Marketable securities are investments that can be easily liquidated through an organized exchange, such as the New York Stock Exchange. If a company also holds securities that are intended for the control of another entity, then these securities should be segregated as a long-term investment. Marketable securities must be grouped into one of the following three categories at the time of purchase and re-evaluated periodically to see if they still belong in the designated categories:

- **Available for sale.** This category includes both debt and equity securities. It contains those securities that do not readily fall into either of the following two categories. It can include investments in other companies that comprise less than 20% of total ownership. These securities are reported on the balance sheet at their fair value, while unrealized gains and losses are charged to an equity account and reported in other comprehensive income in the current period. The balance in the equity account is eliminated only upon sale of the underlying securities. If a permanent reduction in the value of an individual security occurs, the unrealized loss is charged against earnings, resulting in a new and lower cost basis in the remaining investment. Any subsequent increase in the value of such an investment above the new cost basis cannot be formally recognized in earnings until the related security is sold, and so the interim gains will be temporarily "parked" in the unrealized gains account in the equity section of the balance sheet.

  All interest, realized gains or losses, and debt amortization are recognized within the continuing operations section of the income statement. The listing of these securities on the balance sheet under either current or long-term assets is dependent on their ability to be liquidated in the short term and to be available for disposition within that time frame, unencumbered by any obligations.

- **Held to maturity.** This category includes only debt securities for which the company has both the intent and ability to hold them until their time of maturity. Their amortized cost is recorded on the balance sheet. These securities are likely to be listed on the balance sheet as long-term assets.

  If marketable securities are shifted into the held-to-maturity category from debt securities in the available-for-sale category, their unrealized holding gain or loss should continue to be stored in the equity section, while being gradually amortized down to zero over the remaining life of each security.

- **Trading securities.** This category includes both debt and equity securities that the company intends to sell in the short term for a profit. It can include investments in other companies comprising less than 20% of total ownership. They are recorded on the balance sheet at their fair value. This type of marketable security is always positioned in the balance sheet as a current asset.

---

[1] *Much of the information in this section is adapted with permission from Chapter 14 of Bragg,* **Ultimate Accountants' Reference** *(John Wiley & Sons, Inc., Hoboken, NJ, 2006).*

No matter how an investment is categorized, a material decline in its fair value subsequent to the balance sheet date but prior to the release of the financial statements should be disclosed. Further, clear evidence of permanent impairment in the value of available-for-sale securities prior to the release date of the financial statements is grounds for restatement to recognize permanent impairment of the investment.

Examples of available-for-sale transactions

The Arabian Knights Security Company has purchased $100,000 of equity securities, which it does not intend to sell in the short term for profit, and therefore designates as available for sale. Its initial entry to record the transaction is as follows:

Investments—available-for-sale	100,000	
Cash		100,000

After a month, the fair market value of the securities drops by $15,000, but management considers the loss to be a temporary decline, and so does not record a loss in current earnings. However, it must still alter the value of the investment on the balance sheet to show its fair value, and report the loss in Other Comprehensive Income, which requires the following entry:

Unrealized loss on security investment (reported in other comprehensive income)	15,000	
Investments—available-for-sale		15,000

Management then obtains additional information indicating that the loss is likely to be a permanent one, so it then recognizes the loss with the following entry:

Loss on equity securities	15,000	
Unrealized loss on security investment (reported in other comprehensive income)		15,000

Another month passes by and the fair value of the investment rises by $3,500. Since this gain exceeds the value of the newly written-down investment, management cannot recognize it, even though the new value of the investment would still be less than its original amount. Instead, the following entry is used to adjust the investment value on the balance sheet:

Investments—available-for-sale	3,500	
Unrealized gain on security investment (recorded in other comprehensive income)		3,500

Examples of trading transactions

The Arabian Knights Security Company purchases $50,000 of equity securities that it intends to trade for a profit in the short term. Given its intentions, these securities are added to the corporate portfolio of trading securities with the following entry:

Investments—held-for-trading	50,000	
Cash		50,000

After two months, the fair value of these trading securities declines by $3,500. The company recognizes the change in current earnings with the following entry:

Loss on security investment	3,500	
Investments—held-for-trading		3,500

Later in the year, the fair value of the securities experiences a sudden surge, resulting in a value increase of $5,750. The company records the change with the following entry:

Investments—held-for-trading	5,750	
Gain on security investments		5,750

Transfers between Available-for-Sale and Trading Investments

An investment designated as a trading security can be shifted into the available-for-sale portfolio of investments with no recognition of a gain or loss on the value of the investment, since this type of investment should have been adjusted to its fair value in each reporting period already. If a gain or loss has arisen since the last adjustment to fair value, this amount should be recognized at the time of the designation change.

If an investment designated as an available-for-sale security is shifted into the trading portfolio of investments, any gain or loss required to immediately adjust its value to fair value should be made at once. This entry should include an adjustment from any prior write-down in value that may have occurred when securities were classified as available-for-sale.

Example of transfer from the trading portfolio to the available-for-sale portfolio

The Arabian Knights Security Company owns $17,500 of equity securities that it had originally intended to sell for a profit in the short term, and so had classified the investment in its trading portfolio. Its intent has now changed, and it wishes to hold the securities for a considerably longer period, so it must shift the securities into the available-for-sale account. It had marked the securities to market one month previously, but now the securities have lost $350 of value. The company records the following entry to reclassify the security and recognize the additional loss:

Investments—available-for-sale	17,150	
Loss on equity securities	350	
Investments—held-for-trading		17,500

Example of transfer from the available-for-sale portfolio to the trading portfolio

The Arabian Knights Security Company finds that it must liquidate $250,000 of its available-for-sale portfolio in the short term. This investment had previously been marked down to $250,000 from an initial investment value of $275,000, and its value has since risen by $12,000. The incremental gain must now be recognized in current income. The entry is as follows:

Investments—held-for-trading	262,000	
Investments—available-for-sale		250,000
Gain on security investments		12,000

Accounting for Investments in Debt Securities

A debt security can be classified either as held-for-trading or available-for-sale (as previously defined for equity securities), or as held-to-maturity. The held-to-maturity portfolio is intended for any debt securities for which a company has the intent and ability to retain the security for its full term until maturity is reached. An investment held in the held-to-maturity portfolio is recorded at its historical cost, which is not changed at any time during the holding period, unless it is shifted into a different investment portfolio. The only exceptions to this rule are (1) the periodic amortization of any discount or premium from the face value of a debt instrument, depending on the initial purchase price, and (2) clear evidence of a permanent reduction in the value of the investment.

Examples of held-to-maturity transactions

The Arabian Knights Security Company purchases $82,000 of debt securities at face value. The company has both the intent and ability to hold the securities to maturity. Given its intentions, these securities are added to the corporate portfolio of held-to-maturity securities with the following entry:

Investment in debt services—held-to-maturity	82,000	
Cash		82,000

The fair value of the investment subsequently declines by $11,000. There is no entry to be made, since the investment is recorded at its historical cost. However, the company receives additional information that the debt issuer has filed for bankruptcy and intends to repay debt holders at fifty cents on the dollar. Since management considers this to be a permanent reduction, a charge of $41,000 is recorded in current income with the following entry:

Loss on debt investments	41,000	
Investment in debt securities—held-to-maturity		41,000

The company subsequently learns that the debt issuer is instead able to pay 75 cents on the dollar. This increase in value of $20,500 is not recorded in a journal entry, since it is a recovery of value, but is instead recorded in a footnote accompanying the financial statements.

Transfers of Debt Securities among Portfolios

The accounting for transfers between debt securities portfolios varies based on the portfolio from which the accounts are being shifted, with the basic principle being that transfers are recorded at the fair market value of the security on the date of the transfer. The treatment of gains or losses on all possible transfers is noted in Exhibit 7-1.

Exhibit 7-1: Accounting Treatment of Debt Transfers between Portfolios

"From" portfolio	*"To" portfolio*	*Accounting treatment*
Trading	Available-for-sale	No entry (assumes gains and losses have already been recorded)
Trading	Held-to-maturity	No entry (assumes gains and losses have already been recorded)
Available-for-sale	Trading	Shift any previously recorded gain or loss shown in Other Comprehensive Income to operating income.
Available-for-sale	Held-to-maturity	Amortize to income over the remaining period to debt maturity any previously recorded gain or loss shown in Other Comprehensive Income, using the effective interest method.
Held-to-maturity	Trading	Record the unrealized gain or loss in operating income.
Held-to-maturity	Available-for-sale	Record the unrealized gain or loss in the Other Comprehensive Income section of the income statement.

The offsetting entry for any gain or loss reported in the Other Comprehensive Income section of the income statement goes to a contra account, which is used to offset the investment account on the balance sheet, thereby revealing the extent of changes in the trading securities from their purchased cost.

Recognition of Deferred Tax Effects on Changes in Investment Valuations

A deferred tax benefit or tax liability should be recognized alongside the recognition of any change in the fair value of an investment listed in either a trading or available-for-sale portfolio or of a permanent decline in the value of a debt security being held to maturity. The tax impact varies by investment type and is noted as follows:

- **Gains or losses on the trading portfolio.** The deferred tax effect is recognized in the income statement. If there is a loss in value, one should debit the Deferred Tax Benefit account and credit the Provision for Income Taxes account. If there is a gain in value, one should debit the Provision for Income Taxes account and credit the Deferred Tax Liability account.
- **Gains or losses on the available-for-sale portfolio.** The same treatment noted for gains or losses on the trading portfolio, except that taxes are noted in the Other Comprehensive Income section of the income statement.
- **Gains or losses on the held-to-maturity portfolio.** There is no tax recognition if changes in value are considered to be temporary in nature. If there is a permanent reduction in value, the treatment is identical to the treatment of losses in the trading portfolio, as just noted.

The Equity Method of Investment Accounting

There are three ways to account for an investment. The first is to report the investment at its fair value, the second is to report it under the "equity method," and the third is to fully consolidate the results of the investee in the investing company's financial statements. The rules under which each of these methods is applied are noted in Exhibit 7-2.

Exhibit 7-2: Accounting Treatment of Significant Equity Investments

Investment method	Proportion of ownership	Notes
Fair Value	Less than 20% ownership or no significant influence over investee	Record gains or losses based on fair market value of shares held
Equity Method	20% to 50% ownership and significant influence over the investee	Record proportionate share of investee earnings, less dividends received
Consolidation	50%+ ownership of the investee	Fully consolidate results of the investor and investee

The presence of "significant influence" over an investee is assumed if the investor owns at least 20% of its common stock. However, this is not the case if there is clear evidence of not having influence, such as being unable to obtain financial information from the investee, not being able to place a representative on its Board of Directors, clear opposition to the investor by the investee, loss of voting rights, or proof of a majority voting block that does not include the investor.

Income taxes are recognized only when dividends are received from an investee or the investment is liquidated. Nonetheless, deferred income taxes are recognized when a company records its share of investee income, and are then shifted from the deferred income tax account to income taxes payable when dividends are received. A key issue is the assumed income tax rate used, since it can vary based on an assumption of investment liquidation via dividends (which is at a lower tax rate) or sale of the investment (which is at a higher tax rate).

As just noted in the exhibit, the equity method of accounting requires one to record the investor's proportionate share of investee earnings, less any dividends received. However, what if the investee records such a large loss that the investor's share of the loss results in a negative investment? When this happens, the correct treatment is to limit the investment to zero and ignore subsequent losses. One should resume use of the equity method only if subsequent investee earnings completely offset the losses that had previously been ignored. The main exception to this rule is when the investor has committed to fund investee operations or indemnify other creditors or investors for losses incurred.

Example of the equity method of accounting

The Arabian Knights Security Company purchases 35% of the common stock of the Night Patrollers Security Company for $500,000. At the end of a year, Night Patrollers has earned $80,000 and issued $20,000 in dividends. Under the equity method, Arabian Knights reports a gain in its investment of $28,000 (35% investment × $80,000 in earnings), less dividends of $7,000 (35% investment × $20,000 in dividends) for a total investment change of $21,000. The two entries required to record these changes follow:

Investment in Night Patrollers	28,000	
Equity in Night Patrollers		28,000
Cash	7,000	
Investment in Night Patrollers		7,000

In addition, Arabian Knights' controller assumes that the investment will eventually be sold, which requires a full corporate tax rate of 34%. Accordingly, the following entry records a deferred income tax on the $28,000 share of Night Patrollers income, while the second entry records the shifting of a portion of this deferred tax to income taxes payable to reflect the company's short-term tax liability for the dividends received (assuming a 34% tax rate for dividend income):

Income tax expense	9,520	
Deferred taxes		9,520
Deferred taxes	2,380	
Taxes payable		2,380

It is quite common for the investor to pay a premium over the book value of the investee's common stock. When this happens under the equity method, one should informally (i.e., without the use of journal entries) assign the difference in value to other assets and liabilities of the investee to the extent that the fair value of those assets differs from their net book value. Any changes in these assumed assets should be amortized, resulting in a periodic journal entry to reduce the value of the investor's recorded investment.

Example of the amortization of assigned asset valuations

To continue with the last example, 35% of the book value of Night Patrollers Security Company was $350,000, as compared to the $500,000 paid by Arabian for 35% of Night Patrollers. Arabian's controller must assign this differential to the excess fair value of any Night Patrollers assets or liabilities over their book value. The only undervalued Night Patrollers asset category is its fixed assets, to which the controller can assign $30,000. The remaining unassigned $120,000 is designated as goodwill. Given the nature of the underlying assets, the $30,000 assigned to fixed assets should be amortized over five years, resulting in a monthly amortization charge of $500. The monthly journal entry follows:

Equity in Night Patrollers income	500	
Investment in Night Patrollers		500

Any remaining unassigned excess value is considered to be goodwill, and is subject to annual impairment testing that may result in an additional reduction in the recorded level of investment. An impairment test requires a periodic comparison of the fair value of the investment to the current book value of the investment as recorded by the investor. If the fair value is less than the recorded book value, goodwill is reduced until the recorded investment value matches the new fair value. If the amount of the reduction is greater than the informal goodwill associated with the transaction, then the excess is used to proportionally reduce any amounts previously assigned to the investee's assets. In effect, a large enough reduction in the fair value of its investment will result in an immediate write-down of the recorded investment, rather than a gradual reduction due to amortization.

Example of an investment impairment

To continue with the last example, Night Patrollers loses several large security contracts, resulting in a significant reduction in the value of the business. Arabian's controller estimates this loss in value to be $130,000, which requires her to eliminate the entire $120,000 goodwill portion of the initial investment, as well as $10,000 that had been assigned to the fixed assets category. This later reduction results in a decrease in the monthly amortization charge of $166.66 ($10,000 / 60 months).

If a company **reduces** its investment in an investee to the point where its investment comprises less than 20% of the investee's common stock, it should discontinue use of the equity method of accounting and instead record the investment at its fair value, most likely tracking it as part of the company's available-for-sale portfolio. When the transition occurs from the equity method to the fair value method, no retroactive adjustment in the investment account is required—the investor simply begins using the ending investment balance it had derived under the equity method.

If a company **increases** its investment in an investee to the 20% to 50% range from a lesser figure, it must convert to the equity method of accounting on a retroactive basis. This means the investor must go back to the initial investment date and recalculate its investment using the equity method of accounting. The offset to any resulting adjustment in the investment account must then be charged to the Retained Earnings account as a prior-period adjustment. This also requires restatement of prior financial statements in which the fair value method was used to record this investment.

DECISION TREES

Accounting for Gains or Losses on Securities

The flowchart shown in Exhibit 7-3 shows the decision tree for how gains and losses are handled for different types of securities portfolios. The decision flow begins in the upper left corner. For example, if a security is designated as available-for-sale and there is a change in its fair value, then the decision tree moves to the right, asking if there is a permanent value impairment. If so, the proper treatment matches that of a loss for a held-for-trading security; if not, the proper treatment is listed as being reported in the Other Comprehensive Income section of the income statement.

Exhibit 7-3: Accounting for Gains or Losses on Securities

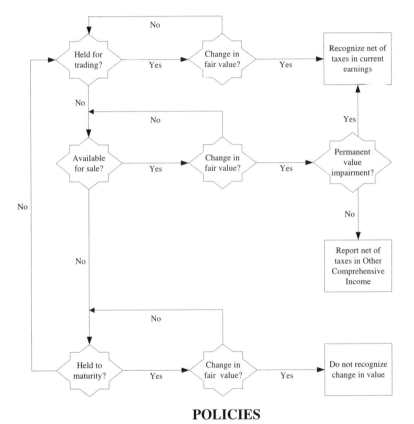

POLICIES

Funds Investment Policies

- **At least $____ shall be invested in overnight investments and in negotiable marketable obligations of major US issuers.** This policy forces the treasury staff to attain a minimum level of liquidity. The fixed dollar amount used in the policy should be regularly reviewed to match upcoming budgeted working capital requirements.

- **No more than ____% of the total portfolio shall be invested in time deposits or other investments with a lack of liquidity.** This policy is similar to the preceding one, except that it ignores a fixed liquidity requirement, focusing instead on a maximum proportion of the total portfolio that must be retained for short-term requirements. This policy tends to require less periodic updating.
- **The average maturity of the investment portfolio shall be limited to ____ years.** This policy is designed to keep a company from investing in excessively long maturities. The policy can be broken down into more specific maturity limitations for different types of investments, such as five years for any US government obligations, one year for bank certificates of deposit, and 270 days for commercial paper.
- **Investments in foreign commercial paper shall be limited to those unconditionally guaranteed by a prime US issuer and fully hedged.** This policy is designed to lower the risk of default on investments in securities issued by foreign entities.
- **Investments in commercial paper shall be limited to those of companies having long-term senior debt ratings of Aa or better.** This policy is designed to limit the risk of default on commercial paper investments by focusing investments on only the highest-grade commercial paper.
- **Investments in bank certificates of deposit shall be limited to those banks with capital accounts exceeding $1 billion.** This policy is designed to limit the risk of default on certificates of deposit, on the assumption that large capital accounts equate to minimal risk of bank failure.
- **Investments shall be made only in investments backed by US government debt obligations.** This policy can be used in place of the preceding ones that specify allowable investments in nongovernment investments. This policy tends to be used by highly risk-averse companies who place less emphasis on the return generated from their investments.

Accounting for Marketable Equity Securities

- **All securities purchases shall be designated as trading securities at the time of purchase.** This policy is intended to avoid the designation of an investment as "available for sale," which would allow management to avoid recording short-term changes in the fair value of the investment in reported earnings. The policy removes the ability of management to alter financial results by shifting the designation of an investment.
- **All losses on securities designated as available-for-sale shall be considered permanent.** Accounting rules allow one to avoid recognizing losses on available-for-sale securities by assuming that the losses are temporary. By using this policy to require an immediate write-down on all losses, management no longer has the ability to manipulate earnings by making assumptions that losses are temporary in nature.

- **Available-for-sale securities shall not be sold solely to recognize related gains in their fair market value.** Accounting rules do not allow ongoing recognition of gains in the value of available-for-sale securities in earnings until they have been sold, so there is a natural temptation to manage earnings by timing their sale. This policy is designed to set an ethical standard for management to prevent such actions from taking place. In reality, this is a difficult policy to enforce, since management can find reasonable excuses for selling securities when their unrecognized gains are needed for bookkeeping purposes.

Transfers between Investment Portfolios

- **The Board of Directors shall be notified of the reasons for any significant shift in the designation of securities between the held-to-maturity, available-for-sale, and trading portfolios, and the approximate impact on different categories of income.** This policy is designed to require management to justify its actions in shifting securities between portfolios, which is likely to reduce the amount of shifting, while also keeping the Board informed of any likely movements of gains or losses between the operating income and Other Comprehensive Income parts of the income statement.

Accounting for Investments in Debt Securities

- **The unrecognized amount of gains or losses on held-to-maturity securities shall be regularly reported to the Board of Directors.** Management may designate poorly performing debt securities as held-to-maturity, in which case any changes in their fair value will not be recognized. This policy is designed to reveal any gains or losses that would be recognized if these securities were to have any other portfolio designation, so the Board is aware of any "hanging" gains or losses.
- **Debt securities shall not be classified as held-to-maturity unless sufficient investments are already on hand to cover all budgeted short-term cash requirements.** GAAP already requires that debt securities not be classified as held-to-maturity if a company does not have the ability to hold the securities for the required time period—this policy is more specific in stating that all anticipated cash flows be fully covered by other investments before any debt securities receive the held-to-maturity classification. The policy makes it more likely that a company will not be forced to prematurely liquidate its held-to-maturity debt portfolio.

Transfers of Debt Securities among Portfolios

- **The Board of Directors must authorize all shifts in investment designation out of the held-to-maturity portfolio.** There are specific accounting instances where the transfer of securities out of the held-to-maturity portfolio will preclude a company's subsequent use of the held-to-maturity portfolio. Accordingly, the Board of Directors should be notified of the reasons for such a designation and give its formal approval before the designation change can be made.

The Equity Method of Accounting for Investments

- **The CFO shall regularly review with the Board of Directors the existing assumptions of significant influence over all entities of whose voting common stock the company owns between 20% and 50%.** Evidence of significant influence requires a company to use the equity method in reporting the financial results of an investee, whereas a lack of influence would require it to record the investment in an investment portfolio category. Regularly reviewing the level of influence over an investee will ensure that the appropriate accounting treatment is used.
- **The tax rate used to recognize taxes under equity method gains shall be the higher of the rates paid on dividend income or sale of the investment.** The income tax rate used to record equity method transactions can be the tax rate either on dividends or from sale of the investment, depending on the investor's intent to eventually dispose of the method. Always using the higher tax rate goes against GAAP to some extent, but keeps the accounting staff from inflating income by using the more conservative tax rate.

PROCEDURES

Funds Investment Procedure

Use the following procedure to invest excess funds in accordance with the corporate investment policy:

1. Review the short-term cash forecast with the treasury staff and determine the amount of funds that are not immediately needed for operations.
2. Using the corporate investment policy and the size of the investable cash balance as guidelines, select the appropriate investment vehicle. For short-term cash investments, select the most liquid investments on the investing policy.
3. Extract a copy of the investment form from the forms cabinet and fill it out, entering the investment initiation date, the type of investment, the broker or bank used to fulfill the order, and the amount of the investment.
4. Have an authorized signer sign the investment form.
5. Fax this form to the company's third-party broker or bank for fulfillment.
6. Call the firm to verify receipt of the fax.
7. Send a copy of the investment form to the general ledger accountant for proper recording in the general ledger.
8. File the original completed investment form, sequenced by date.

Transfers between the Available-for-Sale and Trading Portfolios

Use this procedure not only to specify the correct accounting transactions for a shift between the available-for-sale and trading portfolios, but also to ensure that justification for the change has been documented and approved.

1. Document the reason for the shift between portfolios, and summarize the total impact of gains or losses to be recognized in current income as a result of the change, including the tax impact.
2. If the impact on current earnings is significant, notify the Board of Directors of the prospective change, if required by company policy.
3. Create a journal entry to shift funds between the available-for-sale and trading portfolios, including the recognition of any gains or losses required to bring the recorded value of the securities to their fair market value as of the transaction date.
4. Send the journal entry, documentation of the shift in portfolios, and documentation of Board notification to the general ledger accountant, with instructions to log the journal entry into the general ledger and store the related documentation in the journal entry binder.

The Equity Method of Accounting for Investments

Use this procedure to record an investment under the equity method of accounting.

1. Determine the proper type of accounting methodology to use. If the cumulative investment in the investee is less than 20%, or the investment is less than 50% and there is no significant control over the investee, record the transaction at its fair value. If the cumulative investment in the investment is between 20% and 50% and there is significant control over the investee, use the equity method of accounting. If the investment exceeds 50% of the investee, use consolidated reporting. The remainder of this procedure assumes that the equity method will be used.
2. Multiply the investor's cumulative proportion of ownership in the investee by the investee's book value, and then subtract this amount from the amount paid by the investor.
3. On an electronic spreadsheet, itemize the major categories of investee assets and liabilities, and record in adjacent columns the book and fair values of each category.
4. Create a column in the spreadsheet that calculates the difference between the book and fair values of each asset category.
5. Allocate any difference calculated in step 2 to the investor's share of any excess in fair value over book, as calculated in step 4.
6. If there remains any unallocated excess purchase price after the allocation in step 5 is completed, record the excess as goodwill.
7. Note in another column in the spreadsheet a reasonable amortization period for each asset or liability category to which an allocation was made.
8. Calculate the current period amortization for each asset or liability category to which an allocation was made.
9. Record the initial investment transaction as a debit to Investment in [company name] account and a credit to the Cash account.

10. Record an amortization entry for the current period based on the calculation in step 8, using a debit to the Equity in [company name] account and a credit to the Investment in [company name] account.
11. Send the proposed transaction and all supporting documentation to the company auditors, with a request to review the transaction for errors and conformance with GAAP.
12. Upon auditor approval, send the journal entry to the general ledger accountant for entry in the general ledger.
13. The general ledger accountant attaches all backup materials related to the transaction to the journal entry and stores the entire packet in the journal entry file.

CONTROLS

Transfers between Available-for-Sale and Trading Investments

- **Require Board approval of substantial changes in investment account designations.** Management can modify the amount of reported gains or losses on investments by shifting investment designations from the "available-for-sale" investment portfolio to the "trading" portfolio. If the gain or loss on such a change in designation is significant, the Board of Directors should be notified in advance of the reason for the change and its impact on the level of earnings.

Transfers of Debt Securities among Portfolios

- **Impose investment limits.** When investing its excess funds, a company should have a policy that requires it to invest only certain amounts in particular investment categories or vehicles. For example, only the first $100,000 of funds are insured through a bank account, so excess funding beyond this amount can be shifted elsewhere. As another example, the Board of Directors may feel that there is too much risk in junk bond investments, and so will place a general prohibition on this type of investment. These sorts of policies can be programmed into a treasury workstation, so that the system will automatically flag investments that fall outside a company's preset investment parameters.
- **Require authorizations to shift funds among accounts.** A person who is attempting to fraudulently shift funds out of a company's accounts must have approval authorization on file with one of the company's investment banks to transfer money out to a noncompany account. This type of authorization can be strictly controlled through signatory agreements with the banks. It is also possible to impose strict controls over the transfer of funds **between** company accounts, since a fraudulent person may uncover a loophole in the control system whereby a particular bank has not been warned **not** to allow fund transfers outside of a preset range of company accounts, and then shift all funds to that account and thence to an outside account.

The Equity Method of Accounting for Investments

- **Verify consistent use of the same income tax rate for equity method transactions.** GAAP allows the assumed use of tax rates for either dividend payments or capital gains to record gains from equity method transactions. This can result in improperly switching between different tax rates on successive equity method transactions in order to meet short-term profitability goals. A simple control over this problem is to periodically review the calculation of journal entries in the income tax expense account to see if tax rate usage has been consistent.

- **Require approval of the assumed tax rate used for equity method transactions.** As noted in the preceding control, GAAP allows one to use a range of possible tax rates for equity method transactions, which can result in improperly altering tax rates to meet profitability goals. To avoid this problem, the general ledger accountant should be required to obtain management approval of any journal entries involving the income tax expense account.

- **Require auditor review and approval of excess purchase price allocations to investee assets.** If the amount of an investment exceeds the investee's book value, GAAP requires that as much of the excess investment as possible be allocated to any investee assets for which the fair value exceeds the book value. When this occurs, one must also amortize the incremental value assigned, which will reduce the recorded amount of the investment. Thus, the investor will have an incentive to allocate the minimum amount to assets, if not entirely forgo the allocation process. By having independent auditors review and approve informal asset allocations, as well as the related amortization calculations, one can ensure that a reasonable valuation and resulting amortization of asset values will occur.

- **Add to the monthly closing schedule the amortization of purchase price allocations to investee assets.** If the purchase price of an investment exceeds the book value of the investee and the equity method of accounting is being used, an informal amortization calculation is usually kept that is not integrated into the usual asset depreciation schedule. Because it is maintained separately, there is a strong possibility that this additional amortization will be forgotten and not periodically included in the financial statements. To avoid the problem, the amortization entry should be noted in the formal closing procedure. Also, the amortization should be set up as a recurring journal entry in the general ledger, though inclusion in the procedure is still necessary to ensure that the recurring amortization entry continues to be checked for accuracy.

- **Obtain independent verification of the fair value of investee land assets to which investor goodwill has been allocated.** GAAP requires that the maximum possible amount of excess investment over an investee's book value be assigned to identifiable assets, which are then amortized. By assigning an excessive amount of the investment to land assets, which are not amortized, a company can incorrectly retain a high reported level of investment. Requiring independent verification of the fair value of the land assets is an effective method for ensuring that the correct amount of amortization is entered in the general ledger each month. It is also useful to include in the month-end closing procedure a requirement to obtain a fair value estimate of any new allocation to investee land and compare it to the amount of excess investment informally assigned to the land asset group, thereby formalizing the process.

FORMS AND REPORTS

Investment Approval Form

The investment approval form is a critical document for controlling the types of investments made, as well as how they are designated in the accounting records. The form shown in Exhibit 7-4 contains four blocks that cover key investment information. The first block contains check-off boxes for the various types of approved investments, as noted in the corporate investments policy. The user enters additional information about each type of investment in the "Investment Description" field, followed by the amount to be invested and the maturity date (if any) of the investment. The next block contains check-off boxes for the investment designation to be used in the accounting records, while the third block contains fields for special permissions required for certain types of investments and investment designations. Finally, the fourth block reveals the proper document routing, and includes signature fields to indicate that each step in the process has been completed.

Exhibit 7-4: Investment Approval Form

```
                              INVESTMENT APPROVAL FORM

   Investment Type:
                                                                      Maturity
                                    Investment Description    Amount     Date

   [ ]  Bank Demand Deposit      _____   _____   _____

   [ ]  Certificate of Deposit   _____   _____   _____

   [ ]  US Treasury Bills        _____   _____   _____

   [ ]  Commercial Paper         _____   _____   _____

   [ ]  Other                    _____   _____   _____
   _____

   Investment Designation:

   [ ] Trading          [ ] Available-for-Sale       [ ] Held-to-Maturity
   _____

   Special Approvals:

   Held-to-Maturity Designation   _____   _____
                                  Chief Financial Officer     Date


   "Other" Investments            _____   _____
                                  Chief Financial Officer     Date
   _____

   Routings:

      Investment Approval  ——▶  Investment Transaction  ——▶  G/L Entry


   _____      _____    _____
     Treasurer Signature      Investment Clerk Signature    G/L Clerk Signature


   _____      _____    _____
          Date                         Date                      Date
```

Bond Ledger Sheet

A considerable amount of information must be retained and tracked for each bond in which a company invests, not only to ensure that profits and losses are properly calculated and recorded, but also to maintain a history of all transactions related to it. The Bond Ledger Sheet shown in Exhibit 7-5 is a good example of a computer report that should be printed for each bond purchased and sold. It lists all descriptive information in the header section, while noting individual transactions, such as premium amortization, bond purchase and sale, and interest payments in the detail section at the bottom of the report. The report is also useful for auditors, who will have all needed review information about a bond summarized onto one page.

Exhibit 7-5: Bond Ledger Sheet

Bond Name:_____Intergalactic Coal Mining Co._____

| Purchased | | | | | Nominal Rate___10%___ | | | | | | |
| Through____ABC Bond Sales_____ | | | | | Actual Rate____9.3%___ | | | | | | |

Description:
Numbers:_____B1676,B1677_____   Dated:_____1/1/2007_____
Denomination:____$5,000_____   When Due:_____12/31/2027_____
Where Payable:___Third Trust, Chicago___   Interest Payable:_6/30, 12/31_____
Trustee:_____Third Trust, Chicago___   Redeemable:____Yes_____

Date	Pieces	Memo	Price	Debit	Credit	Balance	Profit or Loss	Due Date	Interest Amount	Paid Date
4/1/05	2	ABC Bond	$107.5	$10,750		$10,750		6/60/07	$500	6/30/07
6/30/05		Premium			$50	$10,700		12/31/07	$500	12/31/07
12/31/05		Premium			$100	$10,600		6/30/08	$500	6/30/08
6/30/06		Premium			$100	$10,500	$100			
7/1/06	1	Denver National	$107.0		$5,200	$5,250				

*SOURCE: Reprinted with permission from p. 693 of Willson et al., **Controllership, 6th ed.** (John Wiley & Sons, Inc., Hoboken, NJ, 1999).*

Stock Ledger Sheet

As was the case for the Bond Ledger Sheet in Exhibit 7-5, information must also be retained for any stock investments. In the Stock Ledger Sheet shown in Exhibit 7-6, the details of all buy and sell transactions can be listed for each stock investment made. The report leaves separate blocks of columns for entries related to stock buys and sells, while showing stock balances on the far right side.

Exhibit 7-6: Stock Ledger Sheet

Stock Ledger Report											
Issued by:_____Intergalactic Coal Mining Co._____											
Class:_____Common_____				Par Value:_____$1.00_____							
Bought				Sold						Balance	
Date	No. of Shares	Price	Cost*	Date	No. of Shares	Price	Total Received*	Profit or Loss	No. of Shares	Average Price	Cost
1/30/2007	100	$30	$3,020						100	$30.20	$3,020
				9/30/2007	25	$36	$890	$135	75	$30.20	$2,265
10/3/2007	50	$35	$1,770						125	$32.28	$4,035
				11/15/2007	25	$38	$940	$133	100	$32.28	$3,228

* *Includes commission*

SOURCE: Reprinted with permission from p. 692 of Willson et al., **Controllership, 6th ed.** *(John Wiley & Sons, Inc., Hoboken, NJ, 1999).*

Report on Investment Position

An alternative to the level of detail shown in the Bond Ledger Sheet and Stock Ledger Sheet is a more summary-level report itemizing the investment, current market value, and return on investment for each investment made. An example is shown in Exhibit 7-7. This approach yields a quick view of a company's overall level of investment and the results thereof.

Exhibit 7-7: Report on Investment Position

Security	Number of shares	Market value	Purchase price	Rate of return	Total dividends Y-T-D
1. ABC Corporation	500	$37,000	$31,000	5.2%	$800
2. Atlas Construction	100	2,400	2,400	6.3	75
3. National Co.	1,000	30,000	31,000	6.5	1,000
4. USA Corporation	1,000	65,500	64,000	7.8	2,000
5. JPC Corporation	100	1,900	1,875	7.5	70
6. Security Co.	500	42,000	38,000	5.3	1,000
Total or average		$178,800	$168,275	6.5%	$4,945

SOURCE: Reprinted with permission from p. 695 of Willson et al., **Controllership, 6th ed.** *(John Wiley & Sons, Inc., Hoboken, NJ, 1999).*

Report on Amortization of Allocated Asset Valuation

If the equity method of accounting is being used for an investment, some portion of any excess amount of the investment price over the investee's book value must be informally allocated to the investee's assets and liabilities. Since the financial presentation of an investment under the equity method is only a single line item, these adjustments must be informally tracked outside the general ledger. An example of such a tracking spreadsheet is shown in Exhibit 7-8, which itemizes the amount of the excess purchase price allocated, the amortization period to be used, and the amortization calculation for each year.

Exhibit 7-8: Report on Amortization of Allocated Asset Valuation

Asset type	Investment allocation	Amortization period	2007	2008	2009
Receivables	$ 20,000	1 year	20,000	0	0
Fixed assets	$ 82,000	5 years	$16,400	$16,400	$16,400
Intangibles	$150,000	10 years	15,000	15,000	15,000
Totals	$252,000		$51,400	$31,400	$31,400

FOOTNOTES

Disclosure of Cash Deposits in Excess of FDIC Insurance Limits

If a company concentrates its cash holdings in accounts exceeding the FDIC insurance limit of $100,000, it should disclose the amount exceeding the limit. An example follows:

> For cash management purposes, the company concentrates its cash holdings in a single account at the Third National Bank of Colorado Springs. The balance in this account may exceed the limit of $100,000 insured by the Federal Deposit Insurance Corporation in case of bank failure. At December 31, 2005, the company had $829,000 in excess of the insurance limit at this bank.

Disclosure of Change in Reported Method of Investment

If a company changes from the cost method to the equity method of accounting or vice versa, a footnote should disclose the change in the level of investment that required the change in method. It should also note the general accounting treatment required by each method, as well as the impact of the change on net income and any change in retained earnings resulting from the retroactive application of the new method. An example follows:

> The company increased its investment in the Alabama Boutiques Company (ABC) in May 2007 from 18% to 35%. Consequently, the company changed from the cost method of accounting for this investment to the equity method. Instead of recording its investment at cost and treating dividends as income, as was the case under the cost method, the company now records its proportionate share of all ABC earnings. The change reduced the company's earnings in 2007 by $109,000, while retained earnings as of the beginning of 2007 were adjusted downward by $128,000 to reflect the retroactive application of the equity method to this investment.

Disclosure of Investments

If a company holds any investments, the accountant must disclose the existence of any unrealized valuation accounts in the equity section of the balance sheet, as well as any realized gains or losses that have been recognized through the income statement. The classification of any material investments should also be noted (i.e., as available-for-sale or held-to-maturity).

If investments are accounted for under the equity method, then the name of the entity in which the investment is made should be noted, as well as the company's percentage of ownership, the total value based on the market price of the shares held, and the total amount of any unrealized appreciation or depreciation, with a discussion of how these amounts are amortized. The amount of any goodwill associated with the investment should be noted, as well as the method and specifications of the related amortization. If this method of accounting is used for an investment in which the company's share of investee ownership is less than 20%, then the reason should be noted; similarly, if the method is not used in cases where the percentage of ownership is greater than 20%, then the reasoning should also be discussed. Finally, the accountant should reveal the existence of any contingent issuances of stock by the investee that could result in a material change in the company's share of the investee's reported earnings. The first example gives a general overview of a company's security classification policies. The second entry reveals the breakdown of security types within its available-for-sale portfolio. The third entry describes gains and losses resulting from both the sale of securities and transfers between security portfolios.

1. The company classifies its investments when purchased and reviews their status at the end of each reporting period. The company classifies those marketable securities bought and intended for sale in the short term as Trading Securities, and records them at fair market value. The company classifies those debt securities it intends to hold to maturity, and has the intent to do so, as Held-to-Maturity Securities. All remaining securities are classified as Available-for-Sale and are recorded at fair market value. Unrealized gains and losses on Trading Securities are recognized in earnings, while they are included in comprehensive income for Available-for-Sale securities.

2. The company's available-for-sale portfolio is recorded at a total value of $1,150,000, of which $650,000 is equity securities and $500,000 is debt securities. The aggregate fair value of investments in this portfolio is $1,050,000, plus $100,000 of gross unrealized holding losses. The contractual maturity dates of $500,000 in debt securities fall into the following categories:

Maturity date range	*Debt reaching maturity*
Less than 1 year	$72,000
1–5 years	109,000
6–10 years	201,000
10+ years	118,000
Totals	$500,000

3. The company recognized $42,000 in gains from the sale of its securities during the period, which was calculated using the specific identification method. It also recognized a loss of $36,000 when it transferred securities from its available-for-sale portfolio to its trading portfolio, due to a change in the intent of management to sell the securities in the short term.

4. The company recorded $1,050,000 of debt securities classified as held-to-maturity. The following table summarizes the debt by type of issuer, and also notes the historical cost at which the debt is recorded on the balance sheet, its fair value, and the gross amount of unrealized gains and losses as of the balance sheet date:

Security issuer	*Historical cost*	*Fair value*	*Gross unrealized gain*	*Gross unrealized loss*
US Treasury debt	$ 450,000	$400,000	--	–$50,000
Mortgage-backed loans	275,000	285,000	$10,000	--
Corporate debt	325,000	310,000	--	–15,000
Totals	$1,050,000	$995,000	$10,000	–$65,000

The contractual maturities of the $1,050,000 in debt securities recorded in the held-to-maturity portfolio fall into the following date ranges:

Maturity date range	Debt reaching maturity
Less than 1 year	$275,000
1–5 years	409,000
6–10 years	348,000
10+ years	18,000
Totals	$1,050,000

Disclosure of Reduction in Market Value of Equity Investments

If management is of the opinion that a permanent decline in an equity investment has occurred, it should note the amount and date of a write-down in the investment valuation, as well as its presentation in the financial statements. An example follows:

> The company wrote down the value of several investments in equity instruments held in its available-for-sale portfolio during August 2007 by $193,000. The write-down was based on management's judgment that the equity instruments have experienced a permanent reduction in value. The write-down is itemized as a Loss on Investments in the operating section of the income statement.

Disclosure of Increase in Value of a Written-Down Held-to-Maturity Investment

If a company writes down the value of a held-to-maturity investment, it cannot record any subsequent recovery of the written-down value in the financial statements, but should do so in the footnotes. A disclosure should note the amount of the initial write-down and the amount of any subsequent value recovery. An example follows:

> The company wrote down the value of its $850,000 held-to-maturity investment in ABC Corporation in July 2007 by $288,000, based on ABC's bankruptcy filing in that month. Subsequently, ABC emerged from bankruptcy with the commitment to pay off its debt at 92% of face value and on the existing payment schedule. This resulted in an increase in the value of the company's ABC holdings of $220,000, which is not reflected in the attached financial statements.

Disclosure of Sale of Held-to-Maturity Investments

If a debt security classified as held-to-maturity is sold, a footnote should disclose the reason for the sale, as well as the amount of any gains or losses recognized and the amount of any as-yet unamortized premiums or discounts. An example follows:

> The company liquidated $2,800,000 of its held-to-maturity portfolio in order to pay for an acquisition. The transaction resulted in the recognition of a gain of $145,000. Also, a previously unamortized discount of $16,500 on the original debt purchase was written off as part of the transaction.

Disclosure of Changes in Investment Fair Value After Balance Sheet Date

If there is a significant change in the value of a company's investments after the balance sheet date but before the issuance of financial statements, the amount of the change should be described in a footnote. Two examples follow:

1. Subsequent to the balance sheet date, the fair value of the company's trading portfolio declined by $98,000, or 17% of the total portfolio value. In addition, the continuing decline of the fair value of the available-for-sale portfolio by an additional $43,000 after the balance sheet date confirms management's opinion that the decline in value of this portfolio has been permanently impaired. For this reason, management recognized a permanent loss of $109,000 in the value of the available-for-sale portfolio subsequent to the balance sheet date.

2. The fair value of the company's available-for-sale portfolio declined by $89,000 subsequent to the balance sheet date. Because the decline is caused by the expected bankruptcy of an investee, management now considers the investment to be permanently impaired. Fair value declines prior to the balance sheet date had not been considered permanently impaired, since the investee had not announced its bankruptcy intentions at that time. The company plans to record the losses in the available-for-sale account as permanent impairments in the next quarterly financial statements.

Disclosure of Shifts between Securities Accounts

If company management feels that the purpose of various investments has changed, it can shift the funds between its held-to-maturity and available-for-sale categories. If so, it should disclose in a footnote the reason for the change, the aggregate amount of securities shifted between accounts, and any related unrealized gain or loss, net of income taxes. An example follows:

> The company shifted approximately half of its securities recorded as held-to-maturity securities to the held-for-trading account during the last quarter of 2007. These securities had a net carrying value of $42 million at the time of the transfer, including unrealized losses net of income taxes of $2.5 million. Management authorized this change in order to reflect its increased need for additional cash in the short term as part of its general upgrade of production facilities.

Disclosure of Nonstandard Reported Method of Investment

If a company chooses to account for an investment in a nonstandard manner, such as using the equity method for a minor investment that would normally require the cost method, then it should disclose in a footnote that it exercises a sufficient degree of control over the investee's operating and financial activities to warrant the change (or vice versa for a larger investment recorded under the cost method). Two examples follow:

1. The company owns a 35% interest in the Arkansas Botox Clinics Company (ABC), which would normally be accounted for under the equity method of accounting. However, due to the considerable resistance of the ABC management to the company's investment, the company's management feels that it has minimal control over ABC's financial and operating activities, and so has chosen to record the in-

vestment under the cost method, whereby it records its investment at cost and only records income on the investment when dividends are received.

2. The company owns a 12% interest in the Alaskan Bear Company (ABC), which would normally be accounted for under the cost method of accounting. However, because the company's CEO is also president of ABC, the company's management feels that it has financial and operating control over ABC, and so has chosen to record the investment under the equity method, whereby it records its proportionate share of ABC's net earnings.

Disclosure of Reduced Equity Method Investment

If an investee has acted to increase its pool of issued shares, or there is a possibility of this occurring through the conversion of convertible securities, options, or warrants, then a footnote should disclose the aggregate amount of the potential reduction in a company's investment, as well as the potential impact on its reported share of the investee's earnings. An example follows:

> As of December 31, 2007, the company had a 39% ownership interest in General Navigation, Inc. (GNI). On that date, GNI issued 1,000,000 options to its employees, which can be exercised at any time at an exercise price of $14.00. If these options were to be converted to common stock, the company's ownership interest in GNI would have been diluted by 4%, resulting in a reduced ownership level of 35%. The potential ownership reduction would have reduced the company's reported share of GNI's 2007 earnings by $355,000.

Disclosure of Reduction in Equity Method Investment

If a company's investment in another entity is accounted for under the equity method, any losses recorded under that method should be adequately described in a footnote, which can include the company's percentage ownership in the entity, the amount of any loss by the entity that is recorded on the company's financial records, and the resulting impact on the company's recorded investment in the entity. The footnote should also disclose any requirement for the company to fund further entity losses, if any. If the reported investment has dropped to zero, the footnote should state that the equity method of accounting will not be used in order to avoid recording a negative investment. Three examples follow:

1. The company has a 35% interest in the Osaka Electric Company, which operates the power grid in the greater Osaka metropolitan area. This investment has been accounted for under the equity method of accounting since 2004. The company's financial results include a loss of $5.3 million, representing its share of Osaka's loss due to a write-down in goodwill on a failed subsidiary. The loss reduced the company's investment balance in Osaka to $4.0 million. The company has no obligation to fund any additional losses reported by Osaka.

2. The company has a 29% interest in the Bogota Power Company, which operates all hydro-electric facilities in Colombia. This investment has been accounted for under the equity method of accounting since 1992. The company's financial results include a loss of $22.8 million, representing its share of Bogota's loss due to reduced maintenance fees paid by the Colombian government. The loss reduced the company's investment balance in Bogota to zero. The company is contractually obligated to provide an additional $100 million in funding if Bogota's losses continue.

Given the current regulatory environment, management feels that the additional funds will be required, so a loss contingency of $100 million has been recognized on the balance sheet.

3. The company has a 40% investment in the Euclid Power Company. This investment has been accounted for under the equity method of accounting since 2005. The company's financial results include a loss of $21 million, representing its share of Euclid's losses. Recognition of this loss has resulted in a reported investment in Euclid of $0. Since the company cannot report a negative investment in Euclid under the equity method, it will not record its share of future Euclid losses until such time as future Euclid profits offset any subsequent losses that would otherwise have resulted in the reporting of a negative investment by the company.

JOURNAL ENTRIES

Accounting for Marketable Equity Securities

Initial investment designated as held-for-trading. To record an investment that management intends to trade for a profit in the short term.

Investment in equity securities—held-for-trading	xxx	
Cash		xxx

Initial investment designated as available-for-sale. To record an investment that management intends to hold as a long-term investment.

Investment in equity securities—available-for-sale	xxx	
Cash		xxx

Gain or loss on investment designated as held-for-trading. The first entry shows the immediate recognition in the current period of a loss due to a drop in the value of an investment designated as a trading security, as well as the related tax effect. The second entry shows the immediate recognition in the current period of a gain due to an increase in the value of an investment designated as a trading security, as well as the related tax effect.

Loss on equity security investment	xxx	
Deferred tax benefit	xxx	
Investment in equity securities—held-for-trading		xxx
Provision for income taxes		xxx
Investment in equity securities—held-for-trading	xxx	
Provision for income taxes	xxx	
Gain on equity security investments		xxx
Deferred tax liability		xxx

Gain or loss on investment designated as available-for-sale. The first entry shows an unrealized loss in the Other Comprehensive Income account on an investment designated as available-for-sale, as well as the related tax effect. The second entry shows an unrealized gain in the Other Comprehensive Income account on an investment designated as available-for-sale, as well as the related tax effect. In both cases, the tax effect is netted against the Investment account, rather than a Provision for Income Taxes account.

Unrealized loss on equity security investment	xxx	
Deferred tax benefit	xxx	
Investment in equity securities—available-for-sale		xxx
Investment in equity securities—available-for-sale	xxx	
Unrealized gain on equity security investment		xxx
Deferred tax liability		xxx

Impairment in value of equity investments classified as available-for-sale. When a drop in the value of an available-for-sale investment is judged to be other than temporary, the first journal entry should be used to recognize the drop in value. The entry includes the initial recognition of a related income tax benefit on the transaction. If one had previously recognized an income tax benefit associated with the loss but prior to its classification as a permanent decline in value, the offset to the deferred tax benefit would have been the investment account itself. If so, one should shift the offset from the investment account to an income tax liability account, as shown in the second journal entry.

Loss on equity securities	xxx	
Deferred tax benefit	xxx	
Unrealized loss on available-for-sale securities		xxx
Provision for income taxes		xxx
Loss on equity securities	xxx	
Unrealized loss on available-for-sale securities		xxx
Provision for income taxes		xxx

Transfers of Equity Securities between Available-for-Sale and Trading Portfolios

Shift investment designation from a trading security to an available-for-sale security. To shift the designation of a security currently recorded as a trading security to that of an available-for-sale security. The journal entry includes provisions for the recognition of any gains or losses on the fair value of the securities transferred since they were last marked to market.

Investments—available-for-sale	xxx	
Loss on equity securities	xxx	
Investments—held-for-trading		xxx
Gain on equity securities		xxx

Shift investment designation from an available-for-sale security to a trading security. To shift the designation of a security currently recorded as an available-for-sale security to that of a trading security, which requires the recognition of all unrealized gains or losses. The first entry assumes the recognition of unrealized losses on securities, while the second entry assumes the recognition of unrealized gains.

Investments—held-for-trading	xxx	
Loss on equity securities	xxx	
Investments—available-for-sale		xxx
Unrealized loss on available-for-sale securities		xxx

Investments—held-for-trading	xxx	
Unrealized gain on available-for-sale securities	xxx	
Investments—available-for-sale		xxx
Gain on equity securities		xxx

Accounting for Investments in Debt Securities

Initial investment designated as held-for-trading. To record an investment in debt securities that management intends to trade for a profit in the short term.

| Investment in debt securities—held-for-trading | xxx | |
| Cash | | xxx |

Initial investment designated as available-for-sale. To record an investment in debt securities that management intends to hold as a long-term investment.

| Investment in debt securities—available-for-sale | xxx | |
| Cash | | xxx |

Initial investment designated as held-to-maturity. To record an investment in debt securities that management has the intent and ability to hold to the debt maturity date.

| Investment in debt securities—held-to-maturity | xxx | |
| Cash | | xxx |

Gain or loss on debt investment designated as held-for-trading. The first journal entry records the immediate recognition in the current period of a loss due to a drop in the value of a debt investment designated as a trading security. The second journal entry records the immediate recognition of a gain due to an increase in the value of a debt investment designated as a trading security.

Loss on debt security investment	xxx	
Investment in debt securities—held-for-trading		xxx
Investment in debt securities—held-for-trading	xxx	
Gain on debt securities—held-for-trading		xxx

Gain or loss on debt investment designated as available-for-sale. The first journal entry records the immediate recognition in the current period of a loss due to a drop in the value of a debt investment designated as an available-for-sale security, which is reported in the Other Comprehensive Income section of the income statement. The second journal entry records the immediate recognition of a gain due to an increase in the value of a debt investment designated as an available-for-sale security.

Unrealized loss on debt security investment	xxx	
Deferred tax benefit	xxx	
Investment in debt securities—available-for-sale		xxx
Investment in debt securities—available-for-sale	xxx	
Unrealized gain on debt security investment		xxx
Deferred tax liability		xxx

Impairment in value of debt investments classified as held-to-maturity. To record a loss on a held-to-maturity debt investment, which occurs only when management considers a drop in value to be permanent in nature.

Loss on debt investment	xxx	
Investment in debt securities—held-to-maturity		xxx

Transfers of Debt Securities among Portfolios

Shift investment designation from the available-for-sale debt security portfolio to the trading debt security portfolio. Any debt security shifted from the available-for-sale portfolio to the trading portfolio must be recorded at its fair market value on the date of the transfer. The first journal entry records the recognition of a loss on the transfer date, while the second entry records a gain.

Investment in debt securities—held-for-trading	xxx	
Loss on debt securities	xxx	
Investment in debt securities—available-for-sale		xxx
Unrealized loss on debt securities—available-for-sale		xxx
Investment in debt securities—held-for-trading	xxx	
Unrealized gain on debt securities—available-for-sale	xxx	
Investment in debt securities—available-for-sale		xxx
Gain on holding debt securities		xxx

Shift investment designation from the available-for-sale debt security portfolio to the held-to-maturity debt security portfolio. Any debt security shifted from the available-for-sale portfolio to the held-to-maturity portfolio must be recorded at its fair market value on the date of the transfer. The first journal entry records the recognition of a loss on the transfer date, while the second entry records a gain.

Investment in debt securities—held-to-maturity	xxx	
Loss on debt securities	xxx	
Investment in debt securities—available-for-sale		xxx
Unrealized loss on debt securities—available-for-sale		xxx
Investments in debt securities—held-to-maturity	xxx	
Unrealized gain on debt securities—available-for-sale	xxx	
Investment in debt securities—available-for-sale		xxx
Gain on holding debt securities		xxx

Shift investment designation from the held-to-maturity debt security portfolio to the available-for-sale debt security portfolio. To record any accumulated gain or loss on a held-to-maturity debt security being transferred into the available-for-sale portfolio, which is recorded in Other Comprehensive Income. The first entry records a loss on the transaction, while the second entry records a gain.

Investment in debt securities—available-for-sale	xxx	
Unrealized loss on holding debt securities	xxx	
Investment in debt securities—held-to-maturity		xxx

Investment in debt securities—available-for-sale	xxx	
Investment in debt securities—held-to-maturity		xxx
Unrealized gain on holding debt securities		xxx

Shift investment designation from the held-to-maturity debt security portfolio to the held-for-trading debt security portfolio. To record any accumulated gain or loss on a held-to-maturity debt security being transferred into the held-for-trading portfolio, which is recorded in earnings. The first entry records a loss on the transaction, while the second entry records a gain. There are no unrealized gains or losses to recognize, since no gains or losses are recognized for held-to-maturity debt investments.

Investment in debt securities—held-for-trading	xxx	
Loss on holding debt securities	xxx	
Investment in debt securities—held-to-maturity		xxx
Investment in debt securities—held-for-trading	xxx	
Investment in debt securities—held-to-maturity		xxx
Gain on holding debt securities		xxx

The Equity Method of Accounting for Investments

Investment (equity method). To record the company's cash or loan investment in another business entity.

Investment in [company name]	xxx	
Cash		xxx
Notes payable		xxx

Investment (equity method), record share of investee income. To record the company's proportional share of the income reported by [name of company in which investment was made]. The second entry records in a Deferred Taxes account the amount of income taxes related to the investor's share of investee income.

Investment in [company name]	xxx	
Income from equity share in investment		xxx
Income tax expense	xxx	
Deferred tax liability		xxx

Investment (equity method), record dividends from investee. To reduce the amount of the original investment by the cash value of dividends received. In the second entry, we assume that a deferred income tax was already recognized when the investor recorded a share of investee income, and now shift the portion of the deferred taxes related to dividends received to the Taxes Payable account.

Cash	xxx	
Investment in [company name]		xxx
Deferred tax liability	xxx	
Taxes payable		xxx

Investment (equity method), record periodic amortization of incremental increase in investee assets due to allocation of excess purchase price. To reduce the equity in the investee's income as recorded by the investor, based on the periodic amortization of any investee assets to which value was assigned as a result of the apportionment of an investment exceeding the book value of the investee.

Equity in [company name] income	xxx	
Investment in [company name]		xxx

Investment (equity method), sale of investment at a gain. To record a cash payment in exchange for liquidation of an investment, including the recordation of a gain on the transaction. The second entry recognizes an income tax on the investment gain above any income tax previously deferred, and also shifts any previously deferred income tax into a current Taxes Payable account.

Cash	xxx	
Investment in [company name]		xxx
Gain on sale of investment		xxx
Income tax expense	xxx	
Deferred tax liability	xxx	
Taxes payable		xxx

Investment (equity method), sale of investment at a loss. To record a cash payment in exchange for liquidation of an investment, including the recordation of a loss on the transaction. The second entry eliminates any previously deferred income tax.

Cash	xxx	
Loss on sale of investment	xxx	
Investment in [company name]		xxx
Deferred tax liability	xxx	
Income tax expense		xxx

RECORDKEEPING

When the designation of securities is changed between the trading account and available-for-sale account, there is an impact on the recognition of unrealized gains on available-for-sale securities. Since a simple designation change can therefore impact reported income, one should sufficiently document the reason for the change to the point where the altered designation is highly credible. This documentation should be attached to the journal entry used to shift securities into a different account.

The bond ledger sheet and the stock ledger sheet described in the Forms and Reports section should be retained in the accounting archives, since they will be needed as evidentiary material for any type of financial or income tax audit. Given the potentially large sums tracked through these sheets, it is best to store them in a locked area, or at least to retain duplicate copies in separate locations. If they are stored in the computer system, be sure to print them out for archiving purposes whenever a year of computer data is being purged from the computer system.

The investment approval form is the primary form of evidence showing that an investment has been properly approved and recorded in the correct investment portfolio. Accordingly, it should be stored as part of the accounting records. Typically, the general ledger accountant will attach a copy of the completed form to the journal entry form used to make the initial investment entry. The treasury staff should also retain a copy of the form, usually filed by date.

When recording investments under the equity method of accounting, one should record an associated income tax expense using the tax rate at which the company eventually intends to liquidate its investment (e.g., the rates applying either to the receipt of dividends or from sale of the underlying stock). The assumption of eventual disposition should be clearly documented in all journal entries recording the income tax expense and changes in the expense.

Under the equity method of accounting, if there is a difference between the amount paid by the investor and the book value of the investee, at least some portion of the difference must be informally assigned to the assets of the investee and amortized, with an amortization entry regularly being made by the investor. A spreadsheet documenting the allocation to assets and the associated amortization must be created and retained in order to provide sufficient evidence for how the amortization entry was derived. A copy of the amortization spreadsheet should be attached to every amortization journal entry.

8 BUSINESS COMBINATIONS AND CONSOLIDATED FINANCIAL STATEMENTS

DEFINITIONS OF TERMS

Acquisition. An entity pays cash, stock, and/or debt to acquire some portion of the voting stock of another entity, and the acquired entity continues to exist as a separate legal entity.

Combination. An entity gains control over the assets of another entity.

Consolidation. A new entity is formed to acquire other entities through an exchange of stock, after which the acquired entities are dissolved as separate legal entities.

Controlling financial interest. Equity investors have voting rights to make decisions about an entity's activities, must absorb the entity's expected losses, and are entitled to the entity's expected residual returns.

Goodwill. The acquisition price of an entity, less the fair value of acquired net assets.

Merger. One entity acquires all the assets of another entity through the payment of cash, stock, and/or debt.

Primary beneficiary. A variable interest holder that is required to consolidate a variable interest entity.

Reporting unit. An operating segment of an acquired entity whose financial results are used to test goodwill impairment.

Reverse acquisition. The acquiring entity issues such a large proportion of its shares to the owners of the entity being acquired that the owners of the entity being acquired become the majority owners of the acquiring entity.

Variable interest entity. An entity for which it is not possible to establish the parties having a controlling financial interest in the company, based on a review of the at-risk investments of those shareholders having voting rights.

CONCEPTS AND EXAMPLES[1]

General Concepts

The key issue surrounding a business combination is how to account for the purchase price. In essence, the acquiring entity records the acquiree's assets and liabilities at their fair values as of the date of the transaction, and then amortizes these fair values over the useful economic lives of the underlying assets. If the purchase price exceeds the fair values of all acquired assets and liabilities, as is usually the case, then the excess amount is recorded by the acquiring entity as goodwill.

It is also possible for a business combination to be completed where the acquisition price is less than the fair market value of the acquiree's assets and liabilities, essentially creating negative goodwill. When this occurs, the negative goodwill is allocated as a cost reduction for all acquired assets that are not required to be carried on the balance sheet at their fair values. If some of the negative goodwill still exists after this cost reduction exercise, then it is recognized as an extraordinary gain. However, if the business combination includes a purchase price that is contingent on future events, then any excess negative goodwill is recorded as a deferred credit (to be used as an offset against any additional payments to the acquiree's shareholders) until the contingent conditions are resolved.

Goodwill is not subject to amortization. Instead, companies must conduct periodic impairments testing, as noted later in the Goodwill Impairment Testing section.

Determining the Fair Value of Acquiree Assets

When a business combination is completed, the acquiring entity must determine the fair value of all acquiree assets and liabilities, and record them on its books at their fair values, subject to the goodwill provisions noted in the last section. The following list itemizes how these assets and liabilities are to be valued:

1. **Marketable securities.** At their fair value.
2. **Accounts receivable.** At their present value, minus a reserve for bad debts.
3. **Inventory.** Finished goods are valued at their estimated selling prices, minus any costs of disposal, less a normal profit. The same calculation is used for work-in-process inventory, except that the estimated costs of completion must also be subtracted from their estimated selling prices. Raw materials are valued at their current replacement cost.

[1] *Some portions of this section are adapted with permission from Chapters 14 and 16 of Bragg,* **Ultimate Accountants' Reference,** *John Wiley & Sons, Inc., Hoboken, NJ, 2006.*

4. **Fixed assets.** At their current replacement cost. However, if any fixed assets are to be sold, then the proper measurement is their current replacement cost minus the estimated sale cost.
5. **Intangible assets.** At their appraised value.
6. **Liabilities.** At their present value.

However, if some acquired assets duplicate those of the acquiring entity and are therefore to be disposed of, then the cost allocated to these assets should equal their estimated net salvage value. If the acquirer plans to dispose of an entire subsidiary of the acquiree, then the expected cash flows from the subsidiary through the expected disposition date are used to assign a value to it. When the subsidiary is sold, any difference between the subsidiary's carrying value on the disposition date and sale proceeds is reapportioned to other company assets. However, if the difference is caused by events occurring after the business combination date, then the difference is reported as a gain or loss.

It may not be possible to precisely determine the fair values of some assets, estimated liabilities, or contingent liabilities as of the date of the business combination. If so, it is possible to reallocate the purchase price when these values are resolved, but only within the first year following the business combination. After one year, any further valuation changes are recorded in the net income of the current period.

Identification and Evaluation of Intangible Assets

One item on the preceding list of assets and liabilities is intangible assets. As part of a business combination, the acquiring entity must identify all of the acquiree's intangible assets, valuing them separately from goodwill. Examples of intangibles that should be separately recognized include

Computer software	Licensing agreements
Construction permits	Noncompetition agreements
Customer lists and relationships	Operating or use rights
Databases	Order backlog
Employment contracts	Patented and unpatented technology
Franchise agreements	Servicing contracts
Internet domain names	Trade secrets
Lease agreements	Trademarks and service marks

These intangible assets are to be recognized at their fair values and amortized by the acquiring entity during the period over which they are expected to directly or indirectly generate cash flows for the entity. Intangible assets may be assigned a considerable proportion of the purchase price of an acquiree, so a large amount of attention should be paid to the proper valuation of these assets.

Example of a purchase transaction

The Arabian Knights Security Company acquires the Templar Security Agency for $800,000 cash. As of the acquisition date, Templar's balance sheet is listed below, showing both the book value and fair value of each item:

	Book value	Fair value
Cash	$ 48,000	$ 48,000
Accounts receivable, net of bad debts	240,000	230,000
Inventory	50,000	20,000
Fixed assets, net of depreciation	190,000	170,000
Intangible assets—databases	--	80,000
Intangible assets—licensing agreements	--	70,000
Total assets	$528,000	$618,000
Current liabilities	$ 90,000	$ 90,000
Long-term debt	400,000	380,000
Stockholders' equity	38,000	148,000
Total liabilities and equity	$528,000	$618,000

The fair value of Templar's long-term debt has declined, since the debt is at a fixed interest rate, and the current market rate at the time of the acquisition has increased from that fixed rate. Independent appraisals are used to determine the decline in the fair value of Templar's fixed assets and inventory, though these appraisals also indicate that significant value can be assigned to several intangible assets.

The computation of goodwill resulting from the acquisition is as follows:

Purchase price		$800,000
Cash	$ 48,000	
Accounts receivable, net of bad debts	230,000	
Inventory	20,000	
Fixed assets, net of depreciation	170,000	
Intangible assets—databases	80,000	
Intangible assets—licensing agreements	70,000	
Current liabilities	(90,000)	
Long-term debt	(380,000)	148,000
Goodwill (excess of purchase price over fair value)		$652,000

The journal entry format used to record a purchase transaction is shown later in the Journal Entries section.

When the acquiring entity records the fixed assets of the acquired entity, it does so using the fair value of those assets as of the acquisition date. None of the depreciation formerly recognized by the acquired entity carries forward to the books of the acquirer.

Goodwill Impairment Testing

The amount of goodwill that a company maintains on its books as an asset must be tested at least annually to see if it has been impaired (though more frequent testing is needed if adverse events arise). If so, any impaired goodwill must be charged to expense in the current reporting period.

Two steps are required for goodwill impairment testing. First, compare the fair value of the reporting unit (which is an operating segment of an acquired entity for which financial information is regularly reviewed by management) to its book value. If the fair value exceeds the book value, then there is no goodwill impairment, and the second testing step is not required.

However, if the book value exceeds the fair value of the reporting unit, then a second step is required. In this second step, allocate the fair value of the reporting unit as of the testing date to its assets (including intangible assets) and liabilities, with the remainder (if any) being assigned to goodwill. If the amount of goodwill resulting from this calculation is less than the carrying amount of goodwill, then the difference is impaired goodwill and must be charged to expense in the current period.

Once any amount of goodwill has been charged to expense, it cannot be written back up at a later date, even if the fair value of the reporting unit has increased.

Example of goodwill impairment testing

The Arabian Knights Security Company acquired the Templar Security Agency (Templar), and operates it as a reporting unit. For the most recent year of operations, Templar had annual revenues of $900,000 and carrying values of assets and liabilities that are as follows:

Cash	$ 32,000
Accounts receivable, net of bad debts	250,000
Inventory	15,000
Fixed assets, net of depreciation	190,000
Intangible assets	135,000
Goodwill	652,000
Current liabilities	(110,000)
Long-term debt	(390,000)
Total	$774,000

In order to determine the fair value of Templar, Arabian locates several similar companies whose operations are similar to those of Templar, and whose stock trades on either the American Stock Exchange or the NASDAQ. These comparison stocks consistently trade at an average multiple of 0.8 times revenues. The management of Arabian believes that this stock multiple is fairly representative of the fair value of Templar, and so uses the multiple in the following assessment:

Fair value of the Templar reporting unit	$720,000
Carrying amount of reporting unit, including goodwill	774,000
Fair value above or below carrying value	$ (54,000)

Templar's carrying amount exceeds its fair value, so additional testing is required to determine the extent of goodwill impairment. To do so, Knight's accounting staff compares the carrying value and fair value of Templar's assets and liabilities in the following table to compute the extent of goodwill impairment:

	Carrying value	*Fair value*
Cash	$ 32,000	$ 32,000
Accounts receivable, net of bad debts	250,000	230,000
Inventory	15,000	10,000
Fixed assets, net of depreciation	190,000	200,000
Intangible assets	135,000	100,000
Goodwill	652,000	--
Current liabilities	(110,000)	(110,000)
Long-term debt	(390,000)	(370,000)
Totals	$774,000	$ 92,000
Fair value of Templar reporting unit		$720,000
Implied fair value of goodwill		628,000
Carrying value of goodwill		652,000
Impairment loss		$ (24,000)

Based on this analysis, Templar must charge $24,000 of its goodwill asset to expense in the current period.

If the acquiring company purchases less than 100% of an acquiree, then goodwill is calculated based on the difference between the acquirer's purchase price and the acquirer's proportionate share of the fair values of the identifiable net assets acquired.

A company can select any date for impairment testing, but once selected, the same date must be used every year.

The aggregate amount of goodwill impairment losses should be reported as a separate line item in the operating section of the income statement.

Contingent Consideration

The shareholders of an acquiree may be due additional consideration if predetermined conditions are met at a date following the original date of the business combination. Such contingent consideration is recognized when the contingency is resolved.

The accounting for contingent consideration is handled differently depending on the reason for the payment. If the consideration is paid based on an earn-out, then the additional payments imply that the original valuation assigned to the reporting unit was too low. Accordingly, the additional payment calls for a prospective revaluation of the reporting unit. This may possibly result in an increase in the value assigned to fixed or intangible assets, as well as related depreciation, though the more likely scenario will be an increase in goodwill.

If the consideration is paid based on a decline in the value of the original purchase package (such as a decline in the acquiring entity's stock), then additional payment must be made to restore the original value of the purchase package. This does not call for a prospective revaluation of the reporting unit. Instead, if the additional shares issued have par values, then the additional amount of par value needed for these shares must be shifted from the additional paid-in capital account to the common stock account.

Noncontrolling Interests

An acquiring company may sometimes acquire less than 100% of the acquiree's stock. When this happens, the acquiring entity presents the entire amount of the acquiress's assets and liabilities and revenue and expenses, as well as offsetting line items for the proportion of each of these items that the acquiring entity does not own. In the income statement, the noncontrolling interest in the income or loss of a subsidiary is deducted from or added to consolidated net income. The format of this offset in the balance sheet is a credit in the stockholders' equity section, based on preacquisition book values.

If the acquiring company increases its ownership share of another entity through the purchase of additional shares of its stock, this additional investment is recorded as an increase in the Investment in Subsidiary account.

Leveraged Buyouts

When a change in control arises in a leveraged buyout (LBO), then it is necessary to step up the reported value of all assets and liabilities of the entity being purchased. If there is no change in control, then the transaction is essentially a recapitalization, in which case the original asset and liability values shall continue to be reported. The determination of a change in control is addressed by a flowchart in the Decision Trees section.

The normal structure of an LBO transaction is that a holding company is formed that acquires an operating company. If the holding company is owned by the current owners of the operating company, then there should be no revaluation of the existing assets and liabilities of the operating company, since the substance of the LBO is that the operating company has not really been sold to a new owner. This is a significant issue, since revaluation can result in significantly different operating results because of changes in depreciation and amortization.

A change in control of the operating company occurs if any one of the following conditions are met:

1. A single shareholder controls the holding company and did not previously control the operating company.
2. A group of new shareholders controls the holding company.
3. A control group controls the holding company, and no subset of that group had previous control of the operating company. The control group can be derived from the following three subsets of the shareholders: (a) management (unless they did not participate in the LBO transaction), (b) those shareholders with an increased ownership percentage in the holding company than they had in the operating company and who own at least 5% of the holding company, and (c) shareholders with the same or lower ownership percentage in the holding company than they had in the operating company and who own at least 20% of the holding company or who own at least 20% of the fair value of cumulative capital (including equity, debt, and guarantees) in the holding company.

In all three cases, control of the holding company must be substantive, genuine, and not temporary.

Reverse Acquisitions

A reverse acquisition occurs when the acquiring entity issues such a large proportion of its outstanding shares to the owners of the acquiree that the owners of the acquiree effectively become the majority owners of the acquiring entity. A reverse acquisition is most commonly used when a public shell corporation nominally acquires a nonpublic operating company.

Because the substance of a reverse transaction is that the owners of the acquiree own the majority of the entire company, the financial statements should show the historical financial results of the acquiree, with the results of the acquiring entity added as of the reverse acquisition date. The financial statements would show the acquiring company's assets and liabilities at fair value, and those of the acquiree at historical cost. In addition, the retained earnings of only the acquiree will appear in the consolidated financial statements.

When a nonpublic company is, in substance, buying a public shell company, no goodwill can be recognized. Further, the valuation of the transaction should be based on the fair value of the net assets acquired, since there may be so little trading in the shell's shares that those shares cannot be accurately valued.

Spin-Off Transactions

A spin-off transaction occurs when a company unilaterally transfers a subsidiary to its shareholders. If the company owns a small percentage of the subsidiary, then the spin-off is essentially a property dividend and is recorded at the fair value of the subsidiary.

If the company owns a majority of the shares of the subsidiary, then the transaction is recorded at the book value of the subsidiary's assets and liabilities. If the subsidiary has a positive net book value, this net worth is recorded as a reduction of the parent company's retained earnings. If the subsidiary has a negative net book value, this is recorded as an addition to the parent company's additional paid-in capital account. These transactions are shown later in the Journal Entries section.

It is also possible to have a reverse spin-off, where the subsidiary being transferred to shareholders has larger assets, revenues, earnings, and fair value than the parent company, and usually retains its senior management. In this case, the proper accounting treatment is to follow the substance of the transaction and treat the spun-off subsidiary as the parent company.

Disposal of a Business Segment

If a company disposes of some portion of a business segment that is a significant proportion of a reporting unit and that constitutes a separate business, then it should allocate to the disposed segment some portion of the goodwill assigned to the reporting unit. This allocation should be based on the relative fair values of the disposed segment and the remainder of the reporting unit. When this occurs, the company should conduct a goodwill impairment test for the remaining reporting unit, to verify that there is no goodwill impairment.

Consolidation Requirements

The acquiring entity must consolidate the results of its majority-owned subsidiaries in its financial statements, with only one exception. Consolidation is not required if it can be clearly shown that the majority owner does not have control over the subsidiary.

If a subsidiary has its own majority-owned subsidiaries, then it should consolidate the results of these lower-tier subsidiaries into its own financial statements, which will in turn be consolidated into the results of the parent company.

Variable Interest Entities

A variable interest entity (VIE) is an entity that is controlled by parties that do not have a majority voting interest. A VIE usually receives minimal capitalization, and is subject to either the risk of significant losses that it cannot absorb or more gains than its ostensible owners could benefit from.

If another entity is exposed to absorbing the majority of the VIE's losses or receives the majority of its residual profits, no matter what level of ownership it has in the VIE, then that party is called the primary beneficiary. This definition is important, because the primary beneficiary must consolidate the results of the VIE in its financial statements (see the preceding Noncontrolling Interests section for the proper reporting of minority shareholders in this consolidation).

DECISION TREES

Determination of Control in a Leveraged Buyout

When an operating company is acquired by a holding company as part of an LBO, the transaction is accounted for as a recapitalization if control over the operating company has not changed since the LBO. Conversely, its assets and liabilities must be recorded at their fair value if control has actually changed. The decision tree shown in Exhibit 8-1 shows the LBO control criteria needed to determine the presence or absence of a change of control.

Exhibit 8-1: Determination of Control in a Leveraged Buyout Transaction

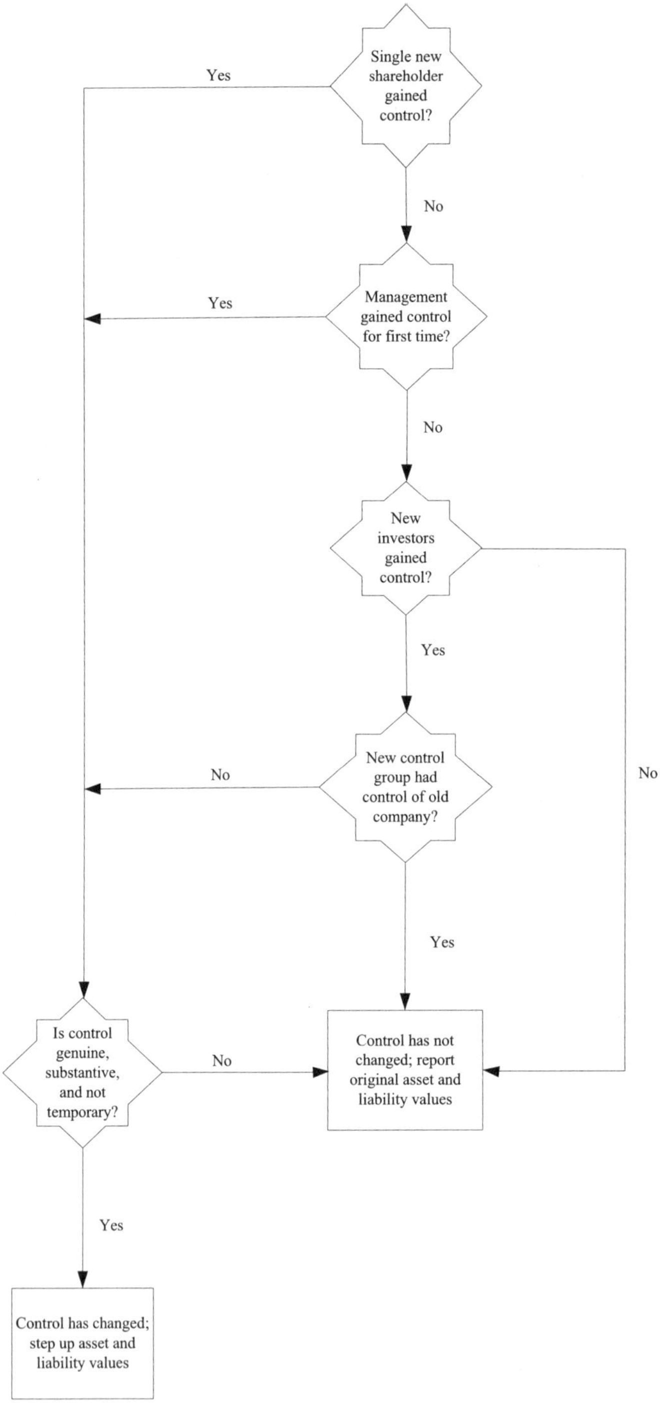

POLICIES

- **The allocation of the acquisition purchase price to an acquiree's in-process research and development (R&D) activities shall not exceed the estimated fair value of those activities.** This policy is designed to keep the accounting staff from assigning an excessive proportion of the purchase price to R&D activities, which are then immediately charged to expense under accounting rules, allowing for the recognition of greater levels of profitability in the future. In practice, the valuation of R&D is extremely difficult, so this policy is primarily designed to stop egregious allocations from occurring.

- **The amortization period of newly acquired assets will be limited to the depreciation periods used for the same asset classes by the acquiring company.** Generally accepted accounting principles (GAAP) allow acquired assets to be amortized over their useful economic lives. This guidance could be construed as allowing for longer amortization periods than the acquiring company uses for similar assets that it acquires by other means, thereby spreading the amortization expense over more periods than normal and inflating reported profits. To avoid this, the acquiring entity should use its standard amortization periods for similar classes of assets as the maximum cap for the amortization periods of acquired assets.

- **Goodwill impairment testing shall be conducted on the same date in every year.** It is possible that a reporting unit's financial results could vary substantially over several reporting periods. If so, the accounting department could be tempted to conduct goodwill impairment testing following a month having excellent reporting results, in an effort to obtain the highest possible fair value for the reporting unit, and thereby avoid any goodwill impairment. This policy is designed to ensure a consistent application of the goodwill impairment methodology on the same date of every year, thereby eliminating the "cherry picking" of testing dates.

PROCEDURES

Use the following procedure to test for goodwill impairment.

1. Use one of two valuation methods to calculate the fair value of the reporting unit. If there are publicly held comparable entities, then determine the average multiple of their market values to revenues, and apply this multiple to the trailing twelve month revenues of the reporting unit to determine its fair value. If there are no comparable market valuations available, then instead calculate the expected present value of cash flows from the reporting unit for the next five years (using the form shown in the Forms and Reports section) to determine its fair value.

2. Compile the carrying value of all assets and liabilities of the reporting unit as of the impairment measurement date.

3. Compare the reporting unit's fair value to the carrying value of its assets and liabilities. If the fair value exceeds the carrying value, then there is no impairment, and no further testing is required.
4. If the carrying value exceeds the fair value, then goodwill has been impaired. Proceed to the next step.
5. Allocate the fair value of the reporting unit to its assets (including intangible assets) and liabilities. After this allocation is completed, any excess fair value should be assigned to goodwill.
6. Compare the newly assigned goodwill value to the previously booked goodwill value. If the previously booked goodwill is higher than the newly assigned goodwill value, then charge the difference to expense in the current period.

CONTROLS

- **Verify that the amount of the purchase price allocated to research and development is not excessive.** A common ploy is for the acquiring entity to allocate an excessive proportion of the purchase price to an acquiree's R&D activities, and to then charge this allocation to expense in the current period, thereby enhancing reported profits in later periods. A recurring internal audit program could require the examination of these allocated amounts for any new acquisitions, comparing them to industry benchmarks or past practice or requiring the use of an independent appraisal. This is an extremely difficult area in which to determine fair value, so the methods used may vary or require the use and comparison of multiple valuation techniques.

- **Verify that all intangible assets were properly identified and adequate values assigned to them.** The single largest problem with accounting for business combinations is that companies can avoid amortization of the purchase price by parking a large proportion of the purchase price in the goodwill asset account. Though an excessive quantity of goodwill may eventually be written off through goodwill impairment testing, this may not take place for some time. Until a write-down occurs, the acquiring company will report excessively high profit levels. To avoid this issue, the acquisition accounting procedure should include the use of an independent appraiser and an outside audit firm to properly designate all intangible assets and ensure that adequate values are assigned to them. In addition, a recurring internal audit program should call for the verification that this procedure is being followed, and that the independent appraiser is truly independent. The result should be a reduction in the proportion of acquisition prices that are allocated to goodwill.

- **Verify the reason for contingent payments.** There is a substantial incentive for the accounting staff to treat a contingent payment as one mandated by a decline in the value of the original purchase package, since this does not call for the creation of an offsetting asset, such as higher fixed asset or goodwill values (as would be the case if the payment were treated as an earn-out). Accordingly, a recurring internal audit program should require the internal audit staff to review the acquisition documents to ensure that the transaction is being treated correctly.

FORMS AND REPORTS

Impairment Testing with Expected Present Value Form

One way to conduct goodwill impairment testing is to periodically compare the carrying value of the assets and liabilities of a reporting unit to the cash flow expected to be generated by that reporting unit. A sample form that can be used for this analysis is shown in Exhibit 8-2. To use the form, enter three scenarios for revenues, expenses, and profits, along with their associated probabilities of occurrence, in the appropriate columns for each of the next five years. Then multiply the cash flow (assumed here to be the earnings before interest, taxes, and depreciation, or EBITDA) for each scenario by its probability to arrive at the expected cash flow by period. Next, use the risk-free interest rate to calculate the present value of the expected cash flows for all five years. Then enter the carrying values of all the assets and liabilities listed in the lower left corner of the form and total them. Finally, compare the expected present value (EPV) of all cash flows to the total carrying value of all assets and liabilities. If the carrying values are higher than the cash flows, then goodwill impairment has occurred.

FOOTNOTES

When a business combination is completed, the acquiring entity should disclose the name and a brief description of the acquiree, as well as the percentage of voting shares acquired. It should also note the period for which the results of the acquiree are included in the income statement of the acquiring entity. The disclosure should also note the cost of the acquisition, the number of shares issued, and the value of those shares, as well as the basis for determining the share value. Contingent payments must also be noted. An example follows:

> In September 2007, the Company completed the acquisition of Superior Night Vision Corporation ("Night"), acquiring all of the issued outstanding shares of Night through a cash tender offer, which was completed at a purchase price of $13.50 per share. Night provides portable night vision equipment to the security and military industries. The transaction was valued at approximately $12 million plus related transaction costs and was funded from borrowings under the Company's credit facility. The purchase price was allocated to assets acquired and liabilities assumed based on estimated fair value as of the date of acquisition. The Company acquired assets of $18 million and assumed liabilities of $7 million. The Company recorded $200,000 in goodwill, which is not deductible for income tax purposes, and intangible assets of $800,000. The $800,000 of intangible assets is attributable to customer relationships and noncompete agreements with useful lives of five years. The operating results of the acquired business are included in the Company's financial statements in the Commercial segment from the effective date of the acquisition, September 2007.

Exhibit 8-2: Form for Impairment Testing with Expected Present Value

Impairment Testing with Expected Present Value (EPV) Analysis

	Year 1			Year 2			Year 3			Year 4			Year 5		
	Scenario 1	Scenario 2	Scenario 3	Scenario 1	Scenario 2	Scenario 3	Scenario 1	Scenario 2	Scenario 3	Scenario 1	Scenario 2	Scenario 3	Scenario 1	Scenario 2	Scenario 3
Probality (sum to 100%)															
Revenue:															
Expenses:															
Cost of goods sold															
Salaries & wages															
Depreciation															
Interest															
Taxes															
Other expenses															
Total expenses:															
Net profit															
EBITDA															

Expected cash flow by period

Interest rate

Present value of cash flows

Current period

Carrying Value Analysis:

Cash

Accounts receivable

Inventories

Fixed assets

Identifiable intangibles

Goodwill

Accounts payable

Debt

Total carrying value

Present value of cash flows

EPV over/under carrying value

If an acquiring entity acquires a number of other business entities that are individually immaterial, but which are material in aggregate, then disclosure must be made of the number of entities acquired and a brief description of their activities. Disclosure must also be made in aggregate of the acquisition cost, the number of shares issued, and the value assigned to those shares. Further, the amounts of acquired goodwill related to each business segment should be noted. An example follows:

> During 2007, the Company acquired the following three entities for a total of $4,900,000 in cash:
>
> - Squelch, Inc., based in Silence, Montana, the developer and patent owner of a technology to reduce the sound emitted by noisy children.
> - ThinKid, Inc., based in LowCal, Massachusetts, a producer of appetite reduction supplements for children.
> - WhereRU, Inc., based in Area 51, New Mexico, a producer of child-tracking GPS wristwatches.
>
> The goodwill recognized in these transactions totaled $3,250,000 and that amount is expected to be fully deductible for tax purposes. All of the goodwill was assigned to the Child Monitoring business segment.

When contingent payments are made by the acquiring entity to shareholders of the acquiree subsequent to the business combination date, the amount of these payments should be disclosed, as well as the nature of the contingent event that caused the payments to be made. Two examples follow:

1. The acquiree's shareholders are eligible to receive contingent consideration in each of the four successive annual periods commencing on January 1, 2007, based on the acquiree's operating results in each period. The contingent consideration in each period consists of a payment equal to 10% of the net income of the acquiree for that period, provided that the cumulative sum of all such contingent consideration does not exceed $2 million. At December 31, 2007, the Company has accrued $92,000 in consideration payable for the first annual period.
2. On June 30, 2008, the Company paid $410,000 to the acquiree's shareholders. Of that amount, $392,000 represented the additional consideration due on the first anniversary and $92,000 represented contingent consideration based on net income.

When intangible assets are acquired as part of business combination, disclosure must include the total amount assigned to each major intangible asset class, the amount of any major class of intangible assets. In subsequent periods, disclosure must be made of the gross carrying amount and accumulated amortization for each class of intangible asset, the aggregate amortization expense for the period, and the estimated amortization expense for each of the next five fiscal years. An example follows:

Other intangible assets consisted of the following as of December 31, 2007:

	Gross carrying value	Accumulated amortization	Net carrying value
Long-term contracts	$320,000	$(180,000)	$140,000
Customer relationships	680,000	(200,000)	480,000
Noncompete agreements	40,000	(35,000)	5,000
Trade names	108,000	(32,000)	76,000
Totals	$1,148,000	$(447,000)	$701,000

Amortization expense was $149,000 for the year ended December 31, 2007. Based on the Company's amortizable intangible assets as of December 31, 2007, the Company expects related amortization expense for the five succeeding fiscal years to approximate $183,000, $148,000, $130,000, $125,000, and $115,000.

In each reporting period, disclosure must be made for each reporting unit of the amount of goodwill, the aggregate amount of impairment losses recognized, and the amount of any goodwill included in the disposal of a reporting unit. Disclosure must also be made of any significant changes in the allocation of goodwill between reporting units. An example follows:

Changes in the carrying amount of goodwill for the year ended December 31, 2007, by reporting segment were as follows:

	Geographical information systems	IT security	Total
Balance at January 1, 2007	$14,600,000	$3,300,000	$17,900,000
ABC Acquisition	2,200,000		2,200,000
Contingent consideration—ABC Co.	200,000		200,000
Contingent consideration—DEF Co.		170,000	170,000
Adjustment to acquired goodwill—ABC Co.	(80,000)		(80,000)
Goodwill impairment—ABC Co.	(710,000)		(710,000)
Goodwill impairment—DEF Co.		(360,000)	(360,000)
Balance at December 31, 2007	$16,210,000	$3,110,000	$19,320,000

If adjustments are made in the current period to the allocation of the purchase price that was recorded in a prior period, the nature and amount of the adjustment should be disclosed. An example follows:

The Company acquired the Templar Security Agency in December 2007. The purchase price of the acquisition exceeded the preliminary fair value of the net assets acquired by $652,000, which was assigned to goodwill. During 2008, the Company completed its fair value analysis of Templar's intangible assets and expensed $70,000 of the excess purchase price representing licensing agreements that had previously been assigned to goodwill. The Company's management concluded that Templar would not recognize significant cash flow from the licensing agreements. The $70,000 charge is aggregated into the "Other operating expenses" line item in the accompanying consolidated statement of income and comprehensive income for the year ended December 31, 2008.

If an impairment loss is recognized, disclosure must include a description of the circumstances causing the impairment, the amount of the loss, and the method used to derive fair value. An example follows:

The Company's judicial case management reporting unit is tested for impairment in the fourth quarter, after the annual forecasting process has been completed. Due to the consolidation of the number of case management providers and the increasing conversion of district court software solutions into state-wide systems, operating profits and cash flows were lower than expected throughout the reporting year. Based on that trend and expectations of similar performance in the future, the earnings forecast of the case management reporting unit for the next five years was revised, and the fair value of that unit was estimated using the expected present value of future cash flows. This resulted in a goodwill impairment loss of $1,045,000 being recognized by the case management reporting unit.

The amount of R&D expense acquired must also be disclosed, as well as the amount written off in the current period, and identification of the line item in the income statement within which this expense is aggregated. An example follows:

> In March 2007, the Company assigned a value of $900,000 to the research and development projects it acquired in a business combination with Squelch, Inc. These projects had not yet been completed as of the date of acquisition; technological feasibility for these projects has not yet been established, nor do they have any future use in research and development activities. Accordingly, the Company recorded a charge of $900,000 for purchased in-process research and development costs in conjunction with this business combination.

JOURNAL ENTRIES

Initial purchase transaction. To record the initial acquisition of another entity. The key element of this entry are the goodwill asset and the form of payment made to the owners of the acquired entity.

Cash	xxx	
Accounts receivable, net of bad debts	xxx	
Inventory	xxx	
Fixed assets, net of depreciation	xxx	
Intangible assets (various)	xxx	
Goodwill	xxx	
Current liabilities		xxx
Long-term debt		xxx
Notes payable (paid to acquired entity shareholders)		xxx
Cash (paid to acquired entity shareholders)		xxx

Negative goodwill offset. To record the offsetting of negative goodwill against accounts that do not have to be carried at fair value. Since the accounts that must be carried at fair value include cash, receivables, and inventory, the primary asset left for offsetting purposes is usually fixed assets.

Negative goodwill	xxx	
Fixed assets		xxx

If there are not sufficient assets available for the complete offsetting of negative goodwill, then the remaining balance of negative goodwill is recognized as an extraordinary item, as shown below.

Negative goodwill	xxx	
Fixed assets		xxx
Extraordinary item—gain on purchase		xxx

Write-off of impaired goodwill. If the fair value of a reporting unit is less than its book value, then some portion of the goodwill asset originally created as part of the acquisition of that reporting unit must be charged to expense in the current period. The entry is shown below.

Impaired goodwill expense	xxx	
Goodwill		xxx

Increased investment in subsidiary. If the acquiring entity does not initially purchase all outstanding shares of an acquiree, but later purchases additional shares, then the additional payment is recorded as an increase in the investment in the subsidiary. The entry is shown below.

Investment in subsidiary	xxx	
Cash		xxx

Spin-off of subsidiary. When a parent company spins off a subsidiary to its shareholders in which it held a majority ownership interest, it must remove the book value of the subsidiary's assets and liabilities from its books. If the net book value of the subsidiary is positive, the parent company records this as a retained earnings reduction, as shown below.

Accounts payable	xxx	
Debt	xxx	
Other liabilities	xxx	
Retained earnings	xxx	
Cash		xxx
Accounts receivable		xxx
Inventory		xxx
Fixed assets		xxx
Other assets		xxx

If the net book value of the subsidiary is negative, the parent company records this as an addition to the additional paid-in capital account, as shown below.

Accounts payable	xxx	
Debt	xxx	
Other liabilities	xxx	
Cash		xxx
Accounts receivable		xxx
Inventory		xxx
Fixed assets		xxx
Other assets		xxx
Additional paid-in capital		xxx

9 CURRENT LIABILITIES AND CONTINGENCIES

DEFINITIONS OF TERMS

Accrued liability. A liability for which there is a clear commitment to pay, but for which an invoice has not yet been received. Typical accrued liabilities are wages payable, payroll taxes payable, and interest payable.

Contingent liability. A liability that will occur if a future event comes to pass, and which is based on a current situation.

Current liability. A liability requiring the use of a current asset to liquidate.

Trade account payable. A payable for which there is a clear commitment to pay, and which generally involves an obligation related to goods or services. Typically, it also involves a payment due within one year, and is considered to include anything for which an invoice is received.

Unearned revenue. Payments made by customers prior to delivery of services or products to them.

CONCEPTS AND EXAMPLES[1]

Current Liabilities—Presentation

If a company has a long-term payable that is approaching its termination date, then any amount due under its payment provisions within the next year must be recorded as a current liability. If only a portion of total payments due under the liability are expected to fall within that time frame, then only that portion of the liability should be reported as a current liability. A common situation in which this issue arises is for a copier leasing arrangement, where the most recent payments due under the agreement are split away from the other copier lease payments that are not due until after one year. This situation commonly arises for many types of long-term equipment and property rentals.

Current Liabilities—Advances

If a customer makes a payment for which the company has not made a corresponding delivery of goods or services, then the accountant must record the cash receipt as a customer advance, which is a liability. This situation commonly arises when a customer order is so large or specialized that the company is justified in demanding cash in advance of the order. Another common situation is when customers are required to make a deposit, such as when a property rental company requires one month's rent as a damage deposit. This may be recorded as a current liability if the corresponding delivery of goods or services is expected to be within the next year. However, if the offset is expected to be further in the future, then it should be recorded as a long-term liability.

Current Liabilities—Bonuses

Rather than waiting until bonuses are fully earned and payable to recognize them, one should accrue some proportion of the bonuses in each reporting period if

---

[1] *Much of the information in this section is adapted with permission from Chapter 18 of Bragg,* **Ultimate Accountants' Reference** *(John Wiley & Sons, Inc., Hoboken, NJ, 2006).*

there is a reasonable expectation that they will be earned and that the eventual amount of the bonus can be approximately determined.

Current Liabilities—Commissions

The amount of commissions due to the sales staff may not be precisely ascertainable at the end of the reporting period, since they may be subject to later changes based on the precise terms of the commission agreement with the sales staff, such as subsequent reductions if customers do not pay for their delivered goods or services. In this case, commissions should be accrued based on the maximum possible commission payment, minus a reduction for later eventualities; the reduction can be reasonably based on historical experience with actual commission rates paid.

Current Liabilities—Compensated Absences

A company is required to accrue for compensated absences, such as vacation time, when employees have already earned the compensated absence, the right has vested, the payment amount can be estimated, and payment is probable. If a company is required to pay for earned compensation absences, then vesting has occurred. A key issue is any "use it or lose it" provision in the company employee manual, which has a dramatic effect on the amount of compensated absences to be accrued. If such a policy exists, then the accrual is limited to the maximum amount of the carryforward. If not, the accrual can be substantial if the vested amount has built up over many years. The payment amount is typically based on the most recent level of pay for accrual calculation purposes, rather than any estimate of future pay levels at the time when the absence is actually compensated.

Example of vacation accrual

Mr. Harold Jones has earned 450 hours of vacation time, none of which has been used. He currently earns $28.50 per hour. His employer should maintain an accrued vacation expense of $12,825 (450 hours × $28.50/hour) to reflect this liability. However, if the company has a "use it or lose it" policy that allows only an 80-hour carryforward at the end of each year, then the accrual is only $2,280 (80 hours × $28.50/hour).

The amount of sick time allowed to employees is usually so small that there is no discernible impact on the financial statements if they are accrued or not. This is particularly true if unused sick time cannot be carried forward into future years as an ongoing residual employee benefit that may be paid out at some future date. If these restrictions are not the case, then the accounting treatment of sick time is the same as for vacation time.

Current Liabilities—Debt

There are a number of circumstances under which a company's debt must be recorded as current debt on the balance sheet. They are as follows:

- If the debt must be repaid entirely within the current operating cycle
- If the debt is payable over a longer term, but it is also due on demand at the option of the lender

- If the company is in violation of any loan covenants and the lender has not waived the requirement
- If the company is in violation of any loan covenants, the lender has issued a short-term waiver, but it is unlikely that the company can cure the violation problem during the waiver period
- If the debt agreement contains a subjective acceleration clause, and there is a strong likelihood that the clause will be activated

If only a portion of a company's debt falls under the preceding criteria, then only that portion impacted by the rules must be recorded as current debt, with the remainder recorded as long-term debt.

If a company intends to refinance current debt with long-term debt, it can classify this debt as long-term on the balance sheet, but only if the refinancing occurs or a refinancing agreement is signed after the balance sheet date but before the issuance date. If this approach is taken, the amount of current debt that can be reclassified as long-term debt cannot exceed the amount of debt to be refinanced, and is also limited by the amount of new debt that can be acquired without violating existing loan covenants.

Current Liabilities—Employee Terminations

If company management has formally approved of a termination plan designed to reduce headcount, the expenses associated with the plan should be recognized at once if the accountant can reasonably estimate the associated costs. The **first requirement** after plan approval is that the plan clearly outlines the benefits to be granted. This information usually specifies a fixed dollar payout based on the amount of time that an employee has been with the company. The **second requirement** is that the plan must specify the general categories and numbers of employees to be let go, since the accountant needs this information to extend the per-person benefit costs specified in the first requirement. Further significant changes to the plan should be unlikely; this locks in the range of possible costs that are likely to occur as a result of the plan, rendering the benefit cost accrual more accurate.

Example of accrual for termination benefits

The Arabian Knights Security Company plans to close its Albuquerque branch office and terminate the employment of all people working there. The action is scheduled for three months in the future. The company's employee manual states that all employees are entitled to one week of severance pay for each year worked for the company. The average number of weeks of severance under this policy is 3.5 for the group to be terminated, and the average pay for the 29 employees affected is $39,500. Thus, the company must immediately accrue a termination expense of $77,101 (29 employees × $39,500 average pay / 52 weeks × 3.5 weeks).

Current Liabilities—Property Taxes

A company should accrue the monthly portion of its property tax liability based on its assessed property tax liability during the fiscal year of the taxing authority.

Example of a property tax accrual

The Arabian Knights Security Company owns property in Arapahoe County, Colorado. Arabian operates under a calendar year, while Arapahoe's fiscal year ends on June 30. Arapahoe sends a notice to Arabian that Arabian's property tax assessment will be $33,600 in the current fiscal year, payable in March of the following year. Accordingly, Arabian's controller begins to accrue 1/12 of the assessment in each month of Arapahoe's fiscal year, beginning in July. The entry is

Property tax expense	2,800	
Property tax payable		2,800

When Arabian pays the assessment in March of the following year, it makes the following entry:

Property tax payable	33,600	
Cash		33,600

Since property taxes are typically paid prior to the end of the taxing authority's fiscal year, this series of transactions will likely result in a debit balance in the Property Tax Payable account for the last few months of the fiscal year, since the company will not have recorded the entire property tax expense until that time.

Current Liabilities—Royalties

If a company is obligated to pay a periodic royalty to a supplier of goods or services that it uses or resells, then it must accrue an expense if the amount is reasonably determinable. A sample royalty calculation worksheet can be found in the Forms and Reports section.

Current Liabilities—Wages

Even if a company times its payroll period-end dates to correspond with the end of each reporting period, this will only ensure that no accrual is needed for those employees who receive salaries (since they are usually paid through the payroll period ending date). The same is not usually true for those who receive an hourly wage. In their case, the pay period may end as much as a week prior to the actual payment date. Consequently, the accountant must accrue the wage expense for the period between the pay period end date and the end of the reporting period. This can be estimated on a person-by-person basis, but an easier approach is to accrue based on an historical hourly rate that includes average overtime percentages. One must also include the company's share of all payroll taxes in this accrual. An example of an unpaid wage accrual form is shown later in the Forms and Reports section.

Current Liabilities—Warranty Claims

If a company has a warranty policy on its products or services and it can reasonably estimate the amount of any warranty claims, it should accrue an expense for anticipated claims. One can also use industry information if in-house warranty claim data are not available. For warranty claims not expected to be received in the current operating cycle, the accrued expense can be split into current and long-term liabilities.

Example of warranty claims

The Halloway Marine Company produces outboard motors for the sport fishing in-dustry. It has historically experienced a warranty expense of 1.5% of its revenues, and so records a warranty expense based on that information. However, it has just devel-oped a jet-powered engine for which it has no warranty experience. The engine has fewer moving parts than a traditional engine, and so should theoretically have a low war-ranty claim rate. No other companies in the industry offer a jet engine, so no compara-ble information is available. The controller chooses to use the 4.8% warranty claim rate applicable to its prior new-engine introductions as the basis for an accrual, since this is the only valid warranty information pertaining to the new product. The controller makes a note to review this accrual regularly to see if the trend of warranty expenses changes after the engine has been on the market for some time.

Contingencies

A **contingent liability** is one that will occur if a future event comes to pass, and which is based on a current situation. For example, a company may be engaged in a lawsuit; if it loses the suit, it will be liable for damages. Other situations that may give rise to a contingent liability are a standby letter of credit (if the primary creditor cannot pay a liability, then the company's standby letter of credit will be accessed by the creditor), a guarantee of indebtedness, an expropriation threat, a risk of damage to company property, or any potential obligations associated with product warranties or defects.

If any of these potential events exists, then the accountant is under no obligation to accrue for any potential loss until the associated events come to pass, but should disclose them in a footnote. However, if the conditional events are **probable** and the amount of the loss can be reasonably estimated, then the accountant must accrue a loss against current income. The amount of the contingent liability must be rea-sonably determinable, or at least be stated within a high–low range of likely out-comes. If the liability can be stated only within a probable range, then the accoun-tant should accrue for the most likely outcome. If there is no most likely outcome, then the minimum amount in the range should be accrued. If the probable amount of a loss changes, then an adjustment should be made in the current period to reflect this change in estimate.

There is a wide range of possible contingent liabilities for which footnote disclo-sure is appropriate. A number of examples are shown in the Footnotes section.

Contingencies—Debt Covenant Violation

If a company violates a debt covenant on long-term debt, it must reclassify the debt as short-term. However, if the lender waives its right to call the debt, the com-pany can leave the existing debt classification alone. The only exception is if the lender retains the right to require compliance with the covenant in the future, and the company is unlikely to be able to comply with the debt covenants on an ongoing basis. In this last instance, the debt must still be classified as short-term.

Contingencies—Debt Guarantees

If a company has guaranteed the debt of a third party, it does not have to record a contingent liability unless there is a reasonable probability that the primary debt holder will be unable to repay the debt. If an ongoing assessment of this probability results in an estimate that the company will be required to cover the debt, a contingent liability should be recorded at that time.

Contingencies—Guaranteed Minimum Option Price

If a company grants stock options that include a minimum payment if the value of the options do not exceed a minimum level, then the amount of this minimum payment should be recognized as a compensation expense, to be ratably recognized over the option service period. If the employee forfeits the options prior to completion of the service period, the compensation expense can be reversed.

POLICIES

Current Liabilities

- **There shall be no carryforward of sick time past the current year.** A common problem is for employees to build up massive reserves of unearned sick time, for which they must be paid when they eventually leave the company. This policy is designed to eliminate all unused sick time at the end of each calendar year, thereby keeping accrued sick time expense to a minimum.
- **The number of hours of vacation time carried forward past the current year is capped at ____ hours.** Some employees have a habit of not taking vacation time, resulting in large vacation accruals that can grow for years. Not only does this represent a significant current liability, but it also presents a control problem, since employees who do not take vacation may be staying on the job in order to hide fraudulent activities. This policy is designed to resolve both problems by allowing only a modest carryforward of earned vacation time.
- **The vacation accrual shall be based on the maximum year-end carryforward amount of vacation hours.** The accrual of vacation time is subject to a great deal of interpretation, since it can be based on the current amount of vacation time existing, the maximum available for the year, the maximum carryforward amount, or an estimate of the carryforward amount. By switching between various estimation methods, one can easily modify the vacation accrual to alter reported financial results. This policy requires one to use just one estimation method, thereby removing the variability from the calculation method. The approach specified in the policy is used as the basis for the vacation accrual form shown in the Forms and Reports section.

PROCEDURES

Current Liabilities—Accounts Payable

This procedure describes the entire transaction cycle for accounts payable.

1. An employee fills out a requisition form for any product she wishes the company to purchase and forwards it to the purchasing department.
2. A purchasing staff person locates the best price for the requisitioned product and issues a purchase order. One copy goes to the supplier, one stays in the purchasing department, and one copy goes to the receiving department. If there is a computerized receiving system, the purchasing person also enters the purchase order into the database.
3. When the product arrives at the receiving dock, the receiving staff compares it to the purchase order and accepts it if the delivery matches the specifications in the purchase order. If the company has a computerized receiving system, the receiving staff calls up the purchase order on the computer and enters the receipt directly into the system. If not, the staff manually enters the receipt in a receiving log and also attaches the bill of lading to the purchase order. These documents are sent to the accounting department at the end of the day.
4. The accounting staff files the documents by supplier name once they arrive from the receiving department.
5. Whenever supplier invoices arrive, the accounting staff matches them to the previously filed purchasing and receiving documents and enters them in the accounting system as approved payables if all documents match. If they do not match, the accounting staff must contact the supplier to resolve any outstanding issues.
6. When a check run is scheduled, the computer system flags those supplier invoices due for payment, and the accounting staff prints the checks. They attach backup materials (invoice, purchase order, and receiving documents) to each check as proof, and forward the check packets to an authorized signer.
7. Once signed, the accounting staff removes the second copy of the remittance advice from each check and staples it to the backup materials, which they file by supplier name. They then mail the checks to suppliers.

CONTROLS

Current Liabilities

- **Include an accrual review in the closing procedure for bonuses, commissions, property taxes, royalties, sick time, vacation time, unpaid wages, and warranty claims.** There are many possible expenses for which an accrual is needed, given their size and repetitive nature. This control is designed to force a continual review of every possible current liability as part of the standard monthly closing procedure, so that no key accruals are missed.
- **Review accrual accounts for unreversed entries.** Some accruals, such as unpaid wage accruals and commission accruals, are supposed to be reversed in the following period, when the actual expense is incurred. However, if an accountant forgets to properly set up a journal entry for automatic reversal in the next period, a company will find itself having recorded too large an expense.

A simple control point is to include in the period-end closing procedure a review of all accounts in which accrual entries are made, to ensure that all reversals have been completed.

- **Create standard entries for reversing journal entries.** As a continuation of the last control point, an easy way to avoid problems with accrual journal entries that are supposed to be reversed is to create boilerplate journal entry formats in the accounting system that are preconfigured to be automatically reversed in the next period. As long as these standard formats are used, there will never be an unreversed journal entry.

- **Include a standard review of customer advances in the closing procedure.** If a company regularly deals with a large number of customer deposits, there is a significant risk that the deposits will not be recognized as revenue in conjunction with the completion of any related services or product sales. This problem can be avoided by requiring a periodic review of the status of each deposit as part of the period-end closing procedure.

- **Include an accrual review in the closing procedure for income taxes payable.** A common practice is to only accrue for income taxes on a quarterly basis, when estimated taxes are due. The trouble is that this is a substantial expense being excluded from all monthly financial statements not falling at the end of each reporting quarter, and so it tends to skew the reported results of those months. By including in the closing procedure a line item requiring the accrual of an income tax liability, the accounting staff is forced to address this issue every time financial statements are issued.

- **Maintain historical expense information about warranty claims both for ongoing product sales and new product introductions.** If a company creates a warranty expense accrual for a new product based on its standard claim rate for existing products, the warranty expense will probably be underaccrued for the initial introductory period of the product, since more product problems will arise early in a product launch that are corrected in later models. A good control over this underreporting is to track warranty expenses separately for new model introductions and ongoing sales, so a reasonable basis of information can be used for each type of accrual.

- **Match the final monthly payroll pay date to the last day of the month.** The unpaid wage accrual can be significant when employee pay dates differ substantially from the last day of the reporting period. This problem can be partially resolved by setting the last (or only) pay date of the month on the last day of the month, and paying employees through that date, which eliminates the need for any wage accrual. This control is most effective for salaried employees, who are typically paid through the pay date. There is usually a cutoff for hourly employees that is several days prior to the pay date, so some wage accrual would still be necessary for these employees.

- **Automate the period-end cutoff.** A common closing activity is to compare the receiving department's receiving log for the few days near period-end to the supplier invoices logged in during that period, to see if there are any receipts for which there are no supplier invoices. This is a slow and error-prone activity. A good alternative is to use the computer system to automatically locate missing invoices. The key requirements are a purchase order system covering all significant purchases, as well as rapid updating of the inventory database by the warehouse staff when items are received. If these features exist, a batch program can be written linking the purchase order, inventory, and accounting databases, and which compares inventory receipts to received invoices. If no invoice exists, the program calculates the price of the missing invoice based on the purchase order. It then creates a report for the accounting staff itemizing all receipts for which there are no invoices, and calculating the price of the missing invoices. This report can be used as the basis for a journal entry at month-end to record missing invoices.

- **Create a standard checklist of recurring supplier invoices to include in the month-end cutoff.** A number of invoices arrive after month-end that are related to services, and for which an accrual should be made. The easiest way to be assured of making these accruals is to create a list of recurring invoices, with their approximate amounts, and use it as a check-off list during the closing process. If the invoice has not yet arrived, then accrue for the standard amount shown on the list.

- **Automate or sidestep the matching process.** The most common way to establish the need for a payment to a supplier is to compare an incoming supplier invoice to the authorizing purchase order, as well as receiving documentation to ensure that the item billed has been accepted. If both these sources of information agree with the invoice, then the accounts payable staff can proceed with payment. The trouble is that this process is terribly inefficient and highly error prone. There are three ways to improve this critical control point.

  1. **Use matching automation software.** Most high-end accounting software packages offer an automated matching system that automatically compares all three documents and highlights mismatches for further review. The trouble is that this software is expensive, requires linked computer databases for accounting, purchasing, and the warehouse, and also still requires manual labor to reconcile any mismatches it locates.

  2. **Authorize payments at the receiving point.** This advanced concept requires the presence of a computer terminal at the receiving dock. Upon receipt of a shipment, the receiving staff authorizes payment by accessing the purchase order in the computer system that relates to the receipt, and checking off those items received. The computer system then schedules a payment without any supplier invoice. This approach is theoretically the most efficient way to control the payables process, but requires considerable custom programming, as well as training of the receiving staff.

  3. **Shift payments to procurement cards.** A large proportion of all purchases are too small to require any matching process, since the labor expended exceeds the value of the control. Instead, create a procurement card system and encourage employees to make purchases with the cards,

up to a maximum limit. This program greatly reduces the number of transactions requiring matching, thereby focusing the attention of the accounts payable staff on just those transactions most likely to contain errors of a significant dollar value.

Contingencies

- **Include an assessment of contingent debt guarantees in the closing procedure.** Companies tend not to review debt guarantees on a regular basis, so the sudden failure of the obligor to pay can come as a considerable surprise, resulting in the recognition of a large debt obligation. This control is designed to force a regular review of any debt guarantees as part of the regular monthly closing schedule.

- **Include an assessment of debt covenant violations in the closing procedure.** It is not at all uncommon for a company to be unaware of debt covenant violations until informed of them by the lender, resulting in the immediate acceleration of debt into the short-term debt category. This problem can be avoided by including a covenant review in the regular monthly closing schedule.

- **Include an assessment of debt covenant violations in the budgeting process and interim financial planning.** Debt covenant violations are sometimes inadvertently caused by specific finance-related activities that could have been avoided if management had been aware of the impact of their actions. These problems can sometimes be avoided by including a covenant violation review in the budgeting procedure.

- **Include an assessment of all contingency reserves in the monthly closing procedure.** Contingency reserves tend to be set up once and forgotten, though the underlying contingencies may change in size over time. A reasonable control is to require a periodic review of the size of all reserves in the monthly closing procedure as a standard line item, thereby repeatedly bringing the issue to management's attention.

FORMS AND REPORTS

Current Liabilities—Commission Calculation Worksheet

There is an infinite array of possible sales commission plans, which frequently call for the creation of a customized spreadsheet or database program to deal with them, sometimes varying by individual salesperson. Given the size of the commissions awarded in some cases, it is important to quickly determine the commission expense accrual at the end of each reporting period, so this information can be accurately reflected in the financial statements. A good way to do this is to update the commission calculation on a weekly basis, and also to update it the day before the end of the reporting period, so that the minimum number of additional sales must be added to the report as part of the closing process. An example of such a report is

Exhibit 9-1: Commission Calculation Spreadsheet

Salesperson Name: [Smith]

June 2005 Commissions

Date	Invoice Number	Amount	Less Supplier Cost	Net Sale	Customer	Product	Commission Type	Commission Rate	Commission Dollars
6/1/2005	5527	$1,117.00	$0.00	$1,117.00	Oregon Land Title	LandTitle Database update	Repeat	4%	$44.68
6/4/2005	5570	-$883.75	$0.00	-$883.75	Arizona Title Search	Credit on customer return	Split	4%	($35.35)
6/30/2005	5638	$14,898.40	$8,332.00	$6,566.40	Iowa Land Equity	LandTitle Database update	Split	4%	$262.66
6/30/2005	5643	$9,191.00	$0.00	$9,191.00	Oregon Land Title	GPS Trak2000 software	Split	4%	$367.64
6/5/2005	5577	$700.60	$0.00	$700.60	Oregon Land Title	LandParcel Database update	New	7%	$49.04
6/5/2005	5578	$9,009.00	$0.00	$9,009.00	Iowa Land Equity	LandParcel Database update	New	8%	$720.72
6/5/2005	5579	$7,850.00	$5,000.00	$2,850.00	Missouri Flood Insurance	GPS Trak2000 software	New	8%	$228.00
6/6/2005	5582	$400.00	$0.00	$400.00	Missouri Flood Insurance	LandTitle Database update	New	7%	$28.00
6/9/2005	5583	$4,229.25	$0.00	$4,229.25	Arizona Title Search	LandParcel Database update	New	8%	$338.34
6/30/2005	5641	$686.80	$0.00	$686.80	Arizona Title Search	GPS Trak2000 software	New	7%	$48.08
		$47,198.30	$13,332.00	$33,866.30					$2,051.80

Manager Override Commissions					
Sales trainee #1	$	2,500	Override	2%	$50.00
Sales trainee #2	$	1,750	Override	2%	$35.00
			Total Commission		$2,136.80

shown in Exhibit 9-1. This spreadsheet itemizes each invoice in the first three columns, and also subtracts out any supplier costs associated with a sale, on the assumption that some sales are actually resales of products drop shipped from other companies. The report also itemizes different commission rates for recurring, split, and new sales, and contains a section at the bottom for override sales commissions.

Current Liabilities—Wage Accrual Spreadsheet

There is typically a gap between the last date through which wages are paid and the end of the reporting period, which can be a substantial time period. To ensure that the expense associated with this unpaid balance is properly accrued, one should use a standard spreadsheet that itemizes the people who are not paid through period-end, as well as their wage rates. It is best to have the spreadsheet automatically calculate a journal entry, as is the case for the sample form shown in Exhibit 9-2. By using this approach, the same account numbers are consistently used across multiple reporting periods, resulting in consistent reported results.

Exhibit 9-2: Wage Accrual Spreadsheet

Wage Accrual Spreadsheet			For the month of:	Jul-05
Department	*Hourly personnel*	*Pay rate per hour*	*Unpaid hours in month*	*Pay accrual*
Marketing	Below, Melissa	$ 40.00	14.00	$ 560.00
Production	Brandon, Andrew	$ 18.15	72.00	$1,306.80
Production	Gutierrez, Pablo	$ 17.25	72.00	$1,242.00
Production	Holloway, Tim	$ 16.43	72.00	$1,182.96
Production	Innes, Sean	$ 15.00	72.00	$1,080.00
Production	Smith, Michael	$ 15.00	72.00	$1,080.00
Consulting	Verity, Thomas	$ 50.00	72.00	$3,600.00

Journal Entry:		*Account number*	*Debit*	*Credit*
	Production Wages	62150-02		
	Production Payroll Taxes	62250-02	$5,891.76	
	Marketing Wages	62150-01	$ 365.29	
	Marketing Payroll Taxes	62250-01	$ 560.00	
	Consulting Wages	50050-03	$3,600.00	
	Consulting Payroll Taxes	62250-03	$ 223.20	
	Wage Accrual	22800		$10,674.97

NOTE: Hourly personnel are paid through the Sunday prior to the payroll date.

Current Liabilities—Royalty Calculation Spreadsheet

If a company must pay out a significant royalty related to its use or resale of another company's products, it should create a periodic accrual of this ongoing expense, which is easily forgotten if the actual royalty payment occurs only infrequently. Though the basic calculation of a royalty could use the format shown in Exhibit 9-3, the form is not a sufficient reminder for a periodic royalty accrual. Consequently, one should also include a periodic accrual in the period-end closing procedure. Exhibit 9-3 shows a standard royalty form suitable for delivery to the entity receiving a royalty, and is based on an ascending scale of royalty percentages, based on increasing revenue volumes. Given the wide array of possible royalty calculations, this format may require significant tailoring to match a specific royalty agreement.

Exhibit 9-3: Royalty Calculation Worksheet

[Supplier Name] Royalty Statement	
for the Third Fiscal Quarter Ended	
[Date]	
Product Name	$ 128,000
Product Name	$ 34,500
Product Name	$ 98,250
Total Product Revenue	$ 260,750
Royalty Calculation:	
4% × First $50,000	$ 2,000
7% × Excess over $50,000, up to $200,000	$ 10,500
11% × Excess over $200,000	$ 6,683
Total Royalty for the Fiscal Year	$ 19,183
Less: Previous Payments Made	$ 14,750
Total Payment	$ 4,433
[Company Name],	
By:_____	Date:_____
Signature of Authorized Officer	

Current Liabilities—Vacation Accrual Spreadsheet

The amount of vacation liability is based on the current amount of earned but unused vacation. However, because vacation time can fluctuate significantly over the course of a year, it is quite common to maintain an accrued vacation expense balance equating to an expected fiscal year-end or quarter-end amount. An example of such an accrual calculation is shown in Exhibit 9-4, where the accrual is calculated for three company subsidiaries. In the example, only 40 hours of vacation can be carried forward by subsidiaries A and C, while 80 hours are allowed for subsidiary B. For each subsidiary, the spreadsheet lists all employees, their annual pay, and the maximum number of vacation hours they can carry forward into the next year. By allowing a maximum vacation carryforward, the accountant can easily calculate the maximum possible vacation accrual that must be on the books at the end of the year. The spreadsheet also compares the maximum accrual to the amount currently booked, and then transfers the required adjustment into a journal entry at the bottom of the page. This is an effective reporting format for periodic adjustments to the vacation accrual.

Exhibit 9-4: Vacation Accrual Spreadsheet

Vacation Accrual

Name	Annualized salary	Maximum hours	Maximum accrual	Division	Maximum accrual	Current accrued balance	Required entry
Adams, Latrone	$45,000	40.00	$865	Subsidiary A			
Benning, Brian	$103,000	40.00	$1,990	Subsidiary A			
Blotten, Charles	$75,250	40.00	$1,447	Subsidiary A	$7,253	$5,250	$2,003
Clarion, Alice	$97,000	40.00	$1,865	Subsidiary A			
Corey, David	$56,400	40.00	$1,085	Subsidiary A			
Brower Franklin	$85,000	80.00	$3,269	Subsidiary B			
Hustle, James	$48,000	80.00	$1,846	Subsidiary B			
Innes, Mandy	$99,000	80.00	$3,808	Subsidiary B	$13,346	$12,000	$1,346
Mandrel, Steven	$65,000	80.00	$2,500	Subsidiary B			
Van den Plee, Joe	$100,000	40.00	$1,923	Subsidiary B			
Chao, Brian	$60,000	40.00	$1,154	Subsidiary C			
Dunwiddy, John	$51,039	40.00	$982	Subsidiary C			
Ephraim, Joe	$48,900	40.00	$940	Subsidiary C	$5,225	$5,000	$225
Horvath, Mark	$37,752	40.00	$726	Subsidiary C			
McKenna, Jason	$74,000	40.00	$1,423	Subsidiary C			

Journal entry:	Account description	Account no.	Debit	Credit
	Salary expense – Subsidiary A	6000-01	$2,003	
	Salary expense – Subsidiary B	6000-02	$1,346	
	Salary expense – Subsidiary C	6000-03	$225	
	Vacation Accrual	22300		$3,574

FOOTNOTES

Disclosure of Collective Bargaining Agreements

If some portion of a company's workforce is unionized, the proportion so organized should be noted, as well as the date when its collective bargaining agreements expire. An example follows:

> The company has 5,000 employees, of which 100% of its hourly production staff of 2,850 is represented by the International Brotherhood of Electrical Workers. The current collective bargaining agreement with this union expires in June 2009. No other company employees are represented by a union.

Disclosure of Contingent Asset Purchase Obligation

If a company has a contingent liability to purchase an asset, one should disclose the terms of the obligation, as well as the range of costs involved if the obligation comes to pass. An example follows:

> The company acquired a below-market lease on its headquarters building in exchange for a contingent liability to purchase the building from the lessor after 15 years for a fixed sum of $20.7 million. If the company chooses not to exercise this option, it will be contingently liable to the lessor for a nonpurchase penalty of 10% of the market value of the building at that time. A recent appraisal of similar buildings in the area indicates that the current market value of the building is approximately $12 million. When

adjusted for probable annual price inflation, the value of the building in 15 years may be approximately $16 million. Thus, the company may be liable for 10% of this amount, or $1.6 million, in 15 years if it chooses not to purchase the building. Since there is a difference of $4.7 million between the eventual purchase price and the expected fair value of the building, the company would capitalize only $16 million if it were to purchase the building, and charge the remainder of the payment to lease expense. Accordingly, the company must recognize either a penalty of $1.6 million or a lease expense of $4.7 million in 15 years. The company is charging 1/15 of the penalty amount to expense in each of the next 15 years in order to recognize the lesser of the two contingent expenses.

Disclosure of Contingent Liabilities

A contingent liability is one where a business entity may be required to pay off a liability, but either the amount of the liability cannot reasonably be determined at the report date, or the requirement to pay is uncertain. The most common contingent liability is a lawsuit whose outcome is still pending. If the contingent amount can be reasonably estimated and the outcome is reasonably certain, then a contingent liability must be accrued. However, in any case where the outcome is not so certain, the accountant should describe the nature of the claim in the footnotes. Also, if a lower limit to the range of possible liabilities has been accrued due to the difficulty of deriving a range of possible estimates, then the upper limit of the range should be included in the footnotes. Finally, if a loss contingency arises after the financial statement date but before the release date, then this information should also be disclosed. Two examples follow:

1. The company has one potential contingent liability. It is for an insurance claim related to earthquake damage to the company's California assembly plant. The insurance company is disputing its need to pay for this claim, on the grounds that the insurance renewal payment was received by it one day after the policy expiration date. Company counsel believes that the insurance company's claim is groundless, and that it will be required to pay the company the full amount of the claim after arbitration is concluded. The total amount of the claim is $1,285,000.
2. The company accepted an obligation to increase the purchase price of a newly acquired subsidiary if it met certain earn-out goals. Management believes the subsidiary will match the earn-out targets, and so has recognized a contingent liability of $2.3 million and increased the goodwill account by an identical amount. The liability will be paid subsequent to the completion of an annual audit that will verify the earn-out results.

Disclosure of Employment Contract Liabilities

A company may enter into a variety of obligations when it agrees to employment contracts, such as a minimum number of years of salary payments, health insurance coverage subsequent to employment termination, and payments for life insurance coverage. If material, the term, potential expense, and descriptions of these agreements should be disclosed in a footnote. It is generally adequate to summarize all employment contract liabilities into a single footnote. An example follows:

The company has entered into five-year employment contracts with its CEO, CFO, and CIO, under which they are collectively guaranteed minimum salaries totaling $748,000 in each of the next five years, assuming their continued employment. In addition, the company has guaranteed payment for all of their term life insurance policies payable to their spouses, aggregating $3,000,000, for the five-year period. Since this is a firm liability, the company has recorded the present value of the expense in the current period, totaling $82,500.

Disclosure of Gain Contingencies

When there is a possibility of a potential future gain, one can describe it in a footnote, including the amount of the gain, payment timing, and situation under which the gain arises. However, the wording should include the risks of **not** receiving the gain, so readers are not misled into assigning an incorrectly high probability to the eventual recognition of the gain. Some examples, involving increasing levels of gain probability, are provided.

1. The company has initiated a suit against ABC Castings in the 4th District Court of Colorado, charging it with the improper design of a casting for a plastic swing sold by the company that has resulted in several million dollars of product warranty costs. The suit seeks recompense for $3.5 million in warranty cost reimbursements. No estimate can be made at this time of the amount of any future gain arising from settlement of this suit.

2. The company was awarded $2.5 million by a jury trial in the 4th District Court of Colorado in July 2007 in its suit against ABC Castings. ABC has filed an appeal, which could result in the substantial reduction or elimination of the awarded amount. Accordingly, the company has elected to not record any gain until cash is received from ABC.

3. The company has reached an out-of-court settlement with ABC Castings, under which ABC has agreed to drop its ongoing appeal of a $2.5 million judgment against it in exchange for an immediate payment of $1.75 million. This payment has been received, so the company has recorded a gain of $1.75 million in the financial statements.

Disclosure of Geographic Risk

If a company's geographic situation renders it more likely to suffer from a future catastrophe based on its geographic location, it can describe this risk in a footnote. Possible situations warranting such disclosure are locating in a floodplain or in a forested area highly subject to wildfires, being near an active earthquake fault line, or in a common area for tornados. An example follows:

The company's primary chemical processing facility is located directly over the San Andreas fault line, which has a history of producing earthquakes ranging up to 6.9 on the Richter scale. The company has attempted to obtain earthquake insurance, but the nature of its business makes the risk of loss so great for insurers that they will not provide coverage. Accordingly, the company is searching for a new facility in central Nevada, and plans to move there within the next three years, shutting down the California facility at that time. In the meantime, the company remains at risk from any earthquake-related incidents, with losses from such an event being potentially large enough to have a material impact on the company's financial results.

Disclosure of Government Investigation

If a company is being investigated by any government division at any level and material penalties or losses could result, one should describe the investigation in a footnote, including the nature and potential cost of any claims made. An example follows:

> The General Services Administration (GSA) has audited the company's billings to the federal government for the past three years, and claims to have found that the billing rates used for several employees were too high, based on their experience levels. The GSA has requested that these invoices be retroactively reduced and the difference paid back to the government. The rebate amount claimed by the GSA is $2.4 million. The company considers the claim to be without merit, and is vigorously defending its position. If a further government review finds the company to be liable for this payment, the company will also be subject to the suspension of its GSA schedule and all contracting with the government for a maximum of two years.

Disclosure of Indebtedness Guarantees

If a company has entered into guarantees of the indebtedness of third parties, it should disclose the nature of the agreement, the amount of the guarantee, and the likely value of any payments that may be made. An example follows:

> The company has guaranteed a term loan to a separate business owned by the company CEO's spouse, under which it is liable for the unpaid balance of the loan, though the lender must first attempt to obtain payment from the separate business. The current unpaid balance of the principal and interest on the loan is $389,000. This amount declines to $214,000 in 2008, and is paid off by the end of 2009.

Disclosure of Industry Risk

If the industry in which a company operates has unique risks related to such factors as intense competition, low barriers to entry, rapidly changing technology, and so on, then a footnote can describe these issues and their potential impact on company operations. An example follows:

> The company's primary business is the design, manufacture, and sale of Christmas ornaments. The company's financial results are influenced by the rapidity with which designs are copied by foreign competitors and reproduced at much lower prices, as well as the company's ability to continue to create new designs finding favor in the marketplace, maintain a large network of distributors, manufacture in sufficient quantities for the Christmas selling season, and dispose of excess inventory without excessive losses. Based on these factors, the company can experience large fluctuations in its future financial results.

Disclosure of Litigation

Companies are frequently the subject of lawsuits for a variety of alleged situations, such as harassment, patent infringement, and environmental liabilities. One should describe in the footnotes the general nature of each lawsuit, the amount of restitution sought, and the opinion of the company's legal counsel regarding the probable outcome of the suit. If there are many similar suits, they may be summarized for descriptive purposes. If lawsuits would have an immaterial impact on company results, then this can be stated in general terms. Some examples follow:

1. The company is the target of a class action lawsuit entitled *Smith v. ABC Company*, currently in the 4th District Court of Colorado. In the case, current and previous hourly staff claim nonpayment of overtime pay, and seek damages of $20,000,000. The company avers that the case is without merit and continues to vigorously defend its position in the case. It is not possible to determine a probable outcome at this time, and since company management feels a material loss from the suit to be remote, the company has not accrued any related expense.

2. The company is the target of a sexual harassment lawsuit entitled *Jones v. ABC Company*, currently in the 4th District Court of Colorado. In the suit, a former employee alleges disparaging comments and actions by her immediate supervisor, and seeks damages of $1 million. Per the advice of company counsel, the company offered to settle the case for $100,000 and accrued for this expense. However, if the offer is not accepted and the case were to go to trial, the company could be liable for the $1 million sought in the suit.

3. The company is the target of a variety of legal proceedings as the result of its normal business operations, generally in the area of personal damage claims related to slips and falls in its warehouse facilities. In management's opinion, any liabilities arising from these proceedings would not have a material adverse impact on the company's financial results.

Disclosure of Outsourced Production Liability

Many companies have outsourced their production to third parties, but are shackled by contingent liabilities under which they are required to purchase minimum quantities from the third parties, and sometimes also to pay for any fixed costs incurred by the suppliers if production is halted before a predetermined quantity of units have been produced. If so, the terms, duration, and general description of the agreement should be included in a footnote. An example follows:

> The company has outsourced its production to the ABC Foreign Company, under a five-year contract that requires the company to purchase a minimum of 10,000 golf carts per year from ABC. If not, the company must pay $650 to ABC for each unit under the minimum on which it did not take delivery. In addition, if the contract is terminated early, the company must pay ABC $200,000 for each year of early termination in order to pay it back for a variety of up-front fixed charges it incurred to create a production line.

Disclosure of Postemployment Benefits

If employees are entitled to benefits subsequent to their employment that are material, then the nature of the transaction, the amount of expense involved, and its treatment in the financial statements should be revealed in a footnote. An example follows:

> The company's former president, Mr. Smith, was asked to step down by the Board on May 5, 2007. As part of the separation agreement, the company agreed to pay Mr. Smith's medical insurance premiums for the next two years, and also paid a lump-sum settlement of $2 million. The present value of the entire medical cost was charged to expense in the current period, as was the lump-sum settlement. The medical expense

was offset against an Unpaid Insurance Premiums liability account, which will be gradually reduced as periodic medical insurance payments are made.

Disclosure of Purchasing Commitments

There may be a minimum purchase agreement extending into future reporting periods, which obligates a company to make purchases in amounts that are material. Also, a company may have made guarantees to pay for the debts of other entities, such as a subsidiary. If these commitments are material, then their nature must be disclosed in the footnotes. The rules are not specific about identifying the exact cost or probability of occurrence of each commitment, so the accountant has some leeway in presenting this information. An example follows:

> The company has entered into a contract to purchase a minimum of 500,000 tons of coal per year for the next twenty years at a fixed price of $20.50 per ton, with no price escalation allowed for the duration of the contract. The company's minimum annual payment obligation under this contract is $10,250,000. The price paid under this contract is $1.75 less than the market rate for anthracite coal as of the date of these statements, and had not significantly changed as of the statement issuance date.

Disclosure of Reseller Liability

Distributors sometimes enter into sole-sourcing agreements with suppliers, whereby they guarantee a minimum amount of sales in exchange for exclusive rights to a sales region. If such an agreement exists, one should disclose its duration, description, and potential amount of payments. An example follows:

> The company has entered into an agreement to be the sole-source New Zealand distributor of Merino lambing shears. The sole distribution agreement will exist for a minimum of two years, as long as the company sells at least 10,000 shears per year. During that two-year period ending in June 2008, the company must pay the supplier $5 for each shears not sold below the minimum annual quantity. If the company were to not sell any shears, this liability would be $50,000 per year for two years. At this time, year-to-date sales indicate that the company will meet the minimum quantity required under the first year of the agreement, so management has elected not to recognize any expenses associated with this contingent liability.

Disclosure of Royalty Payments

A royalty agreement involving potentially material payments should be disclosed. The information in the footnote should include a description and the terms of the agreement, as well as the potential amount of the payments. An example follows:

> The company contracts much of its software game development to third-party developers. These developers receive nonrecoverable advances ranging from $25,000 to $80,000 for each game they create, against which a standard 8% royalty is deducted. Once the full amount of each advance has been earned by a developer, royalty payments are accrued monthly and paid quarterly. All development advances are accounted for as short-term assets in the Development Advances account, which currently contains $2,628,000. The company periodically compares product sales to the remaining amount of advances on each product, and writes off those advances for which sales trends indi-

cate that remaining royalties earned will not be sufficient to eliminate the advances. In the past year, the company wrote off $350,000 of development advances for this reason.

Disclosure of Self-Insurance Liability

If a company has elected to cover some portion of its risk portfolio with self-insurance, one should itemize the types of risk covered by self-insurance, the method by which estimated expenses are calculated, and the recent claims history of the self-insurance program. An example follows:

> The company has set up a self-insurance program to cover its workers' compensation risk. All claims are paid up to an annual limit of $2 million, after which an umbrella policy covers all remaining claims. The company charges to expense all actual claims made during each reporting period, as well as an estimate of claims incurred but not yet reported, based on a one-year rolling history of this information. The amount of claims incurred but not reported is currently $158,000, and is recorded as a liability.

Disclosure of No Insurance

If a company is unable to obtain insurance for coverage of any key business risk, the circumstances of the situation and a statement about potential losses should be noted in a footnote. An example follows:

> Given the spate of wildfires in recent years in the Rocky Mountain region, it is now impossible to obtain fire damage insurance for the company's headquarters, which is located in the midst of a forest in central New Mexico. The company has assertively taken steps to reduce fire danger through the use of forest thinning, in-house fire control teams, and sprinkler systems. Given these risk mitigation steps, the company feels that the potential risk of loss has been much reduced, and so has taken no steps to create a self-insurance fund for this risk.

Disclosure of Supplier Concentration Risk

If a company is highly dependent on a few suppliers for the bulk of its purchases of materials, or if key materials have limited sources, the proportion or types of materials subject to this issue should be noted, as well as commentary on the relationship with these suppliers and how their loss would impact the company. An example follows:

> The printer drum used in the company's primary laser printer product is sole-sourced to a foreign company that is the dominant low-cost producer of this part. If the supplier were to reduce or stop delivering this part, the company would switch to an alternate supplier who is already being used for small production volumes. However, the alternate source's prices are 30% higher, which would have a material impact on the company's cost of goods sold and therefore its financial results. Also, the alternate supplier has unproven experience in producing at the volume levels required by the company. However, management believes the company's relations with its primary supplier to be excellent, and the possibility of a supply shortage to be remote.

Disclosure of Taxation Disputes

A company may be in a variety of stages of investigation by any number of government taxing authorities, ranging from sales and use tax audits to income tax reviews. Disclosure of these reviews can range from a simple statement that an audit is underway, through the initial judgment notice, to a description of a finalized payment settlement. The following footnotes give examples of several options:

1. The company is being reviewed by a California sales tax audit team. Management is of the opinion that this review will not result in any material change in the company's financial results.
2. The company has been audited by a California sales tax audit team, which asserts that the company has established nexus in that state, and so must remit sales taxes for all sales into California for the past three years, which would total $14 million. Management is of the opinion that there are no grounds for establishing nexus, and intends to vigorously contest the issue through the California appeals process, up to and including litigation. Management believes there is no need to establish any loss accrual related to this matter at this time.
3. The company has reached agreement with the State of California, under which a payment of $2.5 million for unpaid sales taxes shall be made. The company intends to collect these taxes from its customers, which management believes will substantially reduce the amount of its liability. Accordingly, it has recognized an expense of $600,000 in the current period to cover any sales taxes it cannot collect from customers, and will modify this amount in the future based on its sales tax collection experience for the amounts due.

Disclosure of Unasserted Claims

Even if a company has not yet received any claims for a specific liability, it should disclose the possibility if such claims are probable, and if losses will result. An example follows:

> The company's construction division has recently learned that some particle board used in its construction of residential homes contains trace amounts of asbestos. Though the company has received no claims arising from this use, other builders in the industry have been targeted by lawsuits, with judgments ranging from $50,000 to $150,000 per home. Since the company plans to vigorously pursue legal action against its particle board supplier if any claims are made, the company feels that the risk of loss, net of pass-through losses to the supplier, is reduced to less than $1 million.

Disclosure of Vacation Liability

If a company is obligated to pay its employees for future time off that has already been earned, it should reveal its method for calculating the obligation, as well as its amount. An example follows:

> The company accrues vacation and sick time for its employees up to a maximum of two weeks per year, since employees cannot accrue more time under a "use it or lose it" policy. The accrual calculation is to multiply the current hourly rate for each employee, plus related payroll taxes, by the accrued amount of time earned by each employee, with a cap of 80 hours earned. The company has accrued $182,000 in the Accrued Vacations liability account under this policy.

Disclosure of Warranty Liabilities

If the amount of warranty liabilities is material, the general product warranty, as well as its duration, should be listed in a footnote. An example follows:

The company warrants its camping equipment products against defects in design and materials for the lifetime of the original owner, and provides replacements at any time with no investigation or evidence of sales receipt. This warranty policy goes well beyond that of the sporting goods industry. Management believes the policy is a key reason why customers consider the company's products to be of high quality, and so intends to retain this policy into the foreseeable future. Warranty reserves are based on the past year of actual warranty claims, which most recently were 5.9% of sales. In addition, warranty reserves may be increased in the short term if there is evidence of problems with specific products that may result in material increases in warranty claims. Reserves are booked at the point of initial sale.

JOURNAL ENTRIES

Current Liabilities

Accrue benefits. To accrue for all employee benefit expenses incurred during the month, for which an associated payable entry has not yet been made.

Medical insurance expense	xxx	
Dental insurance expense	xxx	
Disability expense	xxx	
Life insurance expense	xxx	
Accrued benefits		xxx

This entry should be **reversed** in the following accounting period.

Accrue bonuses. To record an estimated bonus amount. This entry assumes that a separate bonus expense account is charged, though it is also common practice to charge a salaries expense account. The accrual is reversed when the bonus is actually paid.

Bonus expense	xxx	
Accrued salaries		xxx

Accrue commissions. To accrue the estimated commission expense prior to payment. The liability is recorded in an accrued salaries account in order to conserve the number of liability accounts, but can also be recorded in a separate accrued commissions account. This entry is typically reversed in the following accounting period to offset the actual commission payment.

Commission expense	xxx	
Accrued salaries		xxx

Accrue property taxes. To accrue for the property tax liability incurred during the accounting period based on the known base of fixed assets.

Property tax expense	xxx	
Property tax payable		xxx

This entry **should not be reversed** in the following accounting period, since the tax payment will not normally occur in the following period, but instead only once or twice per year. Instead, the actual payment should be charged directly against the accrual account with the following entry:

| Property tax payable | xxx | |
| Cash | | xxx |

Accrue royalties. To accrue the amount of royalties due to a supplier that have been earned but are not yet due for payment. This entry is reversed when the royalty payment is made.

| Royalty expense | xxx | |
| Accrued royalty expense | | xxx |

Accrue salaries and wages. To accrue for salaries and wages earned through the end of the accounting period, but not yet paid to employees as of the end of the accounting period.

Direct labor expense	xxx	
(Salaries—itemize by department)	xxx	
Payroll tax expense	xxx	
Accrued salaries		xxx
Accrued payroll taxes		xxx

This entry should be **reversed** in the following accounting period.

Accrue vacation pay. To accrue vacation pay earned by employees, but not yet used by them, subject to the year-end maximum vacation carryforward limitation. The same entry can be used to record accrued sick time.

Payroll taxes	xxx	
(Salaries—itemize by department)	xxx	
Accrued vacation pay		xxx

This entry **should not be reversed** in the following accounting period, since the vacation time may not be used in the following period. Instead, the actual vacation-related payment should be charged directly against the accrual account.

Accrue warranty claims. To accrue a reserve for warranty claims when a sale is made.

| Warranty expense | xxx | |
| Accrued warranty expense | | xxx |

Record customer advances. To record the liability associated with a customer advance prior to completion of services or delivery of goods to the customer. The second entry assumes an advance is actually a deposit on the use of a company asset, and will be returned once the usage period is completed.

Cash	xxx	
Customer advances		xxx
Cash	xxx	
Customer deposits		xxx

Contingencies

Recognition of minimum option price. To recognize a compensation expense associated with a guaranteed minimum option exercise price. The first entry shows the creation of a liability, while the second entry shows a periodic charge to expense to reflect the ongoing completion of the service period associated with the option grant. The third entry reflects option forfeiture prior to completion of the service obligation.

Deferred compensation	xxx	
Options—additional paid-in capital		xxx
Compensation expense	xxx	
Deferred compensation expense		xxx
Options—additional paid-in capital	xxx	
Compensation expense		xxx
Deferred compensation expense		xxx

RECORDKEEPING

A detailed record should be kept of all advances received by a company from customers, since this is a common area in which liabilities are underreported through the improper immediate recognition of advances as revenue. It is particularly important when the advances are actually deposits and must be returned to customers, since disputes over the amounts payable will be likely if recordkeeping is inadequate.

Bonus payments can be quite large, so an itemization of the plans under which they are authorized and a detailed proof of their having been earned should be stored. This information is usually kept in the human resources file for each person to whom a bonus is paid.

Perhaps the most disputed of all current liabilities is the commission expense, due to both the complexity of many commission plans and the large proportion of pay that this expense represents for the sales staff. Accordingly, the level of documentation in this area should be very high, including a detailed calculation for each commission paid that itemizes every invoice on which payment was made, and a clear notation of all special splits, overrides, and so on related to the payment. One should also retain the annual commission plan for each salesperson, which is used as the basis for the commission calculations.

The amount of accrued vacation and sick time is based on the accrual levels noted in the employee manual, which may change from year to year. A copy of every version of the employee manual should be stored, so that changes in the terms of these compensated absences can be traced. If an override deal is offered to a specific employee, a written copy of the deal should be stored in the employee's human resources file and also documented in the accounting department so it can be readily accessed when compensated absence accruals are made.

If a group of employees are to be terminated, the accrual for termination benefits can be a substantial one, and so should be adequately documented. This should include a copy of the termination plan, as well as written estimates of the number and types of positions to be eliminated, and a summary calculation of termination benefits based on this information.

Royalty payments can cause special problems for a company, because many royalty agreements allow the payee to audit the company's books to ensure that royalty payments are being properly calculated and paid out. Consequently, special care should be made to segregate all royalty information in a separate set of binders where it can be easily accessed. The binders should either include a complete audit trail for the calculation and payment of royalties, or at least document where this information can be located elsewhere in the accounting records.

The wage accrual can be one of the largest period-end accruals, especially if a large proportion of the labor force is paid on an hourly basis, in which case there is typically a lag of several days between the completion of hours worked and the pay date. In these cases, a standard unpaid wage accrual worksheet, such as the one shown earlier in the Forms and Reports section, should be attached to the journal entry recording the accrual and stored in the journal entry binder for future reference.

An accrual for anticipated warranty expenses can be quite large for companies selling particular types of products, such as consumer end products. In these cases, it is worthwhile to record the historical warranty information on which the accrual is based, such as the historical claims information for both new product introductions and products that have been on the market for some time. This information is useful for proving the validity of the accrual if it is challenged during an audit.

Debt covenant violations catch companies by surprise far too often, because they do not regularly track company performance in relation to the covenants or plan in advance to avoid violations. This problem can be controlled to some extent by separately recording the covenants in a place where they are difficult **not** to see, such as in the lead page of the budget, alongside all other assumptions. Even better, covenants can be included in the monthly financial statements, as part of a general comparison of covenants to actual results on a trend line for the past few months. This presentation ensures high visibility and also makes it quite clear which covenants are close to being violated.

The assumptions used to derive the amount of insurance claims incurred but not yet reported under any self-insurance program should be documented and included in the journal entry binder. This information will be used by auditors to determine the most appropriate amount of liability to record in association with unreported insurance claims.

10 LONG-TERM DEBT

DEFINITIONS OF TERMS

Amortization. In the context of long-term debt, the gradual write-off of discounts or premiums associated with debt offerings.

Bond. A debt arrangement with multiple debt holders under which an entity accepts an initial payment in exchange for a promise of periodic interest payments and a principal payment at the end of a specified period.

Callable bond. A bond for which the issuer has the right of early repayment.

Collateral. Assets pledged by a debtor that may be attached by a lender if the debtor does not make payments under a debt agreement in a timely manner.

Convertible debt. Debt that may be converted into stock at the lender's option, depending on specific criteria in the debt agreement.

Debt. Funds owed to another entity.

Discount. A reduction in the value of a bond when it is issued at a stated rate less than the market rate, resulting in bond sales below the face value.

Face value. The principal repayment amount of a bond, as written on the bond document.

Issuance costs. The costs associated with a debt issuance, such as the cost of printing and issuing registration statements, and underwriting, audit, and legal fees.

Long-term debt. A debt for which payments will be required for a period of more than one year into the future.

Note. A debt issued to a single holder, generally with the expectation of repayment within a few years.

Premium. An increase in the value of a bond when it is issued at a stated rate higher than the market rate, resulting in bond sales above the face value.

Stated rate. The interest rate noted on a debt instrument.

CONCEPTS AND EXAMPLES[1]

Overview of Bonds

The typical bond is a long-term (one- to thirty-year) obligation to pay a creditor, and which may be secured by company assets. A traditional bond agreement calls for a semiannual interest payment, while the principal amount is paid in a lump sum at the termination date of the bond. The issuing company may issue periodic interest payments directly to bondholders, though only if they are registered; another alternative is to send the entire amount of interest payable to a trustee, who exchanges bond coupons from bondholders for money from the deposited funds.

The issuing company frequently creates a sinking fund well in advance of the bond payoff date, so that it will have sufficient funds available to make the final balloon payment (or buy back bonds on an ongoing basis). The bond agreement may contain a number of restrictive covenants that the company must observe, or else the bondholders will be allowed a greater degree of control over the company or allowed to accelerate the payment date of their bonds.

---

[1] *Much of the information in this section is adapted with permission from Chapter 19 of Bragg,* **Ultimate Accountants' Reference** *(John Wiley & Sons, Inc., Hoboken, NJ, 2006).*

A bond will be issued at a stated face value interest rate. If this rate does not equate to the market rate on the date of issuance, then investors will either bid up the price of the bond (if its stated rate is higher than the market rate) or bid down the price (if its stated rate is lower than the market rate). The after market price of a bond may subsequently vary considerably if the market rate of interest varies substantially from the stated rate of the bond.

Some bonds are issued with no interest rate at all. These **zero-coupon bonds** are sold at a deep discount and are redeemed at their face value at the termination date of the bond. They are of particular interest to those companies that do not want to be under the obligation of making fixed interest payments during the term of a bond.

The interest earned on a bond is subject to income taxes, except for those bonds issued by government entities. Theses bonds, known as **municipal bonds,** pay tax-free interest. For this reason, they can be competitively sold at lower actual interest rates than the bonds offered by commercial companies.

The **serial bond** does not have a fixed termination date for the entire issuance of bonds. Instead, the company is entitled to buy back a certain number of bonds at regular intervals, so that the total number of outstanding bonds declines over time.

An alternative is the use of attached warrants, which allow the bondholder to buy shares of company stock at a prespecified price. If the warrants are publicly traded, then their value can be separated from that of the bond, so that each portion of the package is recognized separately in a company's balance sheet.

Though some corporations issue their own bonds directly to investors, it is much more common to engage the services of an investment banker, who not only lines up investors for the company, but may also invest a substantial amount of the banker's own funds in the company's bonds. In either case, the Board of Directors must approve any new bonds, after which a trustee is appointed to control the bond issuance, certificates are printed and signed, and delivery is made either to the investment banking firm or directly to investors in exchange for cash.

Debt Classification

It is generally not allowable to reclassify a debt that is coming due in the short term as a long-term liability on the grounds that it is about to be refinanced as a long-term debt. This treatment would likely result in no debt ever appearing in the current liabilities portion of the balance sheet. This treatment is allowable only if the company has the intention to refinance the debt on a long-term basis, rather than simply rolling over the debt into another short-term debt instrument that will, in turn, become due and payable in the next accounting year. Also, there must be firm evidence of this rollover into a long-term debt instrument, such as the presence of a debt agreement or an actual conversion to long-term debt subsequent to the balance sheet date.

If a debt can be called by the creditor, then it must be classified as a current liability. However, if the period during which the creditor can call the debt is at some point subsequent to one year, then it may still be classified as a long-term debt. Also, if the call option applies only if the company defaults on some performance measure related to the debt, then the debt needs to be classified as a current liability only if the company cannot cure the performance measure within whatever period is specified under the terms of the debt. Further, if a debt agreement contains a call provision that is likely to be activated under the circumstances present as of the balance sheet date, then the debt should be classified as a current liability; conversely, if the probability of the call provision being invoked is remote, then the debt does not have to be so classified. Finally, if only a portion of the debt can be called, then only that portion need be classified as a current liability.

Bonds Sold at a Discount or Premium to Their Face Value

When bonds are initially sold, the entry is a debit to cash and a credit to bonds payable. However, this occurs only when the price paid by investors exactly matches the face amount of the bond. A more common occurrence is when the market interest rate varies somewhat from the stated interest rate on the bond, so investors pay a different price in order to achieve an effective interest rate matching the market rate. For example, if the market rate were 8% and the stated rate were 7%, investors would pay less than the face amount of the bond so that the 7% interest they later receive will equate to an 8% interest rate on their reduced investment. Alternatively, if the rates were reversed, with a 7% market rate and 8% stated rate, investors would pay more for the bond, thereby driving down the stated interest rate to match the market rate. If the bonds are sold at a discount, the entry will include a debit to a discount on bonds payable account. For example, if $10,000 of bonds are sold at a discount of $1,500, the entry would be

Cash	8,500	
Discount on bonds payable	1,500	
Bonds payable		10,000

If the same transaction were to occur, except that a premium on sale of the bonds occurs, then the entry would be:

Cash	11,500	
Premium on bonds payable		1,500
Bonds payable		10,000

Example of discount calculation

The Arabian Knights Security Company issues $1,000,000 of bonds at a stated rate of 8% in a market where similar issuances are being bought at 11%. The bonds pay interest once a year, and are to be paid off in ten years. Investors purchase these bonds at a discount in order to earn an effective yield on their investment of 11%. The discount calculation requires one to determine the present value of 10 interest payments at 11% interest, as well as the present value of $1,000,000, discounted at 11% for ten years. The result is as follows:

Present value of 10 payments of $80,000	= $80,000 × 5.8892	= $ 471,136
Present value of $1,000,000	= $1,000,000 × .3522	= $ 352,200
		$ 823,336
	Less: stated bond price	$1,000,000
	Discount on bond	$ 176,664

In this example, the entry would be a debit to Cash for $823,336, a credit to Bonds Payable for $1,000,000, and a debit to Discount on Bonds Payable for $176,664. If the calculation had resulted in a premium (which would have occurred only if the market rate of interest was less than the stated interest rate on the bonds), then a credit to Premium on Bonds Payable would be in order.

Effective Interest Method

The amount of a discount or premium should be gradually written off to the interest expense account over the life of the bond. The only acceptable method for writing off these amounts is through the **effective interest method,** which allows one to charge off the difference between the market and stated rate of interest to the existing discount or premium account, gradually reducing the balance in the discount or premium account over the life of the bond. If interest payment dates do not coincide with the end of financial reporting periods, a journal entry must be made to show the amount of interest expense and related discount or premium amortization that would have occurred during the days following the last interest payment date and the end of the reporting period.

Example of the effective interest method

To continue with our example, the interest method holds that, in the first year of interest payments, the Arabian Knights Security Company's accountant would determine that the market interest expense for the first year would be $90,567 (bond stated price of $1 million minus discount of $176,664, multiplied by the market interest rate of 11%). The resulting journal entry would be

Interest expense	90,567	
Discount on bonds payable		10,567
Cash		80,000

The reason why only $80,000 is listed as a reduction in cash is that the company only has an obligation to pay an 8% interest rate on the $1 million face value of the bonds, which is $80,000. The difference is netted against the existing Discount on Bonds Payable account. The following table shows the calculation of the discount to be charged to expense each year for the full ten-year period of the bond, where the annual amortization of the discount is added back to the bond present value, eventually resulting in a bond present value of $1 million by the time principal payment is due, while the discount has dropped to zero.

Year	Beginning bond present value (4)	Unamortized discount	Interest expense (1)	Cash payment (2)	Credit to discount (3)
1	$823,336	$176,664	$90,567	$80,000	$10,567
2	833,903	166,097	91,729	80,000	11,729
3	845,632	154,368	93,020	80,000	13,020
4	858,652	141,348	94,452	80,000	14,452
5	873,104	126,896	96,041	80,000	16,041
6	889,145	110,855	97,806	80,000	17,806
7	906,951	93,049	99,765	80,000	19,765
8	926,716	73,284	101,939	80,000	21,939
9	948,655	51,346	104,352	80,000	24,352
10	973,007	26,994	107,031	80,000	26,994
	$1,000,000	$0			

(1) − Bond present value multiplied by the market rate of 11%.

(2) = Required cash payment of 8% stated rate multiplied by face value of $1,000,000.

(3) = Interest expense reduced by cash payment.

(4) = Beginning present value of the bond plus annual reduction in the discount.

Debt Issued with No Stated Interest Rate

If a company issues debt that has no stated rate of interest, then the accountant must create an interest rate for it that approximates the rate that the company would likely obtain, given its credit rating, on the open market on the date when the debt was issued. The accountant then uses this rate to discount the face amount of the debt down to its present value, and then records the difference between this present value and the loan's face value as the loan balance. For example, if a company issued debt with a face amount of $1 million, payable in five years and at no stated interest rate, and the market rate for interest at the time of issuance was 9%, then the discount factor to be applied to the debt would be 0.6499. This would give the debt a present value of $649,900. The difference between the face amount of $1 million and the present value of $649,900 should be recorded as a discount on the note, as shown in the following entry:

Cash	649,900	
Discount on note payable	350,100	
Notes payable		1,000,000

Debt Issuance Costs

The costs associated with issuing bonds can be substantial. These include the legal costs of creating the bond documents, printing the bond certificates, and (especially) the underwriting costs of the investment banker. Since these costs are directly associated with the procurement of funds that the company can be expected to use for a number of years (until the bonds are paid off), the related bond issuance costs should be recorded as an asset and then written off on a straight-line basis over the period during which the bonds are expected to be used by the company. This entry is a debit to a bond issuance asset account and a credit to cash. However, if the bonds associated with these costs are subsequently paid off earlier than anticipated, one can reasonably argue that the associated remaining bond issuance costs should be charged to expense at the same time.

Notes Issued with Attached Rights

An issuing company can grant additional benefits to the other party, such as exclusive distribution rights on its products, discounts on product sales, and so on—the range of possibilities is endless. In these cases, one should consider the difference between the present value and face value of the debt to be the value of the additional consideration. When this occurs, the difference is debited to the Discount on Note Payable account and is amortized using the **effective interest method** that was described earlier. The offsetting credit can be to a variety of accounts, depending on the nature of the transaction. The credited account is typically written off either ratably (if the attached benefit is equally spread over many accounting periods) or in conjunction with specific events (such as the shipment of discounted products to the holder of the debt). Though less common, it is also possible to issue debt at an above-market rate in order to obtain additional benefits from the debt holder. In this case, the entry is reversed, with a credit to the Premium on Note Payable account and the offsetting debit to a number of possible accounts related to the specific consideration given.

Example of note issued with attached rights

The Arabian Knights Security Company has issued a new note for $2,500,000 at 4% interest to a customer, the Alaskan Pipeline Company. Under the terms of the five-year note, Alaskan obtains a 20% discount on all security services it purchases from Arabian during the term of the note. The market rate for similar debt was 9% on the date the loan documents were signed.

The present value of the note at the 9% market rate of interest over a five-year term is $1,624,750, while the present value of the note at its stated rate of 4% is $2,054,750. The difference between the two present value figures is $430,000, which is the value of the attached right to discounted security services granted to Alaskan. Arabian should make the following entry to record the loan:

Cash	2,500,000	
Discount on note payable	430,000	
Note payable		2,500,000
Unearned revenue		430,000

The unearned revenue of $430,000 either can be recognized incrementally as part of each invoice billed to Alaskan, or can be recognized ratably over the term of the debt. Since Arabian does not know the exact amount of the security services that will be contracted for by Alaskan during the term of the five-year note, the better approach is to recognize the unearned revenue ratably over the note term. The first month's entry would be as follows, where the amount recognized is 1/60 of the beginning balance of unearned revenue:

Unearned revenue	7,166.67	
Services revenue		7,166.67

Notes Issued for Property

When a note is issued in exchange for some type of property, the stated interest rate on the note is used to value the debt for reporting purposes unless the rate is not considered to be "fair." If it is not fair, then the transaction should be recorded at either the fair market value of the property or the note, whichever can be more clearly determined.

Example of debt with an unfair interest rate, exchanged for property

The Arabian Knights Security Company exchanges a $50,000 note for a set of motion detection equipment from the Eye Spy Company. The equipment is custom-built for Arabian, so there is no way to assign a fair market value to it. The note has a stated interest rate of 3% and is payable in three years. The 3% rate appears to be quite low, especially since Arabian just secured similar financing from a local lender at a 7% interest rate. The 3% rate can thus be considered not fair for the purposes of valuing the debt, so Arabian's controller elects to use the 7% rate instead.

The discount rate for debt due in three years at 7% interest is 0.8163. After multiplying the $50,000 face value of the note by 0.8163, the controller arrives at a net present value for the debt of $40,815, which is recorded in the following entry as the value of the motion-detection equipment, along with a discount that shall be amortized to interest expense over the life of the loan.

Motion-detection equipment	40,815	
Discount on note payable	9,185	
Notes payable		50,000

Extinguishment of Debt

A company may find it advisable to repurchase its bonds prior to their maturity date, perhaps because market interest rates have dropped so far below the stated rate on the bonds that the company can profitably refinance at a lower interest rate. Whatever the reason may be, the resulting transaction should recognize any gain or loss on the transaction, as well as recognize the transactional cost of the retirement, and any proportion of the outstanding discount, premium, or bond issuance costs relating to the original bond issuance.

Example of debt extinguishment

To return to our earlier example, if the Arabian Knights Security Company were to buy back $200,000 of its $1 million bond issuance at a premium of 5%, and does so with $125,000 of the original bond discount still on its books, it would record a loss of $10,000 on the bond retirement ($200,000 × 5%), while also recognizing 1/5 of the remaining discount, which is $25,000 ($125,000 × 1/5). The entry would be as follows:

Bonds payable	200,000	
Loss on bond retirement	10,000	
Discount on bonds payable		25,000
Cash		185,000

If the issuing company finds itself in the position of being unable to pay either interest or principal to its bondholders, there are two directions the accountant can take in reflecting the problem in the accounting records. In the first case, the company may be only temporarily in default, and is attempting to work out a payment solution with the bondholders. Under this scenario, the amortizations of discounts or premiums, as well as of bond issuance costs and interest expense, should continue as they have in the past. However, if there is no chance of payment, then the amortizations of discounts or premiums, as well as of bond issuance costs, should be accelerated, being recognized in full in the current period. This action is taken on the grounds that the underlying accounting transaction that specified the period over which the amortizations occurred has now disappeared, requiring the accountant to recognize all remaining expenses.

If the issuing company has not defaulted on a debt, but rather has restructured its terms, then the accountant must determine the present value of the new stream of cash flows and compare it to the original carrying value of the debt arrangement. In the likely event that the new present value of the debt is less than the original present value, the difference should be recognized in the current period as a gain.

Alternatively, if the present value of the restructured debt agreement is **more** than the carrying value of the original agreement, then a loss is **not** recognized on the difference—instead, the effective interest rate on the new stream of debt payments is reduced to the point where the resulting present value of the restructured debt matches the carrying value of the original agreement. This will result in a reduced amount of interest expense being accrued for all future periods during which the debt is outstanding.

In some cases where the issuing company is unable to pay bondholders, it gives them other company assets in exchange for the interest or principal payments owed to them. When this occurs, the issuing company first records a gain or loss on the initial revaluation of the asset being transferred to its fair market value. Next, it records a gain or loss on the transaction if there is a difference between the carrying value of the debt being paid off and the fair market value of the asset being transferred to the bondholder.

Example of asset transfer to eliminate debt

The Arabian Knights Security Company is unable to pay off its loan from a local lender. The lender agrees to cancel the debt, with a remaining face value of $35,000, in exchange for a company truck having a book value of $26,000 and a fair market value of $29,000. There is also $2,500 of accrued but unpaid interest expense associated with the debt. Arabian's controller first revalues the truck to its fair market value and then records a gain on the debt settlement transaction. The entries are as follows:

Vehicles	3,000	
Gain on asset transfer		3,000
Note payable	35,000	
Interest payable	2,500	
Vehicles		29,000
Gain on debt settlement		8,500

If convertible debt (see the Convertible Debt section) is issued with a conversion feature that is already in the money, then the intrinsic value of that equity component should have been recorded as a credit to the Additional Paid-In Capital account. If so, the intrinsic value must be remeasured as of the debt retirement date and then removed from the Additional Paid-In Capital account. This may result in the recognition of a gain or loss, depending on the difference between the original and final intrinsic value calculations. See the Journal Entries section for sample journal entry formats related to this transaction.

Scheduled Bond Retirement

A bond agreement may contain specific requirements either to create a sinking fund that is used at the maturity date to buy back all bonds, or else to gradually buy back bonds on a regular schedule, usually through a trustee. In either case, the intention is to ensure that the company is not suddenly faced with a large repayment requirement at the maturity date. In this situation, the company usually forwards funds to a trustee at regular intervals, who in turn uses it to buy back bonds. The resulting accounting is identical to that noted under the Extinguishment of Debt section. In addition, if the company forwards interest payments to the trustee for bonds that the trustee now has in its possession, these payments are used to purchase additional bonds (since there is no one to whom the interest can be paid). In this case, the journal entry that would normally record this transaction as interest expense is converted into an entry that reduces the principal balance of the bonds outstanding.

Convertible Debt

The **convertible bond** contains a feature allowing the holder to turn in the bond in exchange for stock when a preset strike price for the stock is reached, sometimes after a specific date. This involves a specific conversion price per share, which is typically set at a point that makes the transaction uneconomical unless the share price rises at some point in the future.

To account for this transaction under the popular **book value method,** the principal amount of the bond is moved to an equity account, with a portion being allocated to the capital account at par value and the remainder going to the additional paid-in capital account. A portion of the discount or premium associated with the bond issuance is also retired, based on the proportion of bonds converted to equity. If the **market value method** is used instead, the conversion price is based on the number of shares issued to former bondholders, multiplied by the market price of the shares on the conversion date. This will likely create a gain or loss as compared to the book value of the converted bonds.

Example of debt conversion using the book value method

A bondholder owns $50,000 of bonds and wishes to convert them to 1,000 shares of company stock that has a par value of $5. The total amount of the premium associated with the original bond issuance was $42,000, and the amount of bonds to be converted to stock represents 18% of the total amount of bonds outstanding. In this case, the amount of premium to be recognized will be $7,560 ($42,000 × 18%), while the amount of funds shifted to the Capital Stock at Par Value account will be $5,000 (1,000 shares × $5). The entry follows:

Bonds payable	50,000	
Premium on bonds payable	7,560	
Capital stock at par value		5,000
Additional paid-in capital		52,560

Example of bond conversion using the market value method

Use the same assumptions as the last example, except that the fair market value of the shares acquired by the former bondholder is $5.50 each. This creates a loss on the bond conversion of $5,000, which is added to the Additional Paid-In Capital account. The entry follows:

Bonds payable	50,000	
Loss on bond conversion	5,000	
Premium on bonds payable	7,560	
Capital stock at par value		5,000
Additional paid-in capital		57,560

Convertible Debt Issued in the Money

The situation becomes more complicated if convertible bonds are issued with a stock conversion strike price that is already lower than the market price of the stock.

In this case, the related journal entry must assign a value to the shares that is based on the potential number of convertible shares multiplied by the difference between the strike price and the market value of the stock. If there are a series of strike prices for different future dates in the bond agreement, then the lowest strike price should be used to determine the intrinsic value of the deal. If bonds are issued with a strike price that is in the money, but contingent on a future event, then any recognition of the intrinsic value of the equity element is delayed until the contingent event has occurred.

Example of bond issuance when the strike price is in the money

An investor purchases $50,000 of bonds that are convertible into 10,000 shares of common stock at a conversion price of $5. At the time of issuance, the stock had a fair market value of $6.50. The intrinsic value of the conversion feature at the time of issuance is $15,000, based on the difference between the fair market value of $6.50 and the conversion price of $5.00, multiplied by the 10,000 shares that would be issued if a full conversion were to take place. The entry would be as follows:

Cash	50,000	
Bonds payable		35,000
Additional paid-in capital		15,000

Example of bond issuance when a sequence of strike prices are in the money

Use the same information as the last example, except that the bond agreement contains a lower strike price of $4.50 after three years have passed. Since this later strike price results in a greater intrinsic value being assigned to equity than the initial strike price, the later price is used for the valuation calculation. The calculation is 11,111 shares ($50,000 divided by a strike price of $4.50), multiplied by the $2 difference between the strike price and the fair market value, resulting in a debit to cash of $50,000, a credit to Bonds Payable of $27,778, and a credit to Additional Paid-In Capital of $22,222.

Example of bond issuance when the strike price is in the money but is dependent on a contingent event

Use the same information as was used for the first example, except that conversion cannot take place until the stock of all Series A preferred shareholders has been bought back by the company. The initial journal entry is a simple debit to Cash of $50,000 and a credit to Bonds Payable of $50,000, since there is no intrinsic value to the equity component at this time. Once the Series A shareholders are bought out, the intrinsic value of the equity is recognized by debiting the Discount on Bonds Payable account and crediting the Additional Paid-In Capital accounts for $15,000.

Convertible Debt—Accrued but Unpaid Interest on Converted Debt

If a convertible debt agreement's terms state that a bondholder shall forfeit any accrued interest at the time the bondholder converts to equity, the company must recognized the accrued interest expense anyway, net of income taxes. The offset to the expense is a credit to the Capital account.

Example of nonpaid accrued interest on converted debt

Mr. Abraham Smith owns $25,000 of the North Dakota Railroad's convertible debt. He elects to convert it to the railroad's common stock, and forfeits the accrued $520 of interest expense that was not yet paid as of the conversion date. The railroad debits the Interest Expense account and credits the Capital account for $520.

Convertible Debt—Subsequent Change in Offering to Induce Conversion

If a company induces its bondholders to convert their holdings to equity by subsequently improving the conversion feature of the bond agreement, it must record an expense for the difference between the consideration given to induce the conversion and the consideration originally noted in the bond agreement.

Example of subsequent change in conversion terms

Mr. Abraham Smith owns $25,000 of the North Dakota Railroad's convertible debt. The bonds were originally issued with a conversion price of $50 per share, which the railroad has subsequently lowered to $40 to induce conversion. The shares have a market value of $38, and a par value of $1. Mr. Smith elects to convert to stock, resulting in the following calculation:

	Before change in terms	*After change in terms*
Face amount of bonds	$25,000	$25,000
Conversion price	50	40
Total shares converted	500	625
Fair value per share	38	38
Value of converted stock	$19,000	$23,750

The difference between the total values of converted stock before and after the change in terms is $4,750, resulting in the following entry to record the entire conversion transaction:

Bonds payable	25,000	
Debt conversion expense	4,750	
Capital account, par value		625
Additional paid-in capital		29,125

Debt Issued with Stock Warrants

A company may attach warrants to its bonds in order to sell the bonds to investors more easily. A warrant gives an investor the right to buy a specific number of shares of company stock at a set price for a given time interval.

To account for the presence of a warrant, the accountant must determine its value if it were sold separately from the bond, determine the proportion of the total bond price to allocate to it, and then credit this proportional amount into the Additional Paid-In Capital account.

Example of bonds issued with attached warrants

A bond/warrant combination is purchased by an investor for $1,100. The investment banker handling the transaction estimates that the value of the warrant is $150, while the bond (with a face value of $1,000) begins trading at $975. Accordingly, the value the accountant assigns to the warrant is $146.67, which is calculated as follows:

$$\frac{\text{Warrant value}}{\text{Bond value} + \text{Warrant value}} \times \text{Purchase price} = \text{Price assigned to warrant}$$

$$\frac{\$150}{\$975 + \$150} \times \$1,100 = \$146.67$$

The accountant then credits the $146.67 assigned to the warrant value to the Additional Paid-In Capital account, since this is a form of equity funding, rather than debt funding, for which the investor has paid. The Discount on Bonds Payable represents the difference between the $1,000 face value of the bond and its assigned value of $953.33. The journal entry is as follows:

Cash	1,100.00	
Discount on bonds payable	46.67	
Bonds payable		1,000.00
Additional paid-in capital		146.67

DECISION TREES

The decision tree shown in Exhibit 10-1 shows the general set of decisions to be made during the life of a bond, beginning with the treatment of discounts or premiums on the initial sale price and proceeding through the presence of attached warrants and early debt extinguishment. The decisions in the top third of the tree will impact nearly all bonds, since it is unusual **not** to have a discount or premium. The middle third impacts only attached warrants, with most of the action items involving in-the-money warrants.

Exhibit 10-1: Decision Points during Lifetime of Bond

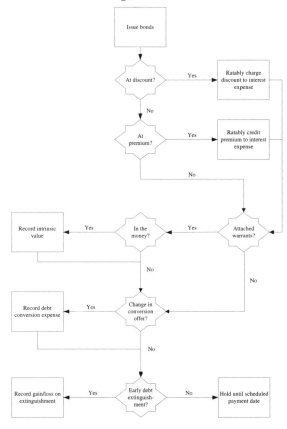

POLICIES

Notes and Bonds

- **All notes and bonds shall only be issued subsequent to approval by the Board of Directors.** This policy gives the Board control over any new debt liabilities. In reality, anyone lending money to the company will require a Board motion, so this policy is likely to be imposed by the lender even if it does not exist internally.
- **Debt sinking funds shall be fully funded on scheduled dates.** This policy is designed to force the treasury staff to plan for the timely accumulation of funds needed to pay off scheduled principal payments on debt, thereby avoiding any last-minute funding crises.
- **Recognition of unearned revenue for attached rights shall match offsetting discount amortization as closely as possible.** This policy is designed to avoid the manipulation of revenue recognition for attached rights. For example, if a value is assigned to an attached right, the debit will be to a discount account that will be ratably recognized as interest expense over the term of the debt; however, the credit will be to an unearned revenue account for which the potential exists to recognize revenue much sooner, thereby creating a split in the timing of revenue and expense recognition. Though this split may be valid in some cases, an effort should be made to avoid any significant disparities, thereby avoiding any surges in profits.
- **The fair market interest rate shall be used to value debt transactions where property is being obtained.** This policy is designed to prevent any manipulation of the value assigned to an acquired asset as part of a debt-for-property transaction. By always using the fair market rate, there is no possibility of using an excessively high or low interest rate to artificially alter the cost at which the acquired property is recorded on the company books.
- **Debt shall always be issued at stated rates as close to the market interest rate as possible.** Though there are valid reasons for issuing debt at rates significantly different from the market rate, this causes a problem with determining the market rate to be applied to debt present value calculations, which has a significant impact on the amount of interest expense recognized. Instead, this policy avoids the problem by requiring debt issuances to have stated interest rates so close to the market rate that there is no possibility of a significant debt valuation issue.

Extinguishment of Debt

- **Debt shall not be extinguished early if the primary aim is to report a gain or loss on the extinguishment.** If a company buys back its bonds when the stated interest rate on the debt is lower than the current market interest rate, it will recognize a gain on the transaction, but must refinance the purchase with more expensive debt at current market rates. Thus, this policy is designed to keep company management from creating transactions that appear to increase profits when the underlying results worsen the company's financial situation.

- **When interest rates allow, the company shall repurchase its debt with less expensive debt.** Though it sounds obvious, this policy is designed to force management to make the correct decision to always use less expensive debt, even though this will result in the recognition of a loss when the older, more expensive debt is eliminated from the company records.

Convertible Debt

- **Debt conversions to equity shall always be recorded using the book value method.** This policy keeps the accounting staff from switching between the book value and market value methods, whereby they could use the market value method to recognize gains and the book value method to avoid losses.
- **Debt conversion calculations shall always be verified by the audit staff.** This policy is designed to ensure that any expenses associated with debt conversions to stock shall be correctly calculated. Either internal or external auditors can be used; the main point is to require independent verification of all journal entries related to debt conversions.

Debt Issued with Stock Warrants

- **Debt issuance calculations incorporating attached stock warrants shall always be verified by the audit staff.** This policy ensures that a separate party comprised of either internal or external auditors reviews the allocation of value between issued bonds and warrants, since the allocation is critical to the amount of bond discount that must be subsequently amortized.

PROCEDURES

Notes and Bonds—Borrowing Short-Term Funds

This procedure is used by the chief financial officer to borrow funds from the corporate line of credit.

1. Review the short-term cash forecast with the financial analyst and determine the immediate cash need from that report.
2. Alter the expected amount based on any unusual cash flows not noted on the standard report.
3. Verify that there is a sufficient amount left on the line of credit to borrow.
4. Extract a copy of the Loan Borrowing/Paydown Form (see the Forms and Reports section) from the forms cabinet and fill it out, entering the amount determined in the first step.
5. Have an authorized signer sign the form.
6. Fax the completed form to the bank.
7. Call the bank to verify receipt of the fax.
8. Send the completed form to the general ledger accountant for proper recording in the general ledger.
9. Follow up with the bank if it does not send a transaction confirmation within a reasonable time period.

Notes and Bonds—Loan Collateralization Report

Use this procedure to update the lender's loan collateralization report (the form is shown in Chapter 2) at the end of each reporting period.

1. Call up the collateralization report in the computer system.
2. Alter the date of the month to reflect the date for which the certificate is being submitted.
3. Alter the month-end balance of accounts receivable and inventory on the report, as well as overdue accounts receivable and obsolete inventory line items.
4. Alter the amount of currently borrowed funds on the report.
5. Review the report and sign it.
6. Mail the loan collateralization report to the lender, along with the detail reports for accounts receivable and inventory that tie to the amounts listed on the report.

Effective Interest Method

Use this procedure to determine the amount of discount or premium to amortize in a given accounting period.

1. Determine the present value of the outstanding bond at the beginning of the calculation period. To do this, determine the present value of all interest payments for the bond instrument, as well as the present value of the principal payment at the end of the borrowing period, using the market rate of interest as the basis for the discount factor.
2. Calculate the interest expense in the reporting period by multiplying the market interest rate by the bond's present value for the number of days in the accounting period.
3. Subtract from the calculated interest expense the actual cash payment made for interest expense to the bondholders, which is based on the stated interest rate rather than the market interest rate. Using the difference between the two numbers, create a journal entry offsetting the outstanding discount or premium.
4. Add this interest rate difference to the outstanding present value of the bond if there is a discount, or subtract it from the bond if there is an outstanding premium.
5. Store the new balance of the bond present value, as well as the newly reduced discount or premium, which will be used as the basis for the effective interest calculation in the next reporting period.

Extinguishment of Debt

Use this procedure to process the repurchase of debt by the issuer.

1. Examine the bond documentation to determine the amount of any extra fees required to extinguish debt early, such as termination fees or premium payments. Calculate the full extinguishment cost including these factors, and

compare it to the cost of replacement financing to see if the proposed extinguishment will result in increased cash flow for the company.

2. Obtain written approval from the Board of Directors to retire the debt, and include this document in the corporate minute book.

3. If there is a trustee managing bondholder transactions, notify the trustee of the proposed extinguishment.

4. Contact bondholders to notify them of the date on which conversion shall occur, and the price they will receive for each bond held. If required by the bond document, this information may require publication to the general public well in advance of the extinguishment date.

5. If the original record of the bond issuance included a recognition of the intrinsic value of its equity portion, this recognition must be reversed. To do so, determine the number of shares that could have been converted on the retirement date. Then calculate the difference between the strike price and the fair market value of the stock on that date, and multiply it by the number of shares that could have been converted. Debit the result to the Additional Paid-In Capital account.

6. If bond issuance costs were incurred and capitalized, then any remaining unamortized amounts left in the asset account as of the date of the debt extinguishment must be recognized as expense.

7. If there is any unamortized discount or premium related to the original bond issuance, recognize that portion of the remaining amount that equates to the proportion of debt being retired.

8. If any premium is being paid to retire the debt, charge this premium to expense at the time of the retirement.

9. On the retirement date, issue settlement funding to the bondholder trustee to retire the bonds.

10. Summarize the transaction and send this information to the general ledger accountant for entry in the general ledger.

Convertible Debt

Use this procedure to process a request by a bondholder to convert that entity's bond holdings to company stock.

1. Verify that a sufficient number of shares are authorized and available to fulfill the request by the bondholder.

2. Send documentation of the request to the general ledger accountant, who records any accrued but unpaid interest expense on the bond, debiting it to expense and crediting the capital account (if the bondholder forfeits the interest). The general ledger accountant should initial the step to signify its completion.

3. If the market value method is used to record the conversion transaction, the general ledger accountant should also note in the procedure the date of the conversion, the market price of the stock on that date, and initial next to this information.

4. Update the bond ledger by recording the retirement of the bond serial number.

5. Create a stock certificate for the bondholder and obtain valid signatures authorizing the certificate. Issue the certificate to the former bondholder by registered mail.

6. Update the stock ledger by recording the stock certificate number and the number of shares issued.

Debt Issued with Stock Warrants

Use this procedure to determine the proper valuation of each component of a debt offering with a warrant attachment.

1. Obtain written approval from the Board of Directors to issue debt with attached stock warrants, and include this document in the corporate minute book.

2. Conduct the bond offering.

3. Determine the value of the bond and stock warrant components of the offering. This can be obtained from the investment banker handling the transaction, who can estimate it based on the value of similar offerings for other clients. Another alternative is to wait until the bonds and warrants are publicly traded and assign values based on their initial trading prices.

4. To assign a price to the warrants, divide the warrant value by the total of both the bond value and the warrant value, and multiply the result by the total purchase price.

5. Have an independent party, such as the internal audit staff, review the calculations splitting the value of the offering between bonds and stock warrants.

6. Credit the resulting warrant value to the Additional Paid-In Capital account and credit the full face value of the bond to the Bonds Payable account. Debit the total cash received from the transaction to the Cash account, and enter any remaining difference to either the Discount on Bonds Payable (if a debit) or to the Premium on Bonds Payable (if a credit).

7. If bond issuance costs were incurred, capitalize them and establish an amortization schedule.

CONTROLS

Notes and Bonds

*   **Require evidence of intent and ability to recategorize debt from short-term to long-term.** If a company shifts the classification of its short-term debt to the long-term debt category, this can mislead investors and creditors in regard to the company's short-term obligations. A good control is to require evidence supporting the reporting shift, such as a Board motion to take on replacement long-term debt, plus a signed long-term loan to pay off the short-term debt. This documentation should be attached to the journal entry that shifts short-term debt into the long-term debt category.

- **Require approval of the terms of all new borrowing agreements.** A senior corporate manager should be assigned the task of reviewing all prospective debt instruments to verify that their interest rate, collateral, and other requirements are not excessively onerous or conflict with the terms of existing debt agreements. It may also be useful from time to time to see if a lending institution has inappropriate ties to the company, such as partial or full ownership in its stock by the person responsible for obtaining debt agreements.

- **Require supervisory approval of all borrowings and repayments.** As was the case with the preceding control point, high-level supervisory approval is required for all debt instruments—except this time it is for final approval of each debt commitment. If the debt to be acquired is extremely large, it may be useful to have a policy requiring approval by the Board of Directors, just to be sure that there is full agreement at all levels of the organization regarding the nature of the debt commitment. To be a more useful control, this signing requirement should be communicated to the lender, so that it does not inadvertently accept a debt agreement that has not been signed by the proper person.

- **Investigate the reasoning for revenue recognition related to attached rights that is not ratably recognized.** When a value is assigned to an attached right, the debit is to a discount account that will be ratably recognized as interest expense over the term of the debt; however, the credit will be to an unearned revenue account for which the potential exists to recognize revenue much sooner, thereby creating a split in the timing of revenue and expense recognition. Whenever revenue recognition related to this credit is not calculated on a ratable basis (which would create an approximate match between revenue and expense recognition), the calculation should first be approved by a manager.

- **Gain management approval of the initial debt entry related to debt issued in exchange for property.** It is quite possible that the stated interest rate on any debt issued in exchange for property will not match the fair market rate at the time of the transaction. Since the stated rate can be used to value the debt transaction unless the rate is not considered to be fair, this can lead to some abuse in asset valuation. For example, if the stated rate is below the market rate and is still used to record the property acquisition transaction, the present value of the debt will be higher, resulting in a larger asset valuation. If the asset is depreciated over a longer period than would the interest expense that would otherwise be recognized if the higher market interest were used, then a company has effectively shifted expense recognition into the future and increased its profits in the short term. Consequently, management approval of the interest rate used to value the acquisition should be obtained, while a justification for the interest rate used should be attached to the journal entry.

- **Include a task for debt issuance cost capitalization in the bond establishment procedure.** There should be a standard procedure describing each step in the recording of an initial bond issuance. The procedure should include a requirement to capitalize and ratably amortize all debt issuance costs. Otherwise, these costs will be expensed at the beginning of the debt issuance, rather than being linked to the benefits of the incurred debt over the life of the debt.

- **Require written and approved justification for the interest rate used to value debt.** When the stated interest rate on debt varies significantly from the market rate of interest, GAAP requires that the debt be valued using the market rate. However, the exact amount of this market rate is subject to interpretation, which has an impact on the amount of interest expense recognized. Requiring justification for and approval of the rate used introduces some rigor to the process.

Effective Interest Method

- **Include in the month-end closing procedure a task to record interest expense on any bonds for which interest payments do not correspond to the closing date.** The payment of interest to bondholders is a natural trigger for the recording of interest expense, but there is no such trigger when there is no payment. To enforce the proper recording not only of unpaid interest expense but also of any amortization on related bond discounts or premiums, a specific task should be included in the closing procedure, as well as a required sign-off on the task.

Extinguishment of Debt

- **Include in the debt procedure a line item to charge unamortized discounts or premiums to expense proportionate to the amount of any extinguished debt.** The general ledger accountant may not remember to write off any unamortized discount or premium when debt is extinguished, so the debt extinguishment procedure should include a line item requiring that this task be addressed. Otherwise, expense recognition could potentially be delayed until the original payment date of the debt, which may be many years in the future.
- **Report to the Board of Directors the repayment status of all debt.** GAAP requires that all unamortized discounts and premiums be recognized in the current period if there is no reasonable chance that the debt will be repaid. Since this acceleration has a significant impact on reported earnings in the current period, there may be some unwillingness to classify debt as unable to be paid. By requiring a standard report to the Board of Directors regarding the status of debt repayments at each of its meetings, the Board can decide on its own when amortization must be accelerated, and can force management to do so.

Convertible Debt

- **Verify the market value of equity on conversion dates when the market value method is used.** If a company uses the market value method to record the conversion of debt to equity, it is possible to influence the gain or loss recorded, depending on fluctuations in the stock price from day to day. Accordingly, the market price of the stock should be independently matched to the date on which the conversion took place. Also, it is possible to include in the conversion procedure a fill-in blank where the stock price can be noted, dated, and initialed. This approach makes it much easier to trace transactions, and also holds accountants responsible for their entries.

- **Verify the market value of equity on debt retirement dates when offsetting equity entries are being reversed.** When a convertible bond is issued with its equity conversion feature already in the money, the intrinsic value of the equity portion of the bond must be credited to the Additional Paid-In Capital account. If the bond is later retired, the equity portion of the bond must then be removed from the Additional Paid-In Capital account at its intrinsic value on the date of the retirement. Any difference between the original and final intrinsic values is charged to either a gain or loss on the extinguishment of debt. The presence of a potential gain or loss on extinguishment makes it more likely for manipulation to occur in both the timing and calculation of the extinguishment transaction. One can match the date of the debt retirement to the equity valuation on that date to ensure that the proper equity value is used. Also, the correct retirement calculation can be included in the corporate accounting procedures manual to ensure that it is handled properly.

- **Include a review of accrued interest expense on all recently converted debt.** If the terms of a company's bond agreements state that bondholders must forfeit accrued interest on converted debt, then there will be a temptation to also avoid recording this accrual on the books as an expense, as is required by GAAP. Consequently, the formal procedure used to convert debt to equity should include a line item for the general ledger accountant to record this accrued interest expense, and also require a signature on the procedure to ensure its completion.

- **Verify expense calculations associated with any sweetened conversion offers.** GAAP requires the recognition of a debt conversion expense associated with any completed conversion from bonds to equity, in the incremental amount of the net increase in fair value of stock obtained through a sweetened conversion offer. Since this results in an added expense, there will be a tendency to simply process the total conversion and not recognize the incremental expense, which could be substantial. Accordingly, a copy of the relevant portions of the original bond agreement should be attached to any journal entry that records a conversion to equity, which provides documentation of the initial conversion price. When the calculation is verified by an internal auditor or senior accounting person, this provides documentation of the initial baseline conversion price.

FORMS AND REPORTS

Notes and Bonds—Loan Borrowing/Paydown Form

It is not sufficient to contact a lender and ask to borrow funds or pay down a loan balance. The bank wants to see a signed form authorizing these changes, preferably on company letterhead. A general-purpose sample form is shown in Exhibit 10-2, which can be used to both borrow funds and pay down debt. The form is designed based on the assumption that there are multiple company accounts or loans outstanding, into or out of which funds can be shifted. The user checks off a "Borrow" or "Paydown" box and circles the appropriate "from" and "to" fields, based on the action requested of the lender, enters the relevant loan number and account number, has an authorized officer sign at the bottom of the form, and faxes it to the lender. Some portions of the form can contain preset information, such as the loan and account numbers, as well as the officer name and confirmation phone number. By using the high degree of standardization in this type of form, one can avoid costly errors in the transfer of funds in and out of loan instruments.

Exhibit 10-2: Loan Borrowing/Paydown Form

Loan Borrowing/Paydown Form
for [Company Name]

To the attention of:
Lending officer name
Lending entity name
Lending entity address

Borrow	Paydown	Dollar Amount		Loan Number		Company Account Number
☐	☐	$ ______	From / To	______	From / To	______
☐	☐	$ ______	From / To	______	From / To	______
☐	☐	$ ______	From / To	______	From / To	______
☐	☐	$ ______	From / To	______	From / To	______
☐	☐	$ ______	From / To	______	From / To	______

Authorization:

Signature	Printed Name	Title/Date
______	______	______

______
Confirmation Phone Number

Notes and Bonds—Loan Collateralization Report

A lender usually requires that a loan collateralization report such as the one shown in the Chapter 2 Forms and Reports section be completed at the end of each month. The agreement usually requires that old receivables be stripped from the reported balance to arrive at a core set of receivables most likely to be collected by the lender in the event of default. In addition, each category of assets used as collateral is multiplied by a reduction percentage (shown in bold in the exhibit), reflecting the amount of cash the lender believes it can collect if it were to sell each type of asset. The reduced amount of all asset types is then summarized and compared to the outstanding loan balance; if the collateral amount has dropped below the loan balance, then the company must pay back the difference. The report is typically signed by a company officer.

Notes and Bonds—Bond Status Report

If a company has made a number of bond issuances, it is useful to maintain a status report, such as the version shown in Exhibit 10-3. The report contains a separate line item for each series of bonds issued, listing the sale price, face value, and

Exhibit 10-3: Bond Status Report

Company Name
Bond Status Report

Beginning serial number	Ending serial number	Sale price	Face value	Stated rate	1st interest payment date	2nd interest payment date	Principle payment date	Total principal	Conversion date	Conversion price
00001	01000	$950	1,000	9.375%	15-Mar	15-Sep	15-Sep-2015	$1,000,000	15-Sep-2020	$50
01001	02000	975	1,000	9.375%	15-Mar	15-Sep	10-Oct-2015	1,000,000	10-Oct-2020	50
02001	03000	990	1,000	9.375%	15-Mar	15-Sep	20-Nov-2015	1,000,000	20-Nov-2020	50
10000	12000	850	1,000	9.100%	15-Feb	15-Aug	15-Feb-2018	2,000,000	15-Feb-2023	52
12001	14000	860	1,000	9.100%	15-Feb	15-Aug	31-Mar-2018	2,000,000	31-Mar-2023	52
14001	16000	845	1,000	9.100%	15-Feb	15-Aug	20-Apr-2018	2,000,000	20-Apr-2023	52
20000	25000	910	1,000	9.250%	1-May	1-Nov	5-May-2020	5,000,000	5-May-2025	55
30000	34000	935	1,000	9.850%	1-Apr	1-Aug	10-Apr-2021	4,000,000	10-Apr-2026	56
40000	48000	980	1,000	9.950%	1-Jun	1-Dec	5-Jun-2022	8,000,000	5-Jun-2027	60
50000	56000	942	1,000	9.450%	1-Jun	1-Dec	11-Jun-2023	6,000,000	11-Jul-2028	62
								$32,000,000		

stated interest rate. It also notes all key dates, including interest payment dates, principal payment dates, and conversion dates (if any) for convertible stock. This report is useful not only for planning when cash payments must be made, but also as the basis for a variety of accounting entries.

FOOTNOTES

Disclosure of Loans

If a company has entered into a loan agreement as the creditor, the accountant should describe each debt instrument, as well as all maturity dates associated with principal payments, the interest rate, and any circumstances under which the lender can call the loan (usually involving a description of all related covenants). In addition, the existence of any conversion privileges by the lender should be described, and any assets to be used as collateral. Other special disclosures involve the existence of any debt agreements entered into subsequent to the date of the financial statements, related-party debt agreements, and the unused amount of any outstanding letters of credit. An example follows:

> The company has entered into a line of credit arrangement with the First Federal Commercial Bank, which carries a maximum possible balance of $5 million. The loan has a variable interest rate that is 1/2% higher than the bank's prime lending rate. The loan's interest rate as of the date of the financial statements is 8 3/4%. As of the date of the financial statements, the company had drawn down $750,000 of the loan balance. Collateral used to secure the loan is all accounts receivable and fixed assets. The loan must be renegotiated by December 31, 2004; in the meantime, the bank can call the loan if the company's working capital balance falls below $2 million, or if its current ratio drops below 1.5 to 1.

Disclosure of Loan Guarantees

If a company is liable for the debt of another entity, a footnote should describe the nature of the indebtedness, the relationship between the two companies, the potential amount of the liability, and the date on which the liability terminates. An example follows:

> The company is contingently liable for the outstanding loans of Excelsior Holdings Ltd., in which it owns a 40% interest. The maximum possible loan balance under the guarantee agreement is $4,200,000, of which $3,800,000 is currently outstanding. The loan is a term loan with required periodic principal payments, resulting in complete termination of the loan and the company's loan guarantee as of May 31, 2011.

Disclosure of Unused Credit Facilities

If a company has entered into a credit facility with a lender and some portion of that potential debt is unused, a footnote should disclose the terms of the agreement, the amount of debt outstanding, and the amount available. If there are covenants associated with the facility, the company's ability to meet the covenants should be noted. An example follows:

> The company has a revolving line of credit with a consortium of banks for a total of $100 million. The debt is secured by the company's accounts receivable and inventory

balances, and carries an adjustable interest rate matching the prime rate. The company must meet the terms of several covenants in order to use the facility; it currently meets all covenant requirements. There was $28.5 million outstanding under the line of credit at year-end, leaving $71.5 million available for further borrowings.

Disclosure of Related-Party Loans

If a company has issued loans to related parties, it should describe the nature of the transactions, as well as the amounts involved, interest rates payable, and the timing of subsequent payments in a footnote. Some examples follow:

1. The company is owed $2,000,000 in various notes receivable from its executive management team. The notes carry interest rates ranging from 5.25% to 7.5%, and will mature within the next two to five years. The Board authorized year-end bonus payments to the executives owing the notes receivable, all of whom chose to forgo payment in exchange for cancellation of their notes payable.
2. The company loaned $175,000 to the CEO in 2005 at an interest rate of 6.5%. Neither the principal nor the accrued interest on the note has been paid. The Board has elected to forgive $100,000 of the outstanding principal and all associated interest, leaving a balance of $75,000 on which interest has continued to accrue since the loan initiation date in 2005.
3. The company has been loaned $350,000 by the CEO. This debt is unsecured, carries an interest rate of 8.2%, and can be repaid only after all bank debt has been retired. The debt is junior to all outstanding bank debt, so the likelihood of debt repayment in the short term is remote. Accordingly, the debt is classified as long-term debt in the financial statements.

Disclosure of Loan Acceleration

If a company cannot maintain the financial covenants called for in a loan document, the lender is usually entitled to require immediate payment of the loan. In such cases, the company should disclose the nature of the covenant violation, the status of any covenant renegotiation, the portion of the debt subject to acceleration, and any reclassification of the debt in the financial statements as a result of this occurrence. An example follows:

> The company was unable to meet the current ratio covenant on its debt agreement with the Fourth National Bank of Wachovia. The bank has elected not to waive its right to accelerate the maturity of the debt. As a result, the bank can require the company to pay the current loan balance of $3,575,000 at any time. Accordingly, the debt has been reclassified as short-term debt on the balance sheet.

Disclosure of Callable Obligations

A company may have a long-term liability that can be called if it violates some related covenants. If it has indeed violated some aspect of the covenants, then the accountant must disclose the nature of the violation, how much of the related liability can potentially be called because of the violation, and if a waiver has been obtained from the creditor or if the company has acted to cancel the violation through some action. An example follows:

The company has a long-term loan with a consortium of lenders, for which it violated the minimum current ratio covenant during the reporting period. The potential amount callable is one-half of the remaining loan outstanding, which is $5,500,000. However, the consortium granted a waiver of the violation, and also reduced the amount of the current ratio requirement from 2:1 to 1:1 for future periods.

Disclosure of Debt Restructuring

If a company restructures its debt, it should disclose any changes in the terms of the debt agreement and changes in income tax liability, as well as any resulting gain or loss. Two examples follow:

1. The company restructured the terms of its $10 million debt with the Fourth National Bank of Wachovia to reduce the interest rate from 10% to 7.5%, which included that portion of the accrued interest expense payable for the past two years. This resulted in a onetime gain on interest expense reduction, net of income tax effects, of $350,000. This has been recorded as an Extraordinary Gain on Debt Restructuring.
2. In December 2007, the company redeemed a portion of its 8% bonds payable in 2014, totaling $14.1 million in principal value. In order to redeem the bonds, the company paid a 12% premium to the bondholders, resulting in an Extraordinary Loss on Debt Reduction of $1.2 million net of a tax benefit of $508,000. The company paid for the bond redemption with funds obtained through a recent preferred stock offering.

Disclosure of Loan Reclassification

If the circumstances under which a loan is assumed to be either short-term or long-term debt have changed, one should disclose the reason for the change and the amount of debt affected by the reclassification. Three examples follow:

1. The company is planning to sell its Russian-based rocket engine business in the near future. At that time, it plans to use the proceeds of the sale to pay off $19 million debt that it acquired in order to originally purchase the business. Accordingly, it has reclassified this debt as short-term debt.
2. The company has entered into a five-year, $10 million loan agreement with a set of lenders that will allow it to retire its $450,000 of short-term debt when it comes due for payment later this year. Since it is the intent of the company to pay for this short-term debt with the new long-term credit facility, the short-term debt has been reclassified as long-term debt.
3. The company is uncertain of its ability to make the next scheduled payment of $500,000 on its long-term debt of $28 million. Accordingly, it has reclassified the entire amount of the long-term debt as short-term debt.

Disclosure of Loan Extinguishment

If a company experiences a gain or loss through a debt extinguishment transaction, the accountant should describe the transaction, the amount of debt extinguished, the amount of the gain or loss, the impact on income taxes and earnings per share, and the source of funds used to retire the debt. Three examples follow:

1. The company retired all of its callable Series D bonds during the period, totaling $7.2 million. The funds used to retire the bonds were obtained from the issuance of Series A preferred stock during the period. The debt retirement transaction resulted

in a gain of $595,000, which had after-tax positive impacts on net income of $369,000 and on per share earnings of $0.29.

2. The company used the proceeds from its recent stock sale to retire $2.9 million in debt payable to the Fourth National Bank of Wachovia. This debt agreement contained a prepayment penalty clause, so the company recorded a $150,000 expense for this penalty at the time of the prepayment. The company had also been amortizing the loan origination cost of the loan, of which $27,000 had not yet been recognized at the time of the prepayment. The company charged the remaining balance of this cost to expense. These charges, net of income tax benefits, resulted in an extraordinary loss of $124,000 and reduced earnings per share by $0.05.

3. In February 2007, the company recorded a loss of $89,000 net of income taxes, related to the write-down of the debt issuance costs for its 9 7/8% bonds. All of these bonds have been called by the company with funds obtained through its recent offering of common stock. The loss is recorded as a Loss on Debt Issuance Costs, and will reduce earnings per share by $0.02.

Disclosure of Convertible Debt

If a company issues debt that is convertible into equity, it should describe the terms of the transaction, including the amount of debt issued, the interest rate, and the conversion features, in a footnote. An example follows:

> The company issued $8 million in convertible debt on November 10, 2007, to help pay for its new Malaysian production facility. The debt carries an interest rate of 7.25%, and requires semiannual interest payments, with a single balloon payment in ten years. Debt holders can convert their debt to company stock at any time at a conversion price of $15 per share. No conversions had occurred as of the date of the financial statements. If all the debt were to be converted to equity, this would represent dilution of 4.7% for the current common shareholders.

Disclosure of Stock Warrants Issued with Debt

If a company issues stock warrants as part of a debt issuance, it should disclose the proportion of warrants issued to debt, as well as the warrant exercise price, the date after which the warrants may be used, the allocation of received funds to the warrant and debt portions of the transaction, how the allocation was derived, and how the allocation was treated in the financial statements. An example follows:

> The company issued $11 million in bonds during January 2007. Each of the 11,000 bonds sold at a price of $1,000 each, and included a warrant to purchase 100 shares of the company's common stock at an exercise price of $14.25, beginning on February 1, 2009. The warrants expire on February 1, 2017. Of the $11 million received, the company allocated $9.8 million to the bonds and $1.2 million to the warrants. This warrant valuation was derived with the Black-Scholes option pricing model, and was recorded as an increase in the Additional Paid-In Capital account. The allocation of funds to the warrants resulted in a discount on the bonds, which will be amortized to Interest Expense over the life of the bonds. The unamortized discount is currently $1,150,000.

JOURNAL ENTRIES

Notes and Bonds

Sale of bonds at a discount. The first entry is made when bonds are sold at a discount from their face value, thereby increasing the effective interest rate. The second entry is made periodically to gradually reduce the discount, charging the offsetting debit to the Interest Expense account.

Cash	xxx	
Discount on bonds payable	xxx	
Bonds payable		xxx
Interest expense	xxx	
Discount on bonds payable		xxx

Sale of bonds at a premium. The first entry is made when bonds are sold at a premium from their face value, thereby reducing the effective interest rate. The second entry is made periodically to gradually reduce the premium, charging the offsetting credit to the Interest Expense account.

Cash	xxx	
Premium on bonds payable		xxx
Bonds payable		xxx
Premium on bonds payable	xxx	
Interest expense		xxx

Sale of debt issued with no stated interest rate. When there is no stated interest rate on a debt instrument, one must record the present value of the note using the market rate of interest at the time of the issuance. The first entry shows the initial recording of the debt sale, while the second entry shows the periodic reduction in interest expense payable.

Cash	xxx	
Discount on note payable	xxx	
Note payable		xxx
Interest expense	xxx	
Discount on note payable		xxx

Issuance of debt for cash and other rights. When debt is issued in exchange for cash and some other form of consideration, the difference between the present value and face value of the debt is recorded as unearned consideration, to be recognized as the consideration is earned by the issuer. The first entry shows the initial recording of such a transaction, while the second entry shows the gradual reduction in unearned revenue.

Cash	xxx	
Discount on note payable	xxx	
Note payable		xxx
Unearned revenue		xxx
Unearned revenue	xxx	
Revenue		xxx

Capitalization of debt issuance costs. Costs associated with the issuance of debt should be capitalized when the related debt is issued, as noted in the first journal entry. This amount should be ratably recognized over the term of the debt on a straight-line basis, as is shown in the second journal entry.

Bond issuance costs	xxx	
Cash		xxx
Bond issuance expense	xxx	
Bond issuance costs		xxx

Notes issued for property. When a company issues debt in exchange for property, it discounts the note either at the stated interest rate on the debt or at the market rate (if the stated rate is not considered to be a fair rate). In either case, the value of the property acquired shall be debited, usually along with a discount on the note payable. The first entry shows this initial transaction, while the second entry shows the periodic reduction in the discount and corresponding recognition of interest expense.

Property (various accounts)	xxx	
Discount on note payable	xxx	
Note payable		xxx
Interest expense	xxx	
Discount on note payable		xxx

Effective Interest Method

Interest, imputed. To recognize the additional interest expense on a bond after it has been issued with a stated rate below the market rate (first entry), or to recognize a **reduced** level of interest expense on a bond after it has been issued with a stated rate higher than the market rate (second entry).

Interest expense	xxx	
Discount on bonds payable		xxx
Cash		xxx
Interest expense	xxx	
Premium on bonds payable	xxx	
Cash		xxx

Extinguishment of Debt

Repurchase of debt. This entry is used when a company elects to buy back issued debt ahead of its expiration date. There is usually a loss on the retirement to reflect the premium usually paid to investors to give up their bonds, while any remaining discount or premium on the debt must also be recognized at this time.

Bonds payable	xxx	
Loss on bond retirement	xxx	
Premium on bonds payable (if applicable)	xxx	
Discount on bonds payable (if applicable)		xxx
Cash		xxx

Repurchase of debt with subsequent gain in intrinsic equity value. When convertible debt is retired for which the intrinsic value of its equity component has already been recorded, the intrinsic value must be determined again at the repurchase date and removed from the Additional Paid-In Capital account. If the value of the equity component has **risen** since the initial entry, then the entry is as follows:

Bonds payable	xxx	
Additional paid-in capital	xxx	
Cash		xxx
Discount on bonds payable		xxx
Gain on debt extinguishment		xxx

Repurchase of debt with subsequent loss in intrinsic equity value. When convertible debt is retired for which the intrinsic value of its equity component has already been recorded, the intrinsic value must be determined again at the repurchase date and removed from the Additional Paid-In Capital account. If the value of the equity component has **fallen** since the initial entry, then the entry is as follows:

Bonds payable	xxx	
Additional paid-in capital	xxx	
Loss on debt extinguishment	xxx	
Cash		xxx
Discount on bonds payable		xxx

Asset transfer to eliminate debt. When a company exchanges an asset with a lender to eliminate a debt, the value of the transferred asset is first written up or down to match its book value to its fair market value, as shown in the first entry. Its fair market value, as well as any accrued and unpaid interest expense, is then netted against the remaining debt, as shown in the second entry. Both entries assume a gain on the transaction, though the entry can be reversed to record a loss.

Asset account	xxx	
Gain on asset transfer		xxx
Note payable	xxx	
Interest payable	xxx	
Asset account		xxx
Gain on debt settlement		xxx

Convertible Debt

Record conversion of convertible debt to equity, book value method. If bondholders wish to convert their bonds into company stock, the following entry is used on the assumption that the remaining balance of the bonds represents the value of the resulting equity.

Bonds payable	xxx	
Premium on bonds payable (if premium existed)	xxx	
Discount on bonds payable (if discount existed)		xxx
Capital stock at par value		xxx
Additional paid-in capital		xxx

Record conversion of convertible debt to equity, market value method. This is a less-used alternative to the preceding book value method, under which any new stock issuance is valued at the market rate. The entry includes a gain or loss to reflect the difference between the market price of the equity and the book value of the bonds being converted, with the offset to the gain or loss being recorded in the Additional Paid-In Capital account.

Bonds payable	xxx	
Loss on bond conversion (if any)	xxx	
Premium on bonds payable (if premium existed)	xxx	
Gain on bond redemption (if any)		xxx
Discount on bonds payable (if discount existed)		xxx
Capital stock at par value		xxx
Additional paid-in capital		xxx

Record issuance of convertible debt with strike price already in the money. This entry is used to record the intrinsic value of the conversion feature at the time of bond issuance, which is based on the difference between the strike price and the fair market value of the stock, multiplied by the number of shares into which the debt can be converted. This intrinsic value is added to the Additional Paid-In Capital account.

Cash	xxx	
Discount on bonds payable (if applicable)	xxx	
Premium on bonds payable (if applicable)		xxx
Bonds payable		xxx
Additional paid-in capital		xxx

Record issuance of convertible debt with strike price already in the money but contingent on a future event. The calculation is the same as for the last journal entry but only after the contingent event has occurred. In the meantime, the strike price issue is ignored, as shown in the first entry. Once the contingent event has occurred, the second journal entry shows a shift in funds to the Additional Paid-In Capital account, with the offset to a discount account.

Cash	xxx	
Bonds payable		xxx
Discount on bonds payable	xxx	
Additional paid-in capital		xxx

Record conversion to equity with accrued but unpaid interest expense. If the terms of a convertible debt agreement require bondholders to forgo any accrued interest expense at the time they convert bonds to company stock, the related journal entry should include the recognition of that expense, as well as an offset to the capital account, as noted in the following journal entry:

Interest expense	xxx	
Long-term debt	xxx	
Capital, par value (various stock accounts)		xxx
Capital (various stock accounts)		xxx

Record conversion to equity following a sweetening of conversion feature. If a company induces its bondholders to convert their holdings to equity by subsequently improving the conversion feature of the bond agreement, it must record an expense for the difference between the consideration given to induce the conversion and the consideration originally noted in the bond agreement. The entry is as follows:

Bonds payable	xxx	
Debt conversion expense	xxx	
Capital account, par value		xxx
Additional paid-in capital		xxx

Debt Issued with Stock Warrants

Initial entry of bonds sale with attached warrants. The first entry is used to assign a value to the warrants attached to the sale of bonds, based on the relative values of the warrants and bonds. The entry includes a provision for any discount or premium on bonds sold. The second entry shifts funds into an expired warrants account, on the assumption that the warrants are never exercised by the holder.

Cash	xxx	
Discount on bonds payable (if applicable)	xxx	
Premium on bonds payable (if applicable)		xxx
Bonds payable		xxx
Additional paid-in capital		xxx
Additional paid-in capital	xxx	
Additional paid-in capital—expired warrants		xxx

RECORDKEEPING

When there is a discount or premium on the issuance of any form of debt, it should be amortized over the life of the debt. Since this amount can be substantial and have an impact on reported results for many years, the calculation of the premium or discount must be fully documented and retained in the accounting archives for the term of the related debt. A copy of the calculation should be retained in the current journal entry binder for easy access by any auditors wishing to review it.

When short-term debt is reclassified as long-term debt on the grounds that the company has the intention and ability to conduct the refinancing, there should be adequate documentation of the company's intent to do so (such as a Board motion), as well as ability to do so (such as a signed loan document). This information should be retained in the accounting archives for as long as the short-term debt transfer is shown in the financial statements. For example, if five comparative financial statements are issued, then the supporting documentation should be kept on file until the year in which the reclassification was made has dropped off the financial statements—a period of five years.

When a right is granted to the lender and attached to a debt (such as a discount on future purchases from the company in exchange for a below-market interest rate), the unearned revenue can be recognized either ratably or in association with a particular event. Since the opportunity exists to manipulate the timing of revenue recognition in this instance, a business case should be documented for all revenue recognition entries that do not evenly spread revenue recognition over the duration of the related debt. The business case should describe the type of event that triggers the revenue recognition and why revenue is most properly recognized at that time.

When a company issues debt in exchange for property and elects to record the value of the debt at an interest rate other than the stated rate of the debt, the reason for doing so as well as the reason for the interest rate selected should be noted as an attachment to the journal entry documentation. This information may be reviewed at any time during the life of either the debt or the acquired property (whichever is longer), so the information should be retained for that time period.

Whenever a convertible bond is issued with the strike price already in the money but contingent upon a future event, the intrinsic value of the equity portion of the bond issuance must be recognized whenever the event comes to pass. This means that a note should be placed in the month-end closing procedure, indicating the contingent event and the action to be taken if it comes to pass. It is also useful to note in the procedure the location of the convertible bond documents that describe the strike price, as well as the accounting entry to be made. This approach will ensure that the equity portion of the convertible bond is accounted for in an appropriate manner.

When convertible bonds are issued with attached warrants, the cash received will be assigned to both the debt and equity parts of the transaction based on their relative valuations. Consequently, a record of the value of the bonds and the warrants as of the date of the transaction should be retained and attached to the journal entry recording the transaction.

11 LEASES

DEFINITIONS OF TERMS

Bargain purchase option. A clause included in a lease agreement that gives the lessee the right to purchase a leased asset at the end of the lease term for an amount substantially lower than its expected fair value at that time.

Capital lease. A lease in which the lessee obtains some ownership rights over the asset involved in the transaction, resulting in the recording of the asset as company property on its general ledger.

Guaranteed residual value. A fixed fee the lessee must pay the lessor at the end of a lease term, representing the predetermined value of the underlying asset.

Implicit interest rate. The discount rate at which the net present value of all lease payments associated with a lease transaction, less executory costs and lessor profit, equals the fair value of the asset being leased.

Operating lease. This is the rental of an asset from a lessor, but not under terms that would qualify it as a capital lease.

Lease. A legal agreement allowing a lessee the right to use an asset provided to it by a lessor, typically under recurring payment terms for a predetermined time period.

Penalty. A clause inserted in the lease agreement requiring the lessee to make a penalty payment or return a leased asset based on its inability to comply with some future condition, such as a late payment or its entry into bankruptcy proceedings.

CONCEPTS AND EXAMPLES

Accounting for Leases—Lessee

A typical lease is recorded by the lessee as an **operating lease**. The lessee must record a lease as a **capital lease** if the lease agreement contains any one of the following four clauses:

1. A bargain purchase option, whereby the lessee can purchase the asset from the lessor at the end of the lease term at a price substantially lower than its expected residual value at that time
2. Transfer of asset ownership to the lessee at the end of the lease term
3. A lease term so long that it equals or exceeds 75% of the asset's anticipated economic life
4. Present value of the minimum lease payments that is at least 90% of the asset's fair value

The decision tree for this transaction is shown later in the Decision Trees section.

The lessee accounts for an **operating lease** by charging lease payments directly to expense. There is no balance sheet recognition of the leased asset at all. If the schedule of lease payments varies in terms of either timing or amount, the lessee should consistently charge the same rental amount to expense in each period, which may result in some variation between the lease payment made and the recorded expense. However, if there is a demonstrable change in the asset being leased that justifies a change in the lease payment being made, there is no need to use straight-line recognition of the expense.

Example of accounting for changing lease payments

The Alabama Botox Clinics (ABC) Company has leased a group of operating room equipment under a five-year operating lease arrangement. The monthly lease cost is $1,000 for the first thirty months and $1,500 for the second thirty months. There is no change in the equipment being leased at any time during the lease period. The correct accounting is to charge the average monthly lease rate of $1,250 to expense during every month of the lease. For the first thirty months, the monthly entry will be

Equipment rent expense	1,250	
Accounts payable		1,000
Accrued lease liability		250

During the final thirty months, the monthly entry will be

Equipment rent expense	1,250	
Accrued lease liability	250	
Accounts payable		1,500

The lessee accounts for a **capital lease** by recording as an asset the lower of its fair value or the present value of its minimum (i.e., excluding taxes and executory costs) lease payments (less the present value of any guaranteed residual asset value). When calculating the present value of minimum lease payments, use the lesser of the lessee's incremental borrowing rate or the implicit rate used by the lessor. The time period used for the present value calculation should include not only the initial lease term, but also additional periods where nonrenewal will result in a penalty to the lessee, or where lease renewal is at the option of the lessor.

If the lessee treats a leased asset as a capital lease because the lease agreement results in an actual or likely transfer of ownership to the lessee by the end of the lease term, then it is depreciated over the full expected life of the asset. However, if a leased asset is being treated as a capital lease when the lessor is still likely to retain ownership of the asset after the end of the lease term, then it is only depreciated for the period of the lease.

Example of a capital lease transaction

The Arkansas Barrel Company (ABC) leases a woodworking machine under a five-year lease that has a one-year extension clause at the option of the lessor, as well as a guaranteed residual value of $15,000. ABC's incremental borrowing rate is 7%. The machine is estimated to have a life of seven years, a current fair value of $90,000, and a residual value (**not** the guaranteed residual value) of $5,000. Annual lease payments are $16,000.

The first step in accounting for this lease is to determine if it is a capital or operating lease. If it is a capital lease, one must calculate its present value, then use the effective interest method to determine the allocation of payments between interest expense and reduction of the lease obligation, and then determine the depreciation schedule for the asset. Later, there will be a closeout journal entry to record the lease termination. The steps are as follows:

1. **Determine the lease type.** The woodworking machine is considered to have a life of seven years; since the lease period (including the extra year at the option of the lessor) covers more than 75% of the machine's useful life, the lease is designated a capital lease.

2. **Calculate asset present value.** The machine's present value is a combination of the present value of the $15,000 residual payment due in six years and the present value of annual payments of $16,000 per year for six years. Using the company incremental borrowing rate of 7%, the present value multiplier for $1 due in six years is 0.6663; when multiplied by the guaranteed residual value of $15,000, this results in a present value of $9,995. Using the same interest rate, the present value multiplier for an ordinary annuity of $1 for six years is 4.7665; when multiplied by the annual lease payments of $16,000, this results

in a present value of $76,264. After combining the two present values, we arrive at a total lease present value of $86,259. The initial journal entry to record the lease is as follows:

Leased equipment	86,259	
Leased liability		86,259

3. **Allocate payments between interest expense and reduction of lease liability.** ABC's controller then uses the effective interest method to allocate the annual lease payments between the lease's interest expense and reductions in the lease obligation. The interest calculation is based on the beginning balance of the lease obligation. The calculation for each year of the lease is as follows:

Year	Annual payment	Interest expense	Reduction in lease obligation	Remaining lease obligation
0				$86,259
1	$16,000	$6,038	$9,962	76,297
2	16,000	5,341	10,659	65,638
3	16,000	4,595	11,405	54,233
4	16,000	3,796	12,204	42,029
5	16,000	2,942	13,058	28,991
6	16,000	2,009	13,991	15,000

4. **Create depreciation schedule.** Though the asset has an estimated life of seven years, the lease term is for only six years, after which the asset is expected to be returned to the lessor. Accordingly, the asset will be depreciated only over the lease term of six years. Also, the amount of depreciation will only cover the asset's present value of $86,259 **minus** the residual value of $5,000. Therefore, the annual depreciation will be $13,543 [($86,259 present value – $5,000 residual value) / 6 years lease term].

5. **Record lease termination.** Once the lease is completed, a journal entry must record the removal of the asset and its related depreciation from the fixed assets register, as well as the payment to the lessor of the difference between the $15,000 guaranteed residual value and the actual $5,000 residual value, or $10,000. That entry is as follows:

Lease liability	15,000	
Accumulated depreciation	81,259	
Cash		10,000
Leased equipment		86,259

Accounting for Leases—Lessor

From the perspective of the lessor, if none of the four criteria previously noted for a lessee lease are met, a lease must be treated as an operating lease. If at least one of the four criteria is met and (1) lease payments are reasonably collectible and (2) there are minimal uncertainties about future lessor unreimbursable costs, then the lessor must treat a lease as one of the following three lease types:

1. **Sales-type lease.** When the lessor will earn both a profit and interest income on a lease transaction.

2. **Direct financing lease.** When the lessor will earn only interest income on a lease transaction.

3. **Leveraged lease.** The same as a direct financing lease, but the financing is provided by a third-party creditor.

The decision tree for this transaction is shown in the Decision Trees section.

Accounting for Operating Leases—Lessor

If the lessor treats a lease as an **operating lease,** it records any payments received from the lessee as rent revenue. As was the case for the lessee, if there is an unjustified change in the lease rate over the lease term, the average revenue amount should be recognized on a straight-line basis in each reporting period. Any assets being leased are recorded in a separate Investment in Leased Property account in the fixed assets portion of the balance sheet, and are depreciated in accordance with standard company policy for similar assets. If the lessor extends incentives (such as a month of no lease payments) or incurs costs associated with the lease (such as legal fees), they should be recognized over the lease term.

Accounting for Sales-Type Leases—Lessor

If the lessor treats a lease as a **sales-type lease,** the initial transaction bears some similarity to a standard sale transaction, except that there is an unearned interest component to the entry. A description of the required entry is contained in the following table, which shows all debits and credits.

Debit	Credit	Explanation
Lease receivable		The sum of all minimum lease payments, minus executory costs, plus the actual residual value
Cost of goods sold		The asset cost, plus initial direct costs, minus the present value* of the actual residual value
	Revenue	The present value* of all minimum lease payments
	Leased asset	The book value of the asset
	Accounts payable	Any initial direct costs associated with the lease
	Unearned interest	The lease receivable, minus the present value* of both the minimum lease payments and actual residual value.

* *The present value multiplier is based on the lease term and implicit interest rate.*

Once payments are received, an entry is needed to record the receipt of cash and corresponding reduction in the lease receivable, as well as a second entry to recognize a portion of the unearned interest as interest revenue, based on the effective interest method.

At least annually during the lease term, the lessor should record any permanent reductions in the estimated residual value of the leased asset. It cannot record any increases in the estimated residual value.

When the asset is returned to the lessor at the end of the lease term, a closing entry eliminates the lease receivable associated with the actual residual value, with an offsetting debit to the fixed asset account.

Example of a sales-type lease transaction

The Albany Boat Company (ABC) has issued a seven-year lease to the Adventure Yachting Company (AYC) on a boat for its yacht rental business. The boat cost ABC

$450,000 to build and should have a residual value of $75,000 at the end of the lease. Annual lease payments are $77,000. ABC's implicit interest rate is 8%. The present value multiplier for an ordinary annuity of $1 for seven years at 8% interest is 5.2064. The present value multiplier for $1 due in seven years at 8% interest is 0.5835. We construct the initial journal entry with the following calculations:

- **Lease receivable.** This is the sum of all minimum lease payments, which is $539,000 ($77,000/year × 7 years), plus the actual residual value of $75,000, for a total lease receivable of $614,000.
- **Cost of goods sold.** This is the asset cost of $450,000, minus the present value of the residual value, which is $43,763 ($75,000 residual value × Present value multiplier of 0.5835).
- **Revenue.** This is the present value of all minimum lease payments, or $400,893 ($77,000/year × Present value multiplier of 5.2064).
- **Inventory.** ABC's book value for the yacht is $450,000, which is used to record a reduction in its inventory account.
- **Unearned interest.** This is the lease receivable of $614,000, minus the present value of the minimum lease payments of $400,893, minus the present value of the residual value of $43,763, which yields $169,344.

Based on these calculations, the initial journal entry is as follows:

Lease receivable	614,000	
Cost of goods sold	406,237	
Revenue		400,893
Boat asset		450,000
Unearned interest		169,344

The next step in the example is to determine the allocation of lease payments between interest income and reduction of the lease principal, which is accomplished through the following effective interest table:

Year	Annual payment	Interest revenue	Reduction in lease obligation	Remaining lease obligation
0				$444,656
1	$77,000	$35,572	$41,428	403,228
2	77,000	32,258	44,742	358,486
3	77,000	28,679	48,321	310,165
4	77,000	24,813	52,187	257,978
5	77,000	20,638	56,362	201,616
6	77,000	16,129	60,871	140,745
7	77,000	11,255	65,745	75,000

The interest expense shown in the effective interest table can then be used to record the allocation of each lease payment between interest revenue and principal reduction. For example, the entries recorded for Year 4 of the lease are as follows:

Cash	77,000	
Lease receivable		77,000
Unearned interest	24,813	
Interest revenue		24,813

Once the lease expires and the boat is returned to ABC, the final entry to close out the lease transaction is as follows:

Boat asset	75,000	
Lease receivable		75,000

Accounting for Direct Financing Leases—Lessor

If the lessor treats a lease as a **direct financing lease,** it will recognize only interest income from the transaction; there will be no additional profit from the implicit sale of the underlying asset to the lessee. This treatment arises when the lessor purchases an asset specifically to lease it to the lessee. The other difference between a direct financing lease and a sales-type lease is that any direct costs incurred when a lease is originated must be amortized over the life of the lease, which reduces the implicit interest rate used to allocate lease payments between interest revenue and a reduction of the lease principal.

A description of the required entry is contained in the following table, which shows all debits and credits.

Debit	*Credit*	*Explanation*
Lease receivable		The sum of all minimum lease payments, plus the actual residual value
	Leased asset	The book value of the asset
	Unearned interest	The lease receivable minus the asset book value

At least annually during the lease term, the lessor should record any permanent reductions in the estimated residual value of the leased asset. It cannot record any increases in the estimated residual value.

Example of a direct financing lease transaction

The Albany Leasing Company (ALC) purchases a boat from a third party for $700,000 and intends to lease it to the Adventure Yachting Company for six years at an annual lease rate of $140,093. The boat should have a residual value of $120,000 at the end of the lease term. Also, there is $18,000 of initial direct costs associated with the lease. ALC's implicit interest rate is 9%. The present value multiplier for an ordinary annuity of $1 for six years at 9% interest is 4.4859. The present value multiplier for $1 due in six years at 9% interest is 0.5963. We construct the initial journal entry with the following calculations:

- **Lease receivable.** This is the sum of all minimum lease payments, which is $840,558 ($140,093/year × 6 years), plus the residual value of $120,000, for a total lease receivable of $960,558.
- **Leased asset.** This is the asset cost of $700,000.
- **Unearned interest.** This is the lease receivable of $942,558, minus the asset book value of $700,000, which yields $260,558.

Based on these calculations, the initial journal entry is as follows:

Lease receivable	960,558	
Initial direct costs	18,000	
Leased asset		700,000
Unearned interest		260,558
Cash		18,000

Next, ALC's controller must determine the implicit interest rate associated with the transaction. Though ALC intended the rate to be 9%, she must add to the lease receivable the initial direct costs of $18,000, resulting in a final gross investment of $978,558 and a net investment (net of unearned interest income of $260,558) of $718,000. The determination of the implicit interest rate with this additional information is most easily derived through an electronic spreadsheet. For example, the IRR function in Microsoft Excel will automatically create the new implicit interest rate, which is 8.2215%.

With the revised implicit interest rate completed, the next step in the example is to determine the allocation of lease payments between interest income, a reduction of initial direct costs, and a reduction of the lease principal, which is accomplished through the following effective interest table:

Year	Annual payment	Unearned interest reduction	Interest revenue	Reduction of initial direct costs	Reduction in lease obligation	Remaining lease obligation (1)	Remaining lease obligation (2)
0						$718,000	$700,000
1	$140,093	$ 63,000	$59,031	$ 3,969	$ 81,062	636,938	622,907
2	140,093	$ 56,062	$52,366	$ 3,696	$ 87,727	549,211	538,876
3	140,093	$ 48,499	$45,154	$ 3,345	$ 94,939	454,271	447,281
4	140,093	$ 40,255	$37,348	$ 2,907	$102,745	351,526	347,444
5	140,093	$ 31,270	$28,901	$ 2,369	$111,192	240,334	238,621
6	140,093	$ 21,476	$19,759	$ 1,717	$120,334	120,000	120,000[*]
	Totals	$260,558[*]		$18,000[*]			

[*] *Rounded.*

The calculations used in the table are as follows:

- **Annual payment.** The annual cash payment due to the lessor.
- **Unearned interest reduction.** The original implicit interest rate of 9% multiplied by the beginning balance in the Remaining Lease Obligation (2) column, which does not include the initial direct lease cost. The total at the bottom of the column equals the unearned interest liability that will be eliminated over the course of the lease.
- **Interest revenue.** The revised implicit interest rate of 8.2215% multiplied by the beginning balance in the Remaining Lease Obligation (1) column, which includes the initial direct lease costs.
- **Reduction of initial direct costs.** The amount in the Unearned Interest Reduction column minus the amount in the Interest Revenue column, which is used to reduce the balance of the initial direct costs incurred. The total at the bottom of the column equals the initial direct costs incurred at the beginning of the lease.
- **Reduction in lease obligation.** The Annual Payment minus the Interest Revenue.
- **Remaining lease obligation (1).** The beginning lease obligation (including initial direct costs) less the principal portion of the annual payment.
- **Remaining lease obligation (2).** The beginning lease obligation, not including initial direct costs, less the principal portion of the annual payment.

Based on the calculations in the effective interest table, the journal entry at the end of the first year would show the receipt of cash and a reduction in the lease receivable. Another entry would reduce the unearned interest balance while offsetting the initial direct costs and recognizing interest revenue. The first year entries are as follows:

Cash	140,093	
Lease receivable		140,093
Unearned interest	63,000	
Interest revenue		59,031
Initial direct costs		3,969

Lease Terminations

On the date that a lessee notifies the lessor that it intends to terminate a lease, the lessee must recognize a liability for the fair value of the termination costs, which include any continuing lease payments, less prepaid rent, plus deferred rent, minus the amount of any sublease payments. Changes in these estimates are recorded immediately in the income statement.

If the lessor has recorded a lease as a sales-type or direct financing lease, it records the underlying leased asset at the lower of its current net book value, present value, or original cost, with any resulting adjustment being recorded in current earnings. At the time of termination notice, the lessor records a receivable in the amount of any termination payments yet to be made, with an offsetting credit to a deferred rent liability account. The lessor then recognizes any remaining rental payments on a straight-line basis over the revised period during which the payments are to be received.

Lease Extensions

If a **lessee** extends an operating lease and the extension is also classified as an operating lease, then the lessee continues to treat the extension in the same manner it has used for the existing lease. If the lease extension requires payment amounts differing from those required under the initial agreement but the asset received does not change, then the lessee should consistently charge the same rental amount to expense in each period, which may result in some variation between the lease payment made and the recorded expense.

If a **lessee** extends an existing capital lease but the lease structure now requires the extension to be recorded as an operating lease, the lessee writes off the existing asset, as well as all associated accumulated depreciation, and recognizes either a gain or loss on the transaction. Payments made under the lease extension are handled in accordance with the rules of a standard operating lease.

If a **lessee** extends an existing capital lease and the structure of the extension agreement requires the lease to continue to be recorded as a capital lease, the lessee changes the asset valuation and related lease liability by the difference between the present value of the new series of future minimum lease payments and the existing balance. The present value calculation must use the interest rate used for the same calculation at the inception of the original lease.

When a lease extension occurs and the **lessor** classifies the extension as a direct financing lease, the lease receivable and estimated residual value (downward only) are adjusted to match the new lease terms, with any adjustment going to unearned income. When a lease extension occurs and the **lessor** classifies an existing direct financing or sales-type lease as an operating lease, the lessor writes off the remaining lease investment and instead records the asset at the lower of its current net book value, original cost, or present value. The change in value from the original net investment is recorded against income in the period when the lease extension date occurs.

Subleases

A sublease arises when leased property is leased by the original lessee to a third party. When this happens, the original lessee accounts for the sublease as though it were the original lessor. This means that it can account for the lease as an operating, direct sales, or sales-type lease. The original lessee continues to account for its ongoing lease payments to the original lessor as though the sublease did not exist.

Sale-Leaseback Transactions

A sale-leaseback transaction arises when a property owner sells the property to another entity, which leases the property back to the original owner. If the transaction results in a loss, then the lessee recognizes it fully in the current period.

If the present value of the rental payments is at least 90% of the property's fair value, the lessee is considered to have retained substantially all rights to use the property. Under this scenario, there are two ways to account for the transaction.

1. If the lease qualifies as a capital lease, the lessee accounts for it as such and recognizes any profits on the initial property sale over the lease term in proportion to the asset amortization schedule.
2. If the lease qualifies as an operating lease, the lessee accounts for it as such and recognizes any profits on the initial property sale over the lease term in proportion to the lease payments.

If the present value of the rental payments is less than 10% of the property's fair value, the lessee should recognize all gains from the transaction fully in the current period. If the rental payments under the transaction appear unreasonable based on market prices at the time of lease inception, the payments are adjusted to make them "reasonable." The difference between the adjusted and existing lease rates is amortized over the life of the asset (if a capital lease) or the life of the lease (if an operating lease).

If the present value of the rental payments is more than 10% but less than 90% of the property's fair value, any excess profit on the asset sale can be recognized by the lessee on the sale date. If the lease is treated as a capital lease, excess profit is calculated as the difference between the asset sale price and the recorded value of the leased asset. If the lease is treated as an operating lease, excess profit is calculated as the difference between the asset sale price and the present value of the minimum lease payments, using the lower of the lessor's implicit lease rate or the lessee's incremental borrowing rate.

DECISION TREES

The decision tree shown in Exhibit 11-1 itemizes the criteria required for the correct classification of a lease by both a lessee and lessor. If at least one of a set of four criteria on the left side of the flowchart is met, the lessee treats a lease as a capital lease; if not, the treatment is as an operating lease. The right side of the flowchart continues with more criteria for a lessor. If none are met, the lease is treated as an operating lease. The flowchart terminates in the lower-right corner, where a lessor can subdivide a capital lease into either a sales-type lease or a direct financing lease.

Exhibit 11-1: Decision Tree for Determination of Lease Type

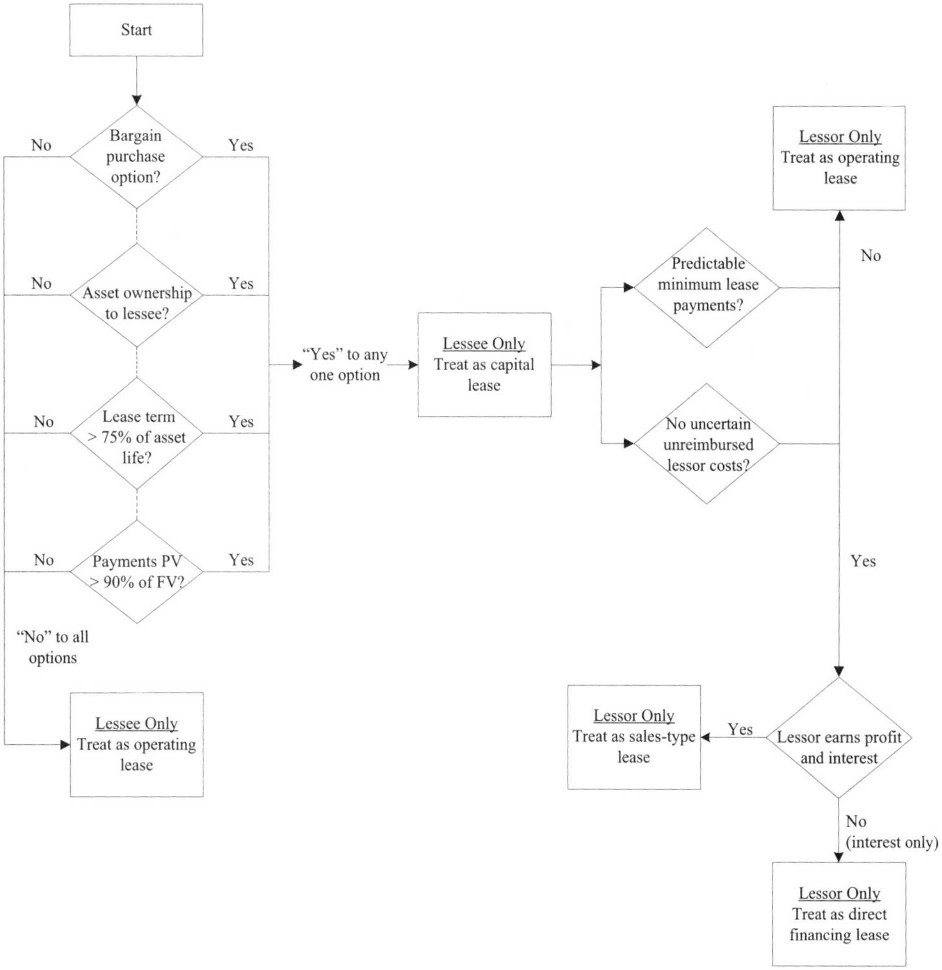

POLICIES

Accounting for Leases—Lessee

- **Lease termination dates shall be regularly reviewed.** It is extremely common for lease agreements to require a written notice of lease cancellation near the end of the lease term. If no written notice is received by the lessor, then the lease payments are contractually required to be continued for some predetermined number of months, which usually is detrimental to the lessee. This policy is designed to ensure a periodic review of lease termination dates, so that lease cancellation notices can be sent in a timely manner.

- **No company leases shall include a guaranteed residual value clause.** A company can negotiate smaller periodic lease payments by guaranteeing the lessor a significant residual value at the end of the lease, which typically calls for a large cash payment back to the lessor. Though such a clause can assist in reducing up-front cash payments, it can also result in an unacceptably high cash liability in the future.
- **The legal department shall send a copy of each signed lease document to the accounting department.** The accounting department must be aware of the amount and timing of all lease payments, so the legal department should be required to provide it this information via copies of all signed leases. For larger companies, this policy would require that leases be sent to the finance department instead of accounting, since the finance staff would be more concerned with cash forecasting.

Lease Terminations

- **Only the Board can approve lease termination agreements.** GAAP requires that the expenses associated with lease terminations be recognized on the date when the lease termination notice is issued to the lessor. Since the expenses recognized can be substantial, there can be a tendency by management to time the termination notice to alter reported financial results. By requiring the Board to issue final approval of such agreements during its regularly scheduled Board meetings, management is less likely to intentionally alter financial results through the use of lease termination agreements. The policy is even more effective if the Board is informed of the amount of any lease expense to be recognized as part of the termination notification.

PROCEDURES

Accounting for a Capital Lease—Lessee

Use this procedure to determine the correct accounting for a capital lease during all phases of the lease term.

1. Upon receipt of the capital lease documents, collect the following information to be used in the determination of lease-related journal entries:
   a. The lease term
   b. The amount of annual lease payments
   c. Any required lease term extensions (i.e., at the option of the lessor, or if a significant penalty will be incurred if the lease is **not** extended)
   d. The corporate incremental borrowing rate
   e. The implicit interest rate used by the lessor
   f. The estimated life of the leased asset
   g. The fair value of the asset
   h. The residual value of the asset at the end of the lease term
   i. Any guaranteed residual value to be paid back to the lessor
   j. The dollar amount of any bargain purchase option
   k. Taxes and executory costs

2. Determine the interest rate to be used for a present value calculation. Use the lesser of the corporation's incremental borrowing rate or the implicit rate used by the lessor in its calculation of lease payments.

3. Calculate the present value of the leased asset. To do so, use a present value table to find the present value multiple for an ordinary annuity of $1 for the lease term, including any required additional lease periods. Multiply this multiple by the annual lease payment (not including any legal or executory costs) due to the lessor. Also, if there is a final payment such as a guaranteed residual value, find the present value multiple for an amount of $1 due at the end of the lease term, including any required additional lease periods. Multiply this multiple by the ending guaranteed residual value due to the lessor. Add together the results of the two present value calculations to arrive at the present value of the leased asset.

4. Assign a value to the asset. Use the lesser of the asset present value, as calculated in the last step, or the fair value of the asset.

5. Record the asset acquisition. Using the value obtained in the last step, record a debit to the appropriate leased asset account and a credit to the Lease Liability account.

6. Calculate the proportion of each lease payment assigned to interest expense and a reduction in the lease obligation. Create a table with one row assigned to each year of the lease. Number the years in the leftmost column, followed by columns containing the annual payment amount, interest expense, reduction in the lease obligation, and the remaining lease obligation. Fill in all rows in the column for annual payments, using the lease payment schedule contained in the lease agreement. Then multiply the predetermined asset value by the predetermined interest rate, resulting in an entry in the Interest Expense column for the first year. Subtract this expense from the annual payment, with the remainder dropping into the Reduction in Lease Obligation column. Then subtract the amount just placed in the Reduction in Lease Obligation column from the beginning asset value, and put the remainder in the Remaining Lease Obligation column. Continue this process for all years of the lease.

7. Enter the asset in the fixed assets register, using the predetermined asset value as the acquisition cost. If the asset is to be returned to the lessor at the end of the lease, then use the lease term as the asset life for depreciation purposes; otherwise, use the full economic life of the asset. For the purposes of calculating depreciation, reduce the asset value by its expected residual value (not the guaranteed residual value to be paid to the lessor, if any such payment clause exists).

8. Upon termination of the lease, remove the asset from the fixed asset register and cancel the lease obligation. Record a debit to the Accumulated Depreciation account for the full amount of depreciation expense charged against the asset, with the offsetting credit going against the asset account for the amount of the original asset entry. Also record a credit for the amount of any guaranteed residual value due back to the lessor. Finally, enter a debit

to cancel the amount of any remaining lease liability, which should be the difference between the guaranteed residual value and the residual value used to initially reduce the asset value for depreciation calculation purposes.

9. Send notice of the lease cancellation to the legal department and accounts payable staff, so the legal staff can archive the leasing documents and the accounts payable staff can halt any recurring lease payments set up in the accounting system.

Accounting for a Sales-Type Lease—Lessor

Use this procedure to determine the correct accounting for a sales-type capital lease by the lessor during all phases of the lease term.

1. Upon receipt of the capital lease documents, collect the following information to be used in the determination of lease-related journal entries:

   a. The lease term
   b. The amount of annual lease payments
   c. Any required lease term extensions (i.e., at the option of the lessor, or if a significant penalty will be incurred if the lease is **not** extended)
   d. The implicit interest rate used by the lessor
   e. The book value of the asset
   f. The residual value of the asset at the end of the lease term
   g. Executory costs

2. Create the initial transaction journal entry for the lease by calculating all components of the entry, as follows:

   a. Determine the amount of the lease receivable by summing all minimum lease payments, minus executory costs, plus the actual residual value of the asset.
   b. Determine the cost of goods sold by subtracting any initial direct costs from the asset book value, less the present value of the actual residual value. Find the present value by calculating the present value multiplier for $1 due at the end of the lease term, using the lessor's implicit interest rate, and multiplying this by the residual asset value.
   c. Determine the lessor total revenue from the lease transaction by calculating the present value of all minimum lease payments. Find the present value by calculating the present value multiplier for an ordinary annuity of $1 due at the end of the lease term, using the lessor's implicit interest rate, and multiplying this by the annual lease payments from the lessee.
   d. Determine the lessor's inventory reduction by locating the book value of the asset being leased to the lessee.
   e. Determine the unearned interest portion of the lessee's prospective lease payments by subtracting from the lease receivable the present value of the minimum lease payments and the actual residual value. Find the present value of the minimum lease payments by calculating the present value multiplier for an ordinary annuity of $1 due at the end of the lease

term, using the lessor's implicit interest rate, and multiplying this by the annual lease payments from the lessee.

3. Once all components of the initial lease entry have been calculated, record the lease receivable and cost of goods sold as debits, and the revenue, inventory, accounts payable, and unearned interest as a credit.

4. Calculate the proportion of each lessee payment assigned to interest revenue and a reduction in the lessee's lease obligation. Create an effective interest table with one row assigned to each year of the lease. Number the years in the leftmost column, followed by columns containing the annual payment amount, interest revenue, reduction in the lease obligation, and the remaining lease obligation. Fill in all rows in the column for annual payments, using the lease payment schedule contained in the lease agreement. Then multiply the predetermined asset value by the predetermined interest rate, resulting in an entry in the Interest Revenue column for the first year. Subtract this revenue from the annual payment, with the remainder dropping into the Reduction in Lease Obligation column. Then subtract the amount just placed in the Reduction in Lease Obligation column from the beginning asset value, and put the remainder in the Remaining Lease Obligation column. Continue this process for all years of the lease.

5. Every time the lessor receives a lease payment from the lessee, record a debit to Cash and a credit to the Lease Receivable account for the full amount of the payment. Also enter a debit to the Unearned Interest account and a credit to the Interest Revenue account for the amount of the interest revenue component of the lessee payment, as noted in the effective interest table constructed in the last step.

6. At least annually, record any permanent reductions in the estimated residual value of the leased asset.

7. Near the end of the lease period, issue a written notification to the lessee regarding the approaching termination date and explaining lease renewal and asset return options.

8. Upon receipt of written notice from the lessee to not renew the lease, notify the lessee of the address to which the asset is to be shipped, and issue a receiving approval to the receiving staff.

9. The receiving staff inspects the asset for any unusual damage and notifies the accounting department of the cost of any required repairs to the asset.

10. The accounting department bills the lessee for any indicated asset repair costs.

11. Upon termination of the lease and return of the asset to the lessor, record a debit to the Asset account and a credit to the Lease Receivable account for the residual value of the returned asset.

Accounting for a Direct Financing Lease—Lessor

Use this procedure to determine the correct accounting for a direct financing capital lease by the lessor during all phases of the lease term.

1. Upon receipt of the capital lease documents, collect the following information to be used in the determination of lease-related journal entries:

    a. The lease term
    b. The amount of annual lease payments
    c. The implicit interest rate used by the lessor
    d. The book value of the asset
    e. The residual value of the asset at the end of the lease term
    f. The total of all initial direct costs

2. Create the initial transaction journal entry for the lease by calculating all components of the entry, which are as follows:

    a. Determine the amount of the lease receivable by summing all minimum lease payments, plus the actual residual value of the asset.
    b. Summarize all initial direct costs associated with the new lease.
    c. Determine the lessor's asset reduction by locating the book value of the asset being leased to the lessee.
    d. Determine the unearned interest portion of the lessee's prospective lease payments by subtracting the asset book value from the lease receivable.

3. Once all components of the initial lease entry have been calculated, record the lease receivable and initial direct costs as debits, and the asset, unearned interest, and any cash paid out for the initial direct costs as a credit.

4. Calculate a revised implicit interest rate for the transaction that allows for the amortization of initial direct costs over the lease term. To do so, summarize by year the annual cash inflows and outflows associated with the lease, including the asset purchase price, initial direct costs, annual lease payments from the lessee, and the amount of the residual value. Incorporate this information into the IRR( ) formula in an Excel spreadsheet to determine the lease's internal rate of return.

5. Calculate the proportion of each lessee payment assigned to interest revenue, a reduction of the initial direct costs, and a reduction in the lessee's lease obligation. To do so, create an effective interest table with one row assigned to each year of the lease. Number the years in the left-most column, followed by columns containing the annual payment amount, unearned interest reduction, interest revenue, reduction of the initial direct costs, reduction in the lease obligation, and separate columns for reductions in the remaining lease obligation where the initial lease obligations both include and exclude the initial direct costs. Fill in all rows in the column for annual payments, using the lease payment schedule contained in the lease agreement. Then follow these steps to complete each row of the table:

    a. Multiply the original implicit interest rate by the beginning balance in the second Remaining Lease Obligation column (which does not include the initial direct costs), resulting in an entry in the Unearned Interest Reduction column for the first year.

b. Multiply the revised implicit interest rate by the beginning balance in the first Remaining Lease Obligation column (which includes the initial direct costs), resulting in an entry in the Interest Revenue column.

c. Subtract the Interest Revenue from the Unearned Interest Reduction and enter the difference in the Reduction of Initial Direct Costs column.

d. Subtract the Interest Revenue from the Annual Payment and enter the difference in the Reduction in Lease Obligation column.

e. Subtract the principal portion of the annual lease payment from the Beginning Lease Obligation column that includes initial direct costs and enter the result in that column.

f. Subtract the principal portion of the annual lease payment from the Beginning Lease Obligation column that does not include initial direct costs and enter the result in that column.

6. Every time the lessor receives a lease payment from the lessee, record a debit to Cash and a credit to the Lease Receivable account for the full amount of the payment. Also enter a debit to the Unearned Interest account, a credit to the Interest Revenue account for the amount of the interest revenue component of the lessee payment, and a credit to the Initial Direct Costs account for the scheduled amortization of that account, as noted in the effective interest table constructed in the last step.

7. At least annually, record any permanent reductions in the estimated residual value of the leased asset.

8. Near the end of the lease period, issue a written notification to the lessee regarding the approaching termination date and explaining lease renewal and asset return options.

9. Upon receipt of written notice from the lessee to not renew the lease, notify the lessee of the address to which the asset is to be shipped, and issue a receiving approval to the receiving staff.

10. The receiving staff inspects the asset for any unusual damage and notifies the accounting department of the cost of any required repairs to the asset.

11. The accounting department bills the lessee for any indicated asset repair costs.

12. Upon termination of the lease and return of the asset to the lessor, record a debit to the Asset account and a credit to the Lease Receivable account for the residual value of the returned asset.

CONTROLS

Accounting for Leases—Lessee

- **Verify existence of leased assets.** A leasing agency could continue to charge a company for lease payments even after the underlying asset has been returned, or a fraudulent employee could sell off or take custody of an asset, leaving the company to continue making the lease payments. In either case, one should periodically trace the assets listed on lease invoices to the actual assets.

- **Verify correct depreciation period for assets acquired under a capital lease.** Under a capital lease, the lessee must depreciate the assets acquired under the terms of the lease. If the asset were to be recorded in the fixed assets tracking module of the accounting system in the normal manner, this is likely to result in a system-designated depreciation period. Such a depreciation period is acceptable if the capital lease involves a transfer of ownership. However, if the lessor retains ownership at the end of the lease, the depreciation period must be limited to the lease term. Using a shorter depreciation period will increase the periodic depreciation expense, so this issue has an impact on earnings. Consequently, verification of the depreciation period should be a standard review item in the month-end closing procedure.
- **Ensure that the financial analysis staff is aware of all scheduled lease payments.** If a company uses leases for a large part of its financing needs, lease payments may comprise a significant part of its cash flow planning. If so, the person responsible for the cash forecast should be kept aware of the stream of required lease payments for all leases, as well as any changes in those payments, and any guaranteed residual values that must be paid to the lessor at the end of a lease. This can be most easily accomplished by requiring the legal department to send a copy of each signed lease document to the accounting department, where the leases can be summarized for cash planning purposes.

Accounting for Leases—Lessor

- **Include in the annual accounting activity calendar a review of residual asset values.** The lessor is required by GAAP to conduct at least an annual review of the residual value of all leased assets, and to adjust those valuations downward if there appear to be permanent valuation reductions. Any such adjustment will result in the recognition of a loss, so there is a natural tendency to avoid or delay this step. By including it in the standard schedule of activities, the accounting staff is more likely to conduct it.

Lease Terminations

- **Match the date of the lease termination notification to the recognition of any losses associated with the termination.** Management can alter the timing of losses related to lease terminations by recognizing the losses later than the date of the termination notification. This control requires one to ensure that the losses are recognized in the period of notification. The control is best included in a standard review procedure, to ensure that it is consistently followed and enforced.

FORMS AND REPORTS

Lease Payments Report

A company should summarize all outstanding leases in a single document, so it can easily determine scheduled changes in lease payments, lease termination dates, and the amount of guaranteed residual values. An example is shown in Exhibit 10-

2. The report identifies the lessor and the asset being leased, as well as the identifying lease number (assuming the leases are stored in some indexed order), payment information, and a "notes" section to cover additional payment information. This report should be reviewed regularly to ensure that all upcoming payments are properly included in the corporate cash forecast; a good way to do so is to schedule a monthly lease review in the accounting department's schedule of activities.

Exhibit 10-2: Lease Payments Report

Lessor	Asset leased	Lease number	Monthly payment	Final payment date	Notes
Awai Leasing	Router	23790	$358.16	5/15/09	Guaranteed residual value payment of $12,000 on 5/15/09
Enoch Leasing	Band saw	24001	200.50	8/01/08	Bargain purchase option of $1 on 8/01/08
Freitag Leasing	Shredder	25329	628.15	3/31/08	Requires replacement lease at termination

Lease Termination Report

Under some lease agreements, the lessor is obligated to notify the lessee of a lease's upcoming termination date within a certain number of days of the end of a lease. Though this information is typically stored within a lease information database, resulting in automatically batched and printed letters to lessees, it can be useful to have a lease termination report such as the one shown in Exhibit 10-3. This report itemizes the types of assets that will shortly be released from leases, so the lessor can make arrangements for disposition of the assets. The report also notes in the BPO column the existence of a bargain purchase agreement, which makes it less likely that an asset will be returned by the lessee. The Asset Residual column contains the original or revised residual value for each asset, and includes a total at the bottom of the report; this information is useful for estimating possible receipts from asset dispositions, or at least the gains or losses likely to arise from asset resales.

Exhibit 10-3: Lease Termination Report

Customer number	Customer name	Termination date	BPO	Asset residual	Asset description
13057	Smith Jones Inc.	8/31/07	No	$42,500	Boston Whaler
14099	Elvis & Sons	8/31/07	No	37,000	Chris Craft
52052	Mobley Assoc.	8/31/07	Yes	128,000	Hudson Boat
				$207,500	

FOOTNOTES

Disclosure of Leases by Lessees

If a company is leasing an asset that is recorded as an operating lease, the accountant must disclose the future minimum lease payments for the next five years, as well as the terms of any purchase, escalation, or renewal options. If an asset lease is being recorded as a capital lease, then the accountant should present the same information, as well as the amount of depreciation already recorded for these assets.

Capital lease information should also include a summary, by major asset category, of the gross cost of leased assets. An example follows:

> The company is leasing a number of copiers, which are all recorded as operating leases. There are no escalation or renewal options associated with these leases. All the leases require the company to pay personal property taxes, maintenance, and return shipping at the end of the leases. There are purchase options at the end of all lease terms that are based on the market price of the copiers at that time. The future minimum lease payments for these leases are as follows:

2007	$195,000
2008	173,000
2009	151,000
2010	145,000
2011	101,000
	$765,000

Disclosure of Lease Termination Costs

An office or equipment lease agreement typically obligates a company to long-term lease payments with no option to stop those payments even if the company is no longer using the space or equipment. Thus, lease termination costs can be quite high, and generally warrant disclosure. A footnote should include disclosure of the pertinent requirements of the lease agreement, the remaining period over which payments are due, and the potential range of costs involved. An example follows:

> Due to the downturn in the company's principal asparagus distribution market, it no longer requires its San Francisco transshipment warehouse, for which it has a lease obligation for another six years. The total lease obligation for this facility through the remainder of the lease is $3,025,000. The company is discussing lease termination options with the lessor, and is also searching for a sublessee. Given the market conditions, the company does not feel that a sublease can be obtained, and so assumes that a lease termination fee will be required. Accordingly, it has recorded a lease termination charge in the current period of $2,405,000, which is the present value of the total lease obligation.

Disclosure of Sale and Leaseback Transactions

If a company has entered into a sale and leaseback transaction, it should disclose the total amount of future minimum lease payments, as well as the amount of this liability in each of the next five years. It should also note the general provisions of the arrangement, and the minimum amount of any payments to be received under the terms of noncancelable subleases. Two examples follow:

1. The company sold its headquarters building under a twenty-year sale and leaseback arrangement. Under the agreement, the company is obligated to make aggregate lease payments of $13.5 million over the term of the lease, which is net of $1.25 million in payments from certain noncancelable sublease agreements. The future minimum lease payments for the next five years and thereafter for these leases are as follows:

2007	$	595,000
2008		613,000
2009		621,000
2010		645,000
2011		701,000
Thereafter		10,325,000
		$13,500,000

2. The company sold its headquarters building under a twenty-year sale and leaseback arrangement. Under the agreement, the company is obligated to make aggregate lease payments of $13.5 million over the term of the lease. This is a financing arrangement under which the lessor's up-front payment of $12 million is recorded as a long-term debt, future lease payments net of interest expense will reduce the balance of the debt, and the company continues to carry the property cost on its books and depreciate that cost. The future minimum lease payments for the next five years and thereafter are as follows…

Disclosure of Leases with Related Parties

If a company has entered into a lease arrangement with a related party, it should reveal the nature and extent of the transaction. An example follows:

> The company's president owns a majority interest in Copier Leases International, from which the company has leased eleven copiers under operating leases. The total amount of payments due under these leases is $93,000, which continue until 2009. Company management is of the opinion that the lease rates obtained are highly competitive to those of other leasing companies.

Disclosure of Treatment of Free Rent Periods

If a company has a rental agreement under which it pays no rent for some portion of the lease period, the proper accounting treatment is to charge to expense the average amount of rent per period, irrespective of the exact timing of payments. This situation should be described in a footnote, as well as how the liability is recorded. An example follows:

> The company has entered into a new five-year rental agreement under which the first five months of rent are free. The company has chosen to charge to expense in each month the average monthly expense over the full lease term, rather than no expense at all for the first five months, since this more accurately reflects the periodic lease cost. The excess amount of lease expense recognized early in the lease period, totaling $85,000, has been recorded in the Other Current Liabilities account.

Disclosure of Sublease Rentals

If a company has subleased any assets under noncancelable agreements, it should disclose the minimum amount of payments to be received under these agreements. An example follows:

> The company has subleased 25,000 square feet of its office building in Montgomery County under a three-year noncancelable lease. The total minimum amount of payments to be received under this agreement is $425,000.

Disclosure of Operating Leases by Lessor

A lessor should disclose the cost of leased property, broken down by major asset classifications, and the aggregate amount of accumulated depreciation. It should also note the total amount of minimum lease payments due under noncancelable leases for each of the next five years, as well as in total. An example follows:

> The company operates a leasing division that issues only leases accounted for as operating leases. The cost of assets leased as of the balance sheet date were $14,700,000 in the farm equipment category, $29,250,000 in the emergency services category, and $41,000,000 in the municipal government category. The company has recorded $21,750,000 in aggregate accumulated depreciation on the assets recorded in all of these categories. The minimum lease payments due under noncancelable leases in each of the next five years are as follows:

2007	$20,000,000
2008	19,250,000
2009	14,750,000
2010	14,500,000
2011	10,000,000
Thereafter	16,500,000
Total	$95,000,000

Disclosure of Direct Financing and Sales-Type Leases by Lessor

A lessor should note the aggregate amounts of unearned interest revenue and unguaranteed residual values in outstanding lease agreements, as well as the total allowance for uncollected lease payments. It should also note the total amount of minimum lease payments due for each of the next five years, with separate deductions for executory costs, as well as in total. In the case of direct financing leases, the amount of initial direct costs must also be disclosed. An example follows:

> The company leases its tractors to local farmer cooperatives. The total amount of unguaranteed lease residuals the company has estimated in aggregate for its outstanding leases is $3,397,000, which represents 9% of the aggregate minimum lease payments due. The company has also reserved $1,510,000 as an allowance for uncollectible lease payments, which is 4% of the aggregate minimum lease payments due. By comparison, the company reserved 3.8% of its aggregate minimum lease payments in 2006 and 3.2% in 2005. There is currently $6,795,000 of unearned interest income recorded as a liability. The minimum lease payments due under noncancelable leases in each of the next five years are as follows:

	Minimum payments due	Less: executory costs	Net minimum payments due
2007	$7,050,000	$141,000	$6,909,000
2008	5,350,000	107,000	5,243,000
2009	6,800,000	136,000	6,664,000
2010	5,000,000	100,000	4,900,000
2011	4,100,000	82,000	4,018,000
Thereafter	9,450,000	189,000	9,261,000
Total	$37,750,000	$755,000	$36,995,000

JOURNAL ENTRIES

Accounting for Leases—Lessee

Lease, capital (initial record by lessee). To record the initial capitalization of a lease, including imputed interest that is associated with the transaction and both the short-term and long-term portions of the associated account payable. A **second entry** records the interest expense associated with each periodic payment on the capital lease. A **third entry** records the depreciation expense associated with the capital lease in each accounting period.

Capital leases	xxx	
Unamortized discount on notes payable	xxx	
Short-term liabilities		xxx
Long-term liabilities		xxx
Interest expense	xxx	
Unamortized discount on notes payable		xxx
Depreciation expense	xxx	
Accumulated depreciation—capital		
leases		xxx

Accounting for Leases—Lessor

Initial lease record by lessor (sales-type lease). To record the initial lease transaction by the lessor, including the recognition of a sale, recording of an unearned interest liability, incurrence of a liability for any initial direct costs, and the transfer of the leased asset out of inventory.

Lease receivable	xxx	
Cost of goods sold	xxx	
Sales		xxx
Inventory		xxx
Accounts payable (any initial direct		
costs)		xxx
Unearned interest		xxx

Receipt of cash payments by lessor (sales-type lease). To record the receipt of cash and the offsetting reduction in the lease receivable when periodic lease payments are made by the lessee to the lessor.

Cash	xxx	
Lease receivable		xxx

Recording of periodic interest revenue by lessor (sales-type lease). To periodically record earned interest by shifting interest from the Unearned Interest account into the Interest Revenue account.

Unearned interest	xxx	
Interest revenue		xxx

Return of asset to lessor at end of lease (sales-type lease). To record the receipt of a leased asset back into inventory upon its return by a lessee who has completed a lease term.

Inventory	xxx	
Lease receivable		xxx

Initial lease record by lessor (direct financing lease). To record the initial lease transaction by the lessor, including the recording of an unearned interest liability, incurrence of a liability for any initial direct costs, and the transfer of the leased asset out of inventory.

Lease receivable	xxx	
Initial direct costs	xxx	
Assets (specify account)		xxx
Unearned interest		xxx
Cash		xxx

Receipt of cash payments by lessor (direct financing lease). To record the receipt of cash and the offsetting reduction in the lease receivable when periodic lease payments are made by the lessee to the lessor.

Cash	xxx	
Lease receivable		xxx

Recording of periodic interest revenue by lessor (direct financing lease). To periodically record earned interest by shifting interest from the Unearned Interest account into the Interest Revenue account, with a portion of the Unearned Interest being allocated to an offset of Initial Direct Costs.

Unearned interest	xxx	
Interest revenue		xxx
Initial direct costs		xxx

Return of asset to lessor at end of lease (direct financing lease). To record the receipt of a leased asset upon its return by a lessee who has completed a lease term.

Asset (specify account)	xxx	
Lease receivable		xxx

Lease Extensions

Conversion of a capital lease to an operating lease. To record a lease extension under which a lease formerly designated a capital lease is now recorded as an operating lease. The existing leased asset is written off, along with all accumulated depreciation. If applicable, either a gain or loss is also recorded on the transaction.

Accumulated depreciation—capital leases	xxx	
Loss on lease conversion	xxx	
Gain on lease conversion		xxx
Capital leases		xxx

Sale-Leaseback Transactions

Sale-leaseback transactions for the lessee (capital lease). The first entry records the initial sale of an asset by the eventual lessee to the lessor, while the second entry records the coincident incurrence of a lease obligation for the same asset. The third entry records any lease payment by the lessee to the lessor, while the fourth entry records depreciation on the leased asset (on the assumption that this is a capital lease). The fifth entry records the periodic recognition of portions of the unearned profit on the initial asset sale.

Cash	xxx	
Asset (variety of possible accounts)		xxx
Unearned profit on sale-leaseback		xxx
Leased asset (variety of possible accounts)	xxx	
Lease obligation		xxx
Lease obligation	xxx	
Cash		xxx
Amortization expense	xxx	
Accumulated amortization		xxx
Unearned profit on sale-leaseback	xxx	
Amortization expense		xxx

RECORDKEEPING

The originals of all signed lease documents should be retained in the legal department, and copies of them in the accounting department. Auditors will want to review the lease documents in order to prepare footnotes for the audited financial statements, while the accounting staff will want to retain the leases in order to determine the dates on which lease payments change or are paid off. Once a lease has terminated, it can be archived with the accounting records for the year in which the lease expired.

12 PENSIONS AND OTHER POSTRETIREMENT BENEFITS

DEFINITIONS OF TERMS

Accrued pension cost. The pension cost accrued in excess of the employer's contribution

Accumulated benefit obligation. The actuarial present value of benefits indicated by the benefit plan formula for employee service and compensation up to (but not beyond) a specified date. It does not address future compensation levels.

Defined benefit pension plan. A pension plan that specifies the amount of benefits to be provided, usually as a function of service time or compensation.

Defined contribution pension plan. A pension plan that specifies the amount of funds contributed to each plan participant's individual account. The plan does not create an obligation to provide specific benefits.

Expected return on plan assets. The rate of return used for calculating the amount of delayed recognition of changes in the fair value of plan assets.

Postemployment benefits. The benefits provided to former employees subsequent to their employment but before their retirement.

Projected benefit obligation. The actuarial present value of benefits indicated by the benefit plan formula for employee service and compensation up to a specified date. It includes assumptions regarding future compensation levels.

Service. The range of employee service dates, including expected future service, that is considered under a pension plan.

Unfunded accumulated benefit obligation. The amount by which accumulated benefit obligations exceed plan assets.

CONCEPTS AND EXAMPLES

A pension plan is considered to be an arrangement whereby a company provides benefits under a specific benefit formula to its retired employees. Companies usually fund their pension plans by making periodic contributions to an independent trustee, who in turn invests the funds and pays benefits to the retired employees.

The key reportable element of the pension plan, from the company's perspective, is the net periodic pension cost, which is comprised of the following five elements:

1. **Service cost.** The actuarial present value of benefits attributed during the current period, which is based on the pension plan's benefit formula.

2. **Interest cost of the projected benefit obligation.** An annual increase in the net periodic pension cost that reflects the time value of money caused by the projected benefits estimated in the previous year now being one year closer to being paid out. This expense is determined by multiplying the assumed settlement discount rate by the projected benefit obligation (as defined later in this section) at the beginning of the year.

3. **Actual return on plan assets.** The change in the fair value of plan assets during the year, adjusted for any contributions in or payments out during the period.

4. **Gain or loss.** Gains or losses caused by changes in (a) plan assumptions, (b) plan assets, or (c) the amount of the projected benefit obligation. Only a portion of these gains or losses is immediately recognized, under the concept that the extent to which short-term fluctuations vary from expected long-term results must be spread out over time. At a minimum, a company must amortize over the average remaining service period of active employees the net gain or loss exceeding 10% of the beginning balances of the market value of plan assets or the projected benefit obligation (as explained at the end of this section). It must also recognize the difference between the expected and actual return on assets held by the pension plan.

5. **Amortization of unrecognized prior service cost.** The cost associated with new amendments to the pension plan that increase benefits. This expense is recognized prospectively, over the estimated remaining service period of active employees (or remaining life expectancy, if most plan participants are inactive).

The preceding five components of the net periodic pension cost describe cost types. However, the net periodic pension cost can also be viewed from the perspective of costs incurred over time. From this perspective, the *accumulated benefit obligation* (ABO) is the actuarial present value of benefit earned based on employee service up until the date of cost measurement. The *projected benefit obligation* (PBO) adds to the ABO the cost of additional benefits associated with expected future compensation increases (assuming that the pension's benefit formula pays more benefits based on increases in compensation, which is not always the case).

POLICIES

- **The expected long-term rate of return must be derived by an independent third party.** A company can significantly alter its reported pension expense each year by changing the expected long-term rate of return that it expects its pension assets to achieve. This policy is designed to keep the expected long-term rate of return from being manipulated internally. Additional layers of control would be requirements to change the third party at regular intervals, as well as to require the third party to hold no investment in the company's securities.

CONTROLS

- **Investigate unusual changes in the expected long-term rate of return.** Since the expected long-term rate of return assumption can have a major impact on the annual pension expense, a recurring audit program should require an investigation of why any changes are made to this rate, as well as the independence of the third party that should be providing the estimate.
- **Audit changes in the assumed rate of compensation increases.** The projected benefit obligation is directly influenced by the assumed rate of compensation increases, if benefits are tied to compensation. To ensure that the assumed compensation rate is not being used to artificially inflate or depress the net periodic pension cost, a recurring audit program should require a review of the justifications made for the assumed rate of compensation increases.

FOOTNOTES

If a company has a defined benefit plan or other postretirement plan, it must disclose a considerable amount of information, which is as follows:

- Reconcile the beginning and ending balances of the benefit obligation, itemizing the service cost, interest cost, participant contributions, actuarial gains and losses, changes in currency exchange rates, benefits paid, plan amendments, business combinations, divestitures, curtailments, settlements, and special termination benefits. An example follows:

    The changes in the projected benefit obligation of plan assets were as follows, for the year ended December 31:

	2007
Net benefit obligation—beginning of year	$257,000
Service costs incurred	4,000
Employee contributions	17,000
Interest costs on projected benefit obligation	15,000
Actuarial loss (gain)	(6,700)
Gross benefits paid	(15,300)
Plan amendment	300
Foreign currency exchange rate change	2,400
Effect of spin-off	(66,000)
Net benefit obligation—end of year	$207,700

- Reconcile the beginning and ending balances of the fair value of plan assets, itemizing the actual return, changes in currency exchange rates, employer contributions, employee contributions, the gross benefit payment, business combinations, divestures, curtailments, and settlements. An example follows:

    The changes in the projected fair value of plan assets were as follows, for the year ended December 31:

	2007
Fair value of plan assets—beginning of year	$295,000
Actual return on plan assets	40,000
Employer contributions (distributions)	1,700
Employer contributions	--
Gross benefits paid	(15,300)
Foreign currency exchange rate change	800
Effect of spin-off	(79,500)
Fair value of plan assets—end of year	$242,700

- Information on the funded status and balance sheet recognition of the unamortized prior service cost, unrecognized net gain or loss, accrued liabilities or prepaid assets, intangible assets, and accumulated other comprehensive income resulting from the recording of an additional minimum liability. An example follows:

  The funded status is as follows for the year ended December 31:

	2007
Over/(under) funded status	$50,500
Unrecognized net transition asset	(2,500)
Unrecognized prior service costs	400
Unrecognized net loss	32,800
Prepaid asset recognized in balance sheets	$81,200

  The amounts recognized in the balance sheet consist of the following as of December 31:

	2007
Prepaid asset	$81,200
Accumulated other comprehensive loss	--
Net amount recognized at year-end	$81,200

- The net benefit cost recognized in the reporting period, showing the service cost, interest cost, expected return on plan assets, amortization of unrecognized transition assets or obligations, any recognized gains or losses, prior service costs, or settlement gain or loss. An example follows:

  The following table provides the components of the net periodic pension benefit income, for the years ended December 31:

	2005	2006	2007
Service costs incurred	$ 3,601,000	$ 4,052,000	$ 2,768,000
Interest costs on projected benefit obligation	15,173,000	14,580,000	10,927,000
Expected return on plan assets	(3,603,000)	(2,953,000)	(2,133,000)
Amortization of prior service cost	165,000	192,000	87,000
Amortization of actuarial cost	--	--	15,000
Amortization of transitional obligation	773,000	772,000	586,000
Net periodic pension benefit (income) expense	$16,109,000	$16,643,000	$12,232,000

- The assumed weighted-average discount rate, weighted-average expected long-term rate on plan assets, and weighted-average compensation rate increase. An example follows:

Assumptions used in the actuarial calculation include the discount rate selected and disclosed at the end of the previous year as well as other assumptions detailed in the table below, for the year ended December 31:

	2007
Discount rate	6.0%
Average salary increase rate	4.5%
Expected long-term rate of return on assets	7.5%

- The percentage of the fair value of total plan assets invested in each category of plan assets. An example follows:

    The following table compares target asset allocation percentages as of the beginning of 2006 with actual asset allocations at the end of 2006:

	Target allocations	Actual allocations
Equities	40–80%	62%
Fixed income	20–50%	11%
Real estate	0–10%	4%
Other	0–20%	23%

- A description of the investment strategies used. An example follows:

    The plan's established investment policy seeks to balance the need to maintain a viable and productive capital base and yet achieve investment results superior to the actuarial rate consistent with our funds' investment objectives. Such an investment policy lends itself to a new asset allocation of approximately 50% investment in equities and property and 50% investment in debt securities. Asset allocations are subject to ongoing analysis and possible modification as basic capital market conditions change over time (interest rates, inflation, etc.).

- A description of the logic used to derive the expected long-term return on assets. An example follows:

    Investment return assumptions for the plan have been determined by obtaining independent estimates of expected long-term rates of return by asset class and applying the returns to assets on a weighted-average basis.

- The accumulated benefit obligation (if the plan is a defined benefit plan). An example follows:

    The Company's accumulated benefit obligation was $85,886,000 in 2007 and $80,450,000 in 2006.

- The benefits the company expects to pay in each of the next five fiscal years, and the aggregate expected payment for the following five years. An example follows:

    The following table provides the expected benefit payments for our pension plan:

2007	$8,553,000
2008	8,447,000
2009	8,377,000
2010	8,466,000
2011	8,527,000
2012–2016	49,231,000

- The expected amount of contributions to be paid into the plan during the next fiscal year. An example follows:

  > The Company's funding policy with respect to its qualified pension plan is to contribute annually not less than the minimum required by applicable law and regulations, or to directly pay benefit payments where appropriate.

- The measurement dates used to calculate the plan benefits. An example follows:

  > The Company uses a December 31 measurement date for its pension plan.

- The trend rate in health care costs used to measure the expected cost of benefits, as well as the time when the company expects that rate to be achieved. An example follows:

	2007	*2006*
Initial health care cost trend rate	10.0%	10.5%
Ultimate health care cost trend rate	5.0%	5.5%
Number of years to ultimate trend rate	6	6

- The effect of a 1% increase and decrease in the assumed health care costs trend rate on the aggregated service and interest costs. An example follows:

  > Assumed health care cost trend rates have a significant effect on the amounts reported for the retiree health care plan. A one percentage point change in assumed health care cost trend rates would have had the following effects:

	One percentage-point increase	*One percentage-point decrease*
Effect on total service and interest cost for the year ended December 30, 2006	$ 454,000	$ (357,000)
Efect on postretirement benefit obligation as of December 30, 2006	4,406,000	$(3,986,000)

- The amount and types of related-party securities included in the plan. An example follows:

  > Equity securities include the Company's common stock in the amounts of $1.8 million (less than 1% of total pension plan assets) and $2.9 million (less than 1% of total pension plan assets) at December 31, 2007 and 2006, respectively. In addition, due to investment strategies used by the Company's asset managers, the pension plan trust also holds short positions in the Company's common stock which had a value of $800,000 at December 31, 2006.

If a company has a defined contribution plan, it must disclose its cost, as well as a description of the effect of significant changes affecting the plan.

JOURNAL ENTRIES

Record net pension cost. The basic entry needed to record changes in the net pension cost is to itemize changes in the service cost, interest cost, and amortization of unrecognized prior service costs. The entry is shown below.

Net periodic pension cost	xxx	
Accrued/prepaid pension cost		xxx

Contribution to pension plan. Whenever a company pays cash into its pension plan, this reduces the amount of its accrued/prepaid pension cost. The entry is shown below.

Accrued/prepaid pension cost	xxx	
Cash		xxx

Record required minimum liability. A company may find it necessary to record a minimum pension liability if the unrecognized net gain or loss exceeds a band of 10% of the greater of the beginning balances of the market-related value of plan assets or the projected benefit obligation. The entry is shown below.

Intangible asset—deferred pension cost	xxx	
Additional pension liability		xxx

The following entry is used if the existing balance of the required minimum pension liability must be subsequently adjusted downward.

Additional pension liability	xxx	
Intangible asset—deferred pension cost		xxx
Excess of additional pension liability		
over unrecognized prior service cost		xxx

Record postretirement benefits. The recording of postretirement benefits besides those contained within a pension plan are very similar to the entry used for a pension plan. Only the name of the expense and related cost change, as noted in the following entry:

Postretirement expense	xxx	
Cash		xxx
Accrued/prepaid postretirement cost		xxx

13 STOCKHOLDERS' EQUITY

DEFINITIONS OF TERMS

Additional paid-in capital. Any payment received from investors for stock that exceeds the par value of the stock.

Best efforts. A stock sale arrangement whereby the underwriter does not undertake to purchase all shares to be offered, instead only taking a commission on those shares it can sell.

Capital. The investment by a company's owners in a business, plus the impact of any accumulated gains or losses.

Dividend. A payment made to shareholders that is proportional to the number of shares owned. It is authorized by the Board of Directors.

Equity. The difference between the total of all recorded assets and liabilities on the balance sheet.

Fair value method. An option valuation method based on the difference between the market price and exercise price of stock, as well as the time value of money net of issued dividends and the value to be gained from a stock's prospective price volatility.

Firm commitment. A stock sale arrangement under which the underwriter purchases a fixed number of shares from the company at a fixed price, which is discounted from the price at which the underwriter will then sell the shares to investors.

Intrinsic value method. An option valuation method based on the difference between the market price and exercise price of stock.

Minimum value method. An option valuation method based on the difference between the market price and exercise price of stock, as well as the time value of money net of issued dividends.

Owners' equity. The total of all capital contributions and retained earnings on a business's balance sheet.

Paid-in capital. Any payment received from investors for stock that exceeds the par value of the stock.

Par value. The stated value of a stock, which is recorded in the capital stock account. Equity distributions cannot drop the value of stock below this minimum amount.

Preferred stock. A type of stock that usually pays a fixed dividend prior to any distributions to the holders of common stock. In the event of liquidation, it must be paid off before common stock. It can, but rarely does, have voting rights.

Retained earnings. A company's accumulated earnings since its inception, less any distributions to shareholders.

Stock certificate. A document that identifies a stockholder's ownership share in a corporation.

Stock option. A right to purchase a specific maximum number of shares at a specific price no later than a specific date. It is a commonly used form of incentive compensation.

Stockholder. A person or entity that owns shares in a corporation.

Unissued stock. Stock that has been authorized for use, but which has not yet been released for sale to prospective shareholders.

CONCEPTS AND EXAMPLES[1]

Legal Capital and Capital Stock

The owners of common stock are the true owners of the corporation. Through their share ownership, they have the right to dividend distributions, to vote on various issues presented to them by the Board of Directors, to elect members of the Board of Directors, and to share in any residual funds left if the corporation is liquidated. If the company is liquidated, they will not receive any distribution from its proceeds until all creditor claims have been satisfied, as well as the claims of holders of all other classes of stock. There may be several classes of common stock, which typically have different voting rights attached to them; the presence of multiple types of common stock generally indicates that some shareholders are attempting some degree of preferential control over a company through their type of common stock.

Most types of stock contain a par value, which is a minimum price below which the stock cannot be sold. The original intent for using par value was to ensure that a

---

[1] *Much of the information in this section is adapted with permission from Chapter 20 of Bragg,* **Ultimate Accountants' Reference** *(John Wiley & Sons, Inc., Hoboken, NJ, 2006).*

residual amount of funding was contributed to the company, and which could not be removed from it until dissolution of the corporate entity. In reality, most common stock now has a par value that is so low (typically anywhere from a penny to a dollar) that its original intent no longer works. Thus, though the accountant still tracks par value separately in the accounting records, it has little meaning.

If an investor purchases a share of stock at a price greater than its par value, the difference is credited to an additional paid-in capital account. For example, if an investor buys one share of common stock at a price of $82, and the stock's par value is $1, then the entry would be

Cash	82	
Common stock—par value		1
Common stock—additional paid-in capital		81

When a company initially issues stock, there will be a number of costs associated with it, such as the printing of stock certificates, legal fees, investment banker fees, and security registration fees. These costs can be charged against the proceeds of the stock sale, rather than be recognized as expenses within the current period.

If a company accepts property or services in exchange for stock, the amount listed on the books as the value of stock issued should be based on the fair market value of the property or services received. If this cannot easily be determined, then the current market price of the shares issued should be used. If neither is available, then the value assigned by the Board of Directors at the time of issuance is assumed to be the fair market value.

Preferred stock comes in many flavors, but essentially is stock that has fewer (or none) of the rights conferred on common stock, but which offer a variety of incentives, such as guaranteed dividend payments and preferential distributions over common stock, to convince investors to buy them. The dividends can also be preconfigured to increase to a higher level at a later date, which is called **increasing rate preferred stock.** This is an expensive form of funds for a company since the dividends paid to investors are not tax deductible as interest expense.

The dividends provided for in a preferred stock agreement can be distributed only after the approval of the Board of Directors (as is the case for dividends from common stock), and so may be withheld. If the preferred stock has a cumulative provision, then any dividends not paid to the holders of preferred shares in preceding years must be paid prior to dividend payments for any other types of shares. Also, some preferred stock will give its owners voting rights in the event of one or more missed dividend payments.

Because this stock is so expensive, many companies issue it with a call feature stating the price at which the company will buy back the shares. The call price must be high enough to give investors a reasonable return over their purchase price, or else no one will initially invest in the shares.

Convertible Preferred Stock

Preferred stock may also be converted by the shareholder into common stock at a preset ratio, if the preferred stock agreement specifies that this option is available. If this conversion occurs, the accountant must reduce the par value and additional paid-in capital accounts for the preferred stock by the amount at which the preferred stock was purchased, and then shift these funds into the same common stock funds.

Example of a preferred stock conversion to common stock

If a shareholder of preferred stock were to convert one share of the Grinch Toy Removal Company's preferred stock into five shares of its common stock, the journal entry would be as follows, on the assumption that the preferred stock was bought for $145, and that the par value of the preferred stock is $50 and the par value of the common stock is $1:

Preferred stock—par value	50	
Preferred stock—additional paid-in capital	95	
Common stock—par value		5
Common stock—additional paid-in capital		140

In the journal entry, the par value account for the common stock reflects the purchase of five shares, since the par value of five individual shares (i.e., $5) has been recorded, with the remaining excess funds from the preferred stock being recorded in the additional paid-in capital account. However, if the par value of the common stock were to be greater than the entire purchase price of the preferred stock, the journal entry would change to bring in extra funds from the retained earnings account in order to make up the difference. If this were to occur with the previous assumptions, except with a common stock par value of $40, the journal entry would be

Preferred stock—par value	50	
Preferred stock—additional paid-in capital	95	
Retained earnings	55	
Common stock—par value		200

Stock Splits

A stock split involves the issuance of a multiple of the current number of shares outstanding to current shareholders. For example, a one-for-two split of shares when there are currently 125,000 shares outstanding will result in a new amount outstanding of 250,000. This is done to reduce the market price on a per-share basis. In addition, by dropping the price into a lower range, it can have the effect of making it more affordable to small investors, who may then bid up the price to a point where the split stock is cumulatively more valuable than the unsplit stock.

A stock split is typically accompanied by a proportional reduction in the par value of the stock. For example, if a share with a par value of $20 were to be split on a two-for-one basis, then the par value of the split stock would be $10 per share. This transaction requires no entry on a company's books. However, if the split occurs without a change in the par value, then funds must be shifted from the additional paid-in capital account to the par value account.

A reverse split may also be accomplished if a company wishes to proportionally increase the market price of its stock. For example, if a company's common stock sells for $2.35 per share and management wishes to see the price trade above the $20 price point, then it can conduct a ten-for-one reverse split, which will raise the market price to $23.50 per share while reducing the number of outstanding shares by 90%. In this case, the par value per share would be increased proportionally, so that no funds were ever removed from the par value account.

Example of a stock split with no change in par value

If 250,000 shares were to be split on a one-for-three basis, creating a new pool of 750,000 shares, and the existing par value per share of $2 were not changed, then the accountant would have to transfer $1,000,000 (the number of newly created shares times the par value of $2) from the additional paid-in capital account to the par value account to ensure that the legally mandated amount of par value per share was stored there.

Stock Subscriptions

Stock subscriptions allow investors or employees to pay in a consistent amount over time and receive shares of stock in exchange. When such an arrangement occurs, a receivable is set up for the full amount expected, with an offset to a common stock subscription account and the Additional Paid-in Capital account (for the par value of the subscribed shares). When the cash is collected and the stock is issued, the funds are deducted from these accounts and shifted to the standard common stock account.

Example of a stock subscription

If the Slo-Mo Molasses Company sets up a stock subscription system for its employees and they choose to purchase 10,000 shares of common stock with a par value of $1 for a total of $50,000, the entry would be as follows:

Stock subscriptions receivable	50,000	
Common stock subscribed		40,000
Additional paid-in capital		10,000

When the $50,000 cash payment is received, the Stock Subscriptions Receivable account will be offset, while funds stored in the Common Stock Subscribed account are shifted to the Common Stock account, as noted in the following entry:

Cash	50,000	
Stock subscriptions receivable		50,000
Common stock subscribed	50,000	
Common stock		50,000

Retained Earnings

Retained earnings is that portion of equity not encompassed by the various par value or additional paid-in capital accounts. It is increased by profits and decreased by distributions to shareholders and several types of stock transactions.

Retained earnings can be impacted if the accountant makes a prior period adjustment that results from an error in the prior financial statements; the offset to this adjustment will be the retained earnings account, and will appear as an adjustment to the opening balance in the retained earnings account. A financial statement error would be one that involved a mathematical error or the incorrect application of accounting rules to accounting entries. A change in accounting **estimate** is not an accounting error, and so should not be charged against retained earnings.

Retained earnings can be restricted through the terms of lending agreements. For example, a lender may require the company to restrict some portion of its retained earnings through the term of the loan, thereby giving the lender some assurance that funds will be available to pay off the loan. Such a restriction would keep the company from issuing dividends in amounts that cut into the restricted retained earnings.

Stock Warrants

A stock warrant is a legal document giving the holder the right to buy a company's shares at a specific price, and usually for a specific time period, after which it becomes invalid. It is used as a form of compensation instead of cash for services performed by other entities to the company, and may also be attached to debt instruments in order to make them appear as more attractive investments to buyers.

If the warrant attached to a debt instrument cannot be detached and sold separately from the debt, then it should not be separately accounted for. However, if it can be sold separately by the debt holder, then the fair market value of each item (the warrant and the debt instrument) should be determined, and then the accountant should apportion the price at which the combined items were sold among the two, based on their fair market values.

Example of value allocation to warrants

For example, if the fair market value of a warrant is $63.50 and the fair market value of a bond to which it was attached is $950, and the price at which the two items were sold was $1,005, then an entry should be made to an additional paid-in capital account for $62.97 to account for the warrants, while the remaining $942.03 is accounted for as debt. The apportionment of the actual sale price of $1,005 to warrants is calculated as follows:

$$\frac{\text{Fair market value of warrant}}{\text{Fair market value of warrant} + \text{Fair market value of bond}} \times \text{Price of combined instruments}$$

or,

$$\frac{\$63.50}{(\$63.50 + \$950.00)} \times \$1005 = \$62.97$$

If a warrant expires, then the funds are shifted from the outstanding warrants account to an additional paid-in capital account. To continue with the last example, this would require the following entry:

Additional paid-in capital—warrants	62.97	
Additional paid-in capital—expired warrants		62.97

If a warrant is subsequently used to purchase a share of stock, then the value allocated to the warrant in the accounting records should be shifted to the common stock accounts. To use the preceding example, if the warrant valued at $62.97 is used to purchase a share of common stock at a price of $10.00, and the common stock has a par value of $25, then the par value account is credited with $25 (since it is mandatory that the par value be recorded), and the remainder of the funds are recorded in the additional paid-in capital account. The entry follows:

Cash	10.00	
Additional paid-in capital—warrants	62.97	
Common stock—par value		25.00
Common stock—additional paid-in capital		47.97

Dividends

Dividends must be authorized for distribution by the Board of Directors. They are not allowed to make such a distribution if the company is insolvent or would become insolvent as a result of the transaction.

When the Board of Directors votes to issue dividends, this is the **declaration date.** At this time, by the Board's action, the company has incurred a liability to issue a dividend. Unless the dividend is a stock dividend, the accountant must record a dividend payable at this time, and debit the retained earnings account to indicate the eventual source of the dividend payment.

The dividend will be paid as of a **record date.** This date is of considerable importance to shareholders, since the entity holding a share on that date will be entitled to receive the dividend. If a share is sold the day before the record date, then the old shareholder forgoes the dividend and the new one receives it. As of the payment date, the company issues dividends, thereby debiting the dividends payable account and crediting the cash account (or the account of whatever asset is distributed as a dividend).

On rare occasions, a company will choose to issue a **property dividend** to its shareholders. Under this scenario, the assets being distributed must be recorded at their fair market value, which usually triggers the recognition of either a gain or loss in the current income statement.

Example of a property dividend

The Burly Book Binders Company declares a property dividend for its shareholders of a rare set of books, which have a fair market value of $500 each. The 75 shareholders receive one book each, which represents a total fair market value of $37,500. The books were originally obtained by the company at a cost of $200 each, or $15,000 in total. Consequently, a gain of $22,500 ($37,500 minus $15,000) must be recognized. To do so, the accountant debits the Retained Earnings account for $37,500, credits the Gain on Property Disposal account for $22,500, and credits its Dividends Payable account for $15,000. Once the books are distributed to the shareholder, the accountant debits the Dividends Payable account for $15,000 and credits the Inventory account for $15,000 in order to eliminate the dividend liability and reflect the reduction in book inventory.

A dividend may also take the form of a **stock dividend.** This allows a company to shift funds out of the Retained Earnings account and into the Par Value and Additional Paid-in Capital accounts, which reduces the amount of funding that the Internal Revenue Service would see when reviewing the company for an excessive amount of retained earnings (which can be taxed). These distributions are also not taxable to the recipient. If the amount of a stock dividend represents less than one-quarter of the total number of shares currently outstanding, then this is considered to be a distribution that will not greatly impact the price of existing shares through dilution; accordingly, the accountant records the fair market value of these shares in the Par Value and Additional Paid-in Capital accounts, and takes the offsetting funds out of the Retained Earnings Account.

Example of a small stock dividend

If the Bobber Fishing Equipment Company wishes to issue a stock dividend of 10,000 shares and their fair market value is $32 per share, with a par value of $1, then the entry would be

Retained earnings	320,000	
Common stock—par value		32,000
Additional paid-in capital		288,000

If more than one-quarter of the total amount of outstanding shares is to be distributed through a stock dividend, then we assume that the value of the shares will be watered down through such a large distribution. In this case, funds are shifted from retained earnings only to cover the amount of the par value for the shares to be distributed.

Example of a large stock dividend

Using the preceding example (and assuming that 10,000 shares were more than 25% of the total outstanding), the entry would change to the following:

Retained earnings	32,000	
Common stock—par value		32,000

If there are not sufficient funds in the retained earnings account to make these entries, then the number of shares issued through the stock dividend must be reduced. However, given the small size of the par values that many companies have elected to use for their stock, the amount of retained earnings required may actually be less for a very large stock dividend than for a small one, since only the par value of the stock must be covered in the event of a large distribution.

A **liquidating dividend** is used to return capital to investors; thus, it is not strictly a dividend, which is intended to be a distribution of earnings. This transaction is impacted by the laws of the state of incorporation for each organization, and so cannot be readily summarized here. However, the general entry in most cases is to credit cash and debit the additional paid-in capital account.

A summary of the entries required for the various types of dividends is provided in the Decision Trees section.

Treasury Stock

If the Board of Directors elects to have the company buy back shares from shareholders, the stock that is brought in-house is called **treasury stock.** A corporation's purchase of its own stock is normally accounted for under the **cost method.** Under this approach, the cost at which shares are bought back is listed in a treasury stock account. When the shares are subsequently sold again, any sale amounts exceeding the repurchase cost are credited to the additional paid-in capital account, while any shortfalls are charged first to any remaining additional paid-in capital remaining from previous treasury stock transactions, and then to retained earnings if there is no additional paid-in capital of this type remaining. For example, if a company chooses to buy back 500 shares at $60 per share, the transaction would be

Treasury stock	30,000	
Cash		30,000

If management later decides to permanently retire treasury stock that was originally recorded under the cost method, then it backs out the original par value and additional paid-in capital associated with the initial stock sale, and charges any remaining difference to the retained earnings account. To continue with the previous example, if the 500 shares had a par value of $1 each, had originally been sold for $25,000, and all were to be retired, the entry would be as follows:

Common stock—par value	500	
Additional paid-in capital	24,500	
Retained earnings	5,000	
Treasury stock		30,000

If instead the company subsequently chooses to sell the shares back to investors at a price of $80 per share, the transaction is:

Cash	40,000	
Treasury stock		30,000
Additional paid-in capital		10,000

If treasury stock is subsequently sold for more than it was originally purchased, the excess amount may also be recorded in an additional paid-in capital account that is specifically used for treasury stock transactions; the reason for this segregation is that any subsequent sales of treasury stock for less than the original buy-back price require the accountant to make up the difference from any gains recorded in this account; if the account is emptied and there is still a difference, then the shortage is made up from the additional paid-in capital account for the same class of stock, and then from retained earnings.

In the less common case where there is no intention of ever reselling treasury stock, it is accounted for at the point of purchase from shareholders under the **constructive retirement method.** Under this approach, the stock is assumed to be retired, and so the original common stock and additional paid-in capital accounts will be reversed, with any loss on the purchase being charged to the retained earnings account, and any gain being credited to the additional paid-in capital account. For example, if a company were to buy back 500 shares at $60 per share and the original issuance price was $52 (par value of $1), then the transaction would be

Common stock—par value	500	
Additional paid-in capital	25,500	
Retained earnings	4,000	
Cash		30,000

Note that under the constructive retirement approach, no treasury account is used, since the assumption is that the shares are immediately retired from use, rather than being parked in a treasury stock holding account.

A special case arises when a company is forced to buy back shares at above-market prices under the threat of a corporate takeover. When this happens, the difference between the repurchase price and the market price must be charged to expense in the current period.

Options

An option is an agreement between a company and another entity (frequently an employee) that allows the entity to purchase shares in the company at a specific price within a specified date range. The assumption is that the options will only be exercised if the fixed purchase price is lower than the market price, so that the buyer can turn around and sell the stock on the open market for a profit. Options are accounted for under either the **intrinsic value method** (promulgated in APB 25) or the **fair value method** (promulgated in SFAS 123).

If stock options are issued at a strike price that is the same as the current market price, then there is no journal entry to record when the **intrinsic value method** is used. However, if the strike price at the time of the issuance is lower than the market price, then the difference must be recorded in a deferred compensation account.

The same rule applies if there is a guaranteed minimum to the value of the stock option grants. In this situation, one must recognize as compensation expense over the service period of the options the amount of the guaranteed minimum valuation.

If the term of the options granted were to be extended, one must compare the difference between the market price and exercise price of the options on the extension date and recognize compensation expense at that time if the exercise price is lower than the market price.

Example of options issued at a below-market strike price using the intrinsic value method

If 5,000 options are issued at a price of $25 each to the president of the Long Walk Shoe Company on a date when the market price is $40, then Long Walk's accountant must charge a deferred compensation account for $75,000 ($40 market price minus $25 option price, times 5,000 options) with the following entry:

Deferred compensation expense	75,000	
Options—additional paid-in capital		75,000

In this example, the options cannot be exercised for a period of three years from the date of grant, so the accountant regularly charges off the deferred compensation account to expense over the next three years. For example, in the first year the accountant would charge 1/3 of the deferred compensation to expense with the following entry:

Compensation expense	25,000	
Deferred compensation expense		25,000

If Long Walk's president elects to use all of the stock options to buy stock at the end of the three-year period, and the par value of the stock is $1, then the entry would be

Cash	125,000	
Options—additional paid-in capital	75,000	
Common stock—par value		5,000
Common stock—additional paid-in capital		195,000

Alternatively, if Long Walk's president were to leave the company at the end of the second year without having used any of the options to purchase stock, the compensation expense thus far recognized would have to be reversed, as well as the deferred compensation associated with the options that would have vested in year three. The entry follows:

Options—additional paid-in capital	75,000	
Deferred compensation expense		25,000
Compensation expense		50,000

If, during the period between the option grant date and the purchase of stock with the options, the market price of the stock were to vary from the $40 price at which the deferred compensation liability was initially recorded, the accountant would not be required to make any entry, since subsequent changes in the stock price are beyond the control of the company, and so should not be recorded as a change in the deferred compensation account.

The Financial Accounting Standards Board has also issued Statement of Financial Accounting Standards (SFAS) 123, which requires a minimum of footnote reporting using a different valuation approach; or a company may use it exclusively for both financial and footnote reporting. If a company chooses to use the SFAS 123 approach for its normal financial reporting of stock option transactions (as opposed to just using it in footnotes), then the decision cannot be rescinded, and the company must continue to use this method (known as the **fair value method**) in the future.

Under the SFAS 123 approach, compensation expense must be recognized for options granted, even if there is no difference between the current market price of the stock and the price at which the recipient can purchase the stock under the terms of the option. A compensation expense arises because the holder of an option does not actually pay for any stock until the date when the option is exercised, and so can earn interest by investing the money elsewhere until that time. This ability to invest elsewhere has a value, and is measured by using the risk-free interest rate (usually derived from the current interest rate on US government securities). The present value of these interest earnings is based on the expected term of the option (i.e, the time period extending to the point when one would reasonably expect them to be used), and is reduced by the present value of any stream of dividend payments that the stock might be expected to yield during the interval between the present time and the point when the stock is expected to be purchased, since this is income forgone by the buyer.

The prospective volatility of the stock is also factored into the equation. If a stock has a history of considerable volatility, an option holder can wait to exercise his options until the stock price spikes, which creates more value to the option holder than if the underlying shares had minimal volatility. The difference between the discounted price of the stock and the exercise price is then recognized as compensation expense.

The calculations required to determine the present value of options are complex and typically require the use of a computer program. Consequently, the following example is extremely simplified and does not account for stock price volatility at all.

Example of SFAS 123 expense recognition for options granted

If the current interest rate on 90-day Treasury bills is 7% (assumed to be the risk-free interest rate), the expectation for purchase of stock is three years in the future, and the option price of the stock is $25, then its present value is $20.41 ($25 times 0.8163).

The difference between $25 and $20.41 is $4.59, which must be recognized as compensation expense.

The use of present value calculations under SFAS 123 means that financial estimates are being used to determine the most likely scenario that will eventually occur. One of the key estimates to consider is that not all stock options will eventually be exercised—some may lapse due to employees leaving the company, for example. One should include these estimates when calculating the total amount of accrued compensation expense, so that actual results do not depart significantly from the initial estimates. However, despite the best possible estimates, the accountant will find that actual option use will inevitably vary from original estimates. When these estimates change, one should account for them in the current period as a change of accounting estimate. However, if estimates are not changed and the accountant simply waits to see how many options are actually exercised, then any variances from the accounting estimate will be made on the date when options either lapse or are exercised. Either of these methods is acceptable and will eventually result in the same compensation expense, but the first approach is technically better, because it attempts to recognize changes as soon as possible, and so results in an earlier representation of changes in a company's compensation expenses.

A major difference between the APB 25 and SFAS 123 approaches to options is their varying treatment of vested options that expire unexercised. Under APB 25, any related compensation expense is reversed, whereas SFAS 123 requires that the compensation expense remain. Depending on the circumstances, this can result in a significant difference in expenses recognized.

If a company elects to cancel options by purchasing them from an option holder, and the price paid is higher than the value of the options as calculated under the fair value method, then the difference is fully recognized as compensation expense at once, since any vesting period has been accelerated to the payment date.

Option Vesting Period

If the APB 25 option expensing system is used, the compensation expense recognition calculation shown in this section must be used. If the SFAS 123 approach is used instead, one can either use the calculation shown in this section or recognize compensation expense on a straight-line basis.

The compensation expense should be recognized ratably over the vesting period. If there is "cliff vesting," where all options fully vest only after a set time period has passed, then the calculation is simple enough—ratably spread the expense over the entire vesting period.

Example of compensation expense recognition with cliff-vested options

The Arabian Knights Security Company issues 9,000 options to its president. The compensation expense associated with the options is $50,000. The option plan calls for cliff vesting after three years, so the company's controller records a monthly charge to compensation expense of $1,388.89 ($50,000 divided by 36 months).

The situation becomes more complex if the vesting schedule calls for vesting of portions of the option grant at set intervals. When this happens, the compensation expense associated with each block of vested options is recognized ratably over the period leading up to the vesting. For example, the compensation associated with a block of options that vest in one year must be recognized as expense entirely within that year, while the compensation associated with a block of options that vest in two years must be recognized as expense over the two years leading up to the vesting date. The net impact of this approach is significantly higher compensation expense recognition in the early years of an option plan that allows incremental vesting over multiple years.

Example of compensation expense recognition with incremental vesting

Assume the same information as the last example, except that the president's options vest in equal proportions at the end of years 1, 2, and 3. The following table shows that 61% of the total compensation expense recognition is now shifted into the first year of the vesting period.

	1st year vesting	2nd year vesting	3rd year vesting
1st 3,000 options	100%		
2nd 3,000 options	50%	50%	
3rd 3,000 options	33%	33%	33%
Percent of total	61%	28%	11%
Expense recognition	$30,500	$14,000	$5,500

Stock Appreciation Rights

Sometimes the management team chooses not to issue stock options to employees, perhaps because employees do not have the funds to purchase shares, or because no stock is available for an option plan. If so, an alternative is the stock appreciation right (SAR). Under this approach, the company essentially grants an employee a fake stock option, and issues compensation to the employee at a future date if the price of company stock has risen from the date of grant to the date at which the compensation is calculated. The amount of compensation paid is the difference between the two stock prices.

To account for a SAR, the accountant must determine the amount of any change in company stock during the reporting period, and charge the amount to an accrued compensation expense account. If there is a decline in the stock price, then the accrued expense account can be reduced. If an employee cancels the SAR agreement (perhaps by leaving the company), then the entire amount of accrued compensation expense related to that individual should be reversed in the current period.

If the company pays the recipients of SAR compensation in stock, then it usually grants shares on the payment date based on the number of shares at their fair market value that will eliminate the amount of the accrued compensation expense. The journal entry required is a debit to the Accrued Compensation Liability account, and a credit to the Stock Rights Outstanding account.

If a service period is required before a SAR can be exercised, the amount of the compensation expense should be recognized ratably over the service period.

Example of a SAR transaction

The Big Fat Pen Company decides to grant 2,500 SAR to its chief pen designer. The stock price at the grant date is $10. After one year, the stock price has increased to $12. After the second year, the stock price has dropped to $11. After the third year, the price increases to $15, at which point the chief pen designer chooses to cash in his SAR and receive payment. The related transactions would be

End of year 1

Compensation expense ($2 net gain × 2,500 shares)	5,000	
SAR liability		5,000

End of year 2

SAR liability	2,500	
Compensation expense ($1 net loss × 2,500 shares)		2,500

End of year 3

Compensation expense ($4 net gain × 2,500 shares)	10,000	
SAR liability		10,000
SAR liability (payment of employee)	12,500	
Cash		12,500

Employee Stock Ownership Plans

An Employee Stock Ownership Plan (ESOP) is one where employees receive additional compensation in the form of stock that is purchased by the ESOP from the corporation. Since the company usually has a legal obligation to provide shares or contributions to the ESOP (which are then used to buy its stock), the ESOP should be considered an extension of the company for accounting purposes. This means that if the ESOP obligates itself to a bank loan in order to buy shares from the company, the company should record this liability on its books even if the company is not a guarantor of the loan. The entry would be a debit to cash and a credit to loans payable. However, a loan from the company to the ESOP does not require an accounting entry, since the company is essentially making a loan to itself.

In addition, if the company has obligated itself to a series of future contributions of stock or cash to the ESOP, it should recognize this obligation by recording a journal entry that debits the full amount of the obligation to an Unearned ESOP Shares account (this is reported as a contra equity account) and crediting the Common Stock account.

When the company makes a contribution to the plan, the funds are usually shifted to the lender who issued a loan to pay for the initial purchase of stock. Accordingly, the Note Payable and Related Interest Expense accounts are both debited, while a second entry also debits a Compensation Expense account and credits the Additional Paid-in Capital and Unearned ESOP Shares accounts to reflect the coincident allocation of shares to ESOP participants. Of particular interest is the treatment of dividends issued by the sponsoring company. When declared, a compensation expense must be recognized for all shares in the ESOP that have **not** been allocated to ESOP participants, rather than the usual charge to Retained Earnings. This tends to be a disincentive for the Board of Directors to declare a dividend, since the declaration immediately triggers an expense recognition.

Example of ESOP Transactions

The Arabian Knights Security Company establishes an ESOP for its employees. The ESOP arranges for a bank loan of $100,000, and uses it to purchase 10,000 shares of no par value stock. The entry is

Cash	100,000	
Notes payable		100,000
Unearned ESOP shares	100,000	
Common stock		100,000

Arabian then contributes $10,000 to the plan, which is used to pay down both the principal and interest components of the debt. The entry is

Interest expense	2,000	
Notes payable	8,000	
Cash		10,000

The ESOP plan requires an allocation of shares to plan participants at the end of each calendar year. For the current year, 2,000 shares are allocated. On the date of allocation, the fair market value of the shares is $13. Since the fair value is $3 higher than the original share purchase price of $10, the difference is credited to the Additional Paid-in Capital account. The entry is

Compensation expense	26,000	
Additional paid-in capital		6,000
Unearned ESOP shares		20,000

Arabian then declares a dividend of $0.50 per share. The dividend applied to the 8,000 remaining unallocated shares is charged to a compensation expense account, while the dividend applied to the 2,000 allocated shares is charged to the Retained Earnings account. The entry is

Retained earnings	8,000	
Compensation expense	2,000	
Dividend payable		10,000

DECISION TREES

Dividends—Recording of Different Types

The decision tree shown in Exhibit 13-1 itemizes the journal entry required for each of the various types of dividends as of the declaration date.

Exhibit 13-1: Dividend Entries on Declaration Date

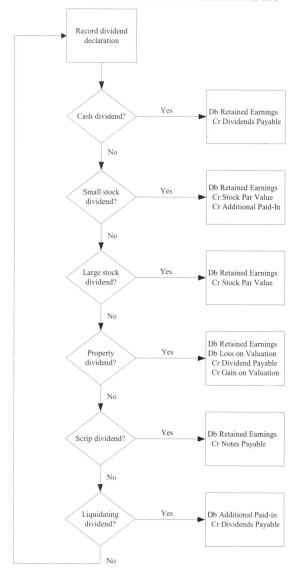

POLICIES

Legal Capital and Capital Stock

Stock issuance costs shall include only certificate printing, security registration, and legal and underwriting fees. This policy is designed to strictly limit the types of expenses that can be charged against the proceeds from a stock offering. By doing so, there is little room for extraneous expenses to be netted against a stock sale.

Stock Subscriptions

Stock subscription plans for employees must be approved by the Board of Directors. This policy requires the Board to authorize the number of shares that may be sold to employees, as well as any discounts on those purchases. By requiring ongoing approval of additions to the number of shares authorized for distribution, the Board can maintain effective control over this program.

Dividends

The Board of Directors shall not time property dividend declarations in order to influence reported earning levels from gains or losses recognized on property to be distributed. A gain or loss on assets must be recognized on the date of a dividend declaration if there is a difference between the fair market and book values of the assets. This can give rise to deliberate timing of dividend declarations in order to recognize gains or losses in specific reporting periods. This policy points out to directors that such behavior is not acceptable.

The Board of Directors shall not time scrip dividend declarations to influence reported levels of indebtedness. A scrip dividend is a note payable issued to shareholders in place of cash, and is generally a bad idea unless there is an immediate expectation of cash receipts to pay off the resulting notes. Further, a Board could time a scrip dividend declaration to immediately follow the issuance of year-end financial statements, so that readers of the statements will not be aware of the sudden increase in indebtedness until the next financial statements are released. This policy is designed to bring the potential reporting issue to the attention of the Board, though it still has the ability to override the policy.

Treasury Stock

The initial sale price of all stock shall be recorded by stock certificate number. When stock is repurchased into the treasury, it is possible that the original sale price of each share repurchased must be backed out of the stock account, depending on the accounting method used. This policy requires that sufficient records be kept to allow such future treasury stock transactions to be properly recorded.

The circumstances of any greenmail stock repurchases shall be fully documented. This policy is designed to provide proper documentation of the amount of any stock repurchased under the threat of a corporate takeover. By doing so, one can more easily determine the price under which shares were repurchased, as well as the market price of the stock on that date. This is critical information for the recognition of expenses related to excessively high repurchase costs, which can have a major negative impact on reported earnings levels.

Options

The current dividend yield shall be used for all option valuation assumptions. When a company uses the popular Black-Scholes option pricing formula to determine the compensation expense associated with its options, it can reduce the amount of expense recorded by assuming an increased dividend yield in the future.

This policy is designed to freeze the dividend assumption, thereby nullifying the risk of deliberate expense modifications in this area.

The expected term of all options shall be based on the results of the last ___ years. When a company uses SFAS 123 guidelines to record compensation expense, part of the calculation is an estimate of the time period over which options are expected to be held by recipients. If this assumed period is shortened, the value of the options is reduced, resulting in a lower compensation expense. Consequently, there is a tendency to assume shorter expected terms. This policy is designed to force the accounting staff to always use a historical basis for the calculation of expected terms, so there is no way to modify the assumption.

Option-based compensation expense shall be adjusted at regular intervals for the forfeiture of options. An estimate of option forfeitures should be made at the time when option compensation expenses are first made under SFAS 123. If actual experience with option forfeitures varies from expectations, the difference must be recognized as a change in accounting estimate in the current period. The trouble is that accountants can ignore the changes for some time and only record them in accounting periods where their impact is most useful to the accountant. This policy is designed to avoid the timing of adjustments by requiring regular adjustments at set intervals. Including this action item in the month-end closing procedure is a good way to ensure compliance with the policy.

Option vesting periods shall be identical for all option and stock grants. When a company reduces the vesting period for its options, it can reasonably justify using a shorter option life if it expenses its stock options using the Black-Scholes model. This policy discourages the Board of Directors from shortening vesting periods by making it necessary to also shorten all types of stock grants at the same time, thereby also introducing some vesting consistency to the complete range of corporate stock grants.

Compensation expenses shall be recognized for both new option grants and those still outstanding from prior years. When a company elects to charge its option grants to expense, a common practice is to ignore outstanding options issued in prior years, and instead only charge new options to expense. This underreports the prospective compensation expense. This policy is designed to force full disclosure of the expense associated with all option grants.

The minimum value model shall be used to calculate compensation expense for option grants as long as the company is privately held. When a company is privately held, it can still use the fair value method promulgated under SFAS 123. The problem is that the fair value method requires the use of a stock volatility measure as part of the calculation, which is entirely a matter of opinion when shares are not publicly traded. To avoid the potential manipulation associated with volatility calculations under this scenario, the policy recommends the use of the minimum value model, which is the same as the fair value method, minus the stock volatility calculation.

Stock Appreciation Rights

Vesting periods for stock appreciation rights (SAR) shall not exceed the standard vesting period used for other stock grants. Since the gradual increases in the value of a SAR grant must be charged to expense in the period when the increases occur, a company could delay this expense recognition by lengthening the service period required before the SAR is earned by an employee. This policy is designed to require the use of a standard vesting period for all types of stock grants, thereby avoiding extremely long SAR vesting periods.

Employee Stock Ownership Plan (ESOP)

The Board of Directors shall not time dividend declarations in order to influence the recognition of a compensation expense for unallocated ESOP shares. When shares held in an ESOP have not yet been allocated to employees, a declared dividend on those shares is charged to compensation expense in the current period. Since this may represent a significant alteration in reported profit levels, there can be a temptation to time the dividend declaration in order to avoid reporting a profit reduction. This policy is designed to bring the potential reporting issue to the attention of the Board, though it still has the ability to override the policy.

Periodic accruals of ESOP compensation costs shall be based on the fair market value of company stock at the end of the current reporting period. It is common practice for a company to allocate shares from its ESOP to plan participants only at the end of each year, at which point compensation expense is recognized for the fair market value of the allocated shares. The amount of this compensation expense should be estimated and partially accrued in each month of the year leading up to the actual allocation. A problem can arise in estimating what the fair market value of the stock will be at the end of the year, since this can result in significant variances in estimates from month to month, with wildly fluctuating compensation expense accruals based on these estimates. The best approach is to use this policy to create the accrual based on the assumption that the actual fair market value at the end of the current reporting period shall match the year-end fair market value, thereby removing valuation estimates from the calculation.

PROCEDURES

Issue Capital Stock

Use this procedure to initially issue shares to the public. This procedure assumes that shares are to be publicly traded, and so lists additional registration steps.

1. Locate an underwriter and negotiate either a best-efforts or firm-commitment stock sale.
2. Determine the initial price at which shares are to be offered to the public.
3. Sign a letter of intent with the underwriter.
4. Undergo a due diligence review by the underwriter.
5. Create a registration statement and send it to the Securities and Exchange Commission (SEC). Respond to any questions the SEC may have.

6. Issue a prospectus version of the registration statement to potential investors.

7. Conduct a road show to meet with institutional investors.

8. Apply to the stock exchange on which the company wishes to list its shares.

9. Submit filings in accordance with the securities laws of all states in which the company expects to sell shares.

10. File the final offering prospectus with the SEC.

11. Sign a lockup agreement, which prevents management from selling shares to the public for a predetermined period.

12. Sell stock to the underwriter if the sale is a firm-commitment arrangement, or issue shares as sold under a best-efforts arrangement.

   a. Remove stock certificates from locked storage. On each one, print the certificate number, the number of shares issued, and the date of issuance. Have the corporate officers sign the certificates as indicated.

   b. Record the number of shares purchased, the purchase price, and the purchaser's name in the stock register and store this document as an attachment to the corporate minute book.

   c. Send the stock certificates to the share purchasers (possibly just the underwriter) by registered mail.

13. Upon receipt of payments from investors, debit Cash and credit the Par Value and Additional Paid-in Capital accounts.

Manage Stock Subscriptions (Employees)

Use this procedure to automatically deduct fixed amounts from employee paychecks and use them to purchase discounted shares of stock on behalf of employees.

1. Obtain authorization from the Board of Directors to create a stock subscription plan, and record the authorization in the corporate minute book.

2. Notify employees of the plan details, including maximum withholdings allowed and any discounts on share purchases.

3. Obtain signed withholding authorizations from participating employees. Forward them to the payroll department for entry in the payroll database as deductions. Then file the forms in employee payroll files.

4. As cash is received, debit the Cash account and credit the Common Stock Subscribed account, noting in the attached journal entry detail the name and Social Security number of each employee from whom the funds were withheld, and the amount withheld.

5. At the end of each month, calculate the fair market price of the stock, less any discount allowed to employees under the stock subscription plan. Issue shares to employees based on the amount of cash withheld. Debit the Common Stock Subscribed account and credit the Additional Paid-in Capital and Par Value accounts for the amount of shares issued.

6. If there is any excess cash remaining that cannot be used to purchase full shares, it is left in the Common Stock Subscribed account until the next month.

7. Periodically calculate the number of shares authorized and not yet issued under the employee stock subscription plan, and report this information back to the Board of Directors.

Issue Property Dividends

Use this procedure to ensure that the Board is aware of any potential gains or losses on property dividends, and that the transaction is properly recorded.

1. If the Board discusses distribution of property, look up the book value net of any amortization or depreciation, and compare it to the fair market value. If there is no ready market for the asset, consult with an appraiser to obtain an approximate valuation range.
2. Determine the difference between the net book value of the property and the fair market value, and note the amount of this gain or loss to be recognized as part of the property dividend. Report this amount to the Board of Directors.
3. If the dividend is approved, record the gain or loss on the dividend declaration date. Credit the Dividends Payable account for the book value of the distribution, the Retained Earnings account for the fair value of the property, and either credit the Gain on Property Disposal or debit the Loss on Property Disposal accounts to show the gain or loss on the adjustment of the property's book value to its fair value.
4. On the distribution date, debit the Dividends Payable account for the net book value of the asset, and credit the asset account to remove the property from the company's accounting records.

Treasury Stock—Record Gains and Losses on Resale of Treasury Stock

Use this procedure to record any gains or losses on the resale of treasury stock. The procedure assumes the use of the cost method when recording the sale of treasury stock.

1. Upon the purchase of stock, record a debit to the Treasury Stock account and a credit to the Cash account for the full amount of the purchase.
2. Note the stock certificate number and number of shares purchased in the corporate stock register.
3. When the stock is resold, record a credit for the full amount of the Treasury Stock account, such that the inflow and outflow to and from this account net to zero. Debit the Cash account for the amount of the cash received. If the difference requires a credit to balance the entry (a gain on the sale), enter a credit to the Additional Paid-in Capital account. If the difference requires a debit to balance the entry (a loss on the sale), enter a debit to the Additional Paid-in Capital account for treasury stock and then to retained earnings if this account balance drops to zero.
4. Note the stock certificate number and number of shares sold in the corporate stock register.

Treasury Stock—Shares Repurchased under a Greenmail Agreement

Use this procedure to determine the proper allocation of a forced stock repurchase under the threat of a corporate takeover between equity and expense accounts.

1. If there is a documented agreement to repurchase shares from an investor at above-market rates, the difference between the market rate and the rate paid on the date of the repurchase must be charged to the Excess Stock Repurchase expense account.
2. If the stock is not publicly traded and the value of other consideration granted by the shareholder is more clearly measurable, then assign the value of the consideration to the Excess Stock Repurchase expense account and record the difference as the repurchase of stock.
3. If there is no way to determine any value for the other consideration granted, and the shares are not publicly traded, then the entire amount of the transaction should be recorded as the repurchase of stock.
4. After determining the proper method for recording the transaction from among the preceding three choices, document the reason for the method chosen and include it in the financial statements as a footnote.

Options—Measurement Using SFAS 123 Requirements

Use this procedure to calculate the initial compensation expense when options are first granted, using the guidelines of SFAS 123.

1. Obtain the signed options agreement.
2. Verify that the option grant has been authorized under a Board-approved option program.
3. Obtain software that calculates the value of options using the Black-Scholes pricing model.
4. Input the exercise price of the options, as listed in the signed options agreement.
5. Input the number of options granted.
6. Input the expected term of the options, based on the most recent rolling three-year history of exercised options.
7. Input the expected percentage of forfeited options, based on the most recent rolling three-year history of forfeited options.
8. Input the risk-free interest rate, using the rate on the most recent issuance of US Treasury ninety-day notes.
9. Input the stock volatility percentage, using the measured volatility for the most recent rolling three-year period. Ignore this step if the company is privately held.
10. Subtract the total exercise price for the options from the option valuation derived from the computer model to arrive at the compensation expense to be recorded.
11. Record the compensation expense ratably over the vesting period of the options granted.

Options—Remeasurement on Option Extension Date (APB 25 Approach)

Use this procedure to calculate any additional compensation expense on the date when an option grant is extended.

1. Verify the accounting method under which compensation expense has been calculated for previous option transactions. If APB 25 was used, then continue with this procedure.
2. Obtain the Board minutes listing any option grant extensions. Be sure to note the date on which the Board granted the extensions.
3. As of the extension date, determine the market value of company shares and the exercise price of the options.
4. If the exercise price is higher than the share market price, there is no entry to make.
5. If the share market price is lower than the exercise price, calculate the difference and multiply it by the number of options whose term has been extended. This is the maximum potential amount of compensation expense to be recognized.
6. Subtract from this potential compensation expense any compensation expense previously recognized on these options.
7. Recognize the remaining compensation expense with a debit to the Deferred Compensation Expense account and a credit to the Options—Additional Paid-in Capital account.

CONTROLS

Legal Capital and Capital Stock

-   **Independent substantiation must be obtained to verify the valuation of stock issued in exchange for goods and services received.** When stock is swapped for goods or services, the stock is valued at the fair value of the goods or services. Since the offsetting debit is to an expense, the amount of this valuation can have a major impact on reported profit levels. This control is designed to force the accounting staff to go through the steps of obtaining outside verification of the fair value at which they have chosen to record the transaction.

Stock Subscriptions

-   **Periodically compare employee-authorized payroll deductions to actual deductions.** If a company's stock is performing well, it is quite possible that employees will complain if the amounts of payroll deductions being taken from their paychecks to pay for the stock have been too low, were ignored, or were started significantly later than the authorization date of the deduction, since employees will be losing money on the appreciation of their stock if any of these problems have arisen. If employees can prove their case, this may even result in the company compensating them for the lost stock appreciation.

Consequently, a periodic comparison of authorized to actual deductions ensures that there is no room for complaints by employees over this issue.

Retained Earnings

- **Password-protect the Retained Earnings account.** Though there are a few instances when the Retained Earnings account can be rightfully altered under GAAP, it is best to control access to the account with password protection, thereby forcing accounting adjustments into the current period, where they can be more clearly seen as a component of the income statement. Adjustments to the Retained Earnings account should only be authorized by the controller after being personally reviewed, and possibly also approved by the external auditors.

Dividends

- **Require Board approval of the fair value justification for all assets used in property dividends.** Since the recognition of the difference between the fair and book value of assets being distributed can have a major impact on reported earning levels, the Board should be made fully aware of the justification for any asset fair values departing significantly from book value, and the impact the resulting gain or loss will have on reported earnings.
- **Obtain Board approval of a specific date range within which dividends are to be declared each year.** This control is designed to keep the Board of Directors from deliberately altering reported financial results through the timing of dividend declarations. For example, the Board can declare either property or scrip dividends on specific dates that are designed to result in gains or losses (for property dividends) or changes in debt levels (for scrip dividends). The same problem applies when dividends are declared for ESOP shares, since the dividends for unallocated ESOP shares are charged to compensation expense in the current period.

Treasury Stock

- **Require the use of a separate additional paid-in capital account for treasury stock transactions.** If treasury stock is resold to investors at a loss, the loss is first charged to any remaining gains from previous treasury stock sales, with remaining losses being offset against the Retained Earnings account. Since a reduction in the retained earnings balance can be construed as a reduced level of financial performance, there is an incentive to charge these losses elsewhere. A typical ploy is to charge the losses to the General Additional Paid-in Capital account, which usually contains a much larger balance than the Additional Paid-in Capital account for treasury stock. By creating the separate Additional Paid-in Capital account for treasury stock and requiring its use in all treasury stock procedures, it is much less likely that treasury stock losses will be diverted away from the Retained Earnings account.
- **Require Board approval of all stock repurchases conducted under greenmail situations.** A normal treasury stock transaction has no impact on ex-

penses, but a greenmail situation does, since the difference between the market price and usually much higher price paid must be charged to expense. It is clearly in the interests of a company to not record this incremental expense, since it can result in a massive reduction in profits during the period when the payment is made. Consequently, the Board should be made aware of the expense consequences when it approves a greenmail stock repurchase.

Stock Appreciation Rights

- **Include SAR compensation expense accruals in the standard closing procedure.** A company could delay or ignore any changes in the value of SAR grants to its employees, thereby avoiding the recognition of any associated compensation expense. This problem can be avoided by including the accrual as a standard action item in the monthly closing procedure. The issue can also be highlighted by including it as a footnote attached to the financial statements, thereby requiring periodic updating of the footnote information.
- **Use a standard stock valuation form when calculating SAR compensation expense.** A company can use a variety of methods for determining the market value of company stock as part of its recognition of compensation expense, especially when the shares are not publicly traded. This can give rise to different methods being used over time, depending on which one results in the smallest compensation expense recognition. The best way to avoid this problem is to create a standard calculation form, such as the one shown in the Forms and Reports section, which forces the use of a single calculation format for all SAR-related compensation expense calculations.

Options

- **Review the assumptions used to determine the compensation cost for options.** The most common formula used to develop the compensation cost associated with stock option grants under the SFAS 123 approach is the Black-Scholes formula, which requires the input of a number of assumptions in order to generate a compensation cost. Even small changes in these assumptions can result in a significant change in compensation costs, so there is a risk of formula manipulation in order to alter reported financial results. In particular, compensation expenses can be reduced by reducing the assumed stock volatility or the assumed life of an option, or by increasing the assumed risk-free interest rate or dividend yield. A periodic review of these assumptions, particularly in comparison to the assumptions used for prior calculations, can spot significant or clearly incorrect assumptions.
- **Verify that option grant extensions are measured on the date of authorization.** When the term of an option grant is extended, one must recognize compensation expense under the terms of APB 25 (if that approach is being used) on the extension date if there is an unrecognized difference between the market and exercise prices of the stock. This rule can give rise to some variation in the date on which the measurement is made, in the hope that the market price of the stock will drop, thereby resulting in a lower compen-

sation expense. By creating a procedure that clearly requires the calculation to be made on the date of authorization, this problem can be eliminated.

- **Use a consistent fair market value estimation method.** If a company is using the terms of APB 25 as the basis for recognizing compensation expense, then it must compare the fair market value of the stock on the option grant date to the exercise price, and charge the difference to compensation expense if the exercise price is lower than the market price. If a company is privately held, it may be difficult to determine the fair market value of the stock, which can result in reduced fair value estimates in order to avoid recognizing any compensation expense. One should require a consistent valuation estimation methodology so a company does not alter its valuation formula every time options are granted.

- **Include a reestimation of option forfeitures step in the closing procedure.** If a company uses SFAS 123 to record its option-related compensation expense, it should regularly review its estimate of how many options will be forfeited, and adjust the compensation expense accordingly to match any revisions in estimate. This can be most easily accomplished by including the step in the closing procedure, so the review can be less easily ignored.

FORMS AND REPORTS

Legal Capital and Capital Stock

When stock certificates are issued, a company must keep track of the number of certificates issued, the number of shares listed on each certificate, to whom the certificates are issued, and information about the dates of issuance and any subsequent cancellation or transfer dates. The example stock record shown in Exhibit 13-2 indicates a typical layout for this type of report.

Exhibit 13-2: Stock Record

Certificate number	Issued to	Number of shares	Issue date	Cancel or transfer date
1	Joel Henderson	1,410,000	3/22/07	
2	Gary Simms	570,000	3/22/07	5/25/07 to Mary Simms
3	Richard Rondo	695,000	3/22/07	5/9/07 cancelled
4	Mark Abercrombie	716,000	7/14/07	
5	Brad Hanley	115,000	7/14/07	

Stock Subscriptions

When a company issues shares to its employees as part of an ongoing stock subscription program, it can assume that employees will periodically ask for a statement detailing the amount of their payroll deductions for this purpose, the number of shares issued based on those deductions, and the residual amount of deductions not yet used to purchase company shares. An example of such a stock subscription statement is shown in Exhibit 13-3. The example assumes payroll deductions twice a month, with a 10% discount from the stock market price for employees.

Exhibit 13-3: Stock Subscription Statement by Employee

Payroll Deductions		Stock Purchases				
Date	*Amount*	*Date*	*Share value*	*10% discount*	*Number of shares*	*Cash remainder*
01/15/2007	$300.00					
01/31/2007	300.00	01/31/2007	$12.15	$10.94	54	$9.24
02/15/2007	300.00					
02/28/2007	300.00	02/28/2007	13.10	11.79	51	7.95
03/15/2007	300.00					
03/31/2007	300.00	03/31/2007	14.05	12.65	48	0.75
04/15/2007	300.00					
04/30/2007	300.00	04/30/2007	13.75	12.38	48	6.51
05/15/2007	300.00					
05/31/2007	300.00	05/31/2007	13.25	11.93	50	10.01

Stock Option Detail Report

If there are many option grants to a large number of employees, it is necessary to maintain a report listing the number of options granted, the exercise price for each grant, and the expiration date of each set of options. The report shown in Exhibit 13-4 shows this information for one sample employee, as well as the number of options vested and the prospective purchase price (good for equity planning) if each block of options were to be purchased.

Exhibit 13-4: Stock Option Detail Report

Date granted	*Options granted*	*Exercise price*	*Options vested*	*Purchase price*	*Expiration date*
Clay, Alfred					
02/01/03	1,317	0.6800	$ 878	$ 597.04	01/31/13
04/03/03	2,633	0.8200	1,755	1,439.10	04/02/13
12/01/03	2,633	0.9000	878	790.20	11/30/13
09/01/04	5,266	0.9800	5,266	5,160.68	08/31/14
12/31/04	1,317	1.0300	1,317	1,356.51	12/30/14
03/08/05	2,633	1.0800	2,633	2,843.64	03/07/15
Totals	15,799		$12,727	$12,187.17	

Stock Appreciation Rights

For many privately held companies, there is no ready method for determining the value of their stock, which can cause problems when the value of stock appreciation rights is calculated. The form shown in Exhibit 13-5 presents a standard approach for creating this valuation, using the revenue multiple for publicly held companies as the benchmark valuation figure. The form is divided into three sections, each one being labeled in the upper left corner in bold. The first section allows one to split the business into its component parts and multiply the revenue for each part by the public sector valuation multiple to arrive at a total estimated company valuation. It is especially important to always use the same "market basket" of public sector companies to derive the valuation multiple in order to achieve consistency in the valuation derivation. The second section is used to itemize the types and amounts of stock outstanding, along with the liquidation participation of each share type, resulting in a valuation per SAR. In the example, a class of preferred stock is assumed to have a double distribution. The third section itemizes the SAR grants by date, listing the number of shares issued on each date and their issuance price. This information is used in the final column on the right to determine the difference between the SAR issuance price and current estimated valuation, resulting in a compensation expense accrual in the lower right corner that can be used as the basis for a journal entry to recognize compensation expense.

Exhibit 13-5: Standard Calculation Form for Stock Appreciation Rights

Stock Appreciation Rights Standard Calculation Form			
Company Valuation:			
Business Segment	*Segment revenue*	*Public sector valuation multiple*	*Estimated company valuation*
Outdoor advertising	$ 4,500,000	1.2	$ 5,400,000
Publishing	12,250,000	1.7	20,825,000
Rentals	8,050,000	1.0	8,050,000
	$24,800,000		$34,275,000

Share Valuation:			
Stock type	*Number of shares*	*Participation percentage*	*Estimated value per share*
Common	12,000,000	100%	$2.2624
Preferred series A	1,500,000	200%	4.5248
Stock appreciation rights	150,000	100%	2.2624
	13,650,000		

SAR Compensation Expense:			
Date of SAR issuance	*Number of shares*	*Issuance price*	*Compensation expense*
05/15/2007	50,000	$1.10	$58,119
08/21/2007	80,000	1.38	70,590
11/03/2007	20,000	1.75	10,248
	150,000		$138,956
	SAR compensation already recognized:		$120,000
	SAR compensation expense accrual:		$18,956

FOOTNOTES

Disclosure of Capital Structure

The financial statements should include a footnote describing the number of shares authorized, issued, and outstanding, their par values, and the rights and privileges associated with each class of stock. A description of these rights and privileges should include dividend preferences and special privileges or unusual voting rights. An example follows:

As of October 31, 2007, the company capital structure consisted of common stock and Series A preferred stock. There were 10,000,000 shares of common stock authorized and 4.2 million shares outstanding, while there were 1,000,000 shares of preferred stock authorized and 800,000 shares outstanding. Both classes of stock have par values of $0.01 per share. The Series A preferred stockholders are entitled to a full return of their original investments in the event of a liquidation or sale of the company, as well as an additional 100% return, before any distributions are made to common shareholders. These shareholders are also entitled to dividend payments matching any declared for shares of common stock. In addition, a two-thirds majority of the Series A shareholders must approve any sale of the company or a significant portion of its assets. Also, Series A shareholders are entitled to elect two members of the company's Board of Directors. Common shareholders are entitled to elect all other members of the Board.

Disclosure of Subsequent Equity Transactions

If a company enters into any equity-related transactions subsequent to the date of the financial statements but before their issuance, these transactions should be described in a footnote. Examples of typical transactions falling into this category would be stock splits, stock issuances, and purchases of stock back into the treasury. An example follows:

> Subsequent to the reporting period, the company issued an additional 100,000 shares of common stock at an average price of $24 per share, resulting in receipts, net of transaction fees, of $2,250,000. Management intends to use the funds to renovate its headquarters building.

Disclosure of Change in the Number of Authorized Shares

If a company elects to either increase or decrease its number of authorized shares through a change in its certificate of incorporation, a footnote should disclose the Board's approval of this action, the change in the number of authorized shares, and any impact on the par value of the stock. An example follows:

> On April 17, 2007, the Board authorized the amendment of the company's certificate of incorporation to increase the number of authorized shares of common stock by 90,000,000 from the prior level of 10,000,000. There was no change in the stated par value of the stock as a result of this transaction.

Disclosure of Stock Sale

If a company sells stock, a footnote should disclose the type and number of shares sold, the price at which the shares were sold, and the general use of the proceeds. An example follows:

> During May 2007, the company sold 4,210,000 shares of its Series B preferred stock at a price of $12 per share, netting $48,500,000 after sale and issuance costs. Management intends to use the proceeds to fund several anticipated acquisitions.

Disclosure of Stock Subscriptions

If investors have subscribed to company shares, the company should reveal the number of subscribed shares not yet issued. An example follows.

> The company offered its common stock for sale to a limited group of investors during the reporting period. The investors subscribed to $4,250,000 of stock at $20.00 per share. Of the amount subscribed, $3,650,000 has been received, resulting in the issuance of 182,500 shares. The share issuance is reflected in all earnings per share information in these financial statements. The unpaid $600,000 of subscriptions will result in

the issuance of an additional 30,000 shares when payment is received, which would have reduced earnings per share in the reporting period by $.03 if the subscription payments had been received during the period.

Disclosure of Converted Bonds

If the holders of convertible bonds have elected to convert their bonds into shares, one should disclose the dollar amount of bonds converted, the conversion ratio, and the resulting number of shares issued. An example follows:

> During the past quarter, 45% of the holders of the company's convertible 8% bonds elected to convert their holdings into the company's common stock. The debt converted was $32 million, leaving $39 million still outstanding. The bond conversion transaction resulted in the issuance of 3,764,705 shares, which is an increase in the company's out-standing common stock of 4.2%.

Disclosure of Redeemable Preferred Shares

If there are any outstanding redeemable preferred shares, a footnote should itemize any determinable redemption requirements in each of the next five years, including call prices and the dates on which they are effective. An example follows:

> The company has 50,000 redeemable preferred shares outstanding. Under the sale agreement for these shares, the company is obligated to repurchase 10,000 shares per year under the following pricing schedule:

Year	Shares to repurchase	Aggregate price
2007	10,000	$50,000
2008	10,000	53,000
2009	10,000	56,000
2010	10,000	59,000
2011	10,000	62,000

Disclosure of Cash Dividends

If a company issues a cash dividend, a footnote should reveal the amount of the dividend, the date on which the dividend was declared, the date on which the dividend will be payable, and the date on which shareholders of record will be identified for the distribution. An example follows:

> On September 10, 2007, the Board declared a cash dividend of $1.07 per share, payable on November 2, 2007, to shareholders of record on September 25, 2007. This dividend distribution does not violate any covenants associated with the company's ex-isting loans.

Disclosure of Noncash Dividends

If a company chooses to pay shareholders dividends with assets other than cash, a footnote should disclose the nature of the assets being used for payment, the fair market value of the amount distributed, any gain or loss recognized by the company as part of the transaction, and how the transaction was handled in the financial statements. An example follows:

The company distributed inventory dividends to its shareholders of record on April 30, 2007, issuing 10 pounds of its hard candy for every 100 shares of common stock held. The candy had a fair market value of $2,000,000 at the time of the dividend distribution. The company recorded no gain or loss on the transaction. It reduced the inventory asset by the amount of the distribution.

Disclosure of Dividends Deferred

If the decision is made to defer payment of declared dividends, a footnote should reveal the reason for the decision, while also specifying which dividends were deferred and the aggregate amount of the deferral, as well as the amount of cumulative and per share dividends in arrears. Two examples follow:

1. The Board deferred the full amount of dividends declared on November 10, 2007, totaling $1,050,000, due to a short-term cash flow problem related to the company's foreign sales receipts. The dividends deferred include $600,000 for common stock and $450,000 for preferred stock.
2. The company has deferred payment of its last two dividend declarations, which total $729,000 in deferred dividends. Based on the number of shares outstanding as of the balance sheet date, there are $1.29 of deferred dividends per share. Due to its declining cash flows, the company is unable to predict when the deferred dividends will be distributed to shareholders.

Disclosure of Employee Stock Ownership Plan

If a company has set up an employee stock ownership plan (ESOP), it should disclose which employees participate in the plan, how dividends received by the plan are used, the formula used to make contributions to the ESOP, how contributed shares are used as collateral on any ESOP debt, how share valuations are assigned to employees, and how the company treats ESOP transactions in its financial reports. The footnote should also disclose any compensation cost recognized during the period. An example follows:

The company makes monthly contributions to its employee stock ownership plan (ESOP) sufficient to make principal and interest payments on its outstanding debt. Shares held by the plan are used as collateral on the debt, but a portion of the shares are released as collateral at the end of each year in proportion to the amount of debt paid down. At that time, the shares are allocated to qualified employees, who are defined as those working at least 30 hours per week as of year-end. Once allocated, shares are included in earnings-per-share calculations. The company records compensation expense each month based on the market value of the shares expected to be released from collateral at year-end. The compensation expense thus recorded in the past year was $189,000. The fair value of shares still held as collateral as of year-end was $4,050,000. At year-end, the ESOP contained 410,000 shares, of which 270,000 was used as collateral and 140,000 had been released from collateral and recorded as compensation expense.

Disclosure of Employee Stock Purchase Plan

If an employee stock purchase plan is in place, a footnote should disclose the amount of any discounts granted to employees, how the discount is calculated, and maximum amounts employees are allowed to purchase. The number of shares reserved for this purpose and the actual number purchased should also be disclosed. An example follows:

> The company operates an employee stock purchase plan that allows its employees to purchase the company's common stock at below-market rates, subject to certain restrictions. Shares are offered at a discount of 10% of the stock's fair market value at the end of each month, as determined by the posted NASDAQ stock price on that date. Employees may purchase shares up to a maximum of 15% of their gross pay. Under the plan, 2.5 million common shares have been reserved for purchase by employees, of which 312,987 shares have thus far been purchased, leaving 2,187,013 available for purchase. In the past year, 82,067 shares were purchased at an aggregate price of $15.85 each.

Disclosure of New Type of Stock

If a company is creating a new type of stock, a footnote should disclose the rights of the new stock, the date on which it was authorized, the number of shares authorized, and the number of any shares issued. An example follows:

> The Board authorized an amendment to the certificate of incorporation that created a new Series B preferred stock in the amount of 10,000,000 shares, with a par value of $0.01 per share. The stock has preferential liquidation rights of 200% of the initial investment prior to the participation of common shareholders, and is also entitled to the same dividend granted to common shareholders. Two million shares of the Series B preferred stock were issued on December 15, 2007, at $8.10 per share, resulting in total proceeds of $16.2 million. The company expects to use these funds to pay down its existing debt.

Disclosure of Par Value Change

Though rare, companies sometimes will alter their certificates of incorporation to change the par value of their stock. This change is typically in a downward direction, resulting in the shifting of funds from the stock account to the additional paid-in capital account. When this happens, a footnote should include the date and amount of the change, as well as the aggregate amount of funds shifted into or out of the stock account. An example follows:

> A majority of the company's shareholders voted on October 10, 2007, to amend the company's certificate of incorporation to reduce the par value of its common stock to $0.01 from $1.00. Due to this change, $990,000 was shifted from the Common Stock account to the Additional Paid-in Capital account.

Disclosure of Retained Earnings Segregation

The Board of Directors may set aside some portion of retained earnings for a specific purpose. If so, a footnote should describe the amount segregated, as well as the reason for and amount of the segregation. An example follows:

> The company has been judged liable for asbestos claims amounting to $14,500,000. The company intends to contest this initial judgment vigorously, and has appealed the decision. Nonetheless, the Board of Directors has segregated the full amount of the initial judgment from retained earnings, so that the company will not find itself with nega-

tive retained earnings in the event that the appeal is denied and it must pay the full amount of the claim.

Disclosure of Reserved Stock

A company may set aside unissued shares for specific purposes, such as the expected exercise of options or warrants, or the conversion of shares from a debt instrument. In these cases, one should disclose the number of shares set aside and the reason for the reservation. An example follows:

> The Board authorized the reservation of 4,025,000 shares as of May 14, 2007. Of this amount, 2 million shares were set aside in expectation of the conversion of the company's 5 7/8% bonds to stock by its bondholders. The remaining 2,025,000 shares were set aside in expectation of the exercise of stock options by employees.

Disclosure of Stock Repurchase Program

One should describe the date on which a stock repurchase program was authorized by the Board of Directors, the maximum number of shares to be repurchased, and the current status of the repurchase program. An example follows:

> The company's Board of Directors authorized a stock repurchase program for its Series A preferred stock on June 30, 2007, up to a maximum of two million shares. As of the balance sheet date, the company had repurchased 1,255,000 shares for a total of $58,500,000. The repurchased shares are held in the corporate treasury and cannot be released without Board approval.

Disclosure of Treasury Stock Held

One should reveal the cost basis used to record any stock held by a company. An example follows:

> The company records the value of its common and preferred stock held in the treasury at cost.

Disclosure of Greenmail Stock Repurchase

If a company elects to buy back shares at a high price under the threat of a takeover or similar situation, it should note the market price of its stock on the date of the transaction, the price per share actually paid, and the amount of the transaction charged to expense. An example follows:

> The company repurchased 450,000 shares from a major shareholder on May 15, 2007. The shareholder had indicated that he was willing to pursue a change of corporate ownership if the company did not agree to pay a premium for his shares. The Board elected to do so, and paid $15 per share for stock having a market price of $11.50 on the date of the transaction. The company charged the difference between the purchase and market prices of $1,575,000 to expense in the current period.

Disclosure of Sale of Treasury Stock

If a company elects to sell some portion of its treasury stock, a footnote should reveal the number of shares sold, the aggregate sale price, the aggregate price at which the shares were originally purchased by the company, and the treatment of any gain or loss on the sale. An example follows:

> The company sold 450,000 shares of common stock for a total of $8,565,000. The company had previously purchased these shares for $8,750,000 and stored them as treasury stock. Since the sale price exceeded the original purchase price by $185,000, the difference was charged to the Additional Paid-in Capital account.

Disclosure of Stock Compensation

If a company has paid employees or outside entities compensation in the form of stock, the number of shares granted, the effective date of the transaction, and its fair market value should be itemized in a footnote. Three examples follow:

1. The Board authorized stock compensation to the company's executive team as of July 31, 2007, in the amount of 340,000 shares of common stock. The stock had a fair market value of $14,900,000 on the date of the grant.
2. The Board authorized the granting of 10,000 shares of common stock with a fair value of $52,000 to the company's legal advisor. The advisor accepted this payment in lieu of a cash payment for ongoing legal services performed.
3. The Board authorized the granting of 150,000 shares of common stock to a director in exchange for the elimination of $800,000 in accrued interest on a loan the director had extended to the company in 2006.

Disclosure of Stock Contribution

If a company donates stock to a nonprofit organization, a footnote should disclose the date of the contribution, the number of shares involved, their aggregate market value, how the transaction was handled in the financial statements, and the amount of any gain or loss recognized as a result. An example follows:

> The company contributed to the My Way Foundation its entire stock holdings in XYZ Corporation, which included 500,000 shares of common stock and 125,000 shares of preferred stock. The market value of the contribution on the transaction date was $842,000. Of this amount, $200,000 was recognized as a pretax loss, while the remaining $642,000 was charged to the Donations Expense account.

Disclosure of Stock Redemption Agreements

If a company has agreements with its shareholders to buy back their shares upon the occurrence of certain events, a footnote should describe the terms of the arrangement and the potential monetary impact. Three examples follow:

1. The company has required all purchasers of its Series B preferred stock to sign redemption agreements under which the company has the right of first refusal if they wish to sell their shares, at fixed prices of $12.50 in 2007 and increasing in increments of $0.75 per share for each year thereafter. If all Series B shareholders were to request redemption of their shares, the total cash payment required of the company would be $31.25 million. The company maintains a sinking fund to cover these payments. The sinking fund currently contains $10 million; the company plans to add $5 million per year to this fund until the full redemption commitment is met.

2. A major company shareholder died during the past quarter. Under the terms of the standard company redemption agreement, the company is required to buy back her shares at their fair market value, which was derived using the average value compiled by three independent appraisers. The fair market value of her shares as determined by this means was $18,900,000, of which $10,000,000 was paid by a company-maintained life insurance policy. Of the remainder, $5,000,000 was paid in cash, and $4,900,000 is payable to her estate at year-end, as well as 7% interest on the unpaid balance.
3. The company redeemed 100,000 shares of its Series A preferred stock, which it issued as part of a financing package arising from its bankruptcy proceedings in 2006. As per the redemption agreement, the company paid a 100% premium over the original $10 sale price of each share, resulting in a total payment of $20 per share or $2,000,000 in aggregate. The incremental increase over the original share price of $1,000,000 was charged to the Additional Paid-in Capital account.

Disclosure of Stock Splits

All stock splits and reverse stock splits should be fully documented in a footnote, itemizing the date on which Board of Directors approval was granted, the ratio of the stock split, and the date on which the split took effect. The footnote should also contain assurances that all stock-related information in the financial statements has been adjusted to reflect the stock split. Two examples follow:

1. The company's Board of Directors authorized a three-for-one reverse stock split on November 15, 2007, to take effect on November 18, 2007. All share and related option information presented in these financial statements and accompanying footnotes has been retroactively adjusted to reflect the reduced number of shares resulting from this action.
2. The company's Board of Directors authorized a three-for-one stock split on November 15, 2007, to take effect on December 20, 2007. Each shareholder of record on November 25, 2007, received two additional shares of common stock for each share held on that date. Additional funds were shifted from the Additional Paid-in Capital account to the Common Stock account to equal the amount of additional par value represented by the additional shares issued under the stock split. All share and related option information presented in these financial statements and accompanying footnotes has been retroactively adjusted to reflect the increased number of shares resulting from this action.

Disclosure of Stock Options

If a company has a stock option plan, it must give a general description of the plan, report the number of shares authorized for option grants, and note vesting requirements and maximum option terms. An example of this "header information" is provided in the following footnote:

> The company maintains a stock option plan under which all employees are awarded option grants based on a combination of performance and tenure. All options may be exercised for a period of 10 years following the grant date, after which they expire. All options fully vest after recipients have worked for the company subsequent to the grant date in a full-time capacity for a period of four years. The Board has authorized the use of 2 million shares for option grants.

It is not yet required to report the fair value of options granted as compensation expense, though some companies have elected to do so. However, any company choosing not to report this information in its financial statements must still show net income and earnings per share in the accompanying footnotes as though the fair value method had been used to determine the compensation expense associated with option grants.

No matter what compensation expense method is used, a footnote must also describe the range of option exercise prices as of the balance sheet date, as well as the weighted-average remaining exercise period for outstanding options, plus the weighted-average-price at which options were converted during the reporting period.

The first of the following footnotes describes an option plan without any associated compensation expense, while the second includes this information. In the first example, the number of shares authorized for option grants, the total outstanding number of options, and the weighted-average exercise price for those options are listed.

1. The company operates a stock option plan, under which 350,000 options to purchase the company's common stock were granted in 2007. The options fully vest 3 years from the date of grant, and will automatically cancel if not used within 10 years of the date of grant. The exercise prices of all options granted matched the market price of the stock on the day of grant. Given this matching of exercise prices to market values, there was no compensation expense associated with the options granted, and therefore no compensation expense was recorded. If the company had used the fair value method of option valuation as recommended by SFAS 123, an additional $94,500 in compensation expense would have been recognized, resulting in a reduction in net income, net of income tax changes, of $61,400, as well as a reduction in earnings per share of $.40. As of this date, the following options in aggregate have been granted, exercised, or canceled since the option plan was created:

	No. of options	Weighted-average exercise price
Options granted	1,890,000	$5.02
Options exercised	−115,000	7.15
Options canceled	−80,000	8.00
Total outstanding	1,695,000	$4.96

2. The company recognizes the compensation costs associated with its stock option grants based on their fair market value on the date of grant. The weighted-average fair value of options granted during the past year was $11.25, which was calculated using the Black-Scholes option pricing formula. When using the formula, company management used as inputs a risk-free interest rate of 3.0%, no dividend yield, an expected option life of eight years, and an expected stock volatility of 39%. The immediate recognition of the compensation cost of stock option grants resulted in a reduction during the past year of $329,000 in net income and a reduction in earnings of $0.32 per share.

If option terms are altered, the terms of the change should be noted in a footnote, as well as any financial changes resulting from the modification. An example follows:

The Board extended the term of 200,000 options previously granted to the management team. The options had been set to expire at the end of 2007, and were extended to the end of 2011. The option exercise price was compared to the fair market value of company shares on the date when the extension was authorized by the Board, resulting in the immediate recognition of $228,000 in compensation expense. There is no deferred compensation expense associated with this transaction, since all extended options had previously been fully vested.

Disclosure of Stock Option Repricing

If stock options have been repriced, a footnote should disclose the reason for doing so, the date on which the change took effect, and the new exercise price. The footnote should also disclose the number of options changed, and the proportion of the total options changed. An example follows:

On August 15, 2007, the Board authorized the repricing of 450,000 options to match the market price on that date, which was $9.65. The change was made in order to retain employees with a better short-term prospect of exercising options at a profit. The options converted represent 18% percent of the total number of options outstanding. None of the options changed belonged to a member of the management team.

Disclosure of Stock Appreciation Rights (SAR)

If a company issues stock appreciation rights, it should indicate in a footnote the group of people covered by the SAR plan, the terms of the plan, the amount of compensation expense accrued, and the amount of compensation expense to be accrued in future vesting periods. An example follows:

The company has issued a total of 150,000 stock appreciation rights to the executive management team, using a baseline stock price of $4.50 per share. Subsequent stock appreciation has resulted in an increase in the value of the SAR of $129,400, of which one-half has vested, resulting in the recognition of compensation expense of $64,700. Of the unvested portion of the increase in stock value, $32,350 will be recognized in 2007 and an additional $32,350 will be recognized in 2008, assuming no further changes in the stock price. No cash payments have yet been made to the SAR holders, which are at the option of the holders until the termination of the plan in 2014.

Disclosure of Warrants Issued

If warrants to purchase stock are issued, a footnote should disclose the reason for the transaction, the number of warrants issued, and the exercise price at which they can be used to purchase shares, as well as the vesting period and expiration date. Two examples follow:

1. The company issued 80,000 warrants to a group of venture capital firms. The warrants allow the firms to purchase the company's common stock at an exercise price of $5.10. There is no vesting period. The warrants expire in 10 years. The warrants were issued as part of the compensation package earned by the firms in assisting the company in the placement of a recent issuance of common stock.
2. During the year ended 2006, certain holders of warrants to purchase shares of the company's common stock exercised a total of 32,000 warrants to purchase 64,000 shares for a total of $326,400.

JOURNAL ENTRIES

Legal Capital and Capital Stock

Initial sale of stock. When a company sells shares to an investor, it allocates a portion of the sale price to a par value account matching the stated par value of each share sold, with the remainder being credited to an additional paid-in capital account, as noted in the following entry:

Cash	xxx	
Stock—par value		xxx
Stock—additional paid-in capital		xxx

Netting of stock issuance costs against sale proceeds. To net stock issuance costs, such as legal, underwriting, certificate printing, and security registration fees, against the proceeds of a stock sale.

Additional paid-in capital	xxx	
Stock issuance expenses		xxx

Stock issued for services rendered or goods received. To record the fair value of services or goods received in exchange for stock.

Expense [reflecting specific services or goods received]	xxx	
Stock—par value		xxx
Additional paid-in capital		xxx

Conversion of preferred stock to common stock. To record the conversion of preferred stock to common stock under a conversion option. The second entry shows this conversion when the par value of the common stock is greater than the entire purchase price of the preferred stock, requiring an additional contribution from the retained earnings account.

Preferred stock—par value	xxx	
Preferred stock—additional paid-in capital	xxx	
Common stock—par value		xxx
Common stock—additional paid-in capital		xxx
Preferred stock—par value	xxx	
Preferred stock—additional paid-in capital	xxx	
Retained earnings	xxx	
Common stock—par value		xxx

Stock split with no change in par value. To record a stock split where the par value of the stock is not proportionately reduced to match the number of new shares issued. This requires a transfer from the Additional Paid-in Capital account to fund the additional amount of par value required for the new shares.

Stock—additional paid-in capital	xxx	
Stock—par value		xxx

Stock Subscriptions

Stock subscription, initial entry. To record the initial commitment by potential investors to purchase shares of company stock, with no cash yet received.

Stock subscriptions receivable	xxx	
Common stock subscribed		xxx
Additional paid-in capital		xxx

Stock subscription, payment of. To record the receipt of cash from investors to fulfill their earlier commitments to purchase stock under a stock subscription agreement.

Cash	xxx	
Stock subscriptions receivable		xxx
Common stock subscribed	xxx	
Common stock		xxx

Warrants

Initial entry of bonds sale with attached warrants. The first entry is used to assign a value to the warrants attached to the sale of bonds, based on the relative values of the warrants and bonds. The entry includes a provision for any discount or premium on bonds sold. The second entry shifts funds into an expired warrants account, on the assumption that the warrants are never exercised by the holder. The third entry shows the proper treatment of a warrant that is converted to stock with an additional cash payment included.

Cash	xxx	
Discount on bonds payable [if applicable]	xxx	
Premium on bonds payable [if applicable]		xxx
Bonds payable		xxx
Additional paid-in capital—warrants		xxx
Additional paid-in capital—warrants	xxx	
Additional paid-in capital—expired warrants		xxx
Cash	xxx	
Additional paid-in capital—warrants	xxx	
Common stock—par value		xxx
Common stock—additional paid-in capital		xxx

Dividends

Dividend declaration, cash payment. To separate the sum total of all declared dividends from retained earnings once dividends have been approved by the Board of Directors.

Retained earnings	xxx	
Dividends payable		xxx

Dividend declaration, property dividend. To record the gain or loss on any property to be distributed as a dividend to shareholders, based on the fair value of the asset to be distributed on the date of declaration.

Retained earnings [asset fair value]	xxx	
Loss on property disposal [if applicable]	xxx	
Gain on property disposal [if applicable]		xxx
Dividends payable [asset net book value]		xxx

Dividend payment, property dividend. To eliminate the dividend payable obligation and remove the asset being distributed from the company's records, including all related accumulated depreciation or amortization.

Dividend payable		xxx	
Accumulated amortization [if needed]		xxx	
Accumulated depreciation [if needed]		xxx	
Asset			xxx

Dividend declaration, small stock dividend. To record a small stock dividend, record the fair value of the issued shares on the declaration date by removing the funds from the Retained Earnings account and shifting them to the Stock and Additional Paid-in Capital accounts.

Retained earnings		xxx	
Stock—par value			xxx
Stock—additional paid-in capital			xxx

Dividend declaration, large stock dividend. To record a large stock dividend, record the par value of the issued shares on the declaration date by removing the funds from the Retained Earnings account and shifting them to the Stock account.

| Retained earnings | | xxx | |
| Stock—par value | | | xxx |

Dividend declaration, scrip dividend. To record the creation of a note payable to shareholders instead of the usual cash dividend.

| Retained earnings | | xxx | |
| Notes payable | | | xxx |

Dividend declaration, liquidating. To record a return of capital to investors, rather than a more traditional dividend that is theoretically based on a distribution of profits.

| Additional paid-in capital | | xxx | |
| Dividends payable | | | xxx |

Dividend payment in cash. To issue cash payment to shareholders for dividends declared by the Board of Directors. The first entry shows the payment of a traditional cash dividend, while the second entry shows the payment of a scrip dividend.

Dividends payable		xxx	
Cash			xxx
Dividends payable		xxx	
Notes payable			xxx

Treasury Stock

Treasury stock, purchase under the cost method. To record the acquisition by a company of its own stock.

| Treasury stock | | xxx | |
| Cash | | | xxx |

Treasury stock, retirement under the cost method. This method is used when there is an assumption that repurchased shares will be permanently retired. The original Common Stock and Additional Paid-in Capital accounts are reversed with any loss on the purchase being charged to the Retained Earnings account, and any gain being credited to the Additional Paid-in Capital account.

Common stock—par value	xxx	
Additional paid-in capital	xxx	
Retained earnings [if there is a loss on the repurchase]		xxx
Cash		xxx

Treasury stock, sale at price higher than acquisition price. To record the sale of treasury stock to investors by the company at a price higher than the price at which the company acquired the shares, with payments in excess of treasury stock cost being credited to the Additional Paid-in Capital account. This entry uses the cost method of accounting for treasury stock.

Cash	xxx	
Treasury stock		xxx
Additional paid-in capital—treasury stock		xxx

Treasury stock, sale at price lower than acquisition price. To record the sale of treasury stock to investors by the company at a price lower than the price at which the company acquired the shares, with the loss on the sale being charged to the Additional Paid-in Capital account until that account is emptied, with any remaining loss being charged to the Retained Earnings account. This entry uses the cost method of accounting for treasury stock.

Cash	xxx	
Additional paid-in capital—treasury stock	xxx	
Retained earnings	xxx	
Treasury stock		xxx

Treasury stock, purchase under the constructive retirement method. This method is used when there is an assumption that the repurchased shares will be permanently retired, or when mandated by state law. The original Common Stock and Additional Paid-in Capital accounts are reversed with any loss on the purchase being charged to the Retained Earnings account, and any gain being credited to the Additional Paid-in Capital account.

Common stock—par value	xxx	
Additional paid-in capital	xxx	
Retained earnings [if there is a loss on the repurchase]		xxx
Cash		xxx

Treasury stock, repurchase under a greenmail agreement. When a company is forced to buy back shares at above-market prices under the threat of a corporate takeover, the difference between the repurchase price and the market price must be charged to expense, as noted in the following entry:

Treasury stock	xxx	
Excess stock repurchase expense	xxx	
Cash		xxx

Options

Options issued with strike price below the market price. If stock options are issued at a strike price that is already below the market price on the date of issuance, then the difference between the two prices must be immediately recognized as deferred compensation. The entry is as follows:

Deferred compensation expense	xxx	
Options—additional paid-in capital		xxx

Options earned over time. Options are typically earned over time as services are performed for a company, or vesting periods are completed. The periodic entry to recognize the deferred compensation expense is as follows:

Compensation expense	xxx	
Deferred compensation expense		xxx

Options used to purchase shares. When an option holder exercises the option to purchase shares, the journal entry is identical to the simple purchase of shares without the presence of an option. This transaction is shown in the first entry. However, if some deferred compensation was recognized at the time of the initial stock grant, then the Options—Additional Paid-in Capital account is reversed as part of the entry. This transaction is shown in the second journal entry.

Cash	xxx	
Common stock—par value		xxx
Common stock—additional paid-in capital		xxx
Cash	xxx	
Options—additional paid-in capital	xxx	
Common stock—par value		xxx
Common stock—additional paid-in capital		xxx

Options lapsed (APB 25 approach). If an option holder elects to let an option lapse, the following entry reverses the accrued compensation expense and any remaining deferred compensation expense associated with the option.

Options—additional paid-in capital	xxx	
Compensation expense		xxx
Deferred compensation expense		xxx

Options lapsed (SFAS 123 approach). If an option holder elects to let a **fully vested** option lapse, the following entry does not reverse the associated compensation expense (as is the case under APB 25), but rather shifts the related equity into a different account.

Options—additional paid-in capital	xxx	
Capital—unexercised options		xxx

Options purchased by the company (SFAS 123 approach). To recognize any compensation expense associated with unvested shares that are being purchased by a company, to the extent that the price paid is higher than the value of the options as measured under the fair value approach. All deferred compensation expense associated with the unvested portion of the options is accelerated and recognized at the time of the purchase.

Compensation expense	xxx	
Deferred compensation expense		xxx
Cash		xxx

Stock Appreciation Rights (SAR)

Record increase in value of SAR grant payable in cash. When an initial SAR grant is made, no entry is required. When there is an increase in value of the underlying share value over the stock price at which the SAR was granted, the difference is recorded as compensation expense. The entry is as follows:

Compensation expense	xxx	
SAR liability		xxx

Record increase in SAR grant payable in stock. When there is an increase in value of the underlying share value over the stock price at which the SAR was granted, the difference is recorded as compensation expense, while the offsetting credit is to a Stock Rights Outstanding equity account.

Compensation expense	xxx	
Stock rights outstanding		xxx

Record exercise of SAR grant payable in cash. When the holder of a SAR wishes to exercise it and the payment is in cash, the amount of the accumulated SAR liability is reversed, with the difference being credited to Cash, representing the payment to the SAR holder. The entry is as follows:

SAR liability	xxx	
Cash		xxx

Record exercise of SAR grant payable in stock. When the holder of a SAR wishes to exercise it and the payment is in stock, the amount of the accumulated stock rights outstanding is reversed, with the difference being credited to the Par Value account and Additional Paid-in Capital account, representing the payment to the SAR holder. The entry is as follows:

Stock rights outstanding	xxx	
Stock—par value		xxx
Stock—additional paid-in capital		xxx

Employee Stock Ownership Plan (ESOP)

Incurrence of loan to purchase shares. To record a loan on the company books when either it or its ESOP obtains a loan with a third-party lender in order to purchase shares from the company.

Cash	xxx	
Notes payable		xxx

Purchase of shares by ESOP from sponsoring company. To record the transfer of company shares to the ESOP entity when it purchases the shares from the company. The shares have not yet been allocated to employees.

Unearned ESOP shares	xxx	
Common stock		xxx

Payments against note payable by ESOP. To record a reduction in the note payable incurred by the ESOP or the company on its behalf. The second entry records the allocation of shares to plan participants, as triggered by the reduction in the note payable.

Interest expense	xxx	
Notes payable	xxx	
Cash		xxx

Compensation expense	xxx	
Additional paid-in capital		xxx
Unearned ESOP shares		xxx

Dividends declared on shares held by ESOP. To record either a reduction in retained earnings (for shares allocated to employees by the ESOP) or compensation expense (for shares held by the ESOP) at the time of a dividend declaration.

Retained earnings [for allocated shares in ESOP]	xxx	
Compensation expense [for unallocated shares in ESOP]	xxx	
Dividends payable		xxx

RECORDKEEPING

When shares are issued, the transaction should be recorded in a stock record, an example of which was shown earlier in the Forms and Reports section. This document should be considered a permanent corporate record, and so should be set aside in a separate archival area to ensure that it is not batched with other documents for destruction at some point in the future. It is common practice to have the corporate law firm or a stock transfer agent maintain this document. If so, one should verify the third party's document safekeeping procedures to ensure that the information is at minimal risk of damage or destruction.

When shares are issued in exchange for goods or services received, the offsetting debit is to an expense account, which can be manipulated by making incorrect assumptions about the value of the goods or services received. Accordingly, one should thoroughly document the reason for the valuation. If the valuation cannot be determined, then the alternative of using the fair value of the issued stock should also be documented, since this valuation can also be subject to opinion when the stock is not publicly traded.

Earnings can be manipulated to a significant extent if the Board of Directors authorizes a property dividend for which there is a significant difference between the book and fair value of the property to be distributed. The asset must be marked up or down to its fair value prior to the distribution to shareholders, so it is necessary to fully document the reasoning behind the determination of fair value. This documentation is necessary in case the basis for the fair value determination is later called into question.

The price of each initial stock sale should be permanently recorded for each numbered stock certificate. This information could be required many years in the future, if those shares are ever bought back into the treasury and the constructive retirement method is used to record the purchase. Under this method, information about the original sale is required in order to determine what part of the share repurchase price is backed out of the stock account and how much is charged to retained earnings. This information is also required if a stock repurchase is initially recorded using the cost method, and then the determination is made that the shares will be permanently retired.

When a company agrees to repurchase shares at an excessively high price, usually due to the threat of a corporate takeover by a shareholder, it should document the circumstances of the repurchase, including the amount by which the repurchase exceeded the market value of the shares on the date of the repurchase. If the shares are not publicly traded, then the estimated market value can be quite difficult to ascertain, so the reasoning for the market value used should be clearly documented. The documentation will likely be reviewed and incorporated into the workpapers of any external auditors, who will use it as proof of the reasonableness of any excess payments charged to expense.

If a company expenses its stock option grants, it should fully document the inputs to its use of the Black-Scholes option valuation model, which is used to calculate the compensation expense associated with the option grants. This information is likely to be carefully reviewed by auditors, as well as by analysts and investors, since changes in the assumptions can be used to alter reported profit levels. For example, if a company has reduced the vesting period for its stock options, this is reasonable evidence for a reduction in the option life assumption in the Black-Scholes model, so a listing of the reduced option vesting periods and the authorizing Board motion should be attached to the journal entry as supporting evidence.

When a company recognizes the compensation expense associated with its option grants, it should document the method under which it ratably spreads the expense over time. There are two techniques available, yielding significantly different expense recognition amounts (as discussed earlier under the Option Vesting Period heading), so this information should be attached to the journal entries used to record the expense.

When a company records a periodic compensation expense as part of its grant of stock appreciation rights to employees, the amount of compensation expense granted may be called into question unless the company can provide a standard means of calculating the expense at the end of each reporting period. Accordingly, the calculation should be noted in a standard format that is attached to the journal entry used to record the expense.

When a company uses an ESOP to allocate shares to its employees, there may be ongoing concerns about who qualifies for the plan, since this determination can completely block an employee from participation, or impact the proportion of total shares allocated. Consequently, all plan documents, including revisions to them, should be stored in the permanent file and also tagged by date, so it is clear when each revision became effective. Also, the calculations for stock allocations should be retained in the permanent file. These calculations should clearly state the basis for stock allocation, show the calculation for each employee, and also have as an attachment any supporting documentation required as evidence of the allocation, such as hours worked by employee and pay levels on the allocation date.

14 INTERIM REPORTING

DEFINITIONS OF TERMS

Discrete view. The measurement of interim-period financial results without regard to the annual reporting period of which it is a part.

Estimated annual effective tax rate. The tax rate expected to be recognized at the end of the annual reporting period that reflects any graduated income tax rates and available tax credits.

Integral view. The measurement of interim-period financial results that considers the results to be an integral part of the annual reporting period of which it is a part. As such, expenses are accrued or deferred in proportion to revenues expected to be recognized for the full annual reporting period.

Interim reporting. Any financial report that covers a period of less than one full year.

Liquidation of last-in, first-out (LIFO) inventories. The excess use of inventories over purchases during an interim reporting period that results in the release of LIFO layers into the cost of goods sold.

Seasonality. A recurring pattern of revenue generation and associated expense recognition that occurs primarily in a small number of interim reporting periods.

CONCEPTS AND EXAMPLES

Interim reporting refers to a requirement by the Securities and Exchange Commission for all publicly held companies to file quarterly information on the Form 10-Q. The intent of this requirement is to provide users of the financial statements with more current information.

There are two views of how interim financial statements should be prepared. The first is the *integral view*, under which each interim period is considered to be an integral part of the annual accounting period. As such, annual expenses that may not specifically arise during an interim period are nonetheless accrued within all interim periods, based on management's best estimates. This heightened level of accrual usage will likely result in numerous accrual corrections in subsequent periods to adjust for any earlier estimation errors. It also calls for the use of the estimated annual tax rate for all interim periods, since the annual tax rate may vary considerably from the rate in effect during the interim period if the company is subject to graduated tax rates.

The second approach to interim statement preparation is the *discrete view*. Under this methodology, each interim period is considered to be a discrete reporting period, and as such is not associated with expenses that may arise during other interim periods of the reporting year. A result of this thinking is that an expense benefiting more than one interim period will be fully recognized in the period incurred, rather than being recognized over multiple periods.

Though the integral view is the more theoretically correct approach to formulating financial statements, there are several exceptions to its use for interim statements, which are outlined below.

- **Calculation of the cost of goods sold.** A normal year-end closing would require the use of a physical inventory count or perpetual recordkeeping system to ensure that the correct cost of goods sold is recorded. However, it is acceptable to instead use the gross profit method for an interim period. Under the gross profit method, one can estimate the cost of goods sold based on the expected gross profit percentage.
- **Recognition of LIFO inventory liquidation.** When some portion of the base-year layer is liquidated at year-end, it cannot be recovered. However, if this occurs during an interim period and the inventory is expected to be replaced by year-end, then the expected inventory replacement cost is added to the cost of sales for the interim period.
- **Lower of cost or market.** When the market value of inventory declines below its cost, the standard practice is to recognize a loss for the difference between the two. However, when reporting for an interim period, this can be avoided if there are seasonal price fluctuations that one would expect to result in a price increase by year-end. Further, if there is a recognized loss on the decline in value of inventory during an interim period, this loss can be offset by a gain in a subsequent interim period if the market price correspondingly increases.

A number of expenses can be assigned to multiple interim reporting periods, even if they are incurred in only one interim period. The key justification is that the costs must clearly benefit all periods in which the expense is recorded. Examples of such expenses are

- Advertising expense
- Bonuses (if they can be reasonably estimated)
- Contingencies (that are probable and subject to reasonable estimation)
- Contingent rental expense (if the contingent expense appears probable)
- Income taxes (based on the estimated annual effective tax rate)
- Profit sharing (if they can be reasonably estimated)
- Property taxes

Example of interim reporting of various expenses

The Arabian Knights Security Company incurs the following costs as part of its quarterly reporting:

- It pays $15,000 of trade show fees in the first quarter for a trade show that will occur in the fourth quarter.
- It pays $32,000 in the first quarter for a block of advertisements that will run throughout the year in *Security Now* magazine
- The Board of Directors approves a profit-sharing plan in the first quarter that will pay employees 20% of net annual profits. At the time of plan approval, full-year profits are estimated to be $100,000. By the end of the third quarter, this estimate has dropped to $80,000, and to $70,000 by the end of the fourth quarter.

Arabian uses the following calculations to record these scenarios:

	Quarter 1	Quarter 2	Quarter 3	Quarter 4	Full year
Trade show[1]				$15,000	$15,000
Advertising[2]	$8,000	$8,000	$8,000	8,000	32,000
Profit-sharing[3]	5,000	5,000	3,000	1,000	14,000

[1] *The trade show expense is deferred until the show occurs in the fourth quarter.*
[2] *The advertising is proportionally recognized in all quarters as it is used.*
[3] *A profit-sharing accrual begins in the first quarter, when the plan is approved. At that time, one-fourth of the estimated full-year profit sharing expense is recognized. In the third quarter, the total estimated profit-sharing expense has declined to $16,000, of which $10,000 has already been recognized. When the profit-sharing expense estimate declines again in the fourth quarter to $14,000, only $1,000 remains to be recognized.*

Extraordinary items and entity disposals are to be recorded in the interim period in which they occurred. Their impact is not to be spread across multiple interim periods.

Any change in accounting *principle* must be applied to all interim periods presented in the financial statements, which may call for retrospective application. However, a change in accounting *estimate* is to be accounted for only on a go-forward basis, so no retrospective application is allowed.

If an adjustment is needed in the interim financial statements that relates to litigation or income taxes, then record in the current interim period only the portion of the expense related to that period. Then restate prior interim financial statements to reflect that portion of the expense pertaining to them, with any remaining expense related to a prior year being recorded in the first interim statement of the current year.

Example of interim reporting of various expenses

The Arabian Knights Security Company is sued over its alleged violation of a patent in its new solar-powered motion detector security product. Under the settlement terms, which are agreed to during the third quarter of the reporting year, Arabian must retroactively pay a 4% royalty on all sales of the product to which the patent applies. Sales of the detector were $20,000 in the first quarter, $35,000 in the second quarter, and $10,000 in the third quarter. In addition, the cumulative total of all sensor sales in prior years was $420,000. Arabian restates its quarterly financial results to include the following royalty expense:

	Quarter 1	Quarter 2	Quarter 3
Sales subject to royalty	$20,000	$35,000	$10,000
Royalty expense	800	1,400	400
Royalty related to prior year sales	16,800		

POLICIES

- **The integral view shall be used for the preparation of all interim financial reports.** This policy is needed to ensure that expenses are recognized in all periods they benefit, rather than being lumped into fewer reporting periods and skewing the results of those periods.
- **The estimated annual effective tax rate shall be used for the income tax accrual in all interim periods.** This policy is needed to ensure that excessively low tax rates are not used in earlier interim reporting periods, and higher tax rates in later periods as the result of graduated tax rates.
- **The lower of cost or market (LCM) analysis shall only be conducted at year-end.** Since interim reporting can allow for the circumvention of LCM rules, one option is to review the LCM only at year-end, thereby avoiding any cost recognition issues earlier in the year.

PROCEDURES

Use the following procedure to ensure that accruals recorded in interim periods that are based on year-end estimates are regularly updated based on revisions to the estimates:

1. Collect the backup information used to compile all accruals from the immediately preceding interim period.
2. For each accrual, review the estimated full-year expense. If the estimate has changed from the preceding reporting period, subtract from the new estimate the expense already accrued, and divide by the number of interim periods left to be reported in the fiscal year. The result is the amount to be accrued in the current period. If the estimate has not changed from the preceding reporting period, then use the last period's accrual amount in the current reporting period.

Use the following procedure to ensure that LIFO layers are not incorrectly reported as liquidated during an interim reporting period:

1. Export the LIFO layer liquidation report to an electronic spreadsheet.
2. Select only those layers that have been liquidated since the last year-end reporting period, and print the report.
3. Review the report with the materials manager to determine which liquidated layers are to be replaced before year-end. For these layers, accrue the anticipated cost of replacing the liquidated inventory.
4. Summarize all other layer liquidations for which no replenishment is expected, and send the report to the controller.
5. During all subsequent interim period closings, review again with the materials manager all liquidated layers for which replacement was considered likely, to ensure that this is still the case.

Use the following procedure to ensure that the LCM analysis in an interim period is correctly reported in subsequent interim periods:

1. Record the detail of all LCM write-downs in each interim reporting period.

2. As part of the next interim reporting period, examine the market prices of items whose values were written down in a previous interim period. If the market price has increased, then record a gain to the extent of the previous loss.
3. Record all gain recognition in the detailed LCM write-down report, so that no additional gain will be recorded in a subsequent interim period.
4. Obtain the approval of the controller before recording the gain.

CONTROLS

*   **Verify that the integral view of interim statement preparation is being used.** A recurring internal audit program should specify that the expense recognition within any interim period be examined to ensure that expenses applying to the annual financial statements are being appropriately recognized.
*   **Verify that the estimated annual effective tax rate is used in each interim statement.** A recurring internal audit program should specify that the income tax rate used in each interim period is based on the estimated annual effective tax rate.
*   **Verify that accruals are being reviewed and adjusted in each interim period.** Part of the closing procedure should require that all accruals involving the recognition of estimated full-year expenses be reviewed and adjusted, based on any changes in the estimated total expense to be incurred.
*   **Verify that liquidated LIFO layer replenishment is still planned.** A recurring internal audit program should require the investigation of all LIFO layers that were liquidated during an interim period. If the layers are expected to be replenished, the amount of the replenishment should be accrued in interim periods. If they are not to be replenished, then no replenishment accrual should have taken place.
*   **Verify the extent of market price increases for inventory items.** Part of the closing procedure for each interim period should include a review of all inventory items for which a loss was recorded under an LCM analysis. This reduces the risk that the company will not recognize an offsetting market price increase in a subsequent period to the extent of the earlier loss.

FOOTNOTES

Disclosure must be made of any changes in accounting principles or the methods of applying them from the preceding interim periods of the current fiscal year or the prior fiscal year. The disclosure must be included in not only the current interim period's financial statements, but also all remaining interim periods of the current year and the annual financial statements. An example follows:

> In the third quarter of 2007, the Company changed its depreciation calculation methodology from the straight-line method used in prior years to the double-declining balance method. The new calculation method has been applied to fixed assets acquired in previous years and interim periods. Management believes that the new method more accurately reflects the Company's level of equipment usage.

If a company's revenue varies materially with the seasons, a company should disclose the seasonality of its sales. This is needed to keep users of the interim financial statements from being misled by large activity changes. Two examples follow:

1. The Company's theme park business is highly seasonal, with 80% of its sales occurring in the second and third quarters.

2. The Company has historically experienced considerable variability on a quarterly basis in its reported level of revenue and net income. A large proportion of this variability is due to seasonal fluctuations in business activity, with activity in its first and fourth quarters being adversely affected by downturns in attendance at its theme parks, particularly in northern climates, where low temperatures can shut down some theme parks entirely. Therefore, the results of operations presented for the three months ended September 30, 2007, are not necessarily indicative of the results of the Company's full-year operations.

RECORDKEEPING

Recordkeeping for interim reporting periods is primarily concerned with tracking variations in inventory levels between interim periods. Recordkeeping is as follows:

*   **Inventory affected by lower of cost or market rule.** Retain information about any inventory for which a valuation write-down occurred during an interim period. This information should include the part number, part description, quantity affected, and the total value of the write-down. The information will be needed if subsequent market price increases result in the recognition of a gain to the extent of the previous loss.

*   **Inventory affected by LIFO liquidation rule.** Retain information about any inventory for which a LIFO layer has been penetrated during a reporting period. If it is estimated that the lost inventory will be replaced by year-end, then retain the backup information describing the expected inventory replacement cost that was added to the cost of sales for the interim period. If this inventory is not replaced by the end of the fiscal year, then the records are needed to reverse the original entry and recognize a gain on the LIFO liquidation.

Once the annual report has been completed, the preceding recordkeeping can be archived, while similar information must now be tracked within each successive year.

15 SEGMENT REPORTING

DEFINITIONS OF TERMS

Chief operation decision maker. The person or group responsible for making decisions about resource allocations to business segments, as well as the evaluation of those segments.

Operating segment. A component of a business entity that earns revenues and incurs expenses, for which financial information is available, and about which the chief operating decision maker (see preceding definition) makes decisions regarding resource allocations and performance assessments.

Segment. A distinct revenue-producing component of a business entity, for which separate financial information is produced internally, and whose results are regularly reviewed.

Segment manager. That person who is accountable to the chief operating decision maker (see preceding definition) for a segment's operating results, financial results, forecasts, and plans.

CONCEPTS AND EXAMPLES

Segment information is required only for public companies. It is reported in order to provide the users of financial information with a better knowledge of the different types of business activities in which a company is involved. This information would otherwise be hidden in the consolidated financial information that a company normally releases in its financial statements.

The determination of a segment is based on how a company organizes its financial information internally, so that external users of the segment information will have access to approximately the same information that company managers use to make decisions.

The general requirement for segment reporting is that the revenue, profit or loss, and assets of each segment be reported, as well as a reconciliation of this information to the company's consolidated results. In addition, it must report the revenues for each product and service, and by customer, as well as revenues and assets for domestic and foreign sales and operations. This information is to be accompanied by disclosure of the methods used to determine the composition of the reported segments.

A reportable segment is a distinct revenue-producing component of a business entity, for which separate financial information is produced internally, and whose results are regularly reviewed by the chief operating decision maker. Some business activities, such as corporate overhead and postretirement benefit plans, are not included in segment reporting.

A segment is considered to be reportable if it is significant to the company as a whole. Significance is assumed if it passes any one of the following three tests:

1. Segment revenue is at least 10% of consolidated revenue.
2. Segment profit or loss, in absolute terms, is at least 10% of the greater of the combined profits of all operating segments reporting a profit, or the combined losses of all operating segments reporting a loss.
3. Segment assets are at least 10% of the combined assets of all operating segments.

When evaluating a segment's reportability with these tests, a segment should not be separately reported if it becomes reportable and due only to a one-time event. Conversely, a segment should be reported, even if it does not currently qualify, if it did qualify in the past and is expected to do so again in the future.

Further, a company may aggregate the results of segments that do not meet any of the 10% tests in order to create a segment that can now be classified as reportable, but only if they have similar economic characteristics and similar products, production processes, customer types, distribution methods, and regulatory environments.

In addition, the combined revenue of the segments designated as reportable must be at least 75% of consolidated revenue. If not, then additional segments must be designated as reportable.

Finally, it is generally best to limit the number of reported segments to no more than ten, after which similar segments should be aggregated for reporting purposes.

As an example of these concepts, the following shows how the three 10% tests and the 75% test may be conducted. The first table shows the operating results of six segments of a reporting entity.

Segment name	Revenue	Profit	Loss	Assets
A	$ 101,000	$ 5,000	$ --	$ 60,000
B	285,000	10,000	--	120,000
C	130,000	--	(35,000)	40,000
D	500,000	--	(80,000)	190,000
E	440,000	20,000	--	160,000
F	140,000	--	(5,000)	50,000
Totals	$1,596,000	$35,000	$(120,000)	$620,000

Because the total reported loss of $120,000 exceeds the total reported profit of $35,000, the $120,000 is used for the 10% profit test. The tests for these segments are itemized in the next table, where test thresholds are listed in the second row. For example, the total revenue of $1,596,000 shown in the preceding table is multiplied by 10% to arrive at the test threshold of $159,600 that is used in the second column. Segments B, D, and E all have revenue levels exceeding this threshold, so an "X" in the table indicates that their results must be separately reported. After conducting all three of the 10% tests, the table shows that segments B, C, D, and E must be reported, so their revenues are itemized in the last column. The last column shows that the total revenue of all reportable segments exceeds the $1,197,000 revenue level needed to pass the 75% test, so that no additional segments must be reported.

Segment name	Revenue 10% test	Profit 10% test	Asset 10% test	Revenue 75% test
Test threshold	$159,600	$12,000	$62,000	$1,197,000
A				
B	X		X	285,000
C		X		130,000
D	X	X	X	500,000
E	X	X	X	440,000
F				
			Total	$1,355,000

DECISION TREES

The decision tree in Exhibit 15-1 shows how to determine which segments must be separately reported, as well as which segments should be aggregated, and which ones can be summarized into the "all other" segments category.

Exhibit 15-1: Decision Tree for Determination of Reportable Segments

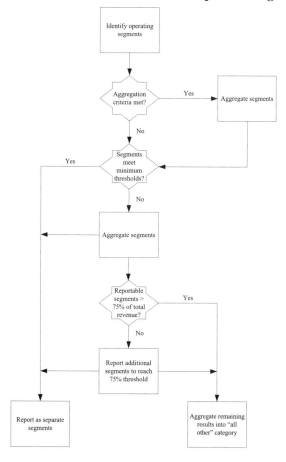

POLICIES

- **Transfer prices used for segment reporting shall match the pricing used for internal reporting purposes.** This policy prevents a company from altering the reported level of segment profitability by shifting profits between segments through the use of transfer pricing.
- **Overhead cost allocations for segment reporting shall match those used for internal reporting.** This policy ensures that financial statement users see the same results shown in internal segment-related financial reports.

PROCEDURES

Segment Determination Procedure

Use the following procedure to determine which business segments must be included in segment reporting:

1. For each business segment, summarize in a table its revenues, profits, losses, and assets. Profits and losses are to be itemized in separate columns.
2. Individually calculate 10% of consolidated company revenues and consolidated segment assets. Also calculate 10% of either total segment losses or profits, whichever is greater.
3. Highlight any segment whose revenues, profits, losses, or assets exceed the 10% threshold figure for each of these categories.
4. Highlight any segments that do not meet these thresholds but have done so in the past and are expected to do so in the future.
5. Remove the highlight from any segment that has exceeded a threshold only as the result of a one-time event, and for which there is minimal expectation that it will exceed a threshold in the future.
6. Summarize the combined revenues of all highlighted segments. If their combined revenue levels do not meet or exceed 75% of consolidated company revenues, then add more segments until this threshold is met or exceeded.
7. If the total number of reportable segments exceeds ten, then aggregate the results of those segments having similar economic characteristics, products, production processes, customer types, distribution methods, and regulatory environments.

Major Customer Reporting Procedure

Use the following procedure to determine which customers comprise 10% or more of consolidated revenues:

1. Print a report showing the trailing twelve months' revenue for all customers, sorted in declining order by total revenue.
2. Aggregate all government sales by top-level entity, so that (for example) all sales to a state government are aggregated into a single sales number, and use the same approach for federal and foreign government sales.
3. Aggregate all customer sales if they are known to be under common control.

4. Calculate the consolidated corporate revenue for the last twelve months, net of intercompany sales. Multiply this amount by 10%.

5. Compare the customer sales (including revenue figures for aggregated governments and customers under common control) to the 10% figure. Report all customers whose sales equal or exceed the 10% figure.

CONTROLS

• **Verify matching of internal and external segment reporting.** The quarterly and annual closing procedures should include a step in which the information issued for segment reporting is compared to the internal segment reports. This information should match. The controller should be notified of any variations between the two reports, which should be reconciled before the segment reports intended for external consumption are released.

FOOTNOTES

The disclosures noted in this section shall be made even if a company has only a single reportable segment. They are as follows:

• A description of how management identifies segments, and whether segments have been aggregated
• Total revenues for product or service, or group of products and services, unless it is impractical to provide this information
• Total revenues from domestic and foreign customers (as well as sales to individual foreign countries, if the amounts are material)
• The amount of long-term assets located in foreign countries, which shall include the amounts held in individual countries if those amounts are material
• Total revenues from any customer with whom its transactions total at least 10% of corporate revenues, as well as the identity of the segments reporting these revenues

For the purposes of these reporting requirements, a group of customers known to be under common control shall be considered one customer, while a local, state, federal, or foreign government shall be considered a single customer. Several examples of segment disclosure follow:

1. **Determination of segment profitability.** Segment profit is determined based on internal performance measures used by the chief executive officer (CEO) to assess the performance of each business in a given period. In connection with that assessment, the CEO may exclude matters such as charges for restructuring, rationalization and other similar expenses, in-process research and development and certain other acquisition-related charges and balances, technology and product development costs; certain gains and losses from dispositions, and litigation settlements or other charges.

2. **Foreign operations (1).** The Company is engaged in business in foreign markets. Our foreign manufacturing and service facilities are located in Australia, Canada, China, Indonesia, and Singapore. Sales to non-US customers were $2,500 million or 32% of total sales, $2,200 million or 38% of total sales, and $1,900 million or 33% of total sales for the years ended December 31, 2007, 2006, and 2005, respec-

tively. These countries have experienced volatile exchange rate fluctuations and interest rates, while cash transfers out of Indonesia are restricted at this time. The Company will continue to be affected by economic conditions in these countries and their surrounding regions, though it is not possible to predict the extent or resulting impact on the Company of these issues.

3. **Foreign operations (2).** The Company earns revenues from both domestic and foreign sources. For the purposes of the following table, revenues are attributed to countries based on the store location from which sales are generated, or the country to which merchandise is delivered:

	Revenue	*Long-lived assets*
United States	$23,470,000	$4,950,000
Foreign countries	12,050,000	2,030,000
Total	$35,520,000	$6,980,000

4. **Reporting of segment results—single segment.** The Company operates a single business segment that includes the installation and servicing of oil rigs for independent oil exploration and production (E&P) companies. The following table summarizes the Company's revenues and long-lived assets in different countries:

	2007	*2006*
Revenues:		
United States	$ 67,000,000	$61,000,000
Canada	31,000,000	26,000,000
Other foreign countries	11,000,000	9,000,000
Total	$109,000,000	$96,000,000
Long-lived assets:		
United States	$ 29,000,000	$28,000,000
Canada	17,000,000	13,000,000
Other foreign countries	4,000,000	4,000,000
Total	$ 50,000,000	$45,000,000

5. **Reporting of segment results—multiple segments.** The Company has determined that there are two reportable segments: (1) geographic information systems, and (2) information technology (IT) security audits. Two unreported segments are the Company's customer relationship management software division and its case management software division, whose results do not meet any of the quantitative thresholds under Financial Accounting Standards Board Statement 131, *Disclosures about Segments of an Enterprise and Related Information.* The following table reveals the operations of the Company's reportable segments:

	Geographic information systems	*IT security audits*	*Other segments*	*Totals*
Revenues	$2,450,000	$5,100,000	$320,000	$7,870,000
Interest revenue	3,400	--	--	3,400
Interest expense	--	63,000	14,000	77,000
Depreciation	93,000	32,000	156,000	281,000
Segment profit	317,000	1,080,000	(43,000)	1,354,000
Segment assets	453,000	190,000	590,000	1,233,000
Expenditures for segment assets	89,000	43,000	25,000	157,000

6. **Major customer reporting (1).** No single customer represents 10% or more of the Company's consolidated revenues.

7. **Major customer reporting (2).** The Company derives a significant portion of its net revenues from a limited number of customers. For the fiscal years ended December 31, 2007 and 2006, revenues from one client totaled approximately $15.7 million and $17.8 million which represented 12% and 15% of total net revenues, respectively. For the fiscal year ended December 31, 2005, revenues from two clients totaled approximately $13.6 million and $10.9 million, which represented 16% and 12% of total net revenues. Net revenues derived from sales to federal government agencies were approximately $126 million, $115 million, and $84 million for the years ended September 30, 2007, 2006, and 2005, respectively.

16 FOREIGN CURRENCY

DEFINITIONS OF TERMS

Conversion. Using an exchange ratio to switch from one currency to another.

Current exchange rate. The respective valuations of two currencies, resulting in a rate at which one currency can be exchanged for the other.

Foreign currency. Any currency other than the one a company designates as the functional currency of its corporate parent.

Foreign currency transaction. A transaction using a currency other than a company's functional currency, where payment or receipt involves a fixed number of units of the foreign currency, irrespective of the exchange rate.

Functional currency. The currency of the region in which a company generates and spends the bulk of its cash.

Highly inflationary economy. For the purposes of currency translation, a country whose economy has experienced cumulative inflation of at least 100% over the last three years.

Local currency. The currency used within a specific country.

Remeasurement. When one must restate an entity's financial statements into its functional currency, because the financial recordkeeping has been in some other currency.

Reporting currency. The currency in which a company reports its financial results.

Spot rate. The exchange rate currently available on the open market at which a specific pair of currencies can be exchanged.

Translation adjustment. Gains or losses resulting from the remeasurement of an entity's financial statements from its functional currency into its reporting currency.

CONCEPTS AND EXAMPLES[1]

The key consideration when making foreign currency translations is that when the conversion is complete, we will see an accurate translation of accounting performance in a foreign currency into precisely the same performance in US dollars. In other words, a foreign subsidiary whose financial statements have specific current ratios, gross margins, and net profits will see the same results when translated into a report presentation in US dollars.

The current rate method and the remeasurement method are the two techniques used to translate the financial results of a foreign entity's operations into the currency of its corporate parent. These methods are explained in the following paragraphs.

The Current Rate Method

The **current rate translation method** is used when a currency besides the US dollar is determined to be the primary currency used by a subsidiary. This approach is usually selected when a subsidiary's operations are not integrated into those of its US-based parent, if its financing is primarily in that of the local currency, or if the subsidiary conducts most of its transactions in the local currency.

However, one cannot use this method if the country in which the subsidiary is located suffers from a high rate of inflation, which is defined as a cumulative rate of 100% or more over the most recent three years. In this case, the **remeasurement method** must be used (as described later in this section). If the local economy is considered to no longer be inflationary, then the reporting method may be changed back to the current rate method; when this happens, the accounting staff must convert the financial statements of the impacted subsidiary back into the local currency using the exchange rate on the date when the determination is made.

To complete the current rate translation method, the first order of business is to determine the functional currency of the subsidiary. In some locations, a subsidiary may deal with a variety of currencies, which makes this a less-than-obvious decision. This should be the currency in which the bulk of its transactions and financing is used. Next, convert all of the subsidiary's transactions to this functional currency. One should continue to use the same functional currency from year to year in order to provide a reasonable basis of comparison when multiple years of financial results are included in the corporate parent's financial results.

---

[1]	*Some portions of this section are adapted with permission from Chapter 13 of Bragg,* **Ultimate Accountants' Reference** *(John Wiley & Sons, Inc., Hoboken, NJ, 2006).*

The next step is to convert all assets and liabilities of the subsidiary to US dollars at the current rate of exchange as of the date of the financial statements. The following conversion rules apply:

- Revenues and expenses that have occurred throughout the current fiscal year are converted at a weighted-average rate of exchange for the entire year. A preferable approach is to convert them at the exchange rates in effect on the dates when they occurred, but this is considered too labor-intensive to be practical in most situations.
- Stockholders' equity is converted at the historical rate of exchange. However, changes to retained earnings within the current reporting period are recorded at the weighted-average rate of exchange for the year, since they are derived from revenues and expenses that were also recorded at the weighted-average rate of exchange.
- Dividends declared during the year are recorded at the exchange rate on the date of declaration.
- Any resulting translation adjustments should be stored in the equity section of the corporate parent's consolidated balance sheet. This account is cumulative, so one should separately report in the footnotes to the financial statements the change in the translation adjustments account as a result of activities in the reporting period.

Example of the current rate method

A division of the Oregon Clock Company is located in Mexico. This division maintains its books in pesos, borrows pesos from a local bank, and conducts the majority of its operations within Mexico. Accordingly, its functional currency is the peso, which requires the parent's accounting staff to record the division's results using the current rate method.

The peso exchange rate at the beginning of the year is assumed to be .08 to the dollar, while the rate at the end of the year is assumed to be .10 to the dollar. For the purposes of this example, the blended full-year rate of exchange for the peso is assumed to be .09 to the dollar. The Mexican division's balance sheet is shown in Exhibit 16-1, while its income statement is shown in Exhibit 16-2. Note that the net income figure derived from Exhibit 16-2 is incorporated into the retained earnings statement at the bottom of Exhibit 16-2, and is incorporated from there into the retained earnings line item in Exhibit 16-1. For simplicity, the beginning retained earnings figure in Exhibit 16-2 is assumed to be zero, implying that the company is in its first year of existence.

Exhibit 16-1: Balance Sheet Conversion under the Current Rate Method

	Pesos	*Exchange rate*	*US dollars*
Assets			
Cash	427	.08	34
Accounts receivable	1,500	.08	120
Inventory	2,078	.08	166
Fixed assets	3,790	.08	303
Total assets	7,795		623

	Pesos	Exchange rate	US dollars
Liabilities & Equity			
Accounts payable	1,003	.08	80
Notes payable	4,250	.08	340
Common stock	2,100	.10	210
Additional paid-in capital	428	.10	43
Retained earnings	14	Note 1	0
Translation adjustments	--	--	(50)
Total liabilities & equity	7,795		623

Note 1: As noted in the income statement.

Exhibit 16-2: Income Statement Conversion under the Current Rate Method

	Pesos	Exchange rate	US dollars
Revenue	6,750	.09	608
Expenses	6,736	.09	607
Net income	14		1
Beginning retained earnings	0		0
Add: Net income	14	.09	0
Ending retained earnings	14		0

The Remeasurement Method

The remeasurement method is used when the US dollar is designated as the primary currency in which transactions are recorded at a foreign location. Another clear indicator of when this method is used is when the subsidiary has close operational integration with its US parent, or when most of its financing, sales, and expenses are denominated in dollars.

Under this method, we translate not only cash, but also any transactions that will be settled in cash (mostly accounts receivable and payable, as well as loans) at the current exchange rate as of the date of the financial statements. All other assets and liabilities (such as inventory, prepaid items, fixed assets, trademarks, goodwill, and equity) will be settled at the historical exchange rate on the date when these transactions occurred.

There are a few cases where the income statement is impacted by the items on the balance sheet that have been translated using historical interest rates. For example, the cost of goods sold will be impacted when inventory that has been translated at a historical exchange rate is liquidated. When this happens, the inventory valuation at the historical exchange rate is charged through the income statement. The same approach is used for the depreciation of fixed assets and the amortization of intangible items.

Other income statement items primarily involve transactions that arise throughout the reporting year of the subsidiary. For these items, it would be too labor-intensive to determine the exact exchange rate for each item at the time it occurred. Instead, one can determine the weighted-average exchange rate for the entire reporting period, and apply this average to the income statement items that have occurred during that period.

Example of the remeasurement method

A simplified example of a corporate subsidiary's (located in Mexico) balance sheet is shown in Exhibit 16-3 (which is the same balance sheet previously shown in Exhibit 16-1). The peso exchange rate at the beginning of the year is assumed to be .08 to the dollar, while the rate at the end of the year is assumed to be .10 to the dollar. The primary difference in calculation from the current rate method shown earlier in Exhibit 16-1 is that the exchange rate for the inventory and fixed assets accounts has changed from the year-end rate to the rate at which they are assumed to have been originated at an earlier date. Also, there is no translation adjustment account in the equity section, as was the case under the current rate method.

A highly abbreviated income statement is also shown in Exhibit 16-4. For the purposes of this exhibit, the blended full-year rate of exchange for the peso is assumed to be .09 to the dollar. Note that the net income figure derived from Exhibit 16-4 is incorporated into the retained earnings statement at the bottom of Exhibit 16-4, and is incorporated from there into the retained earnings line item in Exhibit 16-3.

Exhibit 16-3: Balance Sheet Conversion under the Remeasurement Method

	Pesos	*Exchange rate*	*US dollars*
Assets			
Cash	427	.08	34
Accounts receivable	1,500	.08	120
Inventory	2,078	.10	208
Fixed assets	3,790	.10	379
Total assets	7,795		741
Liabilities & Equity			
Accounts payable	1,003	.08	80
Notes payable	4,250	.08	340
Common stock	2,100	.10	210
Additional paid-in capital	428	.10	43
Retained earnings	14	Note 1	68
Total liabilities & equity	7,795		741

Note 1: As noted in the income statement.

Exhibit 16-4: Income Statement Conversion under the Remeasurement Method

	Pesos	*Exchange rate*	*US dollars*
Revenue	6,750	.09	608
Goodwill amortization	500	.08	40
Other expenses	6,236	.09	561
Remeasurement gain	--		61
Net income	14		68
Beginning retained earnings	0		0
Add: Net income	14		68
Ending retained earnings	14		68

A major issue is that, under the current rate translation method, there was a translation **loss** of $50, while the remeasurement approach resulted in a translation **gain** of $61. This was caused by a difference in the assumptions used in deriving the exchange rate that in turn was used to convert the inventory and fixed asset accounts from pesos into dollars. Consequently, the choice of conversion methods used will have a direct impact on the reported level of profitability.

For smaller companies that only rarely deal with foreign exchange transactions, there is no need to formally recall the details of the preceding translation methods. Instead, if they participate only in an occasional sale transaction, they can simply record the initial sale and related account receivable based on the spot exchange rate on the date when the transaction is initially completed. From that point forward, the amount of the recorded sale will not change—only the related receivable will be altered based on the spot exchange rate as of the date of the balance sheet on which it is reported, adjusting it up or down to reflect the existence of a potential gain or loss at the time of the eventual collection of the receivable. The final gain or loss will be recorded when the receivable is settled, using the spot rate on that date. This procedure will cover the most common transactions that a small business will encounter.

Translation of Foreign Currency Transactions

The gains and losses resulting from various translation adjustments are treated in different ways, with some initially being stored in the balance sheet and others being recorded at once in the income statement. Here are the key rules to remember:

- If a company is directly engaged in foreign exchange transactions that are denominated in foreign currencies, then any translation adjustments to US dollars that result in gains or losses should be immediately recognized in the income statement. It can continue to make these adjustments for changes between the last reporting date and the date of the current financial statements, and may continue to do so until the underlying transactions have been concluded.

Example of foreign currency transaction reporting

The Louisiana Backhoe Company (LBC) sells backhoes to a variety of countries in the European Union, all of which are paid for in euros. It sold $200,000 of backhoes to Germany on March 15. The receivable was still outstanding on March 31, which was the date of the quarterly financial statements. As of that date, the exchange rate of the euro has dropped by 1%, so LBC has an unrecognized loss of $2,000. It records this as a loss on foreign currency transactions, and credits its accounts receivable account to reduce the amount of its receivable asset. When payment on the receivable is made to LBC on April 15, the exchange rate has returned to its level on the sale date of March 15. LBC must now record a gain on its books of $2,000 to offset the loss it had previously recorded.

- Do not report gains or losses on transactions of a long-term nature when accounted for by the equity method. These transactions are defined as those with no settlement date planned in the foreseeable future. Instead, include these transactions in the standard translation procedure used to translate the financial statements of a subsidiary into the currency of its corporate parent.
- If a foreign entity has multiple distinct operations, it is possible that some have different functional currencies. If so, the accountant should regularly review their operations to determine the correct functional currency to use, and trans-

late their financial results accordingly. However, if the results of a selected operation on the financial reports of a foreign entity are insignificant, there is no requirement to break out its financial statements using a different functional currency.

- If there has been a material change in an exchange rate in which a company's obligations or subsidiary results are enumerated, and the change has occurred subsequent to the date of financial statements that are being included in a company's audited results, then the change and its impact on the financial statements should be itemized in a footnote that accompanies the audited results. An example is noted later in the Footnotes section.

Exchange Rates Used for Calculations

There can be some confusion regarding the precise exchange rate to be used when conducting foreign currency translations. Here are some guidelines.

- If there is no published foreign exchange rate available on the specific date when a transaction occurred that requires translation, one should use the rate for the date that most immediately follows the date of the transaction.
- If the date of a financial statement that is to be converted from a foreign currency is different from the date of the financial statements into which they are to be converted into US dollars, then use the date of the foreign currency financial statements as the date for which the proper exchange rate shall be used as the basis for translation.
- If there is more than one published exchange rate available that can be used as the basis for a translation, use the rate that could have been used as the basis for the exchange of funds, which could then be used to remit dividends to shareholders. Alternatively, use the rate at which a settlement of the entire related transaction could have been completed.

Intercompany Transactions

When the results of a parent company and its subsidiaries are combined for financial statement reporting purposes, the gains or losses resulting from intercompany foreign exchange transactions must be reported in the consolidated statements. This happens when the parent has a receivable denominated in the currency of the subsidiary, or vice versa, and a change in the exchange rate results in a gain or loss. Thus, even though the intercompany transaction is purged from the consolidated financial statement, the associated gain or loss must still be reported.

Example of an intercompany transaction

The Seely Furniture Company owns a sawmill in Canada that supplies all of its wood raw materials. The subsidiary holds receivables from the corporate parent that are denominated in US dollars. During the year, there has been a steady increase in the value of the dollar, resulting in a conversion into more Canadian dollars than was the case when each receivable was originally created. By the end of the year, the subsidiary has recorded a gain on currency transactions of $42,000 Canadian dollars. Accordingly, the Seely corporate parent records the gain on its books, denominated in US dollars. Because the year-end exchange rate between the two currencies was $0.73 Canadian per

US dollar, the subsidiary's gain is recorded as a gain in US dollars of $30,660 ($42,000 Canadian × 0.73 exchange rate) on the books of the parent.

DECISION TREES

The decision tree shown in Exhibit 16-5 can be used to determine whether one should use the current rate method or remeasurement method when translating the financial statements of a foreign subsidiary into the currency of the corporate parent.

Exhibit 16-5: Type of Translation Method Decision Tree

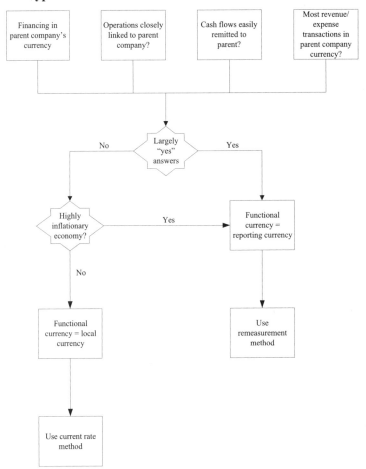

POLICIES

Translation of Foreign Currency Financial Statements

- **Periodically review the status of highly inflationary economies where subsidiaries are located.** This policy is designed to determine the date when a local economy either becomes highly inflationary or is no longer defined as such under accounting rules. This is of importance in determining what type of translation method to use.

Translation of Foreign Currency Transactions

- **Maintain or have access to a database of daily exchange rates for all currencies in which the company conducts transactions.** This policy allows the accounting staff to have ready access to exchange rates for its translation and currency transaction activities.

PROCEDURES

Financial Statement Translation—Highly Inflationary Economy Determination

Use this procedure to determine status changes for highly inflationary economies.

1. Establish the three-year date range over which inflation will be measured.
2. Determine the data source containing inflationary information for the selected time periods.
3. Locate the data source and extract the inflation information.
4. Add together the inflation information for the designated three years. The period over which the inflation is measured in the source document may be different from the corporate fiscal year. If so, also obtain the inflation rate for the year in which any portion of the company's fiscal year falls, and construct a weighted-average inflation rate based on the number of months in each measured year. For example, if a company's fiscal year ends in October, then multiply the inflation rate for year 1 by 2/12 (to address the two beginning months of the fiscal year falling into year 1) and multiply the inflation rate for year 2 by 10/12 (to address the ten final months of the fiscal year falling into year 2). Then add these two calculations together to determine the inflation rate for the first year. Perform the same calculation for years 2 and 3.
5. If the cumulative inflation rate for the three-year period exceeds 100%, use the parent company's currency as the functional currency for the subject subsidiary.

Application of the Current Rate Method

Use the following steps to translate a subsidiary's financial results under the current rate method:

1. Identify the subsidiary's functional currency.
2. Measure all parts of the subsidiary's financial statements in its functional currency.
3. Use exchange rates to translate the subsidiary's financial statements from its functional currency to the currency of the corporate parent. The following items note the different exchange rates to be used for different accounts:

   a. **Use historical exchange rates.** All stockholders' equity accounts, with the single exception noted in the next point.

   b. **Use the weighted-average exchange rate.** All revenues and expenses, as well as changes to retained earnings within the current reporting period.

   c. **Use current exchange rates.** All assets and liabilities.

4. Record any translation gain or loss in a translation adjustment account within the equity section of the balance sheet.

5. Footnote any changes in the translation adjustment account that arose during the reporting period, including the amount of income taxes allocated to the changes.

Application of the Remeasurement Method

Use the following steps to translate a subsidiary's financial results under the current rate method:

1. Verify that the subsidiary's functional currency is the US dollar.

2. Use exchange rates to translate the subsidiary's financial statements into the currency of the corporate parent. The following items note the different exchange rates to be used for different accounts:

   a. **Use historical exchange rates.** All asset and liability accounts that will not be settled in cash, such as depreciation, intangibles, and inventories carried at cost, as well as stockholders' equity.

   b. **Use the weighted-average exchange rate.** All revenues and expenses, except those for which historical exchange rates have already been used.

   c. **Use current exchange rates.** All cash accounts, as well as any account, such as accounts receivable or payable, that will be settled in cash.

3. Record any remeasurement gains or losses in the corporate parent's consolidated income statement.

Translation of Foreign Currency Transactions

Use the following steps to record gains or losses on foreign currency transactions at the end of each reporting period:

1. Obtain a list of all accounts receivable, accounts payable, notes receivable, and notes payable that are outstanding at the end of the reporting period.

2. Obtain the spot exchange rate at the end of the reporting period for the currencies in which all transactions listed in the first step are denominated.

3. Determine the settlement amount of each transaction, assuming that the spot exchange rate will be the exchange rate on the date of settlement.

4. Print out all measurement calculations and attach them to a journal entry form. Note on the form the amount of each spot exchange rate used, as well as the source document and date of the source document for each spot exchange rate. If there is a transaction gain, credit the Gain on Foreign Exchange Transactions account and debit the offsetting asset or liability account associated with the transaction. If there is a loss, then debit the loss

on Foreign Exchange Transactions account and credit the offsetting asset or liability account associated with the transaction.

5. Have the assistant controller verify the calculations and sign off on the journal entry form.
6. Submit the form to the general ledger accountant for entry into the general ledger.

CONTROLS

Translation of Foreign Currency Financial Statements

The following controls should be used to ensure that translation methods are not arbitrarily switched in order to show or avoid translation gains or losses.

- **Gain external auditor approval of any changes in translation method.** A key difference between the current rate and remeasurement methods of translation is that translation adjustments under the current rate method are placed in the balance sheet, whereas adjustments under the remeasurement method are recognized on the income statement as gains or losses. The accounting staff could be tempted to shift between the two methods in order to show specific financial results on the corporate income statement. For example, if there were a translation gain, one would be more likely to use the remeasurement method in order to recognize it on the income statement. This problem is especially likely when the criteria for using one method over the other could be construed either way. The best way to avoid this problem is to have a disinterested third party (i.e., the auditors) approve any change in method over what was used in the preceding year.
- **Require management approval of calculations for the status of inflationary economies.** It is possible to alter the translation method based on the inflationary status of a foreign economy, possibly resulting in the recognition (or not) of translation gains or losses on the income statement. If one were inclined to shift the translation method, a defensible basis for doing so is the inflationary status of the economy in which a foreign entity does business. The inflationary status could be altered by either using incorrect inflation data or shifting the beginning and ending dates of the calculation to correspond to inflation data more in line with one's required result. This issue can be resolved by requiring management or internal audit reviews of these calculations, especially when a change in inflationary status has recently occurred.

Translation of Foreign Currency Transactions

- **Verify that all gains and losses on incomplete currency transactions are updated in the periodic financial statements.** If there have been unusually large fluctuations in the exchange rates of those currencies in which a company has outstanding transactions, there may be a temptation to avoid recording any interim gains or losses prior to settlement of the transactions, on the grounds that the temporary fluctuations will even out prior to settlement. However, this ongoing delay in recognition of gains and losses not only misstates financial statements, but also can build over time into much larger gains or losses, which can come as quite a shock to the users of the financial statements when the changes are eventually recognized. Accordingly, the standard checklist for completing financial statements should itemize the recognition of interim gains and losses on incomplete foreign exchange transactions.

FORMS AND REPORTS

Translation of Foreign Currency Financial Statements

When creating journal entries that include calculations based on a specific exchange rate, it is useful to itemize in the entry not only the exchange rate being used, but also the source and date of this information. Accordingly, the journal entry form shown in Exhibit 16-6 has been modified to include the additional information.

Exhibit 16-6: Modified Journal Entry Form

Journal Entry Form
Date:_____   Approval: _____

Account No.	Account Name	Debit	Credit
_____	_____	_____	_____
_____	_____	_____	_____
_____	_____	_____	_____
_____	_____	_____	_____
_____	_____	_____	_____

Reason for journal entry: _____
_____
_____

Exchange rate used: _____
Exchange rate source document: _____
Date of source document: _____

FOOTNOTES

Aggregate transaction gains or losses related to foreign exchange must be disclosed either within the financial statements, or in the attached footnotes. If the latter option is chosen, a sample footnote would be as follows:

> The company conducts business with companies in several South American countries as part of its ongoing fruit import business. This results in a number of payables denominated in the currencies of those countries, with about $250,000 to $500,000 of such payables being outstanding at any one time. The company does not engage in hedging activities to offset the risk of exchange rate fluctuations on these payables. During the reporting period, the company benefited from foreign exchange gains on these accounts payable totaling approximately $7,500.

If the translation of financial statements using the current rate method results in a gain or loss, the cumulative amount of the gain or loss is shown in the equity section of the balance sheet. In addition, the accompanying footnotes should describe changes in the amount of this balance, the amount of income taxes allocated to it, and any amounts shifted out of this account and recognized as part of the sale or termination of a company's investment in a foreign entity. An example is shown in the following footnote:

> The company summarizes in the equity section of the balance sheet all gains and losses from the translation of the financial statements of its three foreign subsidiaries into the consolidated corporate statements. During the reporting period, the balance in this account declined by $42,500 to a new balance of $108,250, reflecting the cumulative impact of translation losses incurred during the period. Approximately 20% of this decline was attributable to the sale of the company's travel subsidiary located in Indonesia. In addition, 50% of this decline was attributable to the partial write-down on the company's investment in its Peruvian trekking subsidiary.

If there has been a significant change in a foreign currency in which a company has significant outstanding transactions, and this change has occurred subsequent to the financial statement date, then the impact of this change should be reported as a footnote to the statements. An example follows:

> About 40% of the company's revenue is earned from sales to Mexico. On January 14, subsequent to the date of these financial statements, the exchange rate of the Mexican peso dropped 12% from its value on the financial statement date. Since all of the company's sales to Mexico are denominated in pesos, this represents a potential loss of 12% when those revenues are eventually paid by customers in pesos. At this time, the drop in value would represent a foreign exchange loss to the company of approximately $412,000. As of the release date of these statements, no accounts receivable related to the sales had been paid by customers. All receivables related to the sales should be collected by the end of February, and so are subject to further fluctuations in the exchange rate until that time.

JOURNAL ENTRIES

Translation of Foreign Currency Financial Statements

Financial statement translation adjustment. To record the difference between the exchange rate at the end of the reporting period and the exchange rate applicable to individual transactions. The sample entry shows credit adjustments to several accounts, but these entries could easily be debits instead, depending on changes in applicable exchange rates during the reporting period.

Accumulated translation adjustments	xxx	
Various noncash asset accounts		xxx
Net income		xxx
Dividends declared		xxx

Translation of Foreign Currency Transactions

Translation of foreign currency transactions. To record any changes in the spot rate of exchange at which transactions denominated in a foreign currency would be recorded at the date when financial statements are issued. The **first journal entry** records a loss on a decline in the spot rate on an account receivable (resulting in a reduction in the amount of the receivable in US dollars), while the **second entry**

does the same for an account payable (resulting in an increase in the payable in US dollars), and the **third entry** does so for an outstanding loan payable (resulting in an increase in the loan payable in US dollars). For gains on these transactions, the second line of each entry would be reversed, while a credit to a gain account would be substituted for the loss account.

Loss on foreign exchange transaction	xxx	
Accounts receivable		xxx
Loss on foreign exchange transaction	xxx	
Accounts payable		xxx
Loss on foreign exchange transaction	xxx	
Loans payable		xxx

Recognition of the sale of a foreign subsidiary. To recognize any accumulated translation gains or losses as the result of the sale or write-down of a company's investment in a foreign subsidiary. The entry can be reversed if a gain is to be recognized.

Loss on sale of business entity	xxx	
Accumulated translation adjustments		xxx

RECORDKEEPING

The key recordkeeping issue for foreign currency transactions is to keep a continuing record of the exchange rates used to derive transactions. This record should include the exchange rate, the source of this information, and the date of the source document. For example, the exchange rate for transactions used as of the March 31 financial statements might be the *New York Times* on March 31. This information will be used by the external auditors to determine whether the correct exchange rates were used to derive accounting transactions.